REAL ESTATE
A Case Study Approach

William J. Poorvu
Harvard Graduate School of Business Administration

PRENTICE HALL CAREER & TECHNOLOGY
Englewood Cliffs, New Jersey 07632

Library of Congress Cataloging-in-Publication Data

Poorvu, William J.
    Real estate : a case study approach / William J. Poorvu.
        p.   cm.
    ISBN 0-13-763483-8
    1. Real estate business—Case studies.   2. Case method.
I. Title.
HD1375.P664   1993
333.33—dc20   91-28587
                                                                          CIP

Editorial/production supervision and
    interior design: **Janet M. DiBlasi**
Cover design: **20/20 Services, Inc.**
Manufacturing buyer: **Ed O'Dougherty**
Prepress buyer: **Ilene Levy**
Acquisition editor: **James C. Boyd**
Marketing manager: **Tina Culman**

© 1993 Prentice-Hall, Inc.
A Simon & Schuster Company
Englewood Cliffs, New Jersey 07632

Printed in the United States of America

10 9 8 7 6 5 4 3 2

ISBN 0-13-763483-8

Prentice-Hall International (UK) Limited, *London*
Prentice-Hall of Australia Pty. Limited, *Sydney*
Prentice-Hall Canada Inc., *Toronto*
Prentice-Hall Hispanoamericana, S.A., *Mexico*
Prentice-Hall of India Private Limited, *New Delhi*
Prentice-Hall of Japan, Inc., *Tokyo*
Simon & Schuster Asia Pte. Ltd., *Singapore*
Editora Prentice-Hall do Brasil, Ltda., *Rio de Janeiro*

This book is dedicated to Lia
and multigenerations of my family.

CONTENTS

A CONCEPTUAL FRAMEWORK FOR ANALYSIS   xii

PREFACE   xiii

INTRODUCTION   xvii

PART I   Establishing the Framework

1   ANDERSON STREET   1

In June, 1987, Charlie Leonard, a recent college graduate with a full time job and a modest inheritance, is looking for a real estate investment. The case chronicles the process of finding, evaluating, and acquiring a four-unit brownstone in need of renovation in the Beacon Hill area of Boston. The case is designed to encourage students with little or no background in real estate to think through the issues involved in redeveloping a small income producing property.

2   SAVANNAH WEST   16

In August, 1977, Alison Porter, a loan officer with Chemical Bank, has the weekend to decide whether to recommend a $3 million construction loan for a proposed 216-unit garden apartment project in Savannah, Georgia. Though the developer has a good track record with Chemical, and has the potential to become a major player in Georgia development, Porter must justify the loan based on the potential for success of the development itself. In addition to introducing students to the conceptual framework of project evaluation, the case highlights the relationship of lenders to developers.

3 PROSPECT HILL 37

In May, 1989, the Nelson Company is considering the development of a new 274,000 square foot office building in its successful Prospect Hill Office Park on Route 128 in a suburb outside of Boston. Both local market conditions and their relation to national demographic trends predicted for the 1990s are analyzed. The case highlights decisions regarding project economics—the provision of tenant services such as day care and underground parking, the use of interest rate hedges—and examines them in light of the need for the project to compete in an increasingly soft market.

4 FAN PIER 58

In April, 1989, plans for the development of Fan Pier, an ambitious mega-project on Boston's waterfront, have come to a halt as the result of: (1) a major fallout between the property owner and his development partners that in 1987 resulted in litigation and (2) a shift in the political climate that affected the approval process. Both the partners and the city officials have to decide what to do next. The case also presents the successful experience of a similar project, Battery Park City on Manhattan's waterfront, to highlight the overall public and private sector issues relating to large scale urban waterfront development.

5 REGENCY PLAZA 78

In June, 1989, Kris Hodgkins, the project manager for condominium development of the Regency Plaza Hotel complex, is trying to decide how to handle a series of customer requested changes. Condominium sales at the project have been slow and Hodgkins would like to accommodate the owners' requests, but the proposed changes may seriously disrupt the construction process. Hodgkins, as the project manager, has to make a decision that takes into account the design, marketing, sales, construction, and financial aspects of the project. This case also provides an opportunity to take an in-depth look at the design and visual aspects of project development through an exercise in laying out the floor plan for a number of condominium units in the building.

6 SOUTHPARK IV 91

In January, 1990, George Laflin, a local investor, has raised $450,000 to invest in commercial and industrial properties in Houston, Texas. Laflin is interested in purchasing the 80,000 square foot SouthPark IV office/warehouse facility from a local savings and loan institution. Before he proceeds any further, Laflin wants to determine what the potential returns are from the project and calculate a realistic offer. The case takes the student through the mechanics of project valuation using a back of the envelope analysis.

7 ANGUS CARTWRIGHT 103

In January, 1991, Martha and James DeRight, looking to diversify their investment portfolios, have retained Angus Cartwright to identify prospective real estate acquisitions. Mr. Cartwright has four potential properties which merit an in-depth analysis. The case provides an opportunity to examine the various components of real estate return—cash flow, tax benefits, and futures—and measure the profitability of a proposed investment through the calculation of net present value, internal rate of return, and capitalization rate. The class session permits discussion not only about techniques of financial analysis, and their usefulness, but adaptation of those methods to the needs of a particular investor.

PART II Determining Value

8 KING'S PARK 117

In January, 1982, Wolff, Morgan and Company have assembled a 400 acre tract of raw industrial land on the outskirts of Houston. Intending to subdivide the property and market development-ready parcels, Wolff, Morgan evaluates possible financial structures with joint venture partners. The case also discusses the effect of the absence of zoning or other land use regulation on the development climate, and on the valuation of land.

9 TYSONS CORNER 130

In July, 1989, the partnership owning the Tysons Corner Marriott in Virginia is facing a cash flow deficit. The opening of a number of new hotels in the area and the increased trend to product segmentation have resulted in lower occupancy rates and reduced cash flow. This case provides an overview of the hotel industry, the history of this particular hotel, and the dilemma of the general partners in attempting to deal with changes in the market environment.

10 GRAYBAR SYNDICATIONS 150

In March, 1958, the Graybar Building, a one million square foot older office structure in midtown Manhattan, is facing competition from a new generation of buildings. Its proposed acquisition by a syndicate is predicated on a tiered structure of financing and returns to a complex array of participants. The challenge for the student is to wade through the legal documentation of the offering, decipher the priority and breakdown of the cash flow from the property, and decide who gets what return and when. The case deals with many of the issues relating to financial deal structuring.

11   THE COOLIDGE BLOCK   166

In November, 1990, William Jeffries and Eric Gilliland of Chestnut Hill Limited Partners (CHLP) were evaluating their prospective acquisition of the Coolidge Block, a 60,000 s.f. class B office building in Springfield, Mass. Commonwealth Bank was scheduled to foreclose on the property at auction two weeks hence. The case takes us through a discussion of the factors which will impact their determination of the ultimate value of the property in the context of a rapidly declining market both in Springfield in particular and in the industry in general.

12   THE TEXTILE CORPORATION BUILDING   177

In March, 1987, Martin Donwill hopes to submit the winning offer in a sealed bid auction for a 350,000 square foot Boston office complex. Although he feels his skills in management and rehabilitation give him an economic advantage over the competition, he has to quantify the ways in which he can create value, and profitably outbid his competitors. This case offers an opportunity to compare the risk and rewards of new construction with rehabilitation. It also introduces students to the art of bidding, within the greater context of theories of negotiation.

13   THE MIDWEST CORPORATE FUND   191

In January 1992, Donna Jones, the Director of Portfolio Investments for the Midwest Corporate Fund, was preparing to hear the presentations of those three firms which MCF, one of the larger corporate pension plans in the country, had shortlisted as potential real estate advisors. Given the softness of the real estate markets nationally, many pension funds were reassessing their investment positions. With a little over 3% of its $3.5 billion in assets currently invested in limited term real estate assets, MCF was hoping to restructure and perhaps add to its real estate portfolio. Jones knew that each firm was aware of the tremendous investment capacity of a pension fund such as MCF and that each was aggressively looking to grow its client capital under management.

14   THE GLOBAL FUND   216

In January, 1989, Bob Riley, the new Chairman of the Prudential Realty Group, has to decide if Prudential should proceed with the creation of a $2-3 billion global real estate investment fund. Both domestic and international real estate markets are changing rapidly. Does it make sense to invest globally? If it does make sense, what types of properties and locations should Prudential target, and how should it structure and manage the fund?

PART III *Developing the Property*

15 503 RUGBY ROAD 223

In 1970, Mason Sexton, a young, inexperienced developer, made plans to replace a rooming house he had inherited next to the University of Virginia campus in Charlottesville with a new 14 unit, 5 story apartment house. His attempts throughout 1970 and 1971 to assemble the information, approvals, and resources necessary to go ahead point up the steps and risks inherent in the development process. Although the example is of a small scale residential project, the development lessons are applicable to projects of any scale.

16 THE COSTA MESA PROJECT 240

In February, 1981, Copley Real Estate Advisors has to decide whether to proceed as a financial joint venture partner on a major, multi-phased office project in Orange County, California. While the $122 million project fits Copley's portfolio objectives well, the market is uncertain, interest rates are high, and the development partner is new. The case illustrates how the structure of a joint venture arrangement must take into account the players, the property, and projected economics.

17 LAKESIDE CENTER 259

In November, 1989, Maria Sanchez, the leasing agent for a 95,000 s.f. class A office building in Boca Raton, Florida, has to prepare and negotiate lease proposals with three prospective tenants. The building is only 38% occupied, and has fallen behind the project's proforma operating projections. This case is designed to expose students to the leasing process, the strategy and tactics of lease negotiations, and the impact of rental rates and concessions on financial and partnership structures.

18 ONE LEATHER STREET 278

In October, 1987, the Smith brothers, seeking a new real estate niche, elect to rehabilitate a small St. Louis office building. They run into difficulty with their architect, contractor, regulatory officials and their lenders. The case discusses the issues raised by their development problems, economic projections, as well as their highly leveraged financial structure.

19 LYNDON MALL 294

In September, 1988, Joan Carnevali must decide if MKS should bid to purchase the Lyndon Mall. Lyndon Mall is an older regional shopping center in Mississippi that requires both renovation and expansion to compete against a potential new mall. This case explores the criteria for success in shopping center development. It also looks at the business and ethical issues relating to the acquisition of the mall by its current manager.

20 PORTLAND ELDERCARE 308

In September, 1986, Portland, Maine, developer Pam Gleichman is considering entering the field of non-subsidized housing for the elderly. Aware of a national trend toward an aging population, Gleichman wants to investigate the potential of serving the high end of this market. She needs to determine the product which best fits the needs of this segment of the Portland community in terms of location, design, services to be offered and costs. The case discusses the economic and societal implications of three product types—for sale cluster homes, a congregate care development, and a life care facility.

21 THE AMERICAN DREAM 326

The purchase of a single family home is generally the major investment for most young couples. This case shows in some detail the process the Wellingtons go through in August, 1989, to find, finance, and close on a house in Maryland within what they believe to be their financial capabilities. Students are required to identify all the direct and indirect costs involved in home acquisition and compare these costs with the rental alternative.

22 GROSVENOR PARK 349

In September, 1988, Dick Dubin is attempting to gain final approval for a 189 unit single family home subdivision in Bethesda, Maryland targeted to young, upwardly mobile professionals working in the Washington, D.C. area. The case spans the project life cycle from predevelopment to sellout, and addresses issues ranging from land acquisition, construction phasing, finance, design, and marketing, to managing a critical relationship with a powerful local planning board.

PART IV Technical Notes

23 FINANCIAL ANALYSIS OF REAL PROPERTY INVESTMENTS 368

This note examines the methods by which real property investments are analyzed, offers suggestions about those analytical techniques, and provides sources of useful information. The note examines the three components of real estate returns—cash flow, tax effects, and future benefits—and looks at the impact of financial structuring on returns. This note is helpful in providing a conceptual framework for analysis of cases throughout the course.

24 NOTE ON TAXATION 397

This note provides a broad overview of the income tax factors most relevant to real estate ownership and operation. Every real estate transaction is affected substantially by the tax consequences which result from its form and substance. This note is not a definitive guide to the area of taxation, but is intended to help the student better understand basic tax factors and their interrelationships.

25 NOTE ON FORMS OF REAL ESTATE OWNERSHIP 423

This note looks at the advantages and disadvantages of the various legal forms of organization used in owning and operating real estate properties. It examines these structures both from a general management point of view, and from a tax perspective.

Management of the Real Estate Process: Creating Value and Controlling Risk

A CONCEPTUAL FRAMEWORK FOR ANALYSIS

THE PROJECTS:	*THE PLAYERS:*	*THE PANORAMA:*	*THE PROCESS:*
Product	*Stakeholders*	*Industry*	*Conceptual Stage*
Locational Characteristics	Owners	Fragmented	Idea
Business Definition/Time Frame	Investors	Capital Intensive	Strategy Formulation
Design/Physical Conditions	Lenders	Cyclical	Preliminary Investigation
Capital/Operating Costs	Developers	Project Oriented	Projections
Market	Managers	*Economic*	*Pre-Commitment Stage*
Target Use/Advisers	Users	Financial Markets	Approvals
Absorption/Demand	Neighbors	Taxation/Subsidies	Detailed Analysis/Design
Competition/Supply/Comparables	Regulators	General, Regional	Resource Assembly
Timing of Entry	Communities	Characteristics	Organizational Planning
Financial	Suppliers	*Sociological*	*Action Stage*
Operating Projections	Designers	Demographics	Resource Acquisition
Sources/Uses of Funds	Builders	Lifestyles	Financial Commitments
Financial Benefits/Returns:	Brokers	Geography	Construction
Cash Flow Operations	Competitors	Education	Leasing
Taxes	*Characteristics*	*Technological*	*Custodial Stage*
Appreciation	Goals	Communications	Asset Management:
Risk/Reward Allocation	Experience	Infrastructure	Operations
Legal	Competence	Workplace	Rehabilitation
Site Control	Resources	Building Materials, Techniques	Reuse
Regulations	Interrelationships	*Political*	Financial Management/Tax Planning
Ownership Structure	Commitment	Land Use Patterns	Harvesting:
Agreements	Time Frame	Regulatory Environment	Sale
	Compensation	Power/Process	Refinancing
	Risk Profile		
	Integrity		
	Skills		
	Analysis		
	Knowledge		
	Decision Making		
	Negotiation		
	Communication		
	Management		
	Leadership		

PREFACE

The genesis of my attraction to teaching by the case method occurred during my years as an MBA student at Harvard Business School. I found that I prepared more thoroughly for class, paid more attention to the varying points of view expressed by my instructor and co-participants, retained concepts and techniques and learned approaches to solving problems. Not only was I forced to think on my feet, I enjoyed the experience thoroughly.

Although I had no formal courses in the field, after graduation I began working in real estate. I had to start from scratch learning about tenant leasing, mortgage financing, and fixing leaky roofs. However, the training I had received at HBS encouraged me to seek out information in new situations and to be willing to make decisions in a dynamic property world where variable pricing is a given. The multiple negotiations that go on at many levels in the transaction oriented real estate business bear a number of similarities to the classroom. Although the longer time frame before one sees results in the real world is frustrating, and the penalties of failure are more extensive, there is a similar sense of opportunity and excitement.

In the late 1960s when I was given the chance to help start a course in real estate at Harvard Business School on a part-time basis and to write many of the cases, the two worlds came together. Many thousands of students, classes, and cases later, I still feel fortunate to be able to blend two careers, to be exposed to new ideas, and to be continuously challenged by a diverse cross section of people.

To thank only a few of the people who have helped me at Harvard leads to guilt feelings about the many not mentioned. However, I will focus on those who were directly involved in writing cases or notes for this book or providing access to their companies as subjects for our cases.

For many years Professor Howard H. Stevenson has been central to my involvement at the School. His creative and lively mind contributed greatly to the initial structure and teaching of the real estate course and to developing a pedagogical and conceptual framework for looking at the field. Traditionally, the industry had been viewed in academic circles as being too undisciplined and fragmented to lend itself to rational analysis. We focused on the process, asking a common set of questions about the property, the market, and the people that permitted a variety of responses. We saw many firms in the industry adapting their organizational and business practices to the needs of new institutional financial partners, more sophisticated tenants and more demanding regulators. The topic of ethical and socially responsible behavior became an integral part of our class discussions.

Since he joined the faculty, Senior Lecturer Donald A. Brown has brought an extensive background in all aspects of real estate development. As developers and property owners face new challenges, our cases and methods of teaching have to adapt to reflect realities. Since the course began, interest rates have ranged between 6% and 16%. There have been major cyclical market fluctuations at both regional and national levels. The concern for the built environment has become a critical part of our process. Government's role has switched from that of a proponent of growth to that of a gatekeeper. Don Brown's insights, enthusiasm, as well as his commitment to our students have added considerably to the course.

I am grateful for Professor C. Roland Christensen's course in "Teaching by the Case Method" which I took and subsequently co-taught with him. This remarkable communicator made me aware of the potential for using cases effectively in the classroom. Case studies are not just histories of a particular event in time, but an opportunity to shape, to involve, and to raise the level of interaction of the participants. They provide a flexible format for the instructor to develop ideas in a variety of ways. As there is no one way to learn, there is no one way to teach. The instructor's ability to listen, to question, and to respond, heavily influences the process.

Dean John McArthur and the Research Department at the Harvard Business School have been most generous in allowing me to hire recent graduates of the School as research associates. They have suggested ideas and helped in writing and editing the cases and notes in this book. Over the years Richard Crum, Leslie Feder, Katherine Sweetman, and John Vogel have been very involved in this effort. Mart Bakal, Jeff Libert, and Peter Aldrich assisted with case development, and have taught in our program. Sam Plimpton not only wrote cases many years ago, but then became my business partner. Elizabeth McLoughlin deserves special mention not just for having written many of these cases but for returning to work with me a second time. Although in a way she has suffered double jeopardy, her collaboration in so many aspects of this book has been crucial. Lastly, Linda Kelly, my secretary for more years than she will admit, has pitched in to bring order out of an environment that is often times more entrepreneurial than academic.

In the last analysis it is the dynamic "people" aspect of both real estate with its ad hoc series of relationships, and academia with its annual migration of new students bringing new questions, new backgrounds, and new interests that keep me enthusiastic. I am especially grateful for the many former students who have stayed in touch, keeping me up to date with what is going on in markets and companies throughout the world. Most of the cases are direct outgrowths of their experiences.

My hope in writing this book is that in reading and discussing these cases, you will be stimulated to learn more about the real estate industry, to become exposed to an important part of our society, and to discover how you yourselves might become involved in this most challenging and potentially rewarding field. There is an opportunity to do well financially, to meet an exciting variety of people, to have the chance to play a positive role in one's community, and to preserve and enhance the built environment.

INTRODUCTION

The real estate industry has been and continues to be a visible and substantial part of the U.S. economy. The fair market value of all U.S. real estate has been estimated at close to $9 trillion as of 1989, of which slightly under $4 trillion is in commercial, industrial and residential investment property. Approximately $5 trillion is in the hands of non-investment residential property owners.

The industry, as we define it, comprises not only those who develop, own, and operate many types of real estate as separate profit making businesses, but also those who provide them with services. It is dynamic, multi-functional, and multi-disciplinary, with few absolutes over the lifetime of a property.

Triggered by a growing demand for space, the past decades have been ones where a vision for expansion and a willingness to take risks were often key criteria of success. An optimistic view of future prospects attracted an ample supply of project capital. The entrepreneurial opportunity to create equity, the short term price inefficiencies, the fragmentation of real estate markets, and the ease of entry to the industry, attracted many participants. Considerable fortunes were made.

But, the cyclical nature of real estate is well known. Upmarkets have typically inspired an inflow of capital, new construction, and major changes in the built environment. Firms, looking for new opportunities for expansion, found that real estate provided entrepreneurial rewards, high returns, and a hedge against inflation. However, the inevitable downturns resulted in contraction in the industry, more constrained cash flows, and lower property values. Downturns have had a magnified impact on leveraged properties and firms with inadequate cash flows to adjust to changing economic realities. It is the ability to ride out the storms, to take a long term approach to the ownership of real estate that maximizes its value to the individual or firm. Ironically, the best opportunities for beginning to create value often arise during periods of problems or discontinuities.

Real estate professionals have had to adjust to changing industry realities.

Society has rightly become more concerned about regulating growth and as-
sessing its consequences. More sophisticated users have also placed greater demands on those providing services or space. More rigorous codes of ethics in both
the public and private sectors have established higher standards of acceptable
behavior. And finally, as a result of upheavals in most financial markets serving
real estate, lenders and investors have required more in-depth analysis and better
market information. This has been especially true of institutional investors, who
have become major players in recent years.

Although affected by many independent forces, real estate remains a site
specific enterprise, which requires not only local knowledge but hands on attention to details of implementation. That is why case studies based on actual properties located in communities throughout the U.S. are so valuable in helping us
learn about the field. They combine project specific decision making within the
context of broader industry realities.

These real life situations rarely lend themselves to a single solution. People
must act at a particular point in time based upon imperfect information and
their own limited experiences. Discussions of cases allow us to expand horizons,
to see the benefits of rigorous analysis, and to be exposed to multiple points of
view of the same problem. Our goals in this book are twofold: to provide a better
understanding of the real estate industry, and to develop an enhanced ability to
make personal decisions in this challenging field.

The pedagogical framework that we use to examine our cases is divided
into four sections: the *project*, the *players*, the *panorama*, and the *process*. For most
real estate practitioners the *project* is the starting point. We define the project as
specific land and buildings which are owned and developed as separate businesses. A project is typically investigated within the context of a defined market
and certain financial parameters. Then, the appropriateness of the project is
assessed relative to the proposed *players* involved. Do the background, skills,
contacts, and resources of the project team provide the best expertise for making
the project succeed? Likewise, the *panorama*—the regulatory, financial, market,
and socio-economic environments—influences both project decisions and outcomes. Our concern for the *process* stems from our belief that there are patterns
to the acquisition, development, and management of real property, and that
these patterns provide guidance for project specific decisions. Throughout this
introduction we will expand on the issues that are raised within each section.
What is important is to bring the elements together, to see each situation as a
totality, in order to explore and maximize the opportunities for success.

THE PROJECT

As stated, we begin by focusing on the project itself. By concentrating on the
project, we also hope to mirror the industry practice in which most properties
are legally owned and managed as separate businesses, often by small entrepreneurial firms. Since the owner or developer must coordinate all the project

elements, our cases emphasize the enterprise as a whole, at a point in time, recognizing that the project, both as a business and as a building, normally outlasts its original owner.

Questions are asked about the location, market, and physical condition of the individual property, as well as the project's economics. Is the property well sited on its lot? Is it visible, accessible? What can we say about the design? Is the building or its equipment obsolete? Other marketing questions might include: What is happening to the local and regional market? What is the extent of the competition today? What is that competition expected to be like in the future? What are the demographics? How should the property be sold or leased? Is the demand for tenant services changing? What level of tenant fit-up is needed? How should the lease be structured?

From an economic standpoint, there are a range of issues to be discussed. What are the present and projected cash flows? How realistic are the projected rents and expenses? What is an appropriate ongoing vacancy level? What will happen when existing leases expire and rents are adjusted to markets? What are the expenses of re-renting space—commissions, down time, and tenant improvement costs? What are the expectations about future value, growth, or capitalization rate? How can the property be financed? What terms need to be negotiated? What are the income tax consequences? These are but a few of the factors which will affect value.

Each geographical area has its own characteristics. Likewise, each project type has its own subset of variables. If developed for residential use, is the product garden apartments, an urban high rise or a single family subdivision? Is it owned in fee, or by a condominium or a cooperative? If commercial, is it an urban high rise or a research park? Is the shopping center a strip, regional or super-regional? How do we differentiate between raw land or land development, hotel or resort investments? What about public or private mixed use investments? Is the project designed for institutional ownership or occupancy, and if so, how does that affect the way the business is run? How does the scale of the project influence decisions?

For the more experienced students, these questions may be second nature, but for those starting out in this field, it is crucial to begin with the basics, to know what to ask. One should not be afraid to ask or keep asking until one has received an understandable and logical explanation that makes clear the assumptions. The alternative can be expensive.

THE PLAYERS

Since each project or business requires different skills, knowledge, resources, and experience, the project team is often assembled anew for each proposal. Rewards in real estate are often related to the success of each individual transaction or project, rather than to the development of ongoing organizations. Project members may never have worked together. While both the owners and their support team are working toward a common goal, a single leader needs to take responsibility for the successful management of the project to profitable completion. The developer not only has to have a vision, but must be a hands-on manager. In a way he or she is like an orchestra conductor who may not play all the instruments, but must have reasonable familiarity with all of them.

A key element for success is the careful selection, direction, and coordination of the players who can help a project to succeed, such as investors, lenders, brokers, and attorneys. The capabilities and goals of the ad hoc team that is put together must be matched with the unique characteristics of each project. Which players would fit best with this particular project and with each other? Who could make the necessary commitments of time or money, given other obligations? Some participants may have a vested interest and influence over the project, and may benefit little or even lose something from its successful completion. Who are the stakeholders and what are the stakes? What are they betting on? As in venture capital situations, the split of equity among investors, promoters, and workers is to be negotiated upfront.

Real estate projects, owned and managed as entities in and of themselves, enable the allocation of control and returns to many participants. Even a small initial equity contribution can become quite valuable as many projects are highly leveraged. Financing has historically been based on, secured by, and tied to the value or cash flow of an individual project, as well as the experience and history of the borrowers. If personal guarantees are given, the degree of recourse to other assets owned by the borrowers must be considered when evaluating probable risk and return.

A flat organizational structure resulting from a "project team" approach tends to have few preexisting relationships and no existing hierarchy. This creates an informal atmosphere, which greatly influences the process, the results, and the fun one can have working in this field. Even larger financial firms with other institutional characteristics are structured to provide entrepreneurial experiences and rewards. The project leader can tie the financial success of the participants to the performance of the project.

The incentives available to attract high quality participants range from equity participation for financial and development partners to fees for service professionals. Each player may be compensated differently—the architect who understands the site and its potential, the attorney with the appropriate specialties, contacts and experience, or the financial intermediaries who help raise the money. The key is to retain the flexibility to assemble the most appropriate project team and to draft an agreement which will satisfy the project players and bind them together for the common cause.

The well drafted ownership agreement, often structured in the form of a limited partnership, should accommodate the changes that will inevitably take place over the long time frame of property ownership or development. It must deal with management, control, and continuity. The owners should have a strong commonality of interest. The cash distributions, tax benefits, and sharing of future value must reflect the contributions of those involved in the project. Since the project may unexpectedly demand more of one participant than another over time, or may require an additional participant, all parties must understand that ownership interests may need to be restructured at some point. How one gets out of a deal is often more complicated than how one gets in. Changes in bankruptcy laws have altered traditional borrower/lender relationships and the ways in which the parties deal with distressed situations.

In a field of project specific partnerships, there could be the temptation to act only within the letter of the law or the agreement, to find loopholes, and to cut corners. Reputations, like real estate values, are acquired over time, and grow more valuable when well maintained. The value of the individual's word can be his or her most important asset. Ethical behavior and an awareness of the environmental and social impact of real estate can be seen as good business practice, as well as a moral prerogative. What is built, for whom and how it is managed affects others, and economic criteria should not be the only standard for measurement.

Changing attitudes toward development often require close working contacts at the local level. Building regulations, zoning codes, and environmental requirements have to be considered in the planning. The neighboring community acts through its regulators, expressing opinions through the formal approvals process. More informally, neighborhood groups, historical societies, and civic associations have become increasingly sophisticated consumers of the built environment around them. Growth is often regarded as a negative. Who has the power, at what level, and how it is used varies not only from place to place but over time within the same community itself. It is now common to expect the imposition of extra charges or linkage payments to satisfy the demands of a multitude of parties affected directly or peripherally by the project. Managing these tricky and crucial relationships requires tact, sophistication, and cooperation. The project team must expect and have the staying power to withstand a long drawn out process of approval.

Clearly, both the individuals and the organizational structure must be well-matched to the needs of the project. How will real estate firms be structured in the future? What staffing should best be filled in-house as opposed to being purchased from the outside? What types of jobs will be available, and what backgrounds will be needed to fill them? Can a management company experienced in commercial projects handle a shopping center, hotel, or life care center, each of which has operating distinctions that makes it a separate business? Is success dependent upon persistence, instinct, experience, and the willingness to take and juggle risks, or is it a function of being in the right place at the right time? Finally, what degree of risk is the individual or firm willing to take? Whether to work on a fee for service basis or for a share of the upside depends on many factors. How much of one's personal time or resources to commit is always an issue. The scale of project, type of real estate, or geographic locale must be looked at in personal as well as economic terms. Is one more comfortable in an institutional environment, or a small local setting? As has been said before, one can eat well or sleep well, rarely both.

THE PANORAMA

It is critical to think about how a specific project under consideration fits within the broader context of economic, sociological, technological and political trends. Attitudes toward growth vary depending on the times and the specific locality. The development of new construction materials, more efficient building systems, computerized designs, or new applications of construction management techniques affect both the bottom line, and the project's ability to compete in the marketplace. Compliance with handicapped access codes and environmental standards has significant cost implications. Incentives to encourage subsidized housing or historic rehabilitation affect what will be built. Demographic shifts, the availability of capital, projected vacancies in office and hotel space, and innovations in technology all create opportunities for the individual project. The federal government, through the provision of tax subsidies, setting of tax rates and depreciation schedules, and determining the deductibility of interest costs, has a dramatic effect on the profitability of a project over time. Federal and monetary policy influence the rate of inflation. Higher rates of inflation increase the cost of new construction and, eventually, when existing space has been absorbed, result in an upward movement of existing property values.

The fragmented and localized nature of products and markets makes risk assessment and access to capital markets most uneven, a situation that also creates opportunity. The discrepancy between the timing of the infusion of capital into the industry with the needs of the market, especially at the local level, leads to cycles of growth and contraction. In the late 1980s, for example, excess capital availability resulted in the building of products for which market demand was absent. In past decades, inflation, tax subsidies, and growth in demand have often rescued shaky projects. There might not be such easy outs in the future.

It is not easy to incorporate national or industry level trends in the decision making process for an individual project. However, changing financial markets and global shifts in economic power require real estate practitioners to know how and why investment and development practices differ between the U.S. and other parts of the world. Since the individual property owner cannot control many of the events which will affect the property, he or she needs to know how to read the signs, identify the trends, and understand the implications for his or her piece of Main Street, U.S.A. These are often difficult and abstract issues that a busy professional rarely has the time or information to consider. And yet it is often these large exogenous trends that have a significant effect on companies and individuals. To succeed in real estate requires extraordinary skills, common sense, and an understanding of the environment in which we operate.

THE PROCESS

The challenge of making short term decisions in an environment of long term uncertainty is not unique to real estate—just ask any fashion designer, car manufacturer or book publisher. What is special in real estate, what greatly increases the risk, is that after an exploratory period, the major capital commitments and pricing decisions must be made up front based on long term projections of uncertain future cash flows. Real estate has traditionally been an extremely capital intensive business with high fixed costs and few, if any, economies of scale. Once started, it is very difficult to redesign a development to meet changed market needs, and years may pass before major renovation becomes feasible. Thus, the need to determine in advance the optimal combination of variables is crucial.

The first step is to gather and analyze as much information as possible early in the project life cycle. Based on that information, steps can be taken to minimize and reduce risk through options, pre-leasing, and the recruitment of financial partners. The strategy for acquisition or development has to take into account many factors which can be reviewed systematically. The more information that can be established at the outset, the greater the certainty of project returns. Experience with the local market helps enormously at the conceptual stage, especially since it is important to keep out of pocket costs low. A site visit, some phone calls, a couple of meetings and a few back of the envelope calculations cost little, but can be sufficient to make at least a preliminary decision to investigate further or to abandon a deal.

If it is determined that further investigation is worthwhile, questions which were raised at the conceptual phase are investigated more thoroughly, and new questions are asked. The market is reexamined. What similar products are also planned or under construction? How will competition affect this project? How reliable is the market data? How does the location compare to competitive sites? What compromises may be necessary, how much would they cost, and how long will they take to resolve? What approvals are necessary? A hefty premium is often paid for experience and contacts since delays are costly. Because the (often highly leveraged) project may face significant short term debt obligations, efficiently managing the timeline of development is crucial.

The local approval process adds considerable uncertainty and cost to real estate projects. What can be built is not just the decision of the property owner. The U.S. regulatory system continues to limit the property rights of the individual. Zoning regulations, building code requirements, and environmental impact concerns need all be satisfied. Issues of design, scale, and community impact are matters of interpretation, are not easily quantified, and are controlled both by regulations and a legal system that makes it easy for objectors to delay and obstruct through challenges in the court. Cost constraints on local government encourage the shifting of costs to the private developer, be it funding of infrastructure or providing economic benefits to the community.

Since it is hard to find financing for unimproved land, and the major financial commitment from outside lenders and investors is often not finalized until the entire project is ready to move ahead, the developer usually will need to spend his or her own money in the pre-commitment stage. Depending on the situation, the developer may also need to acquire control of the site during this stage through a substantial commitment of resources. Hedging devices which mitigate the need for upfront cash, such as contingent purchase contracts or option agreements can be arranged, but at a price.

The next step, schematic design, usually generates sufficient documentation to submit a credible financing application. The schematic designs, however, lack sufficient detail and scope to obtain accurate construction cost estimates. At some point, the developer has to make the judgment as to when to commission expensive working drawings and specifications. The dilemma is whether to commit funds for working drawings before permanent financing is assured, or to try to get financing without being sure how much money is needed.

The transition from the preliminary stage of investigation with a low level of exposure to the time when resources are committed is critical. The decision must be made at each major investment increment or phase of the process to proceed or, alternatively, to abandon the project and cut one's losses. Inevitably, a decision which should be logical and rational takes on an emotional tone. The optimistic developer may have already invested so much in time, money, pride and reputation that it becomes emotionally difficult to abandon the project. It may even be that the developer cannot afford the loss of money borrowed to fund the preliminary costs, which will be returned from construction loan proceeds only if the project goes forward.

As stated earlier, the developer is working during this difficult period with an ad hoc assembly of consultants, partners, agents, and contractors. Most expect to be paid as their contribution is completed. Some may be willing to forego these payments for higher fees later or promises of equity if the project moves to completion. While most of these arrangements are informal and not legally binding, the integrity with which one maintains these relationships determines the ability to work with the best in the future.

In addition, potential lenders and investors may want some evidence of market interest in the project in the form of pre-leasing commitments. Maintaining a marketing program and keeping all the other elements of the project moving on parallel tracks is a creative challenge for any developer. When to lock in financing, at what level, and on what terms is difficult to determine. Many negotiations must be conducted simultaneously. Experience, contacts, reputation, and pre-leasing can minimize the marketing risk and ensure realistic sale or leasing projections.

When the project proceeds to the action stage, different challenges arise. The developer, or the appointed project manager, must monitor construction progress and problems, and generally oversee and participate in the marketing effort. This requires coordinating the various business functions and monitoring project teams within the context of an overall development schedule, construction budget, and marketing strategy. Regularly scheduled meetings involving all the participants are important to ensure coordination. Depending on the size of the project and the type of tenants sought, a sales force may be dedicated to marketing the space, and must be held accountable for its efforts. Realistic concessions attuned to market conditions are essential tools for the leasing or sale of space.

Once significant construction funds have been committed, the flexibility to adjust the physical project to changes in demand or to the economic climate is limited. The pressure is on to complete the project on time and on budget even if that requires cutting out some of the amenities or reducing the quality of the work. Construction decisions which require modifications to the original plan may result in unanticipated cost overruns, a rethinking of marketing strategy, or the need for more funds. If arrangements have to be made to bring in additional financing, the rights of many parties may have to be renegotiated. For example, institutional partners have needs, resources, and time frames that differ from those of the developer. It is important to have a lender or financial partner that understands the uncertainties in the process and is willing to be flexible.

When construction is completed, the owner's task is not. Work is still required to maintain and enhance value. Proper management looks both to the short term and long term viability of the project. The extent and timing of capital improvements is dependent on many factors. The ability to anticipate and react to real estate cycles is crucial, especially in negotiating tenant leases. The owner's ability to retain tenants minimizes vacancy, marketing costs and commissions, and the need to retrofit the space for new users. In a highly leveraged project, small swings in cash flow can have a major effect on the value of the equity.

The owner needs to assess periodically a harvesting strategy which might include sale, refinancing, or restructuring the equity participation of the partners. What are the advantages, disadvantages, and dangers of each? What is the "real" price in a field of non-standard pricing? Whichever form the harvesting takes, the owner as custodian during the holding period must consider how management decisions may affect returns.

SUMMARY

Much of the discussion in this section has focussed on analyzing properties during the development cycle. The analysis is also applicable to the potential acquisition of existing income properties. Even though the initial construction and marketing risks may have been eliminated, the prudent investor needs to take into consideration the fact that the roll over of leases will require an ongoing marketing strategy, and that the depreciation of property will dictate periodic redevelopment. And, from a competitive standpoint, each site is affected by the new development of others. For investors and developers alike, there is the need for a comprehensive analytic perspective that reflects the dynamics of the field. As one must take into account all elements of the *project*, the *players*, the *panorama*, and the *process* in a field where the capital commitments are upfront, and the returns long term.

Individual success in the industry is dependent on many factors, some of which we have identified below. While not presuming to achieve ten commandment status, the following might help describe the challenges of this most exciting field.

1. The ability to understand, coordinate, and motivate a multitude of ad hoc interrelationships;
2. The creativity and good taste to shape and reshape a vision that will be fixed in concrete in a changing environment;
3. An analytical mind-set that integrates qualitative and quantitative thinking;
4. An attention to detail where the parts are interdependent;
5. The skill to manage risk in a capital intensive environment where commitments must be made upfront;
6. An understanding of how to create value through financial structuring;
7. The willingness to assume individual responsibility as a manager, as a leader, and as a responsible and ethical member of a community;
8. An awareness of and responsiveness to local and national needs;
9. A flair for marketing;
10. The good fortune to be in the right place at the right time with the right people.

While many of the lessons learned throughout these cases are specific to real estate, there are other fundamental lessons which are transferrable across a range of disciplines—issues of ethics, accountability, or even prudent business management. Today's real estate professional must be increasingly well-informed, with an understanding and acceptance of social and environmental issues as well as project economics. Changes in financial markets, fundamental shifts in demographics, and emerging technologies, can be taken advantage of only by increasingly sophisticated practitioners. Yet those with common sense, analytical skills, and an ability to interact with others may be in the best position to create entrepreneurial opportunities.

Future opportunities for creating real estate value may be significantly different than they have been in the past. Increasing institutional and global investment in the industry may make for a more level playing field, wider access to project capital, or less fragmentation of markets. Alternatively, the stakes may be higher, the demographics for development more constraining, or greater equity capital required. Ultimately, however, the creation of value will in all cases rest on project specific criteria, the project as it stands in relation to its own market, its own management, and its own rewards. Real estate will continue to be, in many respects, a hands-on, local industry, with broad, exciting, and potentially rewarding ramifications. The cases that follow are intended to provide exposure to just a few of the dramatic examples that can be found in every community. We hope you will see in them relevance to your own opportunities over the coming decades.

1

ANDERSON STREET

In June, 1987, Charlie Leonard, a recent college graduate with a full time job and a modest inheritance, is looking for a real estate investment. The case chronicles the process of finding, evaluating, and acquiring a four-unit brownstone in need of renovation in the Beacon Hill area of Boston. The case is designed to encourage students with little or no background in real estate to think through the issues involved in redeveloping a small income producing property.

Discussion Questions:

1. How did Leonard go about searching for his property?
2. How did Leonard go about evaluating and buying the property on Anderson Street?
3. What people helped Leonard in the process and what functions did they perform?
4. What are the problems relating to the rehabilitation work proposed?
5. Should Leonard make this investment?

In June of 1987, Charlie Leonard began searching for a small income-producing apartment building in which to invest. Leonard had just graduated from Harvard College, and he was working for a manufacturing firm in Newton, Massachusetts. He had grown up in Boston and was attracted to the investment potential of the Back Bay-Beacon Hill area, which he considered the best residential section of downtown Boston. Many of his contemporaries were renting apartments or had purchased homes there, and he and his wife had attended many of their parties. He considered paying rent to someone else a waste of a capital building opportunity, since he was building up someone else's equity.

Leonard wanted to gain experience in the real estate field, and build an equity base for future real estate investments. He hoped to increase his return by managing and operating his property on weekends and after normal working hours. Leonard had recently received an inheritance from a great aunt of $25,000, and he wanted to achieve maximum leverage for this equity. Although he had no real estate experience, he had a working knowledge of carpentry from three years of designing and building sets for Harvard's Hasty Pudding Show.

BEACON HILL PROPERTIES

Leonard began to spend all his free evenings and weekends becoming familiar with the area. He obtained a copy of the U.S. Census Tract, Boston Standard Metropolitan Statistical Area (SMSA) to check the demographic data on age breakdowns, education, employment, marital status, income, length of stay, and ethnic background of present Beacon Hill residents. Most were transient, and either single or newly married. He checked maps for distances to the city's office, shopping, cultural, and entertainment centers, and found that Beacon Hill was close to all of these urban amenities.

He studied the real estate sections of newspapers for brokers' names and to get an idea of the types of offerings and range of prices available. He found that the Sunday papers had by far the largest real estate advertising sections. He answered some advertisements in order to meet real estate brokers, and learn about the available properties. He specifically attempted to visit those offices that did the most advertising (or that appeared to do the most business in the area).

Adjunct Professor William J. Poorvu prepared this case as the basis for class discussion rather than to illustrate either effective or ineffective handling of an administrative situation.

Many were located around Charles Street, the major commercial street of Beacon Hill. Normally, the brokers wanted to know the type of property in which he was interested, the amount of cash he had to invest, and whether he would live in the building.

Leonard was quite disappointed in the offerings that were shown to him. Although the income and expense statements of one building on Myrtle Street had made it seem quite attractive, the situation was very different when he actually visited the building. It was in a rundown state, and the apartments, occupied by groups of students, were in deplorable condition. The income statement of another property on Myrtle Street showed a 20% return on the cash investment; however, this made no allowance for repairs, vacancies, or management expenses. When considered, these costs reduced the return to 3%. Rentals in another building seemed too high. When Leonard spoke with one of the tenants, he found that the landlord had asked a rental of $810 per month for the apartment, but, when offered $675 per month, accepted on the condition that there be a one-year lease with no rent the first two months and then $810 rent per month for the remainder of the term. This arrangement would enable the landlord to show a higher monthly income after the initial two months.

Most properties sold for $270,000 and higher, and required an investment of more than $25,000. Leonard expected to obtain a bank loan for part of the purchase price through a mortgage (a legal instrument by which property is hypothecated to secure the payment of a debt or obligation). But institutional lenders were reluctant to lend more than 60-80% of the capitalized value of the property. Additional money might be raised by placing a second or junior mortgage on the property, but interest rates on this type of secondary financing were higher, and the personal credit of the borrower was often required as additional collateral. However, sellers were often willing to take a purchase money mortgage to facilitate the sale of the property. Nevertheless, having only $25,000 equity proved a major factor in limiting the building Leonard might purchase.

Leonard became discouraged. Although the real estate brokers were friendly, they never seemed to show him what he considered desirable properties. There rarely appeared to be an opportunity to create value by increasing rents or reducing expenses; if there were, the seller had already taken it into consideration in establishing his price. Leonard soon learned that many of the brokers owned buildings themselves, and were thus, in a sense, competitors of their own customers. Few properties in the area were sold by the owners themselves. Usually they were listed with several brokers who competed to receive a 5% sales commission by selling the property to one of their customers. Since there was considerable investor interest in the area, and listings were rarely exclusive with one broker, the brokers had to act quickly on the desirable properties to make their commissions. Therefore, most of the brokers had a few favored customers to whom they gave first chance. These customers usually had the necessary resources to act quickly to acquire the most desirable situations.

FACTORS AFFECTING VALUE

The same factors which caused Leonard to want to purchase on Beacon Hill had attracted many doctors, engineers, and businessmen also anxious to own real estate. As a result, the market values of many buildings on the Hill had tripled in the past ten years.

The area's location had considerable natural advantages. To the west was the Charles River; to the south was the Boston Public Gardens which led to Newbury Street, Boston's best shopping area; and to the east was the State House and Boston's financial district. The West End slums and the undesirable commercial activity of adjacent Scollay Square to the north had restrained values in the 1940s and 1950s. This had been especially true of the northern slope of the Hill, which had become known as the "back slope" because of its many lower-rent rooming houses. Under Boston's urban redevelopment program, however, in the 1960s and 1970s, the West End slums were torn down and were replaced by Charles River Park, a luxury apartment house development. Scollay Square was replaced by a new Government Center.

As a result of this redevelopment, values all over Beacon Hill had increased, but most drastically on the back or north slope. Rentals and condominium values there had increased as real estate operators began to buy and improve the property. Rents now ranged from $675-$800 for one-bedroom apartments and $900-$1100 for two-bedroom apartments. In spite of this, because most purchasers in this section were real estate speculators who expected a high return on their investment, Leonard felt there would be further growth as investors who were accustomed to lower returns from properties on the lower section of the Hill began to buy buildings on the north slope from these real estate speculators. The recent conversion of rental units to condominiums also caused values to increase.

The Massachusetts State Legislature had established the entire Beacon Hill area as an historic district, and set up a commission to preserve the character of the area. The approval of the commission had to be obtained for any changes to the exterior of a structure before the building department would issue a building permit. The commission would not permit the erection of any new buildings in the area. While this protected and enhanced the values of existing buildings, it provided a ceiling on land values, since land could not be reused for a different, more valuable purpose.

Leonard knew that this activity and interest in the area, which had driven prices up and was proving a disadvantage in his attempts to buy a property, would turn into an advantage once he owned a building. Many investors in Beacon Hill appeared to be satisfied with an 8% return on cash, which meant that for every $1,000 of cash flow, which remained after deducting all charges or costs from gross income, he could expect a buyer to pay $12,500. In some areas an investor might look for a 12.5% return, in which case $1,000 of cash flow would be worth only $8,000.

All of these factors led Leonard to believe that there was considerable safety in an investment in the area. There was little chance of depreciation for functional or economic causes. To obtain maximum capital appreciation, however, he would probably have to narrow his investment search to the back slope of Beacon Hill, where values were still not as high as on the "lower slope." He also realized that he would have to purchase a building that would require considerable renovation. Otherwise, once the income had become established the owner would ask a high selling price that would preclude much short-term growth in value. He had learned that he would have to act quickly if he did find an attractive opportunity. He would also have to check all figures given him carefully since few small buildings had audited financial statements and he could not rely solely on statements made by real estate brokers. Lastly, he knew that his $25,000 equity would limit him to acquiring a relatively small building.

ANDERSON STREET

In August of 1987, Leonard learned of a 4-unit apartment house on Beacon Hill that was for sale. A local broker with whom he was friendly had called to tell him that a building on Anderson Street had just come on the market, and that if he acted quickly, he might be able to outbid several real estate brokers who were interested in the property. Leonard knew that brokers always attempted to convey a sense of urgency, but since he was aware that desirable properties did sell quickly, he decided to investigate the property at once.

The property was located on the "back slope of the Hill" in an improving neighborhood. There had already been some increases in property values, and Leonard expected still greater increases as little new housing was being built in Boston. The property was located in the middle of the block, and was set back 100 feet from the road, which would afford an opportunity for creating an attractive entrance way and garden. The property had been built in the mid-1800s, probably as a middle-income town house. After being used as a rooming house for 20 years it had been gutted by a fire in 1986. Only the structural shell remained. An architect had purchased the shell for $120,000, but after spending $45,000 of what looked to be a $100,000 renovation job, he decided the total cost was beyond his cash available and placed the property on the market. Leonard felt that the architect's plans for renovation were in good taste and that thus far the work had been done well. Each of the first three floors was to have one two-bedroom apartment while the fourth floor would have a large one-bedroom apartment. For the first time, Leonard felt that he had seen a property that met his investment criteria. The property had profit potential; it was aesthetically desirable, in the area he wanted, and, with an asking price of $168,000, was within his price range.

Leonard was told that the $168,000 price was firm because considerable interest had already been shown in the property. A contractor to whom Leonard was referred confirmed that it would cost approximately $55,000 to complete the architect's plans.

Leonard prepared an income and expense statement to see whether the net income of the property would justify its price (see **Exhibit 1-1**). He figured that each of the three two-bedroom apartments could be rented at $990 per month, and the top floor one-bedroom apartment at $880 per month. Rentals would total $46,200 annually. From this figure, he subtracted a 5% vacancy allowance, which would represent two apartments sitting vacant for slightly more than a month. There was the additional possibility that if he did not rent the apartments himself, he would have to pay a broker's commission of 5% of the annual apartment rental. The broker, licensed by the state, received this commission for showing the property to prospective tenants, from bringing the tenants and landlord together, and helping to negotiate the contract between them.

Leonard estimated real estate taxes at 9.5% of the rental income or $4,200. This represented an assessed value of $250,000, which was approximately full market value, and $75,000 above the present $175,000 assessment. He obtained a quotation of a $1,000 annual premium from his real estate broker's firm for a package insurance policy providing protection against fire, extended coverage perils, public liability, loss of rents, and boiler explosion. The tenants would pay the electric bills for their own apartments, but the landlord would pay the bill for the public areas. A janitor would keep the public halls clean, change the light bulbs, and take out the trash. There were several services around Beacon Hill that performed this function for an annual fee of $1,200. Leonard had expected to do some of the repair work and all of the management work himself to increase his cash return, but his broker told him that since potential mortgage lenders or future purchasers would include these costs in their "setups," Leonard would have to do so, too. Also, if he should leave the area, he would have to hire outside firms to perform these services. Therefore, he included an allowance of 5% for repairs and a similar amount for management. His projections showed a cash flow before financing of $30,800, without any allowance for the work he would do himself. (See **Exhibit 1-1**.)

Leonard was very pleased. He told his wife that he had found a building that would be just right. With its skylights, beamed ceiling, and natural brick walls, the top floor apartment was just what they wanted to live in. They could live "rent free," while making money by doing their own managing and renting. They could take out the trash and clean the halls themselves. Although outside management would be more experienced, he would be more attentive and efficient. Rent from the other apartments would pay the other expenses, and he would gain real estate experience.

His wife said that while the apartment seemed very nice, she was not sure she liked the idea of living in a building they owned. They would get tenants' complaints at home. Also, she thought there might be a problem in doing business with their neighbors if they got friendly with them. She doubted that they would be able to charge maximum rents or raise rents.

The real estate broker questioned his decision to act as his own general contractor because of his lack of experience and time. He said that it was difficult, particularly on a part-time basis, to coordinate several subcontractors who never showed up when they said they would. The work might take longer than Leonard anticipated. Also, the Boston Building Department had a maze of rules and many inspectors; his renovation could be quite costly if he were forced to comply exactly with every regulation. Experienced contractors usually found ways of getting around these requirements. He would have to be careful however, to minimize changes and avoid extras once the job had been started, since most subcontractors would charge a premium for extras, because it would be too late to get competitive quotes on small amounts of work.

Leonard replied that any remodeling job would involve changes in adapting to field conditions. One of the reasons he wanted to do the work himself was to avoid the extra charges by subcontractors. Any outside contractor would carry a heavy contingency allowance in bidding the job. Certainly the contractor who gave him the $55,000 estimate to complete the renovation must have carried at least $5,000 for profit. Leonard reasoned that he had at least that $5,000 to spend before his lesson in remodeling began to cost him money.

MORTGAGE FINANCING

Leonard then went to see Jerry Smith, the mortgage officer of the savings bank who had recently given a $180,000 loan on the building for a 20 year period at a 10% interest rate. Smith told him that the existing mortgage was on a constant payment basis of 11.6% or $20,900 per year, which meant that the payments, including amortization and interest, remained the same throughout the entire term of the loan, but that the portion applicable to interest became less as the balance of the mortgage loan decreased. Correspondingly, the portion applicable to amortization increased. The mortgage payment plus a payment of one-twelfth of the estimated real estate taxes were made to the bank monthly. The bank also kept two months' real estate taxes in escrow as additional security. The banker explained that the loan could be paid off at any time, but that it would charge a prepayment penalty of 2% of the unpaid balance.

Leonard explained his plans for finishing the work and gave Smith his projected income and expense statements for the property. Smith noticed that Leonard's rental figures were $5,600 higher than those originally submitted by the present owner. At that time the bank had valued the property at $225,000 and given an 80% mortgage, the maximum permitted by bank policy. He asked whether Leonard knew his total costs. Leonard told him of the contractor's $55,000 bid. Smith told him that he should also consider carrying costs while the renovation work was going on. The bank might waive principal payments on the mortgage for six months during construction, but interest of $9,000 on the $180,000 must be paid, as well as real estate taxes of $1,400 assuming the $175,000 assessment would remain in effect until the renovation was complete. In addition, he still had to pay for six months' insurance at $500 and heat and electricity at $1,100. These costs totalled $12,000. There was also the two-month real estate tax escrow of $1,000, which was a cash outlay even though it would eventually be returned to him. Leonard could but did not need to assume the architect's existing mortgage, thus eliminating the need for new documents and a new title search by the bank's lawyer. (Assumption of a mortgage occurs when, in purchasing a property, the buyer assumes liability for payment of an existing note secured by a mortgage on the property.)

He asked whether the bank would increase its mortgage to $210,000. He explained that he might live in the building, manage it, and do some of the work himself, which would create more cash flow to serve the debt. The banker replied that he could not take this extra income into account in making his decision, since the bank always had to consider a loan in light of the costs the bank would incur if it had to foreclose and run the property itself. (A foreclosure sale occurs when property pledged as security for a loan is sold to pay the debt in the event of a default in payment or terms.)

Smith doubted that the bank would be interested in increasing its loan at this time since it was not certain that Leonard could get the increased rentals. However, Smith added that if the income level was increased when the building became rented and seasoned, the bank might reexamine his request.

Leonard next visited Sarah Harris, the mortgage loan officer at another local savings bank, to find out whether her bank would be interested in a $210,000 mortgage. Leonard showed her the income and expense projections, told her his costs, and explained his plans. Harris said that because of the 80% policy restriction, her bank would have to appraise the property at $262,500 to justify a $210,000 loan. Appraisals, she told Leonard, could be made on the basis of replacement cost, income, or market value based on recent comparable sales. She said that her bank preferred the income approach as the most realistic. Taking a capitalization rate of 11.6% on the $30,800 projected cash flow, she arrived at an appraised value of $265,500. Harris considered it likely that based on this appraisal she could justify a $210,000 mortgage at 10% interest for 20 years. She believed that the $30,800 annual cash flow from operations would be adequate to carry the $24,300 financing charge. She added that she was familiar with the area and considered Leonard's projected figures realistic, although she would have to see the property to be certain of her judgment.

She questioned Leonard about his current personal income. Leonard told her that his present salary was $26,000 per year. Harris said she would require credit references and certain other information about Leonard since he would be signing the note personally as additional protection to the bank against loss. Leonard asked why he would have to become personally liable since there was ample value in the property. He knew that his friends who had bought brownstones in New York had not assumed any personal liability. Harris said that this was the policy of virtually all savings banks in the Boston area for smaller buildings, especially when the loan to value ratio was as high as 80%. If Leonard had confidence in the building, he should not worry. Each year his liability declined as a portion of the mortgage loan was amortized.

Leonard asked whether there were other costs in closing the mortgage. Harris replied that Leonard would be responsible for legal and title expenses at closing, amounting to about $1,000, which would cover the cost of the bank's lawyer. The bank's lawyer is responsible for certifying to the bank that the owner has a valid fee simple ownership in the property, which means that the owner has the right to dispose of it, pledge it, or pass it on to his heirs as he sees fit. Also, the lawyer ascertains that there are no liens on the property senior to the bank's interest. Unless the document's conditions specify otherwise, the seniority of a lien depends on the date it was recorded in the County Registry of Deeds Office. When a lien is paid off a discharge is put on record. There are some liens that are a matter of record that a bank will accept as senior to its position. These include zoning or use regulations, building codes, party wall agreements (where two buildings share the same wall) or certain easements where one party has specific rights or privileges on the land of the other. The certification of title is often done through the issuance of an insurance policy written by a title insurance company at a one-time cost paid by the borrower or purchaser. Harris also told him he should not rely on the bank's attorney to represent him. He should budget about $900 for his own attorney and other miscellaneous costs. Lastly, there would be a 1% loan origination fee of $2,100 payable to the bank upon closing.

LEGAL ADVICE

Leonard then consulted Josh Guberman, his family's attorney, about the whole transaction. Leonard was very disturbed about the bank's requirement that he sign the mortgage note personally. His attorney told him that he did not want to understate the risk, but that this was a customary bank practice in making small mortgage loans in Massachusetts, where banks were often more conservative than in other areas of the country.

Leonard inquired about alternate methods for raising the extra $30,000 besides accepting the new mortgage. Guberman believed that secondary financing could be obtained, but at an interest rate of 15% and only with a personal endorsement. The seller might take back a purchase money second mortgage, but again Leonard would probably have to sign the note personally and repay the entire loan over a 3- to 5-year period. In addition, if the demand for the property were as strong as Leonard indicated an all-cash offer might have a better chance of winning the property than one contingent upon a purchase money second mortgage.

Leonard asked whether he would not be taking a big risk in making an offer for the property without having his financing secured. Guberman explained that while he would have to submit a written offer for the property, together with a deposit to be held by the real estate broker, he could make his offer contingent upon his being permitted to assume the seller's mortgage. This would give him some safety, while still permitting him to attempt to find a higher mortgage.

If Leonard's offer were accepted, a purchase and sales contract would be signed, based on a standard Boston Real Estate Board form (see Exhibit 1-2). Guberman said that in case of forfeiture as a result of the buyer's failure to perform, the sales deposit, normally 5%-10% of the purchase price, would be kept by the seller as liquidated damages. Therefore, Leonard's risk would be limited to $8,400 if the seller would accept a 5% deposit. Also, if the seller could not deliver a quit-claim deed, relinquishing any interest he held in the property and giving a clear title to the buyer, the buyer would be entitled to a refund of his deposit.

Guberman then asked Leonard whether he had adequate funds to complete the project even with a $210,000 mortgage. The asking price for the property was $168,000; the remodeling cost $55,000; carrying costs during construction were now $13,500 because of the higher mortgage; closing costs $4,000; and escrow funds $1,000. These costs totalled $241,500. The $210,000 mortgage or mortgages and his $25,000 equity would still leave him $6,500 short. Leonard replied that he planned to save money by acting as his own general contractor, and he hoped to remodel and rent the property in four months rather than six months. A $210,000 first mortgage with an annual carrying charge of $24,300, although requiring a personal guarantee, would give him leverage, making the pretax return on his $25,000 cash investment 27.0% versus 13.1% on a free and clear or all-cash basis. In addition, he would be amortizing a mortgage. The return would be even greater if he lived in the building and managed it himself.

Guberman asked why Leonard was not selling the units as condominiums. He should be able to get about $80,000 per unit, which could net him $60,000 for all four units after sales costs. Moreover, at a later time a conversion might run into problems given the difficulties of evicting existing tenants. Leonard responded by saying that he wanted to maximize the long-term opportunity of what he considered an excellent market in an excellent area. He was not in it for a short term gain. Rents should increase over time. Although the 1986 tax law reduced the advantages of being able to depreciate real property, he expected that about $8,000 of his income from the property would be sheltered from taxes.

The lawyer said that Leonard's analysis seemed reasonable, but his estimates did not put a dollar value on Leonard's time. He wondered whether this should be considered. Also, he wanted Leonard to realize the seriousness of this time commitment since his full-time job was still his prime responsibility. Finally, he asked him to consider carefully the amount of the offer he was submitting and the risks involved.

Exhibit 1-1

Income

1st floor	$990/month
2nd floor	990/month
3rd floor	990/month
4th floor	880/month
	$3,850 × 12 = $46,200
Allowance for vacancies	2,310
	$43,890

Operating Expenses

Real estate taxes	$4,200
Heat	1,490
Electricity	400
Water	400
Insurance	1,000
Janitor	1,200
Repairs @ 5%	2,200
Management @ 5%	2,200
	$13,090

Cash flow from operations[1] $30,800

[1]Sometimes referred to as free and clear cash flow or net operating income.

Exhibit 1-2

From the Office of:

STANDARD FORM
PURCHASE AND SALE AGREEMENT

1. PARTIES
   (fill in)

   This _____ day of _____ 19 ____

   hereinafter called the SELLER, agrees to SELL and

   hereinafter called the BUYER or PURCHASER, agrees to BUY, upon the terms hereinafter set forth, the following described premises:

2. DESCRIPTION
   (fill in and include title reference)

3. BUILDINGS, STRUCTURES, IMPROVEMENTS, FIXTURES

   (fill in or delete)

   Included in the sale as a part of said premises are the buildings, structures, and improvements now thereon, and the fixtures belonging to the SELLER and used in connection therewith including, if any, all wall-to-wall carpeting, drapery rods, automatic garage door openers, venetian blinds, window shades, screens, screen doors, storm windows and doors, awnings, shutters, furnaces, heaters, heating equipment, stoves, ranges, oil and gas burners and fixtures appurtenant thereto, hot water heaters, plumbing and bathroom fixtures, garbage disposers, electric and other lighting fixtures, mantels, outside television antennas, fences, gates, trees, shrubs, plants, and, ONLY IF BUILT IN, refrigerators, air conditioning equipment, ventilators, dishwashers, washing machines and dryers; and

   but excluding

4. TITLE DEED
   (fill in)
   Include here by specific reference any restrictions, easements, rights and obligations in party walls not included in (b), leases, municipal and other liens, other encumbrances, and make provision to protect SELLER against BUYER'S breach of SELLER's covenants in leases, where necessary.

   Said premises are to be conveyed by a good and sufficient quitclaim deed running to the BUYER, or to the nominee designated by the BUYER by written notice to the SELLER at least seven   days before the deed is to be delivered as herein provided, and said deed shall convey a good and clear record and marketable title thereto, free from encumbrances, except
   (a) Provisions of existing building and zoning laws;
   (b) Existing rights and obligations in party walls which are not the subject of written agreement;
   (c) Such taxes for the then current year as are not due and payable on the date of the delivery of such deed;
   (d) Any liens for municipal betterments assessed after the date of this agreement;
   (e) Easements, restrictions and reservations of record, if any, so long as the same do not prohibit or materially interfere with the current use of said premises;
   *(f)

5. PLANS

   If said deed refers to a plan necessary to be recorded therewith the SELLER shall deliver such plan with the deed in form adequate for recording or registration.

6. REGISTERED TITLE

   In addition to the foregoing, if the title to said premises is registered, said deed shall be in form sufficient to entitle the BUYER to a Certificate of Title of said premises, and the SELLER shall deliver with said deed all instruments, if any, necessary to enable the BUYER to obtain such Certificate of Title.

7. PURCHASE PRICE
   (fill in); space is allowed to write out the amounts if desired

   The agreed purchase price for said premises is
                                                                    dollars, of which
   $ have been paid as a deposit this day and
   $
   $ are to be paid at the time of delivery of the deed in cash, or by certified, cashier's, treasurer's or bank check.

   $ _____
   $ TOTAL

Exhibit 1-2 (*continued*)

8.	**TIME FOR PERFORMANCE; DELIVERY OF DEED** (*fill in*)	Such deed is to be delivered at o'clock M. on the day of 19 , at the Registry of Deeds, unless otherwise agreed upon in writing. It is agreed that time is of the essence of this agreement.

9. **POSSESSION and CONDITIONS of PREMISES.** (*attach a list of exceptions, if any*)

Full possession of said premises free of all tenants and occupants, except as herein provided, is to be delivered at the time of the delivery of the deed, said premises to be then (a) in the same condition as they now are reasonable use and wear thereof excepted, and (b) not in violation of said building and zoning laws, and (c) in compliance with provisions of any instrument referred to in clause 4 hereof. The BUYER shall be entitled to an inspection of said premises prior to the delivery of the deed in order to determine whether the condition thereof complies with the terms of this clause.

10. **EXTENSION TO PERFECT TITLE OR MAKE PREMISES CONFORM** (*Change period of time if desired*).

If the SELLER shall be unable to give title or to make conveyance, or to deliver possession of the premises, all as herein stipulated, or if at the time of delivery of the deed the premises do not conform with the provisions hereof, then any payments made under this agreement shall be forthwith refunded and all other obligations of the parties hereto shall cease and this agreement shall be void without recourse to the parties hereto, unless the SELLER elects to use reasonable efforts to remove any defects in title, or to deliver possession as provided herein, or to make the said premises conform to the provisions hereof, as the case may be, in which event the SELLER shall give written notice thereof to the BUYER at or before the time for performance hereunder, and thereupon the time for performance hereof shall be extended for a period of thirty   days.

11. **FAILURE TO PERFECT TITLE OR MAKE PREMISES CONFORM, etc.**

If at the expiration of the extended time the SELLER shall have failed so to remove any defects in title, deliver possession, or make the premises conform, as the case may be, all as herein agreed, or if at any time during the period of this agreement or any extension thereof, the holder of a mortgage on said premises shall refuse to permit the insurance proceeds, if any, to be used for such purposes, then any payments made under this agreement shall be forthwith refunded and all other obligations of the parties hereto shall cease and this agreement shall be void without recourse to the parties hereto.

12. **BUYER'S ELECTION TO ACCEPT TITLE**

The BUYER shall have the election, at either the original or any extended time for performance, to accept such title as the SELLER can deliver to the said premises in their then condition and to pay therefor the purchase price without deduction, in which case the SELLER shall convey such title, except that in the event of such conveyance in accord with the provisions of this clause, if the said premises shall have been damaged by fire or casualty insured against, then the SELLER shall, unless the SELLER has previously restored the premises to their former condition, either

   (a) pay over or assign to the BUYER, on delivery of the deed, all amounts recovered or recoverable on account of such insurance, less any amounts reasonably expended by the SELLER for any partial restoration, or

   (b) if a holder of a mortgage on said premises shall not permit the insurance proceeds or a part thereof to be used to restore the said premises to their former condition or to be so paid over or assigned, give to the BUYER a credit against the purchase price, on delivery of the deed, equal to said amounts so recovered or recoverable and retained by the holder of the said mortgage less any amounts reasonably expended by the SELLER for any partial restoration.

13. **ACCEPTANCE OF DEED**

The acceptance of a deed by the BUYER or his nominee as the case may be, shall be deemed to be a full performance and discharge of every agreement and obligation herein contained or expressed, except such as are, by the terms hereof, to be performed after the delivery of said deed.

14. **USE OF MONEY TO CLEAR TITLE**

To enable the SELLER to make conveyance as herein provided, the SELLER may, at the time of delivery of the deed, use the purchase money or any portion thereof to clear the title of any or all encumbrances or interests, provided that all instruments so procured are recorded simultaneously with the delivery of said deed.

15. **INSURANCE** * *Insert amount* (*list additional types of insurance and amounts as agreed*)

Until the delivery of the deed, the SELLER shall maintain insurance on said premises as follows:

Type of Insurance	Amount of Coverage
(a) Fire	* $
(b) Extended Coverage	
(c)	

16. **ADJUSTMENTS** (*list operating expenses, if any, or attach schedule*)

Collected rents, mortgage interest, water and sewer use charges, operating expenses (if any) according to the schedule attached hereto or set forth below, and taxes for the then current year, shall be apportioned and fuel value shall be adjusted, as of the day of performance of this agreement and the net amount thereof shall be added to or deducted from, as the case may be, the purchas price payable by the BUYER at the time of delivery of the deed. Uncollected rents for the current rental period shall be apportioned if and when collected by either party.

Exhibit 1-2 (*continued*)

17. **ADJUSTMENT OF UNASSESSED AND ABATED TAXES**

If the amount of said taxes is not known at the time of the delivery of the deed, they shall be apportioned on the basis of the taxes assessed for the preceding year, with a reapportionment as soon as the new tax rate and valuation can be ascertained; and, if the taxes which are to be apportioned shall thereafter be reduced by abatement, the amount of such abatement, less the reasonable cost of obtaining the same, shall be apportioned between the parties, provided that neither party shall be obligated to institute or prosecute proceedings for an abatement unless herein otherwise agreed.

18. **BROKER'S FEE** *(fill in fee with dollar amount or percentage; also name of Broker(s))*

A broker's fee for professional service of
is due from the SELLER to

the Broker(s) herein, but if the SELLER pursuant to the terms of clause 21 hereof retains the deposits made hereunder by the BUYER, said Broker(s) shall be entitled to receive from the SELLER an amount equal to one-half the amount so retained or an amount equal to the Broker's fee for professional services according to this contract, whichever is the lesser.

19. **BROKER(S) WARRANTY** *(fill in name)*

The Broker(s) named herein
warrant(s) that the Broker(s) is(are) duly licensed as such by the Commonwealth of Massachusetts.

20. **DEPOSIT** *(fill in, or delete reference to broker(s) if SELLER holds deposit)*

All deposits made hereunder shall be held in escrow by the Broker(s) subject to the terms of this agreement and shall be duly accounted for at the time for performance of this agreement, provided however that in the event of any disagreement the Broker(s) may retain said deposits pending instructions mutually given by the SELLER and the BUYER.

21. **BUYER'S DEFAULT; DAMAGES**

If the BUYER shall fail to fulfill the BUYER'S agreements herein, all deposits made hereunder by the BUYER shall be retained by the SELLER as liquidated damages unless within thirty days after the time for performance of this agreement or any extension hereof, the SELLER otherwise notifies the BUYER in writing.

22. **RELEASE BY HUSBAND OR WIFE**

The SELLER'S spouse hereby agrees to join in said deed and to release and convey all statutory and other rights and interests in said premises.

23. **BROKER AS PARTY**

The Broker(s) named herein join(s) in this agreement and become(s) a party hereto, insofar as any provisions of this agreement expressly apply to the Broker(s), and to any amendments or modifications of such provisions to which the Broker(s) agree(s) in writing.

24. **LIABILITY OF TRUSTEE, SHAREHOLDER, BENEFICIARY, etc.**

If the SELLER or BUYER executes this agreement in a representative or fiduciary capacity, only the principal or the estate represented shall be bound, and neither the SELLER or BUYER so executing, nor any shareholder or beneficiary of any trust, shall be personally liable for any obligation, express or implied, hereunder.

25. **WARRANTIES AND REPRESENTATIONS** *(fill in); if none, state "none"; if any listed, indicate by whom each warranty or representation was made*

The BUYER acknowledges that the BUYER has not been influenced to enter into this transaction nor has he relied upon any warranties or representations not set forth or incorporated in this agreement or previously made in writing, except for the following additional warranties and representations, if any, made by either the SELLER or the Broker(s):

26. **MORTGAGE CONTINGENCY CLAUSE**

In order to help finance the acquisition of said premises, the BUYER shall apply for a conventional bank or other institutional mortgage loan of $_____, payable in no less than _____ years at an interest rate not to exceed _____ If despite the BUYER's diligent efforts a commitment for such loan cannot be obtained on or before_____ , 19_____ the BUYER may terminate this agreement by written notice to the SELLER(S) and/or the Broker(s), as agent for the SELLER, prior to the expiration of such time, whereupon any payments made under this agreement shall be forthwith refunded and all other obligations of the parties hereto shall cease and this agreement shall be void without recourse to the parties hereto. In no event will the BUYER be deemed to have used diligent efforts to obtain such commitment unless the BUYER submits a complete mortgage loan application conforming to the foregoing provisions on or before _____,19_____.

Exhibit 1-2 (*continued*)

27.	CONSTRUCTION OF AGREEMENT	This instrument, executed in multiple counterparts, is to be construed as a Massachusetts contract, is to take effect as a sealed instrument, sets forth the entire contract between the parties, is binding upon and enures to the benefit of the parties hereto and their respective heirs, devisees, executors, administrators, successors and assigns, and may be cancelled, modified or amended only by a written instrument executed by both the SELLER and the BUYER. If two or more persons are named herein as BUYER their obligations hereunder shall be joint and several. The captions and marginal notes are used only as a matter of convenience and are not to be considered a part of this agreement or to be used in determining the intent of the parties to it.
28.	LEAD PAINT LAW	The parties acknowledge that, under Massachusetts law, whenever a child or children under six years of age resides in any residential premises in which any paint, plaster or other accessible material contains dangerous levels of lead, the owner of said premises must remove or cover said paint, plaster or other material so as to make it inaccessible to children under six years of age.
29.	SMOKE DETECTORS	The SELLER shall, at the time of the delivery of the deed, deliver a certificate from the fire department of the city or town in which said premises are located stating that said premises have been equipped with approved smoke detectors in conformity with applicable law.
30.	ADDITIONAL PROVISIONS	The initialed riders, if any, attached hereto, are incorporated herein by reference.

NOTICE: This is a legal document that creates binding obligations. If not understood, consult an attorney.

_____   _____
SELLER (or spouse)   *SELLER*

_____   _____
BUYER   *BUYER*

_____
Broker(s)

EXTENSION

Date_____

The time for the performance of the foregoing agreement is extended until_____o'clock_____ _____M. on the_____day of_____19_____, time still being of the essence of this agreement as extended. In all other respects, this agreement is hereby ratified and confirmed.

This extension, executed in multiple counterparts, is intended to take effect as a sealed instrument.

_____   _____
SELLER (or spouse)   SELLER

_____   _____
BUYER   BUYER

_____
BROKER(S)

2

SAVANNAH WEST

In August, 1977, Alison Porter, a loan officer with Chemical Bank, has the weekend to decide whether to recommend a $3 million construction loan for a proposed 216-unit garden apartment project in Savannah, Georgia. Though the developer has a good track record with Chemical, and has the potential to become a major player in Georgia development, Porter must justify the loan based on the potential for success of the development itself. In addition to introducing students to the conceptual framework of project evaluation, the case highlights the relationship of lenders to developers.

Discussion Questions

1. Based on the appraisal and other marketing information, do you think there is sufficient justification for building this 216-unit apartment at this site? What do you think of the design and apartment layouts?

2. Evaluate the financial risks, business risks, and rewards from the point of view of the developer, Chemical Bank and Empire Savings Bank. What are the key financial assumptions? Are they reasonable?

3. As Porter, would you recommend that Chemical Bank make this loan and if so, for what amount, and on what terms?

On Friday, August 12, 1977, Alison Porter, a three-year veteran of Chemical Bank's "Real Estate Bank" with medals and scars to prove it, faced the unpleasant prospect of another working weekend. She had just returned from a trip to Savannah, Georgia, where she met with Willy Welsh, an Atlanta developer. Welsh was anxious to get approval for a $3 million construction loan so that he could begin work on Savannah West, a 216-unit "California-style" garden apartment complex in Savannah.

Welsh felt it essential to get started for several reasons. Rumors were afloat that other developers were preparing plans for multi-family projects in Savannah. Welsh wanted to be the first one in the ground and possibly scare off competition. Pressure to start also came from his subcontractors. He had promised them a September 1 starting date. Welsh knew that if the project did not start on time, he could not hold the subcontractors to their initial bids. In addition, if there was a delay, the subcontractors might find other work, and he would have to begin anew the delicate, frustrating job of hiring and scheduling subcontractors to conform to a ten month construction timetable. Welsh was also anxious to get started because the take-out commitment from the Empire State Savings Bank had a time limitation. The $3 million commitment from Empire Savings specified completion of the construction by September 1, 1978. By starting September 1, 1977, Welsh would have ten months to complete the construction, plus a two-month buffer to absorb possible delays.

During her trip to Savannah, Porter promised Welsh a quick answer. Porter had scheduled a meeting of the loan committee for Monday, August 15. At that meeting the committee would either turn down the loan or give it tentative approval. The members of the loan committee would rely heavily on Porter's memorandum explaining the key issues.

WILLY WELSH

Willy Welsh began working in construction during the summers while he was in high school and college. After graduating from the Georgia Institute of Technology, he joined a construction company in Atlanta. In 1968, at the age of 32, he went into partnership with Harry Barnes, an experienced contractor who built

Associate Fellow John H. Vogel, Jr. prepared this case under the supervision of Adjunct Professor William J. Poorvu as the basis for class discussion rather than to illustrate either effective or ineffective handling of an administrative situation. It is based on a case originally prepared by The Harlan Company, Inc.

apartments and light commercial properties. Welsh became president of the company a year later.

In 1970, Welsh created Engineered Concepts, a general contracting firm. He immediately won a bid for the construction of a $5 million, 280-unit apartment development. His firm also took on the supervision of a 288-unit apartment complex as part of a joint venture agreement. Since 1972, Engineered Concepts has completed construction on over $25 million of property. Welsh has also set up a subsidiary which manages income-producing properties (**Exhibit 2-1**).

Welsh came in contact with Chemical Bank in 1976. At that time, Chemical Bank was involved in the troubled Greenbriar Apartments, a 400-unit garden apartment development in Atlanta. A local savings and loan had issued a take-out, contingent upon 80% occupancy by July 1, 1976. The Thomas Herbert Company, Inc. of Atlanta, Georgia, the developer, ran into serious cost overruns and untimely delays. At the same time, a competing project in the neighborhood came on-stream ahead of schedule and drew away potential tenants. When July arrived, the project was less than one-half completed and only 15% occupied; thus canceling the savings bank's commitment.

Without the permanent financing to bail them out, Chemical Bank, the largest of the group of banks involved in the construction financing, realized Herbert would not be able to repay his loan. Chemical also discovered that several of the key subcontractors were displeased with the developer. In an effort to save the project, Chemical decided to step in and arrange for someone else to finish the work. A deal was struck with Herbert, relieving him of personal and corporate liability, and Chemical obtained a deed in lieu of foreclosure. Chemical assigned David Hancock to take charge of the work-out. An old college classmate in the real estate department of one of Chemical's correspondent banks in Atlanta steered Hancock to Willy Welsh.

Welsh's people, in close consultation with Chemical, reviewed the Greenbriar project, and agreed to complete construction on a fee basis for $3.5 million. Welsh recommended several design changes that he felt would improve the marketability of the apartments. Hancock agreed and Welsh proceeded with construction.

Dramatic changes ensued. The project was completed within five months and within the stipulated budget. Welsh's property management subsidiary put together an outstanding marketing program and achieved 40% occupancy in four months and 90% occupancy in nine months. A suitable purchaser was then found, and Chemical Bank received full repayment on its loan.

CHEMICAL BANK

Chemical Bank is the fifth largest bank in New York, and the sixth largest in the United States in terms of both capitalization and deposits. In July 1977 it had over $23 billion in deposits and over $30 billion in assets. There had been an 11% growth in deposits and a 15% growth in assets over the prior twelve months.

Several departments at Chemical Bank are organized as "separate banks." There is, for example, a "Metropolitan Bank," a "Corporate Bank" and a "Trust and Investment Bank." In September 1976, Chemical Bank set up a "Real Estate Bank." The prior two years had been rough ones for the bank's real estate department. The recession of 1974-1975 led to a large volume of real estate problem loans, especially loans made to Real Estate Investment Trusts. The "Real Estate Bank" represented management's recognition of the need for more specialized and sophisticated personnel to deal with existing and new loans in real estate.

By the end of the following year, the "Real Estate Bank" employed 200 people, including 110 loan officers, each of whom was responsible for a specific geographic area in the United States or Canada. In 1977, the "Real Estate Bank" managed a $1.45 billion asset portfolio. Most of this portfolio was inherited. One of the major achievements of 1977 was upgrading this portfolio by reducing loans to Real Estate Investment Trusts from $490 million to $332 million.

In addition to making loans, the "Real Estate Bank" provides a full line of banking services to people in the real estate industry such as lock box facilities, short-term investment management and lines of credit. In creating this separate entity, Chemical Bank hoped to increase its flexibility and improve its service to customers. The goal of the "Real Estate Bank" is to attract new customers on a nationwide basis and to develop and maintain broad customer relationships.

When David Hancock, who had handled the Greenbriar work-out, learned that Willy Welsh was preparing to start a new project in Savannah, Georgia, and had already secured a take- out mortgage from the Empire State Savings Bank, he decided that he had found a stable, competent new customer for the bank. He contacted Alison Porter, detailed the successful Greenbriar work-out, and praised Welsh's efficiency and thoroughness. Porter immediately contacted Welsh and set up a meeting.

SAVANNAH

The city of Savannah is located on the Savannah River, 20 miles upstream from the Atlantic Ocean. It is rich in historical tradition, having been established in 1733 as a Port City in the Georgia colony. Founded by General James Oglethorpe, Savannah was America's first "planned" city and retains today the squares and original street plan.

Savannah is the second largest city in Georgia with a population of 218,000. Eighty percent of these people live in Chatham County. Since 1970 the population of Chatham County has grown at approximately 1% per year. The increase has been mostly in the 20-34 age group. Approximately 60% of the increase has been families with incomes between $12,000 and $20,000. Following the national trend, household size in this area has been declining from 3.5 in 1970 to an estimated 3.2 in 1978. Single-family housing starts in Chatham County are expected to average about 500 per year during the next several years.

The major sources of employment are: the port and related distribution facilities, manufacturing, tourism, and the military. All four areas of employment are growing. The port handles 10 million tons per year, adds about $73 million to the Savannah economy and is currently undergoing a $27 million expansion. The 193 industries that manufacture products in and around Savannah include American Cyanamid, Continental Forest Industries and Savannah Foods. This sector of the economy received a boost from the recent improvements in the federal and state highway network, especially the construction of I-16 giving truckers direct freeway access to I-95 and the rest of the federal highway system. Tourism has grown, especially among foreigners who are taking advantage of the devaluation of the dollar. The Hunter/Stewart army base has always been a major but erratic factor in the Savannah economy. A dramatic build-up is presently underway. The prospects for this army base are enhanced by the fact that the senator from Georgia is chairman of the Armed Services Committee.

As the chart below indicates, the median per capita income in Savannah is projected to rise in the years ahead:

Median Family Income[1] (Savannah SMSA) (constant dollars)

	1975 (ACTUAL)		1980 (PROJECTED)		1985 (PROJECTED)	
	# FAMILIES	INCOME	# FAMILIES	INCOME	# FAMILIES	INCOME
Bryan	2,206	$7,432	2,342	$ 8,852	2,342	$10,272
Chatham	59,960	8,720	65,042	9,802	67,844	10,844
Effingham	4,432	8,944	5,086	10,624	5,640	12,254

[1]These census figures and estimates include the military population.

Unemployment in the civilian work force is estimated at 7.6%, which is close to the 7.4% state average.

SAVANNAH WEST

As vacancy rates began to rise in the Atlanta area, Willy Welsh looked for new opportunities. On a visit to his family in Savannah, Welsh talked with rental agents and learned that the market for apartments was getting tight. There had been little or no multi-family construction in Chatham County in over three years, since the failure of a 200-unit garden apartment project. As a result, vacancy rates in existing apartment complexes were dropping rapidly, from 7% in 1972 to 5% in 1974, and then down to less than 4% in 1976. As far as Welsh was concerned, the market "felt good."

Welsh was determined to move fast. In a short time, he zeroed in on an 11.8-acre property in Chatham County just south of Hunter Army Air Base. This location was excellent, he believed, for a 216-unit garden apartment. It was only 6.5 miles from the Savannah business district. Shopping was available along

Abercorn Extension and at the enclosed 750,000-square- foot Oglethorpe Mall. Although the property was close to Hunter Army Airfield, noise did not seem to be a problem (**Exhibit 2-2**).

Welsh surveyed the multi-family developments in the area and found that vacancies were down to 1%. He felt that he could build a complex that would "completely outclass them" and still rent at a comparable or slightly higher rate (**Exhibit 2-3**). In aiming at what he defined as the "semi-luxury" market, Welsh claimed: "I know what they want. Not the old, stuffy, genteel style so prevalent in Savannah. Our "California" look will sweep them off their feet" (**Exhibit 2-4**).

Based on his survey of neighboring properties, Welsh estimated that he could achieve gross revenues of approximately $600,000 and net income before financing of close to $400,000 (**Exhibit 2-5**). He then estimated his costs as follows:

Land (12 acres±) zoned for 216 units, with on-site water, sewer, and drainage	$ 172,000
Construction and site development	2,578,000
Architectural, engineering and inspection	50,000
Construction interest ($3,000,000 x .5 x 9%)[1]	135,000
Legal and accounting	20,000
Construction loan and permanent loan fees	45,000
	$3,000,000

[1]In August 1977 the prime rate was 7%.

Based on this analysis he negotiated for and purchased the 11.8-acre tract for $172,000.

THE TAKE-OUT

Welsh took his plans and projections to New York to look for permanent financing. He contacted the Empire State Savings Bank, which then hired an Atlanta appraiser to do an appraisal of the property and the project. The appraiser concluded that a 216-unit garden apartment complex constituted the highest and best use of the property. He further stated that when completed, the complex would have a market value of $4,000,000 divided as follows:

Land	$ 200,000
Improvements (see **Exhibit 2-6**)	3,800,000

Empire savings then offered to provide $3 million of permanent financing at 9½% interest for a twelve-year term with a balloon payment due at the end. The constant payment including interest and principal would be 10.23%. Empire offered this financing in the form of a floor-to-ceiling first mortgage. Empire would advance $2,550,000 (the floor) after July 1, 1978 and prior to September 1, 1978. To receive this floor payment, Welsh was required to meet all the terms of the loan covenant including satisfactory completion of all of the construction. Before releasing the $450,000 balance of the mortgage, Empire insisted that occupancy at Savannah West be such that:

> The collectable rentals from the rental units in the buildings shall be at least $552,000 per annum on a nonfurnished basis, exclusive of concessions, and the space shall be rented on a basis so that if the buildings were 100% rented the annual rentals would be at least $601,200.

This ceiling loan would not be made later than January 30, 1979. Welsh secured this $3 million take-out commitment by depositing $30,000 in a noninterest-bearing account. The deposit would be forfeited if the loan were not consummated.

THE DECISION

Like most construction lenders, Chemical Bank did not like to tie up its money in long-term loans and therefore expected most developers to secure take-out financing before applying for a construction loan. Now that Welsh had this permanent financing arranged, he only needed approval from Alison Porter and he could begin construction. In fact, Welsh was so confident of his new relationship with Chemical Bank and so anxious about local competition, that he was prepared to begin construction while waiting for all of the paperwork to be completed. If need be, to get things underway, Welsh was willing to provide some of the initial financing himself. The Savannah subcontractors would be told of the Chemical commitment and asked to postpone their billings for eight weeks.

Porter had reservations about this strategy. She had heard that Savannah subcontractors were inexperienced, undercapitalized and sometimes surly. Would they make a reliable source for the initial financing? In case of problems, would Welsh's proposed strategy lead to mechanics' liens[1] "getting in ahead" of Chemical's claim?

On the positive side, Welsh was exactly the kind of customer Chemical's "Real Estate Bank" was looking for. Chemical was committed to expanding its direct lending in the South Atlantic region. Although the bank had tended to confine most of its activity in that region to participations in loans generated by local correspondent banks, the continuing strong development in the South

---

[1] If a person supplying certain types of labor or material for a building, such as a plumber or electrician, has not been paid within a legislatively designated time period, that person can place a mechanic's lien on the property. Clear title to the property cannot be obtained until this claim is settled. In practice construction lenders often require a certification of clear title with each draw of funds.

Atlantic region and the low level of construction activity in the Northeast had led Chemical to take a more aggressive approach. Welsh might be exactly the right person on whom Chemical should take a chance. He had the potential to become a major regional developer. Here was Chemical's chance to become his bank.

Porter's memorandum, however, would have to concentrate on the specifics of this loan. Did the project make sense financially and otherwise? How helpful was the Empire take-out in minimizing Chemical's risks? What importance should she put on the appraisal showing that the completed property would be worth $4 million?

The loan committee would also want to know about Welsh. What was he putting into the project? What kind of profit was Welsh expecting to make on this project and when would he make it? How valuable was his personal guarantee?

The committee would also expect Porter to recommend terms. What would be an appropriate interest rate relative to prime? What kind of covenants would protect the bank? What covenants would be acceptable to Welsh?

The loan committee liked its officers to begin with a recommendation, rather than just presenting undigested facts. Porter checked her notes and began to write.

Exhibit 2-1

WILLIAM WELSH—PERSONAL BALANCE SHEET ($000—JULY 30, 1977)

Cash	$370	Accounts payable	1
Accounts receivable	162	Loans against	
Insurance policy		life insurance	3
(cash surrender value)	8	Mortgages against	
Stock and securities[1]	1,275	real estate	5,973
Real estate owned[2]	7,761	Net worth	3,599
	9,576		**9,576**

INCOME STATEMENT ($000)

Salary	$110
Bonuses and other payments from Engineered Concepts	300
Other	6
	$416

PERSONAL DATA

Married, 2 children, age 40
Residence: 12 Fairview Road, Atlanta, Georgia

[1]Description of Security	Cost	Estimated Market Value
Georgia Power Bonds	$10,000	$ 10,000
Engineered Concepts		1,213,000
Oilwell-Halsey Project	38,000	1,000
Welsh Property Management Co.		51,000
		$1,275,000

[2]Real Estate Owned	Estimated Market Value
60A Sumpter Road, Clayborn County, Georgia-zoned apartments	$ 112,500
Approximately 36 acres on Old Arkansas Road	108,900
288 unit apartment complex Clark County, Georgia	2,042,500
395 unit apartment complex under construction Dekalb County, Georgia	5,496,783
	$7,760,683

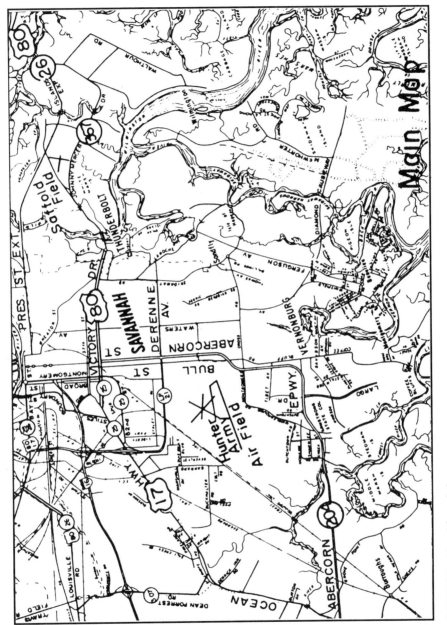

Exhibit 2-2 Map of Savannah Area

25

Exhibit 2-3 Comparable Apartments

The following chart is a summary of the rent comparables. The rental schedules have been analyzed as follows:

COMPARABLE NO.	SIZE	1 BR RENT/SQ. FT.	2 BR RENT/SQ. FT.	3 BR RENT/SQ. FT.
1	172 units	$.28	$.25	$.24
2	278 units	.26	.22	.17
3	160 units	.25	.23	.22
4	58 units	NA	.23	.22
5	238 units	.21	.18	NA
6	232 units	.29	.20	.20
7	216 units	.27	.24	NA
8	168 units	.26	.24	NA
9	102 units	.25	.24	NA

The rent comparables are judged to be similar to the subject with regard to pertinent features such as location, quality and type of construction, and amenities. More detailed information about #6 and #7 follows.

Comparable #6

Project: Spanish Villa
        10599 Abercorn Street Extension
        232 Units

TYPE AND SIZE	RENT MONTHLY/ANNUALLY	MONTHLY RENT/SQ. FT.
64—1 BR, 1 Bath, 664 sq. ft. Gdn.	$195/$2,340	$.29
138—2 BR, 1-1/2 Bath, 1,200 sq. ft. TH	$245/$2,940	$.20
30—3 BR, 2-1/2 Bath, 1,336 sq. ft. TH	$265/$3,180	$.20

Remarks: Project estimated to have been completed in 1972. Buildings are two story with all stucco exterior. Occupancy is reported at 100%. Tenant responsible for all utilities, including water. Standard fully equipped kitchens, including frost-free refrigerator. Drapes included. Amenities include clubhouse, two pools, laundry room, and playground. April 1 rental increase put in effect.

Comparable #7

Project: Club Riviera
        1230 Mercy Boulevard
        216 Units

TYPE AND SIZE	RENT MONTHLY/ANNUALLY	MONTHLY RENT/SQ. FT.
116—1 BR, 1 Bath, 720 sq. ft. (Aug.), Gdn.	$195/$2,340	$.27
100—2 BR, 2 Bath, 1,005 sq. ft. (Aug.), Gdn.	$245/$2,940	$.24

Remarks: Project completed in 1970. Buildings are two story with brick at first level and wood shingle mansard roof at upper level. Occupancy reported at 100%. Tenant responsible for all utilities. Standard fully equipped kitchens. Drapes included. Amenities include clubhouse, two pools, laundry, and volleyball court. Rent increase effective in January 1977.

Exhibit **2-3** (*continued*)   Location of Comparable Apartments

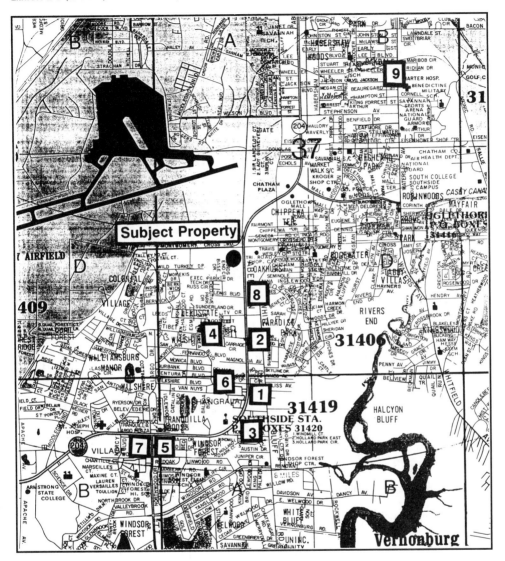

Exhibit 2-4   *Description of Improvements*

The subject is to be improved with a fifteen building, 216 garden unit apartment project, plus clubhouse and auxiliary improvements. Gross building area is approximately 202,244 square feet. A summary of the improvements is as follows:

Total Apartment Area	192,372 square feet
Clubhouse	800 square feet
Paving	130,000 square feet±
Hallways	9,072 square feet
Screen Porch Area	10,368 square feet

Unit Apartment Area

24 - 1 BR units	630 square feet
24 - 1 BR units	707 square feet
72 - 2 BR units	882 square feet
72 - 2 BR units	959 square feet
12 - 3 BR units	1,109 square feet
12 - 3 BR units	1,202 square feet

Foundation:	Poured concrete foundation on slab.
Exterior Walls:	5/8″ exterior plywood over frame structure.
Floors:	Concrete slab at ground level. 1½″ L.W. concrete on ⅝″ plywood deck over 12″ floor joists (24″ O.C.) at upper level.
Floor Covering:	Synthetic carpeting on all floors including bath except kitchens which have vinyl tile.
Roof:	Truss system with asphalt shingles on ½″ plywood decking.
Windows:	Aluminum framed, vertical sliding.
Insulation:	Ceiling insulated with 6″ blow-in and walls with 3″ batts.
Interior Walls and Ceiling:	5/8″ painted gypsum board walls; stippled finish ceilings.
Baths and Plumbing:	Lavatory units with vanity, mirror and small medicine cabinets. Fiberglass wainscot at tubs. Assume copper water lines and cast iron soil and waste line. Individual electric fuel hot water heaters (Rheem); 30 gallon capacity for 1 BR units; 40 gallon capacity for 2 BR and 3 BR units.
Kitchens:	Single bowl sink, free-standing electric range, double door refrigerator, dishwasher, range hood and exhaust fan. Plywood wall and base cabinets.
Heating and Air Conditioning:	Heating and air-conditioning system utilizes an upright closet-type air-handling unit, with an outside mounted condenser. Distribution is through overhead insulated ducts, with a central return air vent. Total electric 1½ to 2 tons per unit (Rheem).

Exhibit 2-4   (*continued*)

Patios/Balconies:	All units have screened-in patios or balconies.
Swimming Pool:	Assume 800 square feet, minimum, concrete deck, fence enclosure, approved filter system.
Landscaping:	Finished landscaping and grounds are typical. Several large mature trees have been saved.
Walks:	4″ concrete slab.
Clubhouse:	Clubhouse includes large recreation room, rest rooms, office, and utility.
Remarks:	In the two-bedroom floor plan, which is available at 882 square feet and 959 square feet, 36 of the 72 smaller units have 2 bathrooms in lieu of 1 bath with laundry room. Also, 36 of the 72 larger units have 2 bathrooms in lieu of 1 bath with laundry room.
Age/Life:	Economic life judged to be 40 years.

Exhibit 2-4 (*continued*)

LG 2 BEDROOM, 2 BATH

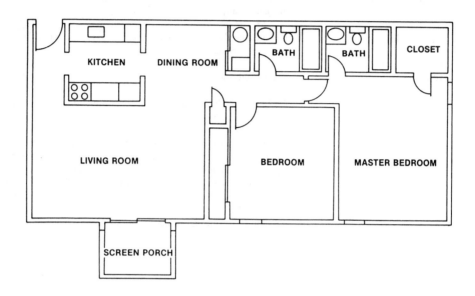

SM 2 BEDROOM

Exhibit 2-4 (*continued*)

LG 1 BEDROOM

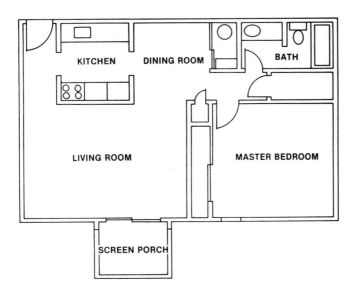

SM 1 BEDROOM

Exhibit 2-5   *Income Projections*

The following rental schedule has been utilized:

1 BR, 1 BA	630 sq. ft. x $.30/sq. ft./mo. =	$189/mo., Say $190
1 BR, 1 BA	707 sq. ft. x .30/sq. ft./mo. =	212/mo., Say 210
2 BR, 1 BA	882 sq. ft. x .25/sq. ft./mo. =	221/mo., Say 220
2 BR, 2 BA	882 sq. ft. x .26/sq. ft./mo. =	229/mo., Say 230
2 BR, 1 BA	959 sq. ft. x .25/sq. ft./mo. =	240/mo., Say 240
2 BR, 2 BA	959 sq. ft. x .26/sq. ft./mo. =	249/mo., Say 250
3 BR, 2 BA	1,109 sq. ft. x .24/sq. ft./mo. =	266/mo., Say 265
3 BR, 2 BA	1,202 sq. ft. x .24/sq. ft./mo. =	288/mo., Say 290

The monthly per square foot rent of the various subject units is in the upper range of the comparables.

Gross annual income is projected as follows:

24—1 BR units @ $190/mo. x 12 mos. =	$ 54,720	
24—1 BR units @ 210/mo. x 12 mos. =	60,480	
36—2 BR units @ 220/mo. x 12 mos. =	95,040	
36—2 BR units @ 230/mo. x 12 mos. =	99,360	
36—2 BR units @ 240/mo. x 12 mos. =	103,680	
36—2 BR units @ 250/mo. x 12 mos. =	108,000	
12—3 BR units @ 265/mo. x 12 mos. =	38,160	
12—3 BR units @ 290/mo. x 12 mos. =	41,760	
Potential Gross Income		**$601,200**

Income Analysis

Projected Gross Rent Income	$601,200
Auxiliary Income[1] ($10.18/unit/month)	26,400
Total	**$627,600**
Less Vacancy/Collection (5%)	31,380
Effective Gross Income	**$596,220**

Expenses

Management Fee	$ 29,900	
Salaries/Taxes	18,500	
Real Estate Taxes	41,915	
Insurance	8,950	
Sanitation	10,750	
Pest Control	2,100	
Common Area Utilities	8,600	
Maintenance, Redecorating	25,600	
General Expenses	26,000	
Total	**$172,315**	
Reserves[2]	**$ 27,336**	
Total Expenses and Reserves	**$199,651**	
Cash flow from operations		**$397,889**

Exhibit 2-5 (*continued*)

[1]Auxiliary income figured as follows:		[2]Reserves		
	Per Month			
Furniture rental	$ 600	Roof:	2,500 squares (10'x10') @ $25/20 years	= $ 3,125
Laundry income	600	Mechanical:	$200/unit/15 years	= 2,880
Cleaning fees	700	Appliances:	$400/unit/12 years	= 7,200
Miscellaneous	300	Floor covering:	14,950 sq. yds. @ $5.25/sq. yd., 8 yrs.	= 9,811
Total	**$ 2,200**	Paving:	14,400 sq. yds. @ $4.50/sq. yd., 15 yrs.	= 4,320
	× 12	**Total**		**$27,336**
Auxiliary income	**$26,400**			

Exhibit 2-6 *Excerpt from Appraisal of Savannah West Garden Apartments*

Correlation and Final Value Estimate

The indication of value from the three approaches are as follows:

Cost Approach	$4,095,000
Income Approach	3,980,000
Market Approach	3,760,000

(See explanation of the approaches below.)

In estimating the Market Value of the subject project, we have given consideration to all three indications of value. In our judgment, the Income Approach is the most reliable indication of value. The Cost Approach and Market Approach set the upper and lower range of value and are felt to be less reliable. Therefore, it is our opinion that the Market Value of the 216-unit apartment development, known as Savannah West Garden Apartments as of April 22, 1977, was Four Million Dollars ($4,000,000) divided as follows:

Land	$ 200,000
Improvements	3,800,000
Total	**$4,000,000**

Cost Approach This estimate is based on "an analysis of cost data obtained from developer/contractors who are knowledgeable about the cost of building apartments. The cost of constructing semi-luxury multi-family apartments" in this area, for example, "range from $13.00 to $16.00 per square foot depending on quality and type of construction and size of units, excluding paving, landscaping, and indirect cost."

A complete breakdown of the costs leading to the $4,095,000 estimate is included at the end of this exhibit.

Income Approach "In order to estimate the value of the subject property by the Income Approach, it is necessary to determine Market Rent typical to the subject neighborhood (**Exhibit 2-3**). . . . The comparison is made on the basis of gross rent per square foot per month."

Based on this survey of comparable apartments, the appraiser concluded that the rents shown in **Exhibit 2-5** "represent market rent" and that the $397,889 net income before financing was reasonable. The appraiser then looked at the net income of four comparable properties that were recently sold and concluded that a 10% capitalization of net income best reflects the current market. He then made the following calculations:

Exhibit 2-6 (*continued*)

Net Income:	$397,889 ÷ .10 = $3,978,880
Indicated Value, Income Approach, Rounded:	$3,980,000

Market Approach "An investigation has been made of sales of properties which possess characteristics similar to the subject. The comparison process is based on a gross rent multiple basis. . . . Adjustments are made for time of sale, location, size, utility, condition of improvement and other factors which, in our opinion, influence value."

SALE NUMBER	GROSS RENT MULTIPLE
1	5.51
2	6.50
3	5.63
4	5.72

The appraiser estimated that Savannah West could be sold for a rent multiple of 6.25 leading to the following calculation:

Projected Gross Income (**Exhibit 2-5**):	$ 601,200
Estimated Gross Rent Multiple	× 6.25
Value by Market Approach:	**$3,757,500**
Rounded to:	$3,760,000

The foregoing description is a simplified summary of the appraisal. The appraisal itself runs to 45 pages plus exhibits.

Reproduction Cost New

Total Apartment Area:		
192,372 sq. ft. @ $15.00	=	$2,885,580
Hallway Area:		
9,072 sq. ft. @ $5.00	=	45,360
Clubhouse:		
800 sq. ft. @ $18.00	=	14,400
Pool:		
1 @ $12,000	=	12,000
Tennis Courts:		
2 @ $10,000	=	20,000
Paving and Parking:		
14,450 sq. yds. @ $4.50	=	65,025
Landscaping, finished site work, etc.		
estimated @ 5% of $3,042,365	=	152,118
Total Direct Construction Cost		**$3,194,483**
Indirect Costs:		
Construction Loan Interest, 10% of		
$3,194,483 × .60	=	$ 191,669
Miscellaneous, including Entrepreneurial		
Profit, Loan fees, and Off-site Overhead	=	507,923
Reproduction Cost New		**$3,894,075**
Less Depreciation, None Observed		0

Exhibit 2-6 (*continued*)

Depreciated Reproduction Cost New	**$3,894,075**
Plus Land Value	200,000
Value Indicated by Cost Approach	**$4,094,075**
Rounded to:	$4,095,000

Exhibit 2-7 *Summary of Key Clauses in Chemical Bank's Standard Commitment Letter for a Construction Loan*

General Terms and Conditions

1. Amount of the loan $_____.
2. Construction of the improvements shall commence within 30 days of the loan closing.
3. The loan shall mature in _____ months and interest shall be payable monthly on the outstanding balance at a rate of ____% or ____% plus the prime rate.
4. Loan will be secured by a first (second) mortgage or deed of trust.
5. Signed commitment letter together with a commitment fee must be returned to Lender within _____ days.
6. The loan closing shall be held within 60 days of the date of issuance of this letter.
7. All leases shall be assigned to Lender.

Fees

1. A commitment fee of $_____ shall be deemed earned by Lender upon Borrower's acceptance of the commitment letter. If loan does not close Lender may retain all of such good faith deposit as liquidated damages.
2. Borrower agrees to pay all fees, commissions, costs, charges, taxes, and other expenses incurred in connection with this commitment letter and the making of the loan. These fees include: a. Lender's New York counsel and local counsel, b. appraisal fees, c. survey fees, d. title examination fees, e. mortgage title insurance, f. hazard insurance, g. bond premiums, h. mortgage and transfer taxes, i. recording fees and charges.

Some of the Usual Conditions for the Commitment

1. Joint and several guarantee of payment of the note by the principals and their wives.
2. Joint and several guarantee of completion of the improvements.
3. A permanent loan commitment for the long-term mortgage financing.
4. An appraisal indicating a value in the real property equal to not less than $_____.
5. One hundred percent payment and performance bond.
6. Final plans and improvements approved in writing by independent inspecting architects and engineers designated by the Lender.
7. Current certified financial statements of Borrower and all guarantors.
8. Evidence of compliance with all zoning, environmental and other laws, ordinances, rules and regulations.
9. A detailed breakdown of the cost of the improvements and an itemization of nonconstruction and land costs. In no event shall the amount of the loan exceed these estimated costs.
10. Evidence from utility companies and municipalities servicing the Premises that water, sewer, electric, telephone and gas service will be available upon completion.
11. Full insurance on the property in the form of an "all risk," 100% nonreporting policy.

Exhibit 2-7   (continued)

12. All instruments and documents affecting the premises, securing the loan, or relating to the development and construction shall be subject to the approval of the Lender, the Lender's New York counsel and the Lender's Local counsel.

During Construction

1. Borrower shall furnish a revised survey showing location of foundation, plus an affidavit from the surveyor that set-backs conform with zoning restrictions.
2. All contracts shall be assigned to the Lender. Borrower shall furnish all such information about the architect, construction manager, general contractor and subcontractors as the Lender requests. All these people shall be subject to approval by the Lender. All shall continue performance in Lender's behalf under the respective contracts without additional cost in the event of a default by the borrower.
3. Advances shall not be made more frequently than monthly and shall be based upon inspections and certifications by the Supervising Engineers. The total amount retained from Borrower by Lender shall, in no event, be less than 10%.

Grounds for Termination

1. Lender may terminate commitment if Borrower misrepresented any feature.
2. Lender may terminate commitment if an adverse change occurs to the premises.
3. Lender may terminate commitment if any part of the premises is taken for condemnation or if any person connected with the loan is involved in bankruptcy or insolvency.
4. Borrower shall keep permanent loan commitment in full force.
5. Loan may become payable immediately upon sale or transfer of the property.

Chemical Bank does not require all borrowers to conform to all of these terms and conditions. On the other hand, it may insert additional terms and conditions in a specific loan commitment to cover unique or unusual situations.

3

PROSPECT HILL

In May, 1989, the Nelson Company is considering the development of a new 274,000 square foot office building in its successful Prospect Hill Office Park on Route 128 in a suburb outside of Boston. Both local market conditions and their relation to national demographic trends predicted for the 1990s are analyzed. The case highlights decisions regarding project economics—the provision of tenant services such as day care and underground parking, the use of interest rate hedges—and examines them in light of the need for the project to compete in an increasingly soft market.

Discussion Questions

1. What do you think of Nelson's strategy for Prospect Hill?
2. Should the Nelson Company go forward with the Hillside Building, given the market conditions? What would your decisions be concerning the amenities, the parking alternatives, and the interest rate hedge?
3. How might the development problems for a quality office building in a suburban location in Waltham differ from those in a downtown site?

Bill Hassett, a partner in The Nelson Companies, looked out the window of 200 Fifth Avenue in the Prospect Hill Executive Office Park (Prospect Hill) on Route 128 in Waltham, MA in May of 1989. From his third floor office, he could see the toddlers of The Children's Place, the Prospect Hill day care center, tricycling excitedly around their playground. The children were a pleasant distraction, but Hassett had important decisions to make regarding the expansion of Prospect Hill. He needed to decide how to handle some important pre-development issues concerning the new Hillside Building which was scheduled for groundbreaking in June of 1989. His major concerns were how to position this class A office building in a softening market, how to handle certain parking issues, and whether expanded day care facilities would enhance lease-up or merely increase the expenses. He also considered whether it would be wise to negotiate some sort of hedge on the adjustable interest rate construction loan. The construction loan would become operative when construction started in June 1989, and would be replaced with permanent financing for a ten year term with interest only at 10% but only after the building was 80 percent leased. The target date for that occupancy level was June 1991.

PROSPECT HILL EXECUTIVE OFFICE PARK

The creative force behind The Nelson Companies was its founder Arthur Nelson (see **Exhibit 3-1**). Nelson's goal was not to be merely another developer of reflective glass suburban office boxes but to create sane and healthy environments for living and working. Recognizing early the economic and demographic changes reshaping the American work force, Nelson was among the first developers in the nation to include childcare and employee healthclub facilities on the grounds of an office park.

A suburban developer since 1974, Nelson had assembled piecemeal a large expanse of hillside on Route 128 between the Massachusetts Turnpike and Route 2 interchanges. Prime territory for suburban office users, Route 128 was considered to be the high tech corridor of the Northeast. By 1988, The Nelson Companies had completed 550,000 square feet of office space in four 6 and 7 story

Research Assistant Katherine Sweetman prepared this case under the supervision of Adjunct Professor William J. Poorvu as the basis for class discussion rather than to illustrate either effective or ineffective handling of an administrative situation.

buildings. Much of the rest of the site had existing low rise industrial buildings. Only 25 acres, including the Hillside site, were left to be developed.

The Nelson Companies had developed the site gradually, building only what the market could absorb at a given time. By November of 1988, Hassett and Nelson had decided that the time was right to expand Prospect Hill by adding the Hillside Building on 6.5 acres of land. The 6-story Hillside building would be built to its maximum allowable F.A.R.[1] of 1.0 and would contain 274,000 net rentable square feet of office space and require 279,000 gross square feet of parking for 800 cars. Hassett analyzed the price tag for building the underground parking and concluded that it would be well over four times that of surface parking and almost twice as much as a 3-level structure for parking above grade. He wondered if they had chosen the right course of action. Building the structured parking required that they charge top rates, and the market was threatening to soften before Hillside would start its leasing. They had decided to build 6 levels of underground structured parking to conserve land, believing the future value of the 2 to 5 acres of land saved to be high. Since comparable land with a similar FAR traded at $40 per square foot, he feared that surface or above-ground structured parking would squander the future development value of the land.

THE ROUTE 128 PHENOMENON

When built in 1954, Massachusetts Route 128 was nicknamed the Road to Nowhere. A swathe of asphalt curving through farmland, Route 128 carried light traffic for two decades before the area was "discovered" by high tech ventures. During the 1970s and 1980s, the region grew at a very fast clip, and the Road to Nowhere became a congested avenue connecting businesses to Boston, Hartford, New York and beyond.

By 1988, business began to slow. Reductions in high tech employment reflected several factors dampening the growth and profitability of the high tech business. Route 128's Digital, Data General, Prime, and Wang Laboratories had all focused on mini computers and had become the best in that field. Unfortunately, consumers increasingly demanded personal computers and independent work stations which were primarily made in Silicon Valley in California. Many experts predicted that the mini-computer industry faced consolidations which would likely lead to lay-offs and a reduced need for office space on Route 128. Other firms also reduced their work forces due to business slow-downs and corporate consolidations.

Hassett was further troubled by a recent report from Salomon Brothers, "Oversupply in the Office Market: The Legacy of the 1980s," which made him

[1]F.A.R. = Floor Area Ratio. The ratio of the number of square feet of buildable area that can be built on a site for each square foot of land area. Parking is not included in the above calculation.

fear that the vacancy rate may be less cyclical than structural (see **Exhibit 3-2**). How would this national trend apply to Boston or even more specifically Route 128 and Waltham?

He also looked at an excerpt from another Salomon Brothers report "Demand for Office Space" which highlighted the expected reduction in growth rates from the demand side (see **Table 3-1**).

Despite such negative news, Hassett and Nelson believed that it would be hard for other parts of the country or the world to duplicate the concentration of brainpower in the Boston area, largely due to the world renowned universities in Boston and Cambridge. The two partners remained optimistic about the future of Route 128.

ROUTE 128 OFFICE MARKET

The suburban office market surrounding Boston on Route 128 is divided into three submarkets: North, West, and South (see **Exhibit 3-3**). Waltham, the site of Prospect Hill, is in the West Suburban market on the North Suburban border.

The density of development on Route 128 has resulted in a series of submarkets along the length of the highway which are distinguished from one another primarily by the nature of their particular interchanges and the particular community in which they are located. Waltham, for example, was very well located: the Totten Pond Road exit to Prospect Hill was only a five-minute drive from the Route 128/Massachusetts Turnpike interchange (connecting downtown Boston to Hartford and New York City), and Prospect Hill offices were only minutes from executive housing in Weston, Wellesley, Newton and Lexington, as well as employee housing in Waltham, Belmont and Watertown.

By 1988, the North Suburban submarket, containing almost 10 million square feet, had somewhat recovered from extremely high vacancy rates ranging up to 30 percent experienced during the mid-1980s. Vacancy rates for first class office projects still hovered over 12.2 percent. Reduced vacancy was largely due to cutbacks in construction. Office space totalling one million square feet was scheduled to be delivered during 1989 and 1990. Asking rents for first class office space averaged $22.00 per square foot per year.

The South Suburban market was comprised of 6.6 million square feet of office space primarily located in Quincy, Braintree and Norwood. The vacancy

Table 3-1   Demand for Office Space

ANNUAL COMPOUND GROWTH RATE	1972-79	1979-86	1986-88	1988-2000 Est.
Civilian labor force	2.71%	1.66%	1.64%	1.10%
Office workers in selected industries	5.25%	5.10%	4.83%	2.64%
Space per worker	2.31%	2.41%	1.45%	0.56%

Source: Salomon Brothers, *Bond Market Research*, May 1989.

rates in these areas improved in 1988, dropping from 21 percent to 9.2 percent. Nervous developers delayed construction of projects slated to open in 1988, deferring to 1989 and 1990 construction of over 863,000 more square feet of first class office space. Asking rental rates for new first class office space ranged from $18.50 to $26.00 per square foot in 1988.

The West suburban market was considered to be the healthiest segment of the suburban office market belt around Boston in 1988 and the largest at 19 million square feet. In recent years this subsegment had experienced absorption rates averaging 500,000 square feet annually. The prime office locations were on Route 128 near the Massachusetts Turnpike in Newton and Wellesley. Although the overall vacancy rate for the West was 13.1 percent, this Route 128 subsegment enjoyed a vacancy rate of 6.2 percent in 1988, a rate which was projected to decline even further in the near-term since other than the space referred to below no new building was planned in the immediate future. Other subsegments in the western suburbs experienced vacancy rates from 7 to 15 percent. Waltham's vacancy rate was 12.1% but the area ran a close second to Newton/Wellesley in terms of desirability and was expected to benefit greatly in the future from Newton/Wellesley's construction slowdown. Over 800,000 square feet of new first class office space is scheduled to be delivered in the West by the end of 1990. Of this space, 274,000 square feet will be in Prospect Hill's Hillside Building. Asking rental rates for new first class office space in the west market ranged from $23.50 to $27.00.

NELSON'S PHILOSOPHY

With the construction of the third building, 200 Fifth Avenue, in 1981, Nelson began to implement his vision of a well-balanced work environment. Amenities in this building include a 6,000 square foot fitness center, one of the first childcare centers in an American office park (4,000 square feet to accommodate 45 children ranging in age from eight weeks through pre-school), a 5,000 square foot employee cafeteria and a small convenience store. A helipad soon to be licensed would shuttle travelers back and forth to Boston's Logan International Airport in eight minutes at a cost of $15.00 per passenger. A one-way cab ride to the same destination would take up to an hour and cost $40.00.

The space for amenities was donated by The Nelson Companies. The operations were run at a breakeven basis with some of the operating costs of these amenities shared equally among Prospect Hill's tenants on a square foot basis. The assessments averaged $.20 per square foot per year.

By 1988, the scope of Prospect Hill's amenities had enlarged dramatically. The day care center now accommodated 70 children. The fitness center instituted a comprehensive wellness program for employees and grew to contain 60 nautilus machines, aerobics classes and saunas. The fitness center easily reached its breakeven level of 800 members at a membership fee of $300 each, a sum often partially funded by employers. The firm also maintained 7 miles of jogging trails through the Waltham woods. Nelson was discussing forming an area Wellness Council in conjunction with the Harvard School of Public Health.

The day care center was run by national day care expert Joan Bergstrom who had studied Scandinavian methods of group child care. Space for the childcare center was donated to the operators who ran it on a break-even basis ($190 per week for infants, $175 per week for toddlers and $115 per week for pre-schoolers in 1988). By 1988, she had expanded her services to aid corporate clients throughout the region in finding child care facilities for their employees near home or work through a computer matching service. In September of 1988, The Nelson Companies opened the first fully-accredited kindergarten in an American office park in the 400 building. The kindergarten accommodated 20 children.

The Nelson Companies developed an innovative use for one floor of 20,000 square feet in the 400 building after the departure of Polaroid in 1988: the 128 Entrepreneurs' Center. "We recognize that the world is a hostile place for entrepreneurs," said Arthur Nelson. "People who had been protected in a big company were now completely vulnerable. They are involved with, but don't know much about law, marketing, accounting. They need support during their first couple of years. They have a real need to *look* legitimate but can't afford to pay much. Entrepreneurialism is lonely . . . they need to see others and share problems."

Nelson established a board which screened entrepreneurs who applied for entrance to the center. Entrepreneurs who were admitted received office space as well as secretarial, telephone and conference room service, all heavily subsidized. The Nelson Companies paid for operating expenses and taxes associated with the building. These costs totaled about $200,000 in 1988 on an annualized basis. Those businesses that succeeded moved up to the fifth floor where they paid a modest rent.

The goal was for businesses which became established to graduate to the greater office park, although no obligation was made that they remain there. Nelson was also aware that most new jobs in the U.S. were created by small businesses. Between 1980 and 1988, large Fortune 500 companies had experienced a net loss of three million employees, while all other employers experienced a net gain of 17 million. Of these, 12 million were jobs created by small firms with fewer than 100 employees. Nelson calculated that business incubated in the 400 building would have no reason to leave since he was determined to create the best office park on Route 128. By 1988, the 550,000 square feet of office space in Prospect Hill were 96 percent leased (see **Exhibits 3-4** and **3-5**).

THE FUTURE OF PROSPECT HILL

In addition to the amenities mentioned above, Nelson's organization moved forward with larger plans. These included commencing construction on the first world class luxury hotel on Route 128 and reviewing the blueprints for a high tech communications center to be called the Spacebridge Building.

The Nelson Companies arranged a management agreement with Hilton International and had already erected part of the skeleton of the hotel/restaurant/convention center at the front of Prospect Hill near its entrance to Route 128. With 400 companies located within one mile of the facility, the 350 room facility was almost guaranteed to succeed.

The Spacebridge Building was to be a single purpose structure providing corporate communication via satellite on a time-share basis to tenants of Prospect Hill and to other 128 tenants who paid to join the service. The Spacebridge concept was based on an idea used by 25 existing companies in America. Ford Motor Company, for example, used corporate "television" to personalize communications between its sales staff and its corporate headquarters. Rather than acting for a single large company, air time in the Spacebridge Building would be set up on a time-share basis, charging $7,000 per time-share hour. Virtually all of the costs were fixed. At this rate, the Spacebridge operator would break even at 54 hours per month. Nelson also felt that the facility had potential for education, beaming Massachusetts-grade education to less advantaged regions in the country.

Nelson believed that these two services would help solidify his office park's position as the consummate full-service office park, as well as make money as separate businesses.

PROSPECT HILL PROJECT ECONOMICS

Hassett used the comparables shown in **Exhibit 3-6** to make his estimates for the Hillside Building income projections. From his net figure of $20.50 per square foot per year in income, Hassett subtracted the debt service on the $48.6 million loan which covered the full project cost exclusive of land. Calculated at the rate of an interest-only mortgage at 10.0 percent, the Hillside building was left with a cash flow after financing of $757,000 on the 274,000 square foot building. The numbers below assume that the underground parking was built.

Hassett's back of the envelope calculations:

Income	
Rent @ $27.00/sq. ft.	$7,398,000
Expenses	
Vacancy @ $1.00/sq. ft.	(274,000)
Operating Expenses @ $3.50/sq. ft.	(959,000)
Taxes @ $2.00/sq. ft.	(548,000)
Cash Flow from Operations	**$5,617,000**
Debt service on $48.6 million interest only loan at 10.0%	(4,860,000)
Cash Flow after Financing	**$ 757,000**

Given the market uncertainty, Nelson was uncomfortable with the bottom line in the event of changes in the real estate market or financial market. He worried that if income went down and interest rates went up The Nelson Companies would have a big problem meeting its cash flow obligations. He thought it would make sense to do some sensitivity analysis.

PARKING

Hassett decided to rethink the parking decision. Parking conditions were not expected to affect gross rents as long as sufficient parking spaces were available to the tenants. Parking was included as part of the tenants' base rental. Most office campuses on Route 128 used surface parking despite the disadvantages during the long cold New England winters. Sharpening his pencil, Hassett recalculated the cost of each form of parking and tried to arrive at a decision. Using an area standard of one square foot of parking space for each square foot of net leasable office space, and an industry standard of 350 square feet per parking space, he estimated the cost to build each form of parking. Surface parking cost $3,000 per space; structured parking above grade cost $7,000 per space; and structured underground parking cost $13,000 per space. The maintenance on the underground parking would be about 50 cents per square foot per year, versus 15 cents per square foot per year for the other options. Could they afford the price tag?

DAYCARE

Nelson also thought about daycare as a possible competitive advantage in a soft market. He and his partners considered whether firms would be more likely to lease in a building where office workers could bring their children. He calculated the costs of placing a 3,000 square foot daycare space for 34 children in the lower level, and building a play area outside:

	UPFRONT COST	ANNUAL COST
Cost of buildout	$150,000	
Annual lost income for space (net)		$40,000
Insurance		$10,000
	$150,000	**$50,000**

He had recently received a copy of a Massachusetts tabulation of the problems people had in child care search (see **Exhibit 3-7**). He also was aware that the percentage of women in the labor force between ages 25 and 54 was 40%

higher in 1988 than 1972 and was expected to be 60% greater than 1988 in the year 2000.

FINANCING

The construction loan which Hassett had negotiated for the Nelson Companies from the Shawmut Bank called for interest at prime plus 1.25 percent over its two year term. The prime was assumed to be 8.75 percent, leaving Hassett no cushion from his pro forma projection of a 10 percent interest rate. Many forecasters predicted increased interest rates, however, and, given the other risks the project faced, Hassett was anxious to avoid being swamped by debt service. Hassett met with Ed Hogan of Citibank in New York City and, with his advice, narrowed his hedge options down to four choices: the swap, the cap, the collar, and the participating interest rate agreement.

The interest rate swap would allow The Nelson Companies to convert its floating debt into fixed rate debt without renegotiating the existing prime plus 1.25 percent loan with Shawmut. Under a separate agreement with Citibank, The Nelson Companies would receive and pass on to Shawmut a payment from Citibank covering the prime portion of the payment they owed to Shawmut. Nelson would pay to Citibank a fixed rate of 9.25 percent and pay 1.25 percent to Shawmut bringing the total debt payment by Nelson to a predictable 10.5 percent.

The interest rate cap was a somewhat simpler instrument which Nelson could also arrange with Citibank without disturbing the underlying loan with Shawmut. Nelson could set the cap level, say 10 percent, and be guaranteed that the total payment to Shawmut would not exceed that amount. Citibank would require a fee of $250,000 to cover its future cap obligations.

With an interest rate collar, Nelson could substantially reduce or even eliminate the fee by "selling back" some of the developer's potential benefits from any fall in interest rates. As in the cap, if the rate exceeded a predetermined "ceiling," the bank would reimburse Nelson. But if the rate fell below a certain "floor," Nelson would pay Citibank the difference between the floor rate and the market rate. Citibank offered to eliminate any up-front fee if Nelson would agree to a floor of 10 percent and a ceiling of 11 percent.

One reason why Hassett was having a hard time choosing an alternative was because of a difference of opinion among Nelson Company partners regarding the future of interest rates. While Bill Hassett was more concerned about protecting his downside risk, other partners voiced concern that too conservative an approach toward hedging would cost them a lot of money. Ed Hogan, aware of the conflict, offered a new instrument, a Participating Interest Rate Agreement (PIRA), which would allow Nelson Companies to gain only part of the benefit from the floating rate. As in a cap, there was protection above a certain level, say, 10.0 percent. If the current borrowing rate was lower, Citibank would take

33 percent of the spread and Nelson would receive 67 percent. The two-thirds is called the "Participation Rate." If the rate rose, Citibank would pay 67 percent of the spread and Nelson 33 percent.

THE DECISION

With a projected opening date of June 1990, Hassett needed to decide soon how to handle the parking and whether to begin negotiations with a daycare provider. He also wanted to arrange an interest rate hedge as soon as possible if he decided that it was the best course of action for fear that the real estate market might turn worse and increase the perceived risk to the bank. Lastly, he wanted to rethink whether now was the right time to start the overall building. Having spent so much time and about $15 million bringing all the elements of the project together, he knew the temptation was to keep going, but he didn't want to do so if the economics no longer made sense.

Exhibit 3-1 *Arthur Nelson Curriculum Vitae*

1940-1943	Physics major at Kansas State.
1943-1946	Radar research at MIT's Radiation Laboratory.
1946-1949	Harvard Law School.
1952-1963	Founded General Electronic Labs, a small firm involved in electronics research and development.
1954-Present	Founded Associates for International Research, a consulting firm, to capitalize on the emerging globalization of large American businesses after World War II. AIR evaluates the cost of living by locality to help establish compensation levels for American executives living abroad. Clients include Mobil Oil, and the U.S. government.
1965-Present	Founded Technical Education Research Centers. TERC develops curricula for emerging technical industries, including medical equipment, laser technology and electromechanics. TERC is considered to be a first-mover in its field. Executive development on computers in the classroom.
1974-Present	Nelson built his first project on Route 128, a successful office building. Encouraged, he began to assemble the future site of the Prospect Hill Executive Office Park with the goal of creating a distinctive office park over ten years.

Exhibit 3-2

Bond Market Research

Real Estate

May 16, 1989

Salomon Brothers

Sandon J. Goldberg
(212) 747-3296
Sharon A. Meyers
(212) 747-5841

Oversupply in the Office Market: The Legacy of the 1980s

Overview

We believe that fundamental changes, both structural and cyclical, in the supply and demand for office space prohibit a return to the low-vacancy equilibrium environment of the 1978-81 period. Over the past ten years, the national metropolitan office vacancy rate has risen from roughly 5% to 20% (see Figure 1). Vacancy rates overall have fallen little from their 1986 peak — near 17% in the downtowns and 24% in the suburbs — as the recent decline in the rate of supply has, been matched closely with a drop in new demand. In other words, there has not been a sufficient decline in construction or increase in absorption to significantly erode the surplus of vacant space.

Figure 1. Metropolitan, Suburban and Downtown Office Vacancy Rates, 1978-89

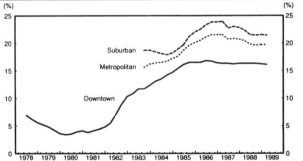

Source: Coldwell Banker.

In our semiannual survey of more than 50 metropolitan office markets, we found 475 million vacant square feet of office space, representing 19.1% of the total inventory. In addition, we estimate that a further 216 million square feet will be constructed by 1990, while only 190 million square feet will be absorbed (see Figure 2). Thus, while the vacancy *rate* may decline, the *absolute amount* of vacant office space nationwide will continue to increase.

This means that the current glut of available space will not disappear, because this is not merely a cyclical oversupply that is due to correct itself. We believe that the structural vacancy rate has risen to approximately 8% for central business districts (CBDs) and to 15% for suburban areas.[1] In

---

[1] We define the structural vacancy rate to be that proportion of vacant space that exists independent of cyclical factors. The numbers cited reflect the fact that only the tightest markets have reached these levels.

Exhibit 3-2 (*continued*)

Figure 2. U.S. Office Market Supply and Demand Conditions, Year-End 1988
(Square Feet in Millions)

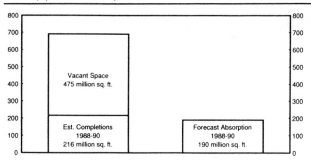

Source: Salomon Brothers Inc.

1984-85, when overbuilding became widespread, many developers and
owners considered it a temporary condition, signing five-year leases with
deep concessions to avoid cutting contract rents. Now that these leases are
rolling over, owners are finding that market conditions have improved only
marginally, and competition has at best kept real effective rents at or near
their earlier levels.

Supply: Fueled by Availability of Capital

The pace of new office supply in the United States has peaked. Throughout
most of this decade, supply has led demand, glutting the national office
market. However, new construction starts, as measured by F.W. Dodge
contract awards, have steadily declined since the mid-1980s (see Figure 3).
Contract awards have dropped by 40% from their 1985 peak, and owing to
a continuing decline in underlying demand, we expect them to fall by an
additional 10% by year-end 1989.

Figure 3. Office Employment Growth versus Office Construction Contract Awards,
1972-89 (Year-to-Year Absolute Change in Employment; 12-Month Moving
Average of Construction Contracts in Square Feet Indexed With Jan 72=100)

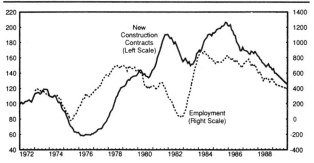

Note: Shaded area indicates forecast.
Sources: U.S. Bureau of Labor Statistics and F.W. Dodge/DRI Construction and Real Estate Information Service.
Reproduction or dissemination of this contract data in any form prohibited without prior written permission
of Dodge/DRI, McGraw-Hill, Inc.

Exhibit 3-2 (*continued*)

The surge in construction in the early 1980s resulted primarily from a substantial increase in the availability of capital. The dominant funding sources for real estate have shifted from local banks to national pension funds, life insurers and global lenders. Foreign capital now plays a greater role than ever in U.S. office investment. In addition, the Tax Act of 1981, which roughly doubled the tax advantages of owning real estate, elicited significant development capital from syndicators. Finally, as the value of diversification among financial assets and real estate began to be accepted more widely, large pools of additional domestic capital became available to fund institutional real estate investments. Pension funds' planned asset allocation to real estate rose from nothing in the early 1970s to 10%-15% currently, although actual allocation is now around 5%. In the mid-1970s, quality property was available at a relatively high yield, but these properties are currently in short supply, yields are low, and more money is available than there are premier assets to buy.

Consequently, institutions that formerly had provided permanent "takeout" financing for newly completed, leased buildings saw the profitability in this market diminished by competition. They also earned negative real returns through fixed-rate lending in the highly inflationary environment of the early 1980s. Lenders therefore sought to earn higher returns by participating at the beginning of the development process rather than at project completion and either partially or completely on an equity rather than a debt basis. Many institutional investors became joint venture partners with established developers, thereby adding capital to and further fueling the construction boom.

In the early 1980s, these capital flows to development, coupled with a boom in office-intensive industries, meant that buildings could be built speculatively, as developers and construction lenders generally agreed that tenants would eventually materialize. Now, however, the market has changed, and tenants are less abundant. Speculative buildings, therefore, are no longer in vogue with lenders, who now almost invariably require some preleasing. Recent market conditions that have made lenders and investors wary of risky projects are curtailing some of the more aggressive development, as well. In addition, the ongoing consolidation of the thrift industry will decrease competition among lenders and make funds more difficult and expensive to obtain.[2] Construction will naturally fall in response.

Regardless of the level of future construction, however, the current supply of vacant space will take a number of years to absorb. If construction continues at its current pace, given a constant forecast rate of absorption, the supply of available space in the nation's CBDs would continue to grow, as construction is outpacing absorption, pushing the vacancy rate to 20% by the year 2010 (see Figure 4). Vacant space in the suburbs is being absorbed, yet so slowly that even in 20 years these markets will still be 15% vacant (see Figure 5). Should construction fall to 50% of its current pace, suburban markets would still require seven years to reach an arbitrary threshold vacancy rate of 10%, while the CBDs would need eight years. Even at these substantially reduced rates of construction, an ample supply of office space will likely remain well into the next millennium.[3]

---

[2] See *The Thrift Reform Program: Summary and Implications*, Barbara Pauley, Salomon Brothers Inc, April 1989.
[3] Our analysis excludes the effect of inventory reduction due to the demolition of functionally obsolete buildings, the magnitude of which is difficult to measure.

Exhibit 3-2 *(continued)*

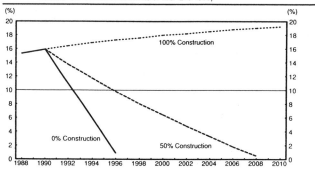

Figure 4. Central Business District Office Vacancy Implications, 1988-2010
(Forecast Vacancy Rate Given Constant Forecast Absorption and Varying
Rates of Current Construction as of Year-End 1988)

Source: Salomon Brothers Inc.

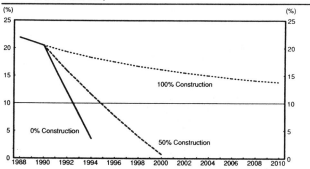

Figure 5. Suburban Office Vacancy Implications, 1988-2010 (Forecast Vacancy Rate
Given Constant Forecast Absorption and Varying Rates of Current Construction
as of Year-End 1988)

Source: Salomon Brothers Inc.

Demand: Difficult to Sustain 1980s Growth

Demand for office space in the United States through 2000 will increase at
a decidedly slower pace than it has for most of this decade. Population
growth, the changing composition of the work force, the increasing
dominance of the service economy, and the allocation of more space per
worker have all given impetus to office absorption in recent years.[4] Long
term, these trends will abate and will limit the demand for office product.
This strain on demand will be further exacerbated by a worsening
educational system that is failing to provide adequately skilled office
employees.[5] Construction will taper off in response to these trends.

---

[4] See *Demand for Office Space*, Sherman J. Maisel, Salomon Brothers Inc, May 1989.
[5] See *America's Educational Failures: How Will They Affect Real Estate?*, Anthony Downs, Salomon
Brothers Inc, May 1988.

Exhibit 3-2 (*continued*)

In the near term, a shortage of labor, high home prices in coastal areas and limited employment growth, particularly in the office sector, will contribute to a falloff in demand. The enormous growth of office-intensive industries, such as financial services, consulting and real estate, was a onetime happening and cannot be expected to recur. Office employment growth has already slowed because of corporate restructuring and retrenchment in the defense and financial services industries.[6] Finally, the growth rate in labor force participation and the unemployment rate have hit cyclical levels just about as high and low, respectively, as they can go. As these trends gain momentum, it will be evident that new office buildings are becoming less and less necessary.

One further hindrance to absorption is that, in most markets, tenants have taken advantage of overbuilt conditions to upgrade and expand their space in low-rent environments and will not need additional space for some time. Lately, a great deal of leasing activity has resulted from developers "churning" the markets by offering substantial concessions to tenants to move between buildings while not expanding significantly. Other tenants have availed themselves of the concessionary environment and taken more space than they currently needed to lock in lower rental rates while providing for future growth, effectively borrowing from future absorption. Thus, an additional excess of inventory exists at the tenant level, and the reported vacancies may even understate the true amount of vacant space.

Implications for the Office Market

We have experienced a fundamental shift in the market for office space. The confluence of events that caused the office boom of the 1980s has left an excess of office space in its wake. Developers and other office market participants should not expect the current high vacancy rate environment to change in the foreseeable future. Rental growth assumptions and lease-up projections ought to acknowledge these conditions.

The glut of available space nationally means that competition for tenants will prevent real rent gains. Effective real rents thus will continue to remain soft, as current vacancies approach their structural levels. In addition, capitalization rates will likely rise somewhat, as the weakness in office employment growth becomes more evident. Recognizing these realities will help the office market regain its balance.

*   *   *   *   *

---

[6] See *The Restructuring of Corporate America: Implications for Real Estate America*, David Shulman, Salomon Brothers Inc, March 13, 1989.

Exhibit 3-3   *General Area Road Map*

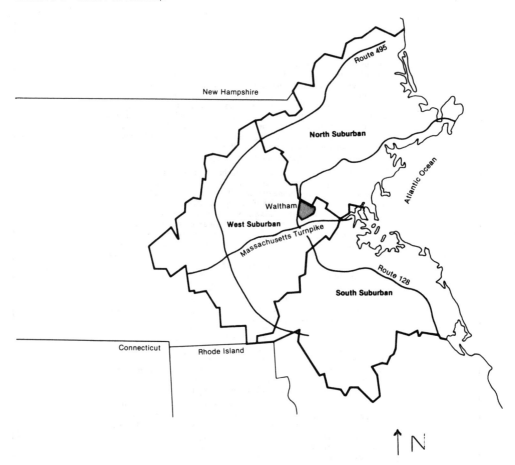

Exhibit 3-4 *Prospect Hill Development History*

Goal: **To transform the standard suburban office park into a business and living center.**

1977   Nelson buys 25 acres along a powerline easement near Route 128. Existing abandoned shell for a three-year-old building containing 120,000 square feet is the only improvement. Surrounding area yet relatively undeveloped. Buildings nearby all low-lying research and development.

1978   Polaroid takes a 10-year lease on the rehabilitated shell, renamed 400 Fifth Avenue. Requests 136,000 more square feet: Nelson Companies builds 300 Fifth Avenue.

1980   Management Decision Systems takes 80,000 of the 150,000 square feet in 200 Fifth Avenue. Remainder of building leases quickly.

1981   100 Fifth Avenue leases up quickly with a variety of smaller tenants.

1988   Construction begins on the Hilton International Hotel and preliminary drawings completed on the Spacebridge telecommunications building.

1977-1988   Nelson assembles parcels of 16 adjacent landowners. Holdings by 1988 total 125 acres.

BUILDING	YEAR BUILT	SQUARE FOOTAGE
400	1977	120,000
300	1979	136,000
200	1980	150,000
100	1981	144,000

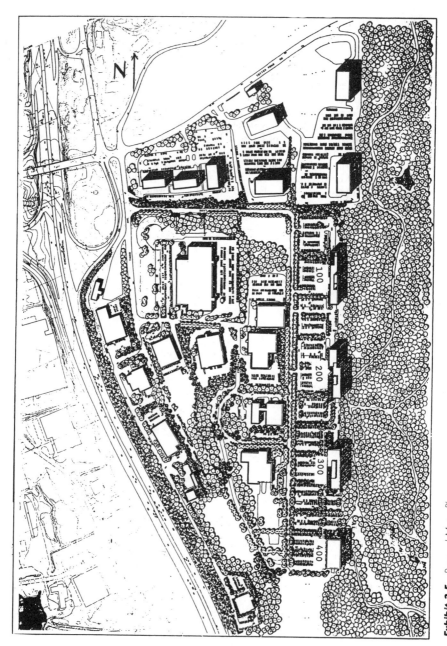

Exhibit 3-5 Proposed Master Plan

Exhibit 3-6 *Current Market Vacancy Report*

WALTHAM EXISTING BUILDING	DATE COMPLETED	# FLOORS	TOTAL RENT AREA	SQUARE FEET AVAILABLE	ESTIMATED RENT PER SQ. FT.	PERCENT VACANT
235 Bear Hill Road	1963	4	21,000	1,500	$17.00	7.1%
255 Bear Hill Road	1980	5	26,000	6,500	18.00	25.0
260 Bear Hill Road	1976	3	27,000	3,062	17.00	11.3
300 Bear Hill Road	1978	2	30,000	8,500	18.00	28.3
135 Beaver Street	1985	4	95,300	26,000	18.50	27.3
100 Fifth Avenue	1981	7	144,000	22,050	22.00	15.3
200 Fifth Avenue	1980	7	150,000	Full	16.00	0.0
300 Fifth Avenue	1979	6	136,000	Full	20.00	0.0
400 Fifth Avenue	1977	6	120,000	Full	21.00	0.0
69 Hickory Drive	1964	2	21,600	4,200	16.00	19.4
610 Lincoln Street	1971	3	81,000	Full	21.00	0.0
1430 Main Street	1985	2	39,000	Full	19.00	0.0
1446 Main Street	1982	3	64,000	7,000	18.50	0.0
1 Moody Street	1981	4	40,000	Full	18.00	0.0
Reservoir Place I	1982	3	162,000	50,000	24.00	30.9
Reservoir Place II	1986	3	368,000	180,000	26.00	48.9
204 Second Avenue	1981	3	41,000	Full	22.00	0.0
230 Second Avenue	1985	2	38,000	5,500	19.25	0.0
200 Smith Street	1968	3	323,570	Full	14.00	0.0
230 South Street	1984	6	206,000	2,938	26.00	1.4
125 Technology Drive	1986	7	130,000	3,700	23.00	2.8
138 Technology Drive	1984	3	45,000	Full	17.50	0.0
75 Third Avenue	1963	1	14,000	Full	19.00	0.0
214 Third Avenue	1963	1	11,000	Full	18.00	0.0
300 Third Avenue	1969	2	20,000	Full	22.00	0.0
391 Totten Pond Road	1967	4	15,000	1,750	16.00	11.7
393 Totten Pond Road	1966	4	15,000	2,650	16.00	17.7
395 Totten Pond Road	1969	4	15,000	Full	16.00	0.0
401 Totten Pond Road	1970	4	80,000	4,398	16.00	5.5
402 Totten Pond Road	1969	4	80,000	Full	16.00	0.0
440 Totten Pond Road	1969	4	15,000	Full	15.00	0.0
460 Totten Pond Road	1971	7	120,000	33,948	16.00	28.3
470 Totten Pond Road	1970	5	67,000	Full	22.00	0.0
486 Totten Pond Road	1969	3	31,253	Full	22.00	0.0
504 Totten Pond Road	1968	3	31,253	Full	22.00	0.0
Tracer Lane Executive Center	1980	3	73,000	73,000	18.00	100.0
1 University Office Park	1980	3	108,000	Full	23.50	0.0
2 University Office Park	1986	6	152,000	Full	23.50	0.0
411 Waverly Oaks Road	1982	5	141,000	72,902	19.00	51.7
245 Winter Street	1983	4	92,000	12,282	16.00	13.4
265 Winter Street	1983	4	92,000	13,355	16.00	14.5
281 Winter Street	1985	4	67,000	Full	26.00	0.0
950 Winter Street	1985	4	275,000	Full	26.00	0.0
225 Wyman Street	1954	2	135,000	Full	21.00	0.0
235 Wyman Street	1985	4	98,000	3,500	21.00	3.6
275 Wyman Street	1963	3	80,000	6,500	22.00	8.1
303 Wyman Street	1979	3	90,000	7,300	23.00	8.1
333 Wyman Street	1981	3	87,000	Full	22.00	0.0
400 Wyman Street	1965	3	70,000	Full	21.00	0.0
404 Wyman Street	1988	3	210,000	Full	27.00	0.0
Total Existing Waltham			**4,628,976**	**558,035**		**12.1**

Exhibit 3-6 (continued)

56

RENTAL RANGE	# OF BUILDINGS	TOTAL OFFICE RENTABLE SQ. FT.	TOTAL OFFICE AVAILABLE SQ. FT.	AVAILABLE %	BUILDINGS WITH AVAILABLE SQ. FT.	OWNER OCCUPIED SQ. FT.	OWNER OCCUPIED %	TOTAL R&D RENTABLE SQ. FT.	TOTAL R&D RENTABLE SQ. FT.	AVAILABLE %
South Suburban Office Market										
$36.00 and Up	0	0	0	0.00	0	0	0.00	0	0	0.00
$33.00–$35.99	0	0	0	0.00	0	0	0.00	0	0	0.00
$30.00–$32.99	0	0	0	0.00	0	0	0.00	0	0	0.00
$27.00–$29.99	0	0	0	0.00	0	0	0.00	0	0	0.00
$24.00–$26.99	1	95,000	0	0.00	0	0	0.00	0	0	0.00
$21.00–$23.99	9	1,124,022	121,874	10.83	5	240,000	21.35	0	0	0.00
$18.00–$20.99	21	3,342,608	258,259	7.73	10	669,820	20.04	0	0	0.00
$15.00–$17.99	24	1,303,324	145,215	11.14	13	53,324	4.09	0	0	0.00
$12.00–$14.99	16	457,480	56,921	12.44	9	0	0.00	0	0	0.00
Below $12.00	49	357,232	33,000	9.24	3	0	0.00	1,616,695	267,698	16.56
Total	**120**	**6,679,666**	**615,179**	**9.21**	**40**	**963,144**	**14.42**	**1,616,695**	**267,698**	**16.56**
West Suburban Office Market										
$36.00 and Up	0	0	0	0.00	0	0	0.00	0	0	0.00
$33.00–$35.99	0	0	0	0.00	0	0	0.00	0	0	0.00
$30.00–$32.99	1	71,324	0	0.00	0	0	0.00	0	0	0.00
$27.00–$29.99	3	585,500	414,000	70.71	2	14,381	2.46	0	0	0.00
$24.00–$26.99	21	2,244,830	393,700	17.54	12	60,000	2.67	0	0	0.00
$21.00–$23.99	55	4,256,326	308,888	7.26	27	40,980	0.96	0	0	0.00
$18.00–$20.99	77	6,162,835	505,810	8.21	40	165,200	2.68	0	0	0.00
$15.00–$17.99	76	3,939,436	646,764	16.42	45	26,600	0.68	213,761	26,000	12.16
$12.00–$14.99	19	637,300	160,800	25.23	8	0	0.00	335,600	47,600	14.18
Below $12.00	51	1,388,880	105,050	7.56	11	0	0.00	2,793,443	267,019	9.56
Total	**303**	**19,287,431**	**2,535,012**	**13.14**	**145**	**307,161**	**1.59**	**3,342,804**	**340,619**	**10.19**
North Suburban Office Market										
$36.00 and Up	0	0	0	0.00	0	0	0.00	0	0	0.00
$33.00–$35.99	0	0	0	0.00	0	0	0.00	0	0	0.00
$30.00–$32.99	0	0	0	0.00	0	0	0.00	0	0	0.00
$27.00–$29.99	0	0	0	0.00	0	0	0.00	0	0	0.00
$24.00–$26.99	9	887,747	61,646	6.94	3	138,000	15.54	419,000	93,000	22.20
$21.00–$23.99	21	1,342,056	189,876	14.15	12	21,711	1.62	0	0	0.00
$18.00–$20.99	54	3,069,769	433,468	14.12	32	12,315	0.40	96,000	5,150	5.36
$15.00–$17.99	36	2,467,790	216,741	8.78	20	76,500	3.10	88,900	55,000	61.87
$12.00–$14.99	38	1,335,761	157,686	11.80	14	0	0.00	426,398	41,137	9.65
Below $12.00	99	657,300	149,000	22.67	5	300	0.05	6,219,324	1,095,453	17.61
Total	**303**	**9,760,423**	**1,208,417**	**12.38**	**86**	**248,826**	**2.55**	**7,249,622**	**1,289,740**	**17.79**

Source: Builders Owners and Managers Association, *Market and Occupancy Survey: 1988.*

Exhibit 3-7 *Childcare*

Problems in Child Care Search	
Cost	26%
Type of care	9
No openings	41
Schedule problems	16
Program issues	4
Location	16
Quality	14
Other	26
Satisfaction with Child Care	
Very good	48%
Good	30
Satisfactory	18
Poor/Very Poor	4

Source: Massachusetts Executive Office of Human Services: Office for Children. Information based on 7,357 calls from parents seeking care for 9,601 children.

4

FAN PIER

In April, 1989, plans for the development of Fan Pier, an ambitious mega-project on Boston's waterfront, have come to a halt as the result of: (1) a major fallout between the property owner and his development partners that in 1987 resulted in litigation and (2) a shift in the political climate that affected the approval process. Both the partners and the city officials have to decide what to do next. The case also presents the successful experience of a similar project, Battery Park City on Manhattan's waterfront, to highlight the overall public and private sector issues relating to large scale urban waterfront development.

Discussion Questions

1. What were the goals of each of the players in forming this partnership? How would you evaluate the relationship of Athanas and HBC over the years?
2. Assess the approval process governing this megaproject.
3. What would you recommend be built on the site at this point in time? What might be the recommendation of a South Boston community leader, or the Director of the Boston Redevelopment Authority?
4. Compare the story of Fan Pier to that of Battery Park City. What lessons can be learned?

The Superior Court of the State of Massachusetts handed down its decision in the case of HBC v. Athanas on April 18, 1989. The decision did not decide the fate of the Fan Pier site on Boston Harbor in South Boston, but did deliver a strong opinion as to why the partnership collapsed, why the development stalled and where the fault lay. Judge Abrams ruled that the owner of the land comprising Fan Pier, Anthony Athanas, had unlawfully obstructed the efforts of his development partner, HBC Associates, headed by Richard Friedman, in obtaining the approvals necessary to build the $800 million mixed use project they had planned together. The extent of the damages would be determined by the trial starting in the fall of 1989 unless the feuding partners found another solution outside the courts.

The spectrum of potential outcomes from the trial was broad: the court could order that Athanas pay HBC amounts ranging from the $13 million HBC declared it had invested to date up to an amount equal to the net present value of the profits HBC had been denied through Athanas' actions, plus damages. Some guessed this number to be over $100 million. The court could also rule for "specific performance," requiring that HBC be permitted to develop the project as planned. Of course, Athanas could appeal any of these outcomes and delay satisfying any court-ordered reparations for years. Meanwhile, the site would continue to sit as vacant land.

Any new solution for the development of the site would have to take into account important changes which occurred in the development environment during the two-year litigation between the partners. First, both the first class office and residential condominium markets had softened significantly between 1987 and 1989. First class office vacancies had risen from 6 percent in 1987 to 10 percent in 1989 and were predicted to rise to 13 percent by 1991. The luxury condominium market stagnated after rapid rises in the early 1980s and was considered to be overbuilt. Secondly, the area in which Fan Pier was located fell under the guidelines of the Boston Redevelopment Authority's new master plan. It reduced the buildable square footage of the area by 30 percent and significantly downsized allowable heights. The master plan also included a lengthy community review and approval process for any development in the area.

Anthony Athanas was a 77 year old restauranteur who was badly disappointed by the stumble of the megaproject for which he had begun assembling

Research Assistant Katherine Sweetman prepared this case under the supervision of Adjunct Professor William J. Poorvu as the basis for class discussion rather than to illustrate either effective or ineffective handling of an administrative situation.

parcels in the early 1960s. Richard Friedman, although happy to be vindicated by the court ruling, was still frustrated by the uncertainty surrounding the ultimate outcome of the project. Each of the parties tried to consider what went wrong and what would be an appropriate strategy for the future. They were aware that another major development, Battery Park City, a megaproject on New York City's waterfront was reputed to be a great success (see **Exhibit 4-1**). Did it provide any lessons for Fan Pier?

FAN PIER DEVELOPMENT

Fan Pier is the collective name for Piers 1, 2 and 3 on the Boston Harbor in the Fort Point channel section of South Boston next to downtown Boston (see **Exhibits 4-2** and **4-3**). Fan Pier is comprised of 18.5 acres, of which 2.6 are underwater and therefore unbuildable. Fan Pier had once served an important maritime function, benefitting from New England's shipping and fishing industry and its own location near Boston's downtown. By the early 1960s, however, Boston's piers lay abandoned and in disrepair due to declines in the regional maritime economy. Boston itself was going through an economic slump with little office growth and considerable social unrest. Few, if any, other than Athanas saw much value in those piers in South Boston.

The history of the attempted development of the Fan Pier can be divided into three stages: 1) the land assemblage, the initial joint venture agreement, and the early plans under Mayor White's administration, 2) the reexamination of the plan under Mayor Flynn's administration, and 3) the breakdown of the joint venture agreement and the subsequent lawsuit.

THE INITIAL STAGES

In 1963, on the 16.4 acre Pier Four site, Anthony Athanas built Anthony's Pier Four, a large seafood restaurant. The site was so removed from the dinner circuit that Athanas inaugurated the restaurant by inviting all area taxi drivers to a gala opening. The restaurant was an immediate success and enjoyed many cabdriver referrals for years. He later assembled at favorable prices the various adjoining parcels that now comprise Fan Pier.

Although the land was purchased in the 1960s, it was not until the late 1970s that growth in downtown Boston was sufficient to justify development on the Fan Pier parcel. Initially, Athanas envisioned a large convention hotel which would spark a revitalization of the entire area and encourage a steady source of patrons for his restaurant business. In 1979, local Boston broker/developer Richard Friedman, head of Carpenter & Co., brought together his client, Hyatt Corporation, and Athanas. Athanas agreed to lease the Fan Pier site and grant certain development rights to a Hyatt and Carpenter joint venture partnership named HBC.

The January 1981 agreement defined the roles. HBC would act as developer, hiring the master planning/architectural team and lawyers who would help the project through the approvals process. Athanas would retain rights of review on Fan Pier and the future development rights to the undeveloped portion of Pier Four.

The early plans were being made during the administration of Mayor Kevin White and reflected the optimism of an innovative development proposed to a pro-growth mayor. Most of the rest of the Boston waterfront had been redeveloped during White's tenure, and he helped to make the Fan Pier site economically feasible by more than doubling the permissible floor area ratio (FAR) from 2.0 to 4.2.

HBC proposed to develop the site in two parts over a ten year period (see **Exhibit 4-4**). The first would be a commercial development including at least one hotel of not less than 1,000 rooms. The commercial development would comprise at least 8 acres and be located on Northern Avenue frontage. The residential component would be at least 6 acres and would be developed slightly later. The 1981 Agreement set rent for the commercial ground lease at $90,000 per acre per year. The residential land would be sold to HBC for $1 million per acre.

In 1983, at Athanas' suggestion, HBC modified the original agreement and arranged to pay the restauranteur ten percent of HBC's share of net sales and net rental profits in addition to the land sale and ground lease amounts agreed upon in 1981. The Outside Closing Dates for construction to begin on the various phases were extended to June 30, 1988 and December 31, 1988.

The next step was to go through the approval process—city zoning, city planning, state environmental review and a buzzing confusion of other agencies who control the permits necessary for construction. The State of Massachusetts requested that both the Fan Pier and Pier Four projects be viewed together since the projects both involved Athanas and were closely linked physically and politically. After all, the surrounding neighborhood viewed the projects essentially as one. This requirement forced Athanas to hire an architect to prepare his own plan for Pier Four.

Despite strong community concerns, the project proceeded apace. In the fall of 1983, Cesar Pelli & Associates of New Haven was selected by HBC to design the hotel. Pelli's firm became master planner of the entire project in fall of 1984. Pelli had a large vision for Fan Pier which reflected his experience as the primary architect for the commercial portion of the Battery Park City development in Manhattan which was soon to open.

THE FLYNN YEARS

While Pelli busily sketched his plans, Boston elected a new mayor, Raymond Flynn, in 1984. Where White had been distinctly pro-development, Flynn had run on a political ticket promising to decentralize Boston, to give more power back to the individual neighborhoods, to listen to and empower people like those in South Boston. Most significantly, South Boston was Mayor Flynn's home base and greatest source of support.

Surrounding South Boston was a homogeneous, primarily Irish-American community with a strong tradition of extended families living within blocks of each other. Household incomes in South Boston were more modest than the average household income throughout the region as a whole. Even though South Boston had suffered during the recession of the 1970s, losing 16 percent of its workforce, the residents retained a strong loyalty to their homes. They feared that pier development would raise property values to the point where the neighborhood would become unaffordable to their own children.

Residents were also concerned about transportation issues. The influx of cars, buses and trucks would require complicated rerouting of transportation, construction of new roads, repairs to the Northern Avenue Bridge, perhaps an additional stop on the subway's Red Line. Nearby, at the edge of downtown, construction of a $4 billion underground roadway and new tunnel to the airport were expected to cause major congestion for the next 12 years regardless of what happened at Fan Pier.

Flynn and Stephen Coyle, the director of the Boston Redevelopment Authority, encouraged the formation of the Citizens Advisory Committee (CAC) to solicit input from the residents of abutting neighborhoods regarding development on Fan Pier. The agenda which emerged from the CAC included developer contributions toward affordable housing, guaranteed jobs for local residents, rent protection for members of the arts community currently located in the Fort Point Channel area, mandatory inclusion of harbor uses, and careful attention to transportation issues. Such requirements are known as "linkage payments" because they are public benefits directly linked to the approval of private development.

It was apparent that it was no longer Athanas and the BRA alone who would review HBC's project.

In April of 1985, Pelli unveiled his $800 million master plan (see **Exhibits 4-5** and **4-6**). The project encompassed a public waterfront park and a vast mixed use complex with an average FAR of 4.63:

LAND USE	GROSS SQ. FT.
Residential	834,000
Hotel (850 rooms)	854,000
Office	1,400,000
Retail	150,000
TOTAL	3,238,000

Pelli's ambitious concept featured a waterfront "island" to be formed by dredging a 90 foot wide "canal" strip inland. The island would house the hotel complex and three apartment buildings, each exceeding twenty stories. Two bridges from the island would extend to the office segment fronting on Northern Avenue. The hotel was especially controversial, a tall thin spire which some critics feared would permanently damage the Boston Harbor skyline. However, by connecting the project by bridges to the surrounding community, the architect tried to blunt criticism of the earlier master plan which was more focused internally.

One objection to the project was that its style, scope, density and height made Fan Pier an extension of the downtown highrises which had punctuated the Boston's modest skyline in recent years. The Pelli plan was considered by some insensitive to the low scale and low density of the existing South Boston neighborhoods. Pelli felt that the site plan and proposed buildings were an exciting use of urban space, where the public would be encouraged to use the waterfront and its walks.

In addition, Athanas' architects announced plans for his Pier Four site: a 300 room hotel, 750 apartments, a 55,000 square foot restaurant, 13,500 square feet of retail and a 1,500 car garage.

Between the two projects, the office space planned for Fan Pier and Pier Four was sufficient to absorb more than 40 percent of the new space needs predicted for downtown Boston in the near future. Negative press reinforced the neighborhood's fears about transportation issues. Owners of large neighboring parcels complained that the scale of Fan Pier would limit the potential development of their sites.

In December 1986, a Joint Draft Environmental Impact Statement for Fan Pier and Pier 4 was submitted by the developers to the State of Massachusetts. In January 1987, the South Boston community again voiced rising concern over the threat of traffic in its neighborhood. In February, the community became more organized and strident. Environmental, housing and civic groups urged rejection of the Fan Pier project by both city and state officials, primarily on the basis of height and density. Mayor Flynn made it clear that it would be the developer's job not only to satisfy the surrounding community, but also to pay the costs associated with meeting their linkage demands.

In February and March of 1987, the two projects were reviewed jointly by the BRA and the Boston Zoning Commission with Athanas' support. Both received the necessary first round approvals. In March, HBC offered $8 million in public benefits including off-site affordable housing to the community. To provide more variety, a number of well-known architects had been selected to design the individual buildings.

In April, HBC received BRA approval of the development plan with some reductions in size. But at the State level, after considerable political pressure, the environmental agency ruled that it needed more information, a declaration which essentially put the project on hold for six to nine months, until the end of 1987.

THE BREAKDOWN

Athanas was beginning to chafe under the constraints, and question the adequacy of his return from the project. A booming Boston economy pushed downtown real estate values higher every year in the mid 1980's, and Athanas felt that even the deal he had renegotiated in 1983 was insufficient. The vacancy rate for first class office space in Downtown Boston in 1987 was only 6 percent and rental rates seemed to increase daily. The residential condominium market was hot: the newest waterfront condominiums across the harbor next to downtown Boston sold in the million dollar range, about $500 per square foot.

From February through May of 1987, Athanas requested a new agreement from HBC in exchange for his continued cooperation during the approvals process. When HBC replied that the 1983 deal was firm, Athanas forcefully criticized the project on the eve of a critical public hearing and officially withdrew all support. He claimed that HBC had dragged its heels since 1981 and that it would not be able to meet the December 1988 deadline for start of construction. The restauranteur argued that he had been grievously harmed financially by the downscaling and delays.

Athanas' action compounded HBC's problems in meeting its obligatory Closing Date. Also as a consequence, two major downtown Boston law firms who had announced their intention to move to the project began to look elsewhere. The financial commitment from the Japanese bank which had agreed to participate in the project was put on hold at least temporarily. The result was litigation between HBC and Athanas for almost two years.

BRA'S NEW PLAN

The Boston Redevelopment Authority and the community groups of South Boston seized the opportunity granted by the court battle and pushed forward their own plans while the sparring partners poked and jabbed.

In March 1989, the BRA announced plans for the 900 acre area it called the Fort Point District. Geographically, Fan Pier represented only a small part of the plan in terms of size, but its ambitious plans, as well as its location near the downtown and transportation made it an important site (see **Exhibit 4-6**). Of all the BRA's new goals for the area, the one most affecting the Fan Pier was the declared intent to manage growth through zoning and community controls. Overall FAR was reduced to 3.0, a dramatic decrease from the Pelli plan.

New height and use restrictions would define what could be built, while "Capacity Based Planning" would temper growth to match the capacity of the transportation and utility infrastructure. For example, guidelines stated that for every two square feet of new office space, one square foot of new housing must be built. A proper mix of service (office), manufacturing, industrial and water-dependent uses in the district would be encouraged to even out cycles in the economy.

The BRA and the community also shared a social agenda which mandated that private developers use some of their profits from commercial development to finance up to 2,500 units of market-rate and affordable rate housing.

In terms of design, the district would avoid any superblock proportions; instead a well-scaled street grid reflecting the surrounding neighborhood would be required. This would also help to maintain and improve existing water views and help create new ones.

PROJECT ECONOMICS

Clearly, the potential returns to the project and to the partners were dependent on the market and the allowable build-out. An outside viewer had calculated the following table in an effort to evaluate what the project might have been worth to all the partners when completed. Since the area was new, comparables were at best an estimate. Real estate rents and values had been weakening.

In any case, the numbers below would have to be considered optimistic. The real return would have to be discounted to reflect the risk involved, the long time frame before receipt of profits and the portion of the returns that would have to be allocated to financial partners who might furnish debt and equity capital.

Total Project Costs and Expected Profit

	SQ. FT. (000)	COST PER SQ. FT.	TOTAL COST (000)[1]	NET OPERATING INCOME	VALUE (000)	PROFIT (000)
Residential	834	$250	$208,500	N.A.	$250,200[2]	$ 41,700
Office	1,400	200	280,000	$35,000[3]	350,000	70,000
Retail	150	160	24,000	3,300[4]	33,000	9,000
	2,384	$610	$512,500	$38,300	$633,200	$120,700
Hotel	850	$180,000	$153,000	$18,830	$188,300	$ 35,300
Total	N.A.	N.A.	$665,500	$57,130	$821,500	$156,000[5]

[1]including infrastructure and soft costs; excluding land value
[2]value of $300 per square foot as condominiums
[3]net operating income of $25 per square foot per year
[4]net operating income of $20 per square foot per year
[5]before payments to Athanas

CONCLUSION

Some observers felt that an out-of-court settlement would be the best way to conclude the dispute and allow both Athanas and Friedman to get on with their lives. The legal system did not lend itself to quick or inexpensive settlement.

Each had to evaluate not only where he wanted to end up but how to get there. Given the past history, each knew it would not be easy. The development process in the United States was certainly fragmented, but in megaprojects such as this one, the problems seemed to be compounded. On the other hand, neither party wanted to give up a dream that had been so long a major part of their lives.

Exhibit 4-1 *Battery Park City Development*

Battery Park City is on a 92 acre site created from landfill during the 1960s and 1970s located in Lower Manhattan along the Hudson River (see **Exhibit 4-1a**). The project was first proposed in the mid 1960s and underwent many political, economic and architectural changes. Four stages can be identified in the 20 years of planning and development of Battery Park City. The first stage marks the beginnings: 1963-1967, when early notions of a high-rise, futuristic megaproject were promoted. During the second stage, between 1968 and 1972, negotiations between the City of New York and the State of New York established control over the site. Construction of the infrastructure and the marketing of the site was started. From 1972 to 1979, the project was stalemated by a variety of factors and threatened with bankruptcy. Finally, in the 1980s, a reworking of the plan and its control systems (with the good fortune of a renewed economy) enabled Battery Park City to be developed in its present form. In the end, the project has been a tremendous commercial success.

Stage 1: 1963-1967

In the 1950s, the combination of new transportation technologies, shifting economies and competitive pressures depressed the maritime industry of Lower Manhattan. As maritime activity slowed and the piers gradually rotted with neglect, certain areas of the waterfront in lower Manhattan were filled in. State and civic leaders, notably New York State Governor Nelson Rockefeller and New York City Mayor John Lindsay took strong interest in the site on the Hudson River.

The plan Rockefeller announced in early 1966 included housing for 14,000 families, including 6,000 middle income and 1,500 low income families in sixteen 31 story buildings and several town-houses. The plan also included a hotel of 2,200 rooms, two office buildings of 67 stories each, plus space for manufacturing below a covered deck. There would be recreation and shopping facilities, indoor parking and parks. This plan was modified three months later, eliminating the manufacturing component but retaining the scale. The governor announced that he would seek legislation to create a public benefit corporation which would oversee the development (see **Exhibit 4-1b**).

Stage 2: 1968-1972

But at the start of Stage 2, from roughly 1968 to 1972, the Mayor of the City of New York John Lindsay had *his* own plans for the site. With a mayoral election coming up in 1969, Lindsay was anxious to retain control over this important property. He felt pressure to promote a socially progressive political agenda which would appeal to voters who were feeling the pain of increasing housing prices. The governor and the mayor negotiated, arriving at a compromise plan which increased the ratio of lower and middle class units to two-thirds of the residential component. The City would receive a rent set at 6 percent of fair market value of the land, certain payments in lieu of taxes, and ground rents, as well as any surplus revenue earned by the Authority. The Master Lease required that the project be completed in ten years, that is, by mid-1978. The Battery Park City Authority would have to comply with a Master Development Plan and be subject to City review bodies. In 1969, the City of New York created the Special Battery Park City District to expedite the development of the landfill.

Architect Phillip Johnson was commissioned to design the Master Plan. In keeping with the

Exhibit 4-1 (*continued*)

large spirit of Rockefeller's idea, Johnson envisioned an integrated complex connected by a spine. The infrastructure would be financed by project bonds issued with the moral backing of the State of New York. While the State would not be legally bound to back these bonds, it was expected that the State would take care of any default.

Stage 3: 1973-1979

During Stage 3 there were problems. By 1973, a recession had fouled Manhattan's expectations for growth and Manhattan office space was glutted. Six million square feet of office space lay vacant in 1973; an additional seven million square feet was coming to market when the World Trade Center across the street from Battery Park was completed. Annual absorption rates led experts to predict that the excess space would be absorbed by 1976 at best.

Second, the plan for Battery Park City had been adjusted to help New York alleviate its chronic housing crisis. Only one-third of the 14,100 residential units would reflect conventional (market rate) rents or sales. The remaining two-thirds would be subsidized by the State and would house middle, moderate and low income families. But by the mid 1970s, it was no longer easy to find the subsidy dollars required.

Third, the City of New York suffered severe and well-publicized financial difficulties at this time which interfered with the financing of the residential component. The Authority had originally planned to borrow $80 million from investors, but the default by the State Urban Development Corporation on other bond issues made these bonds unsaleable.

Stage 4: 1979-1989

Thus in 1979 began the final stage. Decision makers at both the City and State level realized that changes had to be made quickly. A major reworking of the City/State agreement was imperative.

The work-out of Battery Park City included five elements: 1) takeover of the Authority by the State Urban Development Authority under the control of newly-elected Governor Hugh Carey; 2) the removal from the commercial portion of onerous review specifications imposed by the City of New York; 3) the substitution of a simpler, less expensive design; 4) the guarantee that the State would honor its moral obligation on the debt payment; and 5) a mandate to develop the entire project at market rates without the subsidized housing. In addition, the City gave up its claim to ground rents and tax equivalency payments. The City even agreed to provide a tax abatement for the first of the office buildings. In return, the City would own the site after the retirement of the bonds and the repayment of any state advance.

The newly streamlined Authority was encouraged by the recovering real estate market of 1979. Absorption rates were increasing and the World Trade Center was leasing quickly. A new, much simplified Master Plan by Alexander Cooper of the firm Cooper/Eckstut was commissioned. This plan organized the site as an extension of Lower Manhattan, with traditional streets and blocks, public access to the waterfront, and large amounts of open space. The "superblock" motif was abandoned in favor of a contextual solution which would provide the residential segment the variety of building types and design which make distinctive older New York neighborhoods (see **Exhibit 4-1c** and **4-1d**).

The total cost of the development was re-estimated to be $4 billion, including the privately financed $1.5 billion commercial portion. When fully developed, the working population of Battery Park City was estimated to be 40,000 and the residential population estimated to be 25,000.

A major factor in the success of the commercial component was the selection of Canadian developer Olympia & York in November of 1980. O&Y proposed to help take care of the Authority's existing debt problem by paying it $2 million per year starting immediately. This ground rent would rise modestly thereafter, and the Authority would receive a participation in the net income from the office space after 10 years. In exchange, O&Y wanted the 6 million square feet of office space to be

Exhibit 4-1 (*continued*)

built at one time in only four interconnected buildings called the World Financial Center. O&Y felt that larger-sized floors would better meet the needs of major financial institutions who were fast outgrowing the smaller spaces available in the Wall Street area.

O&Y was right. The four buildings with floorsizes averaging 40,000 square feet were soon taken by Merrill Lynch, American Express, Oppenheimer and Dow Jones. A fifth financial tower is now planned to the north.

The residential segment, which eventually will have 14,000 units, also benefited from the economics propelling the expansion of those same financial institutions. The Authority established strict zoning and building regulations and then selected a number of firms to develop their own individual buildings within these restrictions. The market rate rentals and condos were quickly filled by well-educated young professionals, or "Yuppies", working in the financial district who needed convenient places to stay and who could afford to pay. Rental rates quickly approached top of the market, and many of the condos developed in recent years ranged in prices from $300,000 to $500,000. The two components together were such an economic success that excess Authority revenues have been committed to pay the debt service for $400 million of bonds that will support low and middle income housing in *other* parts of New York City.

The project characteristics changed greatly over the decades. A number of people tried to draw conclusions from what had happened. While the location was always desirable and there was no surrounding residential community to raise objections, many external factors came into play. The perception of planning in the sixties with respect to Battery Park City was seen as being visionary. The focus was on dramatic design and idealistic social goals with less regard for economic realities and the scale of day to day living. Large scale federal and state subsidies were expected to absorb the costs. The seventies were considered a time of upheaval, when profound readjustments in the economics and politics of the city paralyzed new development including Battery Park. The eighties, however, saw a strong pragmatism on the parts of the politicians, the planners and the developers in regard to this site. A single authority with a clear mission controlled both land and the approvals process, funded the infrastructure, reacted quickly to an improved economy and with the help of strong private developers capitalized on growth segments in both the commercial and residential sectors.

Exhibit 4-1a *Map of Lower Manhattan*

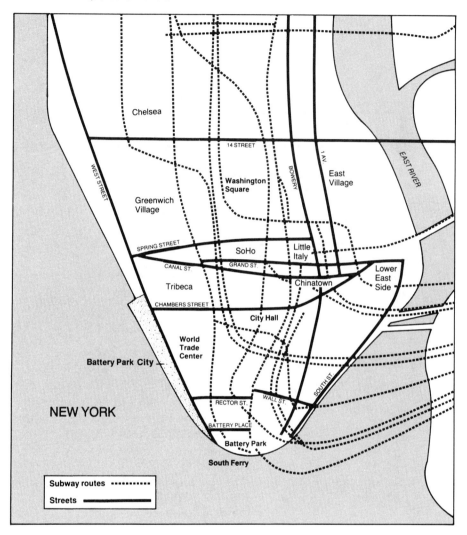

Exhibit 4-1b *Rendering of Proposed Buildings Based on Early Plan for Battery Park City (with the two World Trade Center Towers in the background)*

Exhibit 4-1c *New Site Plan for Battery Park City*

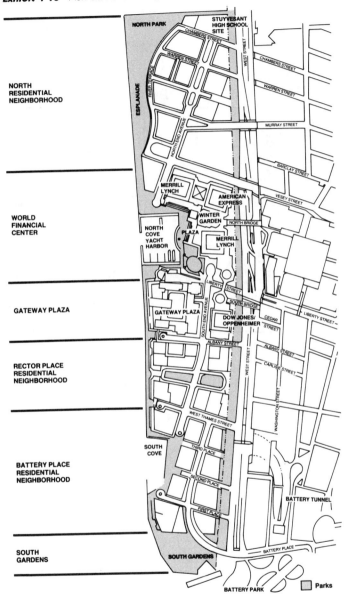

Exhibit 4-1d *Rendering of Proposed Buildings in Battery Park City*

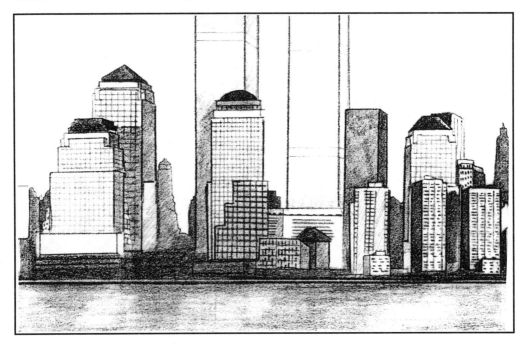

Exhibit 4-2   *Plan of Downtown Boston and Fan Pier Area*

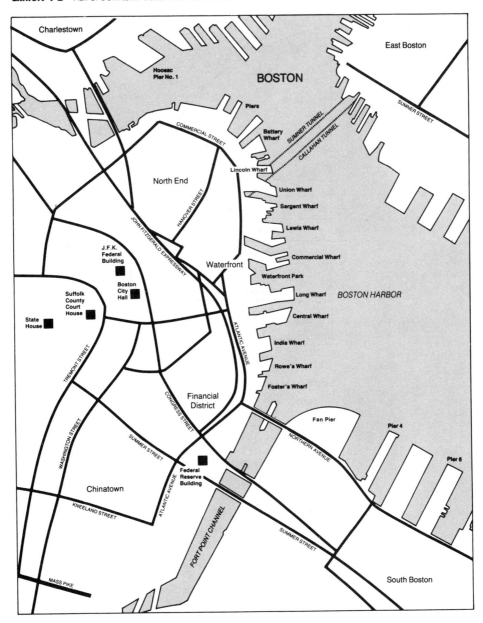

Exhibit 4-3 *Plan of Piers on Fort Point Channel*

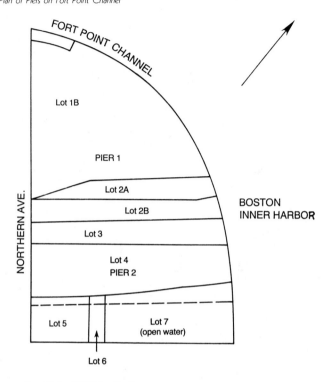

Open Water: 113,158 ± Sq. Ft. = 2.598 ± Ac.

Total: 807,408 ± Sq. Ft. = 18.536 ± Ac.

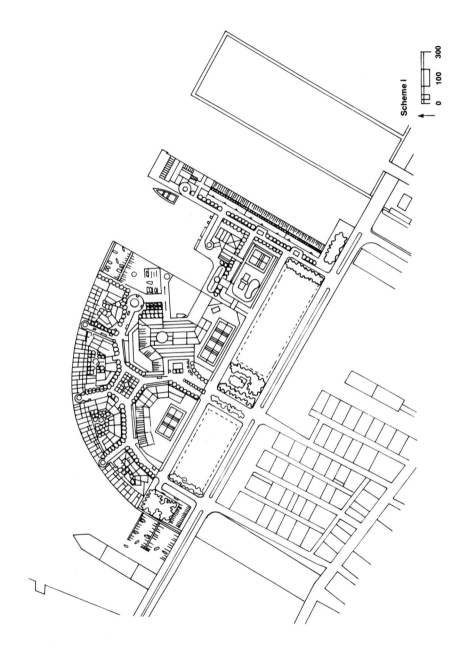

Scheme I

0   100   300

Exhibit 4-4 1981 Master Plan for Fan Pier

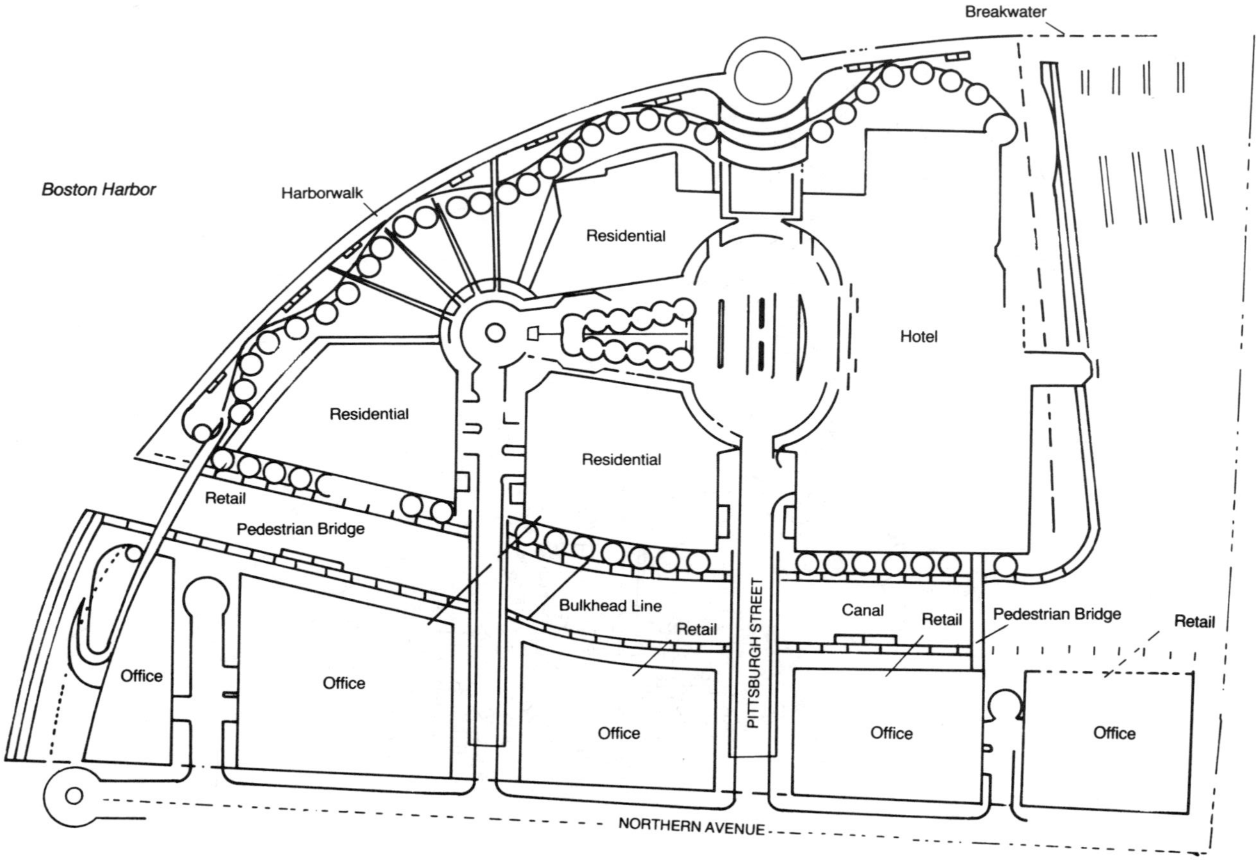

Exhibit 4-5 *Revised Fan Pier Master Plan*

Breakwater

Boston Harbor

Hotel

Residential

Residential

Residential

Harborwalk

Retail

Pedestrian Bridge

Office

Office

Office

Office

Office

Pedestrian Bridge

Retail

Canal

Retail

Bulkhead Line

Retail

PITTSBURGH STREET

NORTHERN AVENUE

Exhibit 4-6   *Rendering of Proposed Buildings for Fan Pier*

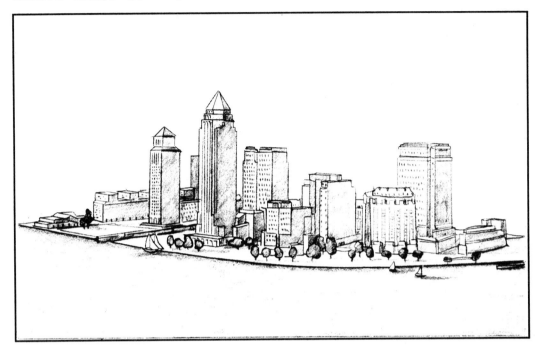

5

REGENCY PLAZA

In June, 1989, Kris Hodgkins, the project manager for condominium development of the Regency Plaza Hotel complex, is trying to decide how to handle a series of customer requested changes. Condominium sales at the project have been slow and Hodgkins would like to accommodate the owners' requests, but the proposed changes may seriously disrupt the construction process. Hodgkins, as the project manager, has to make a decision that takes into account the design, marketing, sales, construction, and financial aspects of the project. This case also provides an opportunity to take an in-depth look at the design and visual aspects of project development through an exercise in laying out the floor plan for a number of condominium units in the building.

Discussion Questions

1. What has been the role of the project manager up to now? Have the marketing and design processes been set up properly? What, if anything, would you have done differently?

2. What should Hodgkins do about the Miller's requested changes? How should she implement her decision? What are the construction implications of her decisions, both now and at earlier stages?

3. How would you lay out six to nine units on the floor plan on **Exhibit 5-1**? *Note:* The class may work in groups of up to four students on this question. Each group should prepare a transparency with the group's design on it for presentation in class. Your design should be at a level of detail similar to the unit layout in **Exhibit 5-4**.

Kris Hodgkins, the project manager for condominium development at the Regency Plaza hotel complex, worked her way through the half finished units on the twelfth floor of the building. It was early on a Thursday morning in late June of 1989, and the sounds of construction workers and equipment being mobilized for work filtered up through the floor. All around her, Hodgkins could see the skeletal forms of luxury condominium units taking shape.

She carried with her several hand drawn sketches that detailed a series of changes to the layout of condominium unit 1203. She could see that the sketches were a radical departure from the standard floor plan and that some of the already installed work would have to be ripped out. She had scheduled an afternoon meeting with the owners, the Millers, their interior designer, the project architect, and the general contractor's project manager to discuss the changes.

Hodgkins was worried about the project. Condominium sales were slow and the local economy appeared to be weakening. The project was behind schedule and over budget. The general contractor was angry about both the number and frequency of changes that were taking place on the project and the cost of estimating changes that did not go through. Several of the buyers had begun to complain about slower service, bad workmanship, and delayed closings.

Senior management at the Regency Hotel Group, however, remained committed to a high level of customer service and to their strategy of allowing buyers to customize their condominium units so long as he or she was willing to pay for any additional costs. Should she allow these changes to go through? Who would pay for the delays and wasted materials?

THE PROJECT

The Regency Plaza was a mixed use project consisting of the 280 room Regency Plaza hotel and 96 luxury condominiums. The building was a 22 story steel and concrete structure with a brick and granite facade that blended well with the older buildings that surrounded it. The first two floors consisted of common areas that would be used by both the hotel and the condominium owners. The next eight floors were hotel rooms and the last twelve floors contained the

Research Assistant Richard E. Crum wrote this case under the supervision of Adjunct Professor William J. Poorvu as the basis for class discussion rather than to illustrate either effective or ineffective handling of an administrative situation.

condominium units. Two levels of underground parking provided 450 parking spaces for both the condominiums and the hotel.

The site was located on the east side of the Boston Common. Spectacular views of the park and city were available from the units facing westward. Units on the back of the building looked onto a city owned garage located on the lower end of Washington Street.

Amenities at the project would include a four star restaurant, an exclusive health club, valet parking, and concierge service. Condominium owners would have access to all of the hotel's services. They could, for example, order room service from the hotel's main dining room. The condominium units were projected to sell for between $250,000 and $800,000.

THE REGENCY HOTEL GROUP

The Regency Hotel Group was the owner and operator of 24 luxury hotel properties that were located in major urban centers throughout the world. The company was renowned for both its emphasis on service and the extensive range of amenities that it offered at its hotels. Regency had developed all of its hotel properties in the past but this would be the first project that would include condominium units. Room rates at Regency hotels started at $200 per night.

THE PROJECT MANAGEMENT TEAM

Hodgkins was hired as a project manager by Regency in the spring of 1987 to manage the design, construction, and marketing of the condominium units. A three person sales staff would report directly to her. In addition, Regency hired Russell Farley, a well known condominium marketing consultant, to help with the initial design and marketing of the units. A separate project team would manage the hotel construction process.

KDS Associates was hired as the project architect. KDS specialized in hotel design and it had developed a strong working relationship with Regency on previous projects. A small local architecture firm, O'Brian and Sinclair, was retained by Regency to coordinate any condominium buyer changes with the base building design.

THE DESIGN PROCESS

Hodgkins was hired just as the conceptual design of the project was nearing completion. The size, massing, and exterior details of the project had been arrived at through a series of tortuous discussions between Regency, KDS, the Boston Redevelopment Authority (BRA), and a number of vocal neighborhood groups. The size and layout of the floor plate were further complicated by the difficulty of designing a structure to accommodate condominiums over hotel rooms over a parking garage. The column spacing and the elevator core location, for example, were essentially fixed by these constraints. As a result, the floor plate could not be changed and the floor to ceiling height was a tight 8'-6" (see **Exhibit 5-1** for a typical floor plate).

One of the first decisions Hodgkins faced was the number, size, and mix of condominium units that would be offered. Farley recommended that Regency should build larger units even though this meant that only 72 units could be built. KDS argued that Regency should build 96 units since this was the maximum allowed by the BRA. Hodgkins knew that she was expected to hit the project's pro forma projections of $53.4 million in gross sale proceeds and $10 million in net profit from the condominium sales. Ultimately, she decided to build 96 units averaging 1,400 square feet.

More mundane considerations, such as the length of the hallways, the efficiency of the floor plans, the relationships of the room locations, and the placement of windows, also needed to be addressed. Should there be a mix of apartment sizes and types or should there be concentrations in either the large or small sizes? How should the units be priced?

The project was initially targeted toward wealthy couples in late middle age. It was hoped that these couples would either sell their suburban homes and move back into the city or purchase a condominium unit as a second home. The design and finishes of these units would obviously have a dramatic impact on unit sales and, ultimately, on the overall success or failure of the project.

THE BIDDING PROCESS

Because they wanted a firm commitment on the cost of the project, senior management at Regency decided to use a fixed sum contract. They had also considered using either a cost plus contract, in which the general contractor would be paid for its costs plus a management fee, or a guaranteed maximum price contract (GMP), in which the general contractor would be paid for its actual cost plus a management fee up to a fixed ceiling.

During this time, KDS began to develop a set of bid documents from the original design drawings. The bid documents would consist of separate sets of architectural, structural, civil, mechanical, electrical, and plumbing drawings as well as a book of written specifications. These specifications described aspects of the project, such as material types, test requirements, warranties, and finishes, that could not be easily communicated on the drawings.

The drawings, specifications, and a written contract formed the contract documents that governed the construction process. Changes would be issued as addenda to the original contract documents and a contract change order would be issued to authorize the additional work. These were also the documents Regency would use to obtain building permits and certificates of occupancy for the hotel and the individual condominiums.

THE BIDS

When the bids came in, there was a wide range of prices. Many of the bids had a number of exclusions and exceptions. The Regency project management team spent the next four weeks meeting with each of the bidders to conduct a scope review during which they tried to ensure that each bid covered the full scope of work shown on the bid documents. Finally, after a series of adjustments to the bids, Regency decided to negotiate with the three lowest bidders.

Kelly Construction emerged as the lowest bidder with a bid of $72 million. They were also convinced to cut three months off their original estimate of 32 months. The schedule would be tight but as long as there were minimal changes, they could make it.

CONSTRUCTION MANAGEMENT

Throughout the fall of 1987, preparations for construction continued at a rapid pace. Kelly awarded a series of subcontracts for the major portions of the construction. Shop drawings and samples began to pour in for review. Items with long lead times, such as elevators and marble, were released for production by the manufacturers. Schedules for the project and for each trade were developed.

The shop drawings were detailed drawings that were prepared by each subcontractor. The shop drawings showed the location, finish, and details of the work that the subcontractor would be doing. When the drawings came in, they would be reviewed by the general contractor and then sent on to the architects and engineers for their review. Often, drawings would be reviewed three or four times before they would be approved. Each cycle could take up to a month. Kelly estimated that there would be close to 5000 shop drawings on this project.

Each subcontractor also submitted a schedule of values that broke out each major area of expense within its contract. The schedule of values, after Kelly approved it, became the basis for the subcontractor's monthly pay request. Each month, the subcontractor would submit an invoice which detailed the hours of labor and how much material had been put in place. Both Kelly and Regency would review and approve the pay requests.

The pay requests would then be consolidated for the project and submitted to the construction lender in order to receive a draw against the construction loan. Normally, 10% of the contract amount would be retained in order to ensure that the work was promptly and properly completed.

When a subcontractor began to complete its work, Kelly would prepare a "punch list" of items or areas that needed to be corrected to bring them into compliance with the contract documents. The 10% retention was often used to force the subcontractor to correct punch list items.

MARKETING

Hodgkins created a comprehensive marketing and service program for the condominium units. Each of the condominium units would be sold with a package of appliances and finishes. On a small number of items, such as bathroom fixtures, the buyer would be given an allowance to use towards the purchase of these items.

Typically, Hodgkins would send each buyer a series of letters that described their options. Each letter described a default option that would be automatically selected if the buyer didn't respond by the specified cutoff date.

In general, however, Hodgkins hoped that changes would be minimal, not disruptive to hotel guests or other condo owners, and that most of them could be done by the buyer after the building was completed. For this reason, Hodgkins did not initiate discussions about customizing individual units. Senior management at Regency also hoped that it would not have to sell units to investors since they felt this would adversely affect the reputation of the project.

THE CURRENT SITUATION

By late June, construction work on the hotel was nearing completion. It was scheduled to open on July 15 and the hotel area was swarming with workers. Work slowed on the finish of the condominium units during May and June as manpower had been switched to the hotel in order to maintain the schedule. Now, however, Hodgkins could sense the pace of work in the condominium area picking up. There were over 250 construction workers at a time on the project and most of them would be working on the condominium floors within two weeks.

During the spring, the relationship between Regency and Kelly had begun to sour. A series of design changes delayed the project and raised costs. Kelly's project manager, Paul Grogan, had become increasingly frustrated by the increasing number of specialty items and unusual details. It was next to impossible for him to get good production runs and obtain sizable efficiencies.

Jeff Cunningham, Regency's project manager for the hotel portion of the project was also unhappy. As the project began to slip behind schedule, Cunningham noticed that manpower on the job had been decreasing. When he questioned Grogan, Grogan replied that he couldn't maintain the manpower levels due to the constant changes that were still being made to the project design.

Cunningham also had to pay for an extensive segment of hardwood flooring that needed to be replaced. Cunningham had verbally instructed Grogan to change the type of flooring in the master ballroom. When a brief spell of humid weather hit in early June, the flooring buckled. Grogan claimed that the flooring had been installed according to standard industry practice and that it was Cunningham's responsibility. Cunningham felt that the flooring should have been installed using a slower but more secure method.

The marketing of the condominium units went slowly. Only 30 out of 96 units pre-sold. Hodgkins hoped that as the units took shape and as the early buyers began to move in, the project would begin to gain some momentum. Hodgkins knew that the target market for this type of product was very thin and that word of mouth advertising would be critical. Even though the buyers were generally particular about details, Hodgkins wanted to minimize the cost of reconfiguring units in order to make sales.

THE CHANGES AT THE MILLERS' UNIT

Hodgkins could see from the sketches that the interior designer had, with a few strokes of a pen, made a series of major changes: the entrances to both bathrooms were reoriented, the master bedroom gained a new walk in closet, the den was enlarged, and the living room fireplace was shifted slightly (see **Exhibit 5-2** for the base building unit floor plan and the interior designer's sketch). Hodgkins knew that all of the trades would be affected by these changes. Ceilings would have to be dropped for recessed lights, sprinklers changed, and electric outlets and switches moved.

If she had the time, Hodgkins would have sent the sketches to O'Brian and Sinclair to have them turned into a set of working drawings. She would then have sent the drawings to Grogan who in turn would have sent them to each of the subcontractors. After Grogan collected the quotes from the subcontractors and prepared an estimate for the work, he would meet with Hodgkins to review the quotes. If they were acceptable, Hodgkins would submit them to the owner for approval; if Hodgkins felt that some portion needed to be reworked, the process would go through another iteration. Unfortunately, each iteration would take several weeks.

Grogan told Hodgkins that he could not continue to make extensive changes to the base building construction work and meet his budget and schedule requirements. If she wanted to make changes to the unit, she would have to give him written authorization stopping work on the unit and she would have to be prepared to pay subcontractor claims for up to $10,000 for out of sequence work. He further warned that the scheduled completion of the twelfth floor might be delayed by as much as two months if the changes affected the base building electrical, mechanical, plumbing or fire safety systems.

THE MEETING

Hodgkins felt it was necessary to act quickly. A face to face meeting was the only way to obtain consensus on the many details to be resolved. She arranged a meeting inside the unit itself. Present would be Sam and Helen Miller, their interior designer Susan Randolph, Tom Sinclair from O'Brian and Sinclair, Paul Grogan from Kelly Construction, and Hodgkins. She was concerned, however, that the meeting could be explosive if she didn't handle it carefully.

THE MILLERS

Sam and Helen Miller decided to buy a condominium at the Regency Plaza to use as an apartment when they were in town and for entertaining business and personal friends. Sam was the president of a local high tech manufacturing firm and both of the Millers were active in the social circles of Boston. The Millers also had a large and beautiful home in Manchester, Massachusetts.

The Millers agreed to pay $600,000 for the unit and planned to spend an additional $100,000 for architectural changes. Furniture and furnishings could cost $50–$75,000 per room. It was important to both of them that the unit be well laid out and beautifully decorated.

Helen Miller had become increasing concerned about the condominium over the past four months. The original closing date of June 1, 1989 had passed, and Regency unilaterally "extended" their closing date to August 1, 1989. Very little work had been done on the unit over the past two months and she doubted it would be ready by August 1.

She had also received several invoices from Hodgkins. One was for work that Tom Sinclair claimed to have performed. He had billed at $75 per hour and the total was over $500 for a minor kitchen cabinet change that affected the plumbing. A second invoice for $120 was for the addition of two wall outlets. Similar work at their Manchester home had cost $30. She was beginning to wonder if they made a mistake when they signed a purchase and sale agreement and put down a 5% deposit five months earlier.

SUSAN RANDOLPH

Susan Randolph was hired by the Millers in late April to customize their unit and furnish it. A well executed design would bring prestige and additional work to her business. Randolph would be judged on the basis of the finished unit and on the amount of money that it cost her client.

Randolph felt that neither Hodgkins nor Grogan paid enough attention to the aesthetics of the unit design. It was important that light fixtures be centered, the sight lines be clean, and that traffic flow be efficient and comfortable. She felt they were both focused on speed and efficiency rather than quality. This apartment would be here for years and she felt they should build it the right way.

She also felt that they were taking advantage of her clients' naivete about construction costs and practices. She felt that part of her responsibilities were to fight for her clients' rights. Each dollar of contractor profit that she managed to cut could be used to upgrade her design. She understood the delays and frustrations involved in getting quotes, but she also didn't want to expose her clients to surprises about the cost after the work had already been done.

TOM SINCLAIR

Tom Sinclair was hired by Regency to coordinate any customer changes with the base building design. The work was fairly straightforward and simply required him to coordinate a whole host of details. A mistake on his part, however, could be quite costly.

He had recently begun to get some pressure from Hodgkins to cut down on his billable hours. This was frustrating since many of the designs that she forwarded to him were incomplete, inconsistent or confusing. It wasn't surprising that it took him hours to coordinate the new designs and lay out the new floor plans and details. Now, Hodgkins wanted him to commit to changes on short notice and with incomplete information. After all, he knew that many of the changes would not be adopted once the cost of the work became clear.

PAUL GROGAN

Grogan was trying to manage 32 subcontractors and almost 250 construction personnel. Kelly originally budgeted a contingency of $3.8 million and a profit of $5 million for the entire project. Most of the contingency was gone. Under the fixed sum contract, any further cost overruns that weren't authorized by the owner would come out of Kelly's profits and out of Grogan's hide.

In order to win the competitively bid contract, Kelly had to assume that it would be able to run the project efficiently. Union labor was paid between $20 and $40 per hour including benefits, depending upon the trade, and overtime was often twice that amount. Wasted time and mistakes were very expensive.

Kelly subcontracted out most of the work but this only partially solved Grogan's problems. If his subcontractors were losing money, they would make his life miserable. His job was to make sure that the job ran smoothly and a big part of this was controlling changes.

Grogan had already begun to assess the impact of the changes in the Millers' unit. The drywall studs had already been installed, the sprinkler system was in, the rough electrical wiring completed, and the mechanical ducts were in place. In addition, the appliances, fixtures, and door hardware for the unit were all stored in the bottom of the parking garage. There would be some demolition, layout, and additional construction work to do.

But these were only the direct costs. Many of the subcontractors had a limited number of supervisory people. The new layouts would require additional supervision. The costs of any mistakes would have to be eaten by the subcontractor. The crews would also be a lot slower as they grappled with new dimensions and details. There was also the issue of doing the work out of sequence.

Grogan's immediate problem was that his drywall contractor had three teams of four men apiece that were ready to begin work on the condominium units on Monday morning. Behind them, the other trades were ready to move in and start work as soon as the drywall was up. He needed a commitment from Hodgkins about what he should do.

Hodgkins asked him for a price for the work but he told her he needed completed drawings in order to get quotes from his subcontractors. He was not willing to commit to a price unless he had a commitment from his subcontractors. He knew that many of his subcontractors were planning on charging a substantial premium to make the changes.

Grogan began to rough out in his own mind what he felt the changes would cost. He realized that clients never believed him when he told them his actual costs. In this case, he felt that his hard costs would be roughly $35,000. He wondered how much he should add for delays, inefficiencies, contingency, profit, and overhead.

HODGKINS'S OPTIONS

Hodgkins felt that she had five main options. The first and simplest option was to tell the Millers it was too late to customize the unit. They could, after they closed on the unit, make the changes themselves, although sprinkler changes could involve shutting down the entire floor and would require careful coordination.

The second option would involve trying to push through the changes. This would minimize the amount of work that would have to be ripped out. Grogan had told Hodgkins that he couldn't wait. It would be expensive to put a hold on the unit.

Unfortunately, Hodgkins knew that the Millers would not commit to the changes until they knew the cost. That would probably take several weeks. If she put a hold on the unit, estimated the cost of making the changes, and then the Millers decided not to make any changes, who would pay for the hold?

She was also worried that the estimates for the work would be outrageous. Some contractors bid jobs on a break even basis and then make their profit on change orders.

Her third option was to hire a small general contractor to come in and finish out the unit before the closing. It was extremely difficult to get other contractors to come onto a job site for small items though. Their mobilization and overhead expenses would make their quotes prohibitive. Other drawbacks to this approach were that Kelly would probably give a very small credit for the work done and materials that had already been purchased and that managing two general contractors was difficult. If the second general contractor used nonunion labor there was always the possibility of violence and vandalism, not to mention arguments over who would be responsible for which punch list items.

Her fourth option involved stopping work on the unit and turning it over to the Millers as an empty shell that they could finish at their convenience. There were several problems with this option. Most banks would not lend against a unit until the developer obtained a certificate of occupancy for the unit. Some banks would make exceptions for special clients or for buyers who would be putting up very large down payments. Hodgkins wasn't sure if the Millers would be able to do this. For the other units in the building, it would further shrink an already small target customer pool. This option would also reduce Regency's control over the project. The hotel management team was concerned about the impact of continuing construction operations in a building that also held a luxury hotel.

The fifth option was to move the Millers to a different unit on a higher floor where the interior work had not yet started. This would buy some additional time. Unfortunately, the building floor plate changed as the building stepped back as it went up. An identical unit was not available on a higher floor. Higher floor units were also more expensive and Susan Randolph had already spent several days working on her design.

Hodgkins tried to estimate the cost impact of the various options. Units of an average of 11,400 square feet were now selling at an average price of $532,000 or $380 per square foot. She felt this price was lower than the prices that had been obtained in the area a year ago. At that time, she had hoped to sell the units at $400 per square foot. But now, the market was tighter and buyers were more cost conscious.

If she turned over units in a "shell" condition with only a base electrical system, an HVAC base unit and rough plumbing stacks, she could give the buyer an allowance of $50 per square foot. If a buyer later wanted one of the standard layouts it would cost about $100 per square foot more to do the work since the work would not be done in sequence. If the owners designed their own unit, the costs might range from $90 to $150 per square foot, depending on the layout and the quality of the finishes.

The Millers' redesign of their unit also raised the question as to whether or not the sales rate or the sale prices for the condominium units would be increased if the floor plans of the units were revised. Many of the early buyers had made extensive revisions to their units. Obviously, there were elements of the condominium unit layouts that many of the prospective owners did not like. Some were, in fact, spending significant amounts of money to rip out existing work. Maybe there was a better design.

Even though she knew it was unlikely that major changes would be made at this late date, Hodgkins decided to take the typical floor plan shown on **Exhibit 5-1** and try a new set of layouts. There was 11,200 square feet of salable space on this floor and she hoped to lay out six to nine units in this space. Even if she decided not to revise the floor plan, she felt that this exercise would help her to better understand the constraints of the shape of the building. She might be able to anticipate buyer concerns earlier and minimize changes late in the process. Changes were not only costly, but generally led to resentments by everyone. Still, she might make more sales by providing potential buyers with additional layouts.

Irrespective of the overall marketing issues, she had to make a decision on how to handle the Millers' unit. Balancing a "big picture" approach with a need to solve myriad detailed problems seemed to be the norm for a project manager in real estate. The excitement and variety kept her going.

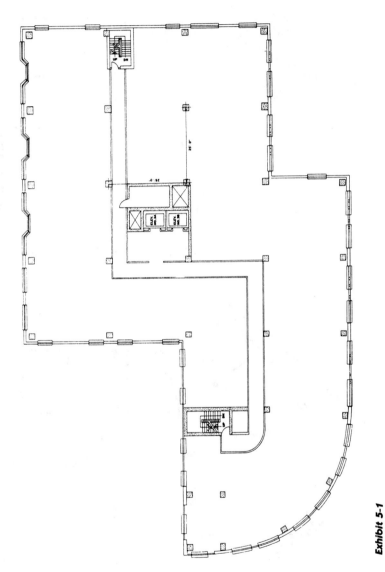

Exhibit 5-1

Exhibit 5-2

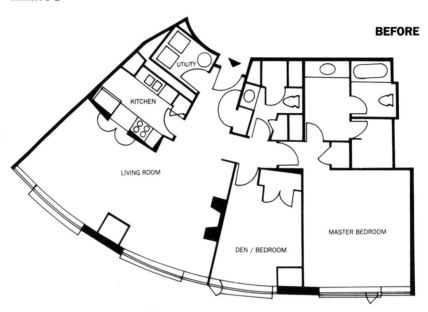

BEFORE

UTILITY

KITCHEN

LIVING ROOM

DEN / BEDROOM

MASTER BEDROOM

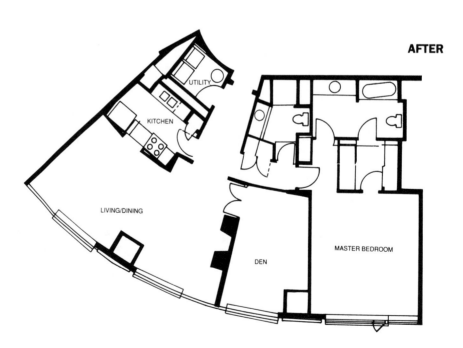

AFTER

UTILITY

KITCHEN

LIVING/DINING

DEN

MASTER BEDROOM

6

SOUTHPARK IV

In January, 1990, George Laflin, a local investor, has raised $450,000 to invest in commercial and industrial properties in Houston, Texas. Laflin is interested in purchasing the 80,000 square foot SouthPark IV office/warehouse facility from a local savings and loan institution. Before he proceeds any further, Laflin wants to determine what the potential returns are from the project and calculate a realistic offer. The case takes the student through the mechanics of project valuation using a back of the envelope analysis.

Discussion Questions

1. Is this a good property for Laflin to acquire?
2. What assumptions has Laflin made in creating his setup for SouthPark IV? What changes, if any, would you make to his setup? What is your projected return for SouthPark IV?
3. What price should Laflin offer for SouthPark IV? What conditions should he attach to his offer? How might Lonestar try to justify a higher price? What might SouthPark IV be worth in five years?
4. Why are there wide variations in the valuation of real property assets?

George Laflin was intrigued by the packet of papers that lay in front of him. The papers comprised a brochure that Lonestar Savings & Loan had put together in an effort to sell the SouthPark IV Distribution Center in Houston, Texas. SouthPark IV was an 80,000 square foot office/warehouse facility located on the south side of Houston. Lonestar was asking $1.5 million for the property.

It was January of 1990 and the Houston real estate market was beginning to show a few signs of recovering from a decade long slump. Laflin had recently raised $450,000 to invest in troubled properties and he wondered whether SouthPark IV would make a good investment.

GEORGE LAFLIN

Laflin had been born and raised in Houston. After graduating from Rice University with a degree in electrical engineering, he had accepted a job with a large computer manufacturer in Houston. During the past ten years, he had seen both explosive growth and rapid declines in real estate values. Now, at the age of 32, he wanted to invest in real estate and hopefully build equity through appreciation.

He had convinced eight friends to join him in committing $50,000 each to buy one or two troubled properties within the greater Houston area. Laflin had decided to initially focus on office/warehouse properties due to their relatively small size and their strong historical performance.

During his initial discussions with his friends, Laflin had expressed his hope that the properties would achieve both a reasonable current return and substantial appreciation. Laflin would take 10% of the deal for putting it together and acting as an asset manager. He would hire a professional property management firm to manage any properties that were purchased.

SOUTHPARK IV

Built in 1980, the SouthPark IV Distribution Center was located in the 100 acre SouthPark Industrial Center. The building had 185 foot bay depths and 22 foot clear ceilings. Approximately 15% of the space was finished as office space (see **Exhibit 6-1** for a floor plan). The exterior walls were simple concrete panels.

Research Assistant Richard E. Crum prepared this case under the supervision of Adjunct Professor William J. Poorvu as the basis for class discussion rather than to illustrate either effective or ineffective handling of an administrative situation.

Loading docks were located in the front of the building and access to rail service was available from the back of the building. There was parking for 80 cars.

In general, the building was considered to be in excellent condition. The one exception was the roof which needed to be repaired. Lonestar had recently received an estimate of $50,000 to repair the roof.

As part of the sales book, Lonestar had provided a summary of SouthPark IV's operating results as of October 1989. Lonestar's numbers projected that SouthPark IV would have $252,000 in total income, $52,000 in total expenses, and $200,000 in cash flow from operations for 1989.

The building was fully leased to four tenants. The leases ranged in size from 12,000 square feet to 30,000 square feet. All four leases were due to expire on June 30, 1990 (see **Exhibit 6-2** for a summary of the lease terms). The leases were net of common expenses, taxes, and insurance. Lonestar paid these expenses and then was reimbursed by each tenant on a per square foot basis. These payments were shown on the income statement as expense reimbursement.

All four tenants had indicated to Lonestar that they would be willing to extend their leases for five years but only at the current market base rental rate of $2.00 per square foot. If Laflin purchased the property and extended the leases, he would incur no additional costs. If he brought in new tenants, however, he would most likely incur a tenant improvement expense of $2.50 per square foot and a leasing expense, on a five year lease, of 15% of the first year's rent. The tenant improvement expense represented a negotiated amount that an owner often gave to a new tenant to customize the tenant's space.

The land under SouthPark IV had recently been appraised at $300,000 and the building at $1,200,000. In arriving at his result, the appraiser had used three methods to calculate the property value: cost, income, and market data. Under the cost approach, the appraiser had applied current construction costs to the appropriate square footages within the building (see **Exhibit 6-3**). For the income approach, he had set up a ten year discounted cash flow (see **Exhibit 6-4**). Finally, the market data approach used recent comparable sales to arrive at a value (see **Exhibit 6-5**).

Lonestar had foreclosed on the property when the original developer had been forced into bankruptcy by the failure of another project. When no one else had bid at the foreclosure auction, Lonestar had bid in at its mortgage amount in order to protect its position. Federal regulators were pushing the bank to dispose of its real estate holdings. Lonestar had responded by aggressively marketing its properties and by offering attractive financing terms.

FINANCING

Lonestar was offering a $1,200,000 loan secured by a purchase money first mortgage on the property with a 10 year term, 30 year amortization period and an 8% interest rate. (See **Exhibit 6-6** for the interest and principal payments associated with this loan.) The mortgage payment constant for this loan was 8.9%. Both the promissory note and the mortgage had an exculpatory clause which meant that the bank had no recourse to the personal assets of the borrower. The property being pledged was the sole security for repayment.

A purchase money mortgage is a mortgage from the seller to the buyer. It may or may not be similar in its terms to a "market rate" mortgage. In this case, Lonestar had sweetened the deal by offering a below market interest rate and a long amortization period. The current market terms for this type of loan were 11% interest with a 20 year amortization period and a 10 year term. The resulting constant was 12.4%.

ANALYSIS

Laflin had looked at a lot of brochures over the past six months. Before he spent any more time or money on market research, he wanted to do a rough, back of the envelope valuation of the property. If the returns to his investors didn't make sense, he knew that there would be no reason to waste his time on detailed financial analysis.

As a starting point, Laflin decided to create a "setup" for the project using the financial information that Lonestar had supplied. A setup was a real estate term for a simplified cash flow statement for a project. From the Lonestar numbers, Laflin deducted a 5% vacancy allowance, a 4% management fee, and a $15,000 structural reserve allowance.

SouthPark IV Setup ($000s)

	ORIGINAL	REVISED
Base rent (80,000 s.f.)	$200	$200
Expense reimbursement	52	52
Gross Income	252	252
Vacancy (5%)		−13
Net Income	252	239
General expenses	−12	−12
Real estate taxes	−30	−30
Insurance	−10	−10
Management fee (4%)		−10
Structural reserve		−15
Total expenses	−52	−77
Cash flow from operations	200	162

The $1.5 million asking price reflected a capitalization rate of 13.3% on the original projection of $200,000 in cash flow from operations. With a cash flow from operations of $162,000, the capitalization rate was 10.8%. As an investor,

Laflin was more interested in the cash flow after financing (CFAF) and the cash flow after taxes (CFAT). To determine these two numbers, he had to calculate the interest and principal payments on the Lonestar loan and the taxable income or loss that the property would incur.

SouthPark IV Setup (Including Financing and Taxes) ($000)

Cash flow from operations	162
Interest	− 96
Principal	− 10
Cash flow after financing	56
+ Principal	10
+ Structural Reserve	15
− Depreciation	− 38
Taxable Income	43
Income Tax (28%)	− 12
Cash flow after taxes	44

The interest and principal payments had been fairly straightforward to calculate. The loan had constant monthly payments of $8,882. As the outstanding mortgage balance was reduced by each principal payment, the amount of interest in each payment would decrease and the amount of principal would increase. Since the term of the loan was 10 years, the outstanding mortgage balance would come due as a lump sum payment at either the end of the 10th year or upon the sale of the building.

To calculate taxable income, Laflin had added back the principal and the structural reserve allowance, since neither was tax deductible, and then subtracted depreciation. He had calculated the depreciation figure by taking the $1,200,000 appraised value of the building and dividing by its depreciable life of 31.5 years. Laflin then multiplied the taxable income by the current tax rate of 28% to arrive at the income tax. In this case, there was no state or county tax to consider.

The $44,000 in cash flow after tax represented a 14.7% current return on a $300,000 equity investment. If he could achieve this level of return, he knew that his investors would be quite happy. If his numbers were accurate, he knew that he didn't need to spend much time or effort calculating the benefits of future rental increases or sale proceeds. But how accurate were his numbers, especially given the problems in the rental market?

THE HOUSTON MARKET

By 1990, the Houston economy was slowly recovering from the collapse of the oil industry in the early eighties. Both employment and population levels had crept to roughly at or past 1985 levels (See **Tables 6-1** and **6-2** for population

Table 6-1 Houston Area Population (1960-1987)

	1985	1986	1987	1988
Houston CMSA	3,663,700	3,545,900	3,553,100	3,580,800
Harris County	2,755,000	2,714,400	2,718,900	2,742,900

Note: The City of Houston is located within the Houston-Galveston-Brazoria Consolidated Metropolitan Statistical Area (CMSA) and it is the county seat of Harris County.

and employment data.) Oil prices, which had been as high as $35 per barrel in 1982 and as low as $14 per barrel in 1986, had recently risen to $16 per barrel.

The outlook for the real estate industry in Houston was not clear. Economic growth would generate fresh demand for space, although almost every category of real estate had a tremendous supply of vacant space. There was also a concern that the collapse of the Savings & Loan industry in Texas might further depress prices and rents by flooding the market with deeply discounted properties.

Houston, with almost 210 million square feet of industrial space, was the 9th largest industrial market in the U.S. Between 1981 and 1985 approximately 35,000,000 square feet of industrial space was added. From 1986–1989, there has been no speculative construction in the area. A limited amount of build-to-suit construction had taken place during this period (See **Table 6-3** for Houston industrial occupancy data).

Within the submarket in which SouthPark IV was located, there were nine buildings that were considered to be competitive to SouthPark IV. Occupancy and rental rate information, based on their current tenants, are shown below in **Table 6-4**.

Most of these leases, however, were written many years ago at higher rents. At the current market rental rate of $2.00 per square foot, Laflin realized that

Table 6-2 Houston Employment (1980-1989)

YEAR	SERVICES	CONSTRUCTION	MANUFACTURING	OTHER	TOTAL
1980	281,800	134,900	428,500	606,900	1,452,100
1981	307,800	142,800	481,200	643,700	1,575,500
1982	301,500	134,500	405,300	642,200	1,483,500
1983	310,700	118,700	369,600	649,600	1,448,600
1984	339,200	111,000	371,000	679,300	1,500,500
1985	341,100	102,800	353,700	681,600	1,479,200
1986	342,000	86,200	305,200	655,900	1,389,300
1987	361,900	81,400	310,100	647,900	1,401,300
1988	386,900	87,900	324,900	666,200	1,465,900
1989	395,600	88,900	324,300	660,900	1,469,700

Source: Texas Employment Commission

Table 6-3 Houston Industrial Occupancy Data (000s)

YEAR	TOTAL	OCCUPIED	NEW SUPPLY	ABSORPTION	VACANCY
1981	175,580	154,738	9,800	9,600	11.9%
1982	185,380	164,338	7,400	2,200	11.4%
1983	192,780	166,538	8,000	1,900	13.6%
1984	200,780	168,438	5,900	500	16.1%
1985	206,680	168,938	3,300	1,400	18.3%
1986	209,980	170,338	0	600	18.9%
1987	209,980	170,938	0	5,500	18.6%
1988	209,980	176,438	0	6,238	16.0%
1989	209,980	182,676	0	7,434	13.0%

he would not obtain Lonestar's projected rents. Obviously, the returns would be lower.

But Laflin had been following the local real estate market closely. He felt that the local economy was gaining strength and that a resurgence in economic activity would cause a rise in rental rates and real estate values. He also felt that the near collapse of the Savings & Loan industry in Texas presented a unique opportunity to invest in troubled real estate properties at a substantial discount.

Somehow he would have to incorporate both current market rates and potential future rates in his analysis. If he didn't, he felt that someone else would outbid him for the property.

If the partnership invested in SouthPark IV, Laflin assumed that the partnership would hold the property for five years. Over this period, he believed that both income and expenses for office/warehouse properties in Houston would grow at a 3% annual rate. He also believed that he would be able to sell the property at a 10% cap rate.

Table 6-4 Competitor Occupancy & Rental Rates October, 1989

BUILDING	TOTAL AREA	% OCCUPIED	AVG. BASE RENT
1.	95,600	100%	$2.40
2.	287,350	35%	$2.30
3.	546,717	97%	$2.50
4.	342,510	98%	$2.20
5.	228,900	98%	$2.15
6.	117,692	100%	$2.60
7.	198,944	80%	$2.40
8.	113,420	78%	$2.00
9.	102,840	53%	$2.30
Total	2,033,973	84%	$2.34

To complete his analysis, Laflin had to calculate the net cash flow from a sale. To do this, he would take the net selling price and subtract the net book value in order to get the gain on sale. He would then calculate the tax liability by multiplying the gain on sale by the 28% tax rate. This would allow him to calculate the net cash from sale by taking the net selling price and subtracting the mortgage balance and the tax liability. Net book value was defined as the purchase price plus capital improvements minus accumulated depreciation. He assumed that the cost of selling the project would be 5% of the gross sales price.

Laflin wondered if the asking price itself was too high. Even with future rental increases and future sale proceeds included, it was difficult to make the numbers work. The fixed mortgage payments could lead to either positive or negative leverage depending on the actual rental rate that he achieved. If he could negotiate a lower sales price with Lonestar, he might be able to improve the returns to his investors. Of course, he also knew that Lonestar would not lend the partnership more than 80% of the purchase price.

It was time for Laflin to do some calculations: a revised income statement, a five year projection, and, using the back of the envelope approach, an analysis of the impact of a lower purchase price. Only then could he see if SouthPark IV was the right investment for his group. There were opportunities in Houston but he also had to consider the risks. After all, the numbers were at best projections.

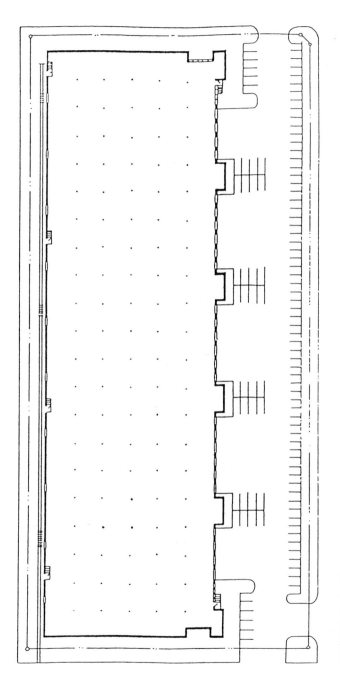

Exhibit 6-1 *Floor Plan*

Exhibit 6-2 *Rent Roll—October 1989*

TENANT	S.F.	RATE (PSF)	ANNUAL RENT	EXPIRATION
Tower Distribution	30,000	$2.70	$81,000	30-June-90
Bayview Nissan	22,000	$2.50	$55,000	30-June-90
Ace Products	16,000	$2.35	$37,600	30-June-90
Boyertown Gaskets	12,000	$2.20	$26,400	30-June-90
Totals/Averages	80,000	$2.50	$200,000	30-June-90

Exhibit 6-3 *Cost Valuation*

DIRECT COSTS

Site Preparation:	Preparation	109,497 sf × $ .12 psf	$ 13,140
	Fill for Floors	185,055 sf × $ .17 psf	31,459
Concrete Foundation:	Non-Bearing Walls	80,000 sf × $ 1.18 psf	94,400
Frame:	Steel	80,000 sf × $ 4.07 psf	325,600
Floor Structure:	Concrete on Ground	80,000 sf × $ 2.03 psf	162,400
Floor Cover:	Vinyl Tile	5,759 sf × $ 1.03 psf	5,932
	Carpet/Pad	7,755 sf × $ 1.75 psf	13,571
Ceiling:	Suspended Fiber, Insulation	13,514 sf × $ 1.55 psf	20,947
Frame, Interior Partitions:	Tenant Space	13,514 sf × $ 8.06 psf	108,923
	Demising Walls, Block	12,210 sf × $ 2.28 psf	27,839
	Demising Walls, Gypsum	8,140 sf × $ 2.36 psf	19,210
Plumbing:		80,000 sf × $ 1.29 psf	103,200
Fire Sprinklers:		80,000 sf × $ 1.05 psf	84,000
HVAC:	Heat	80,000 sf × $ 0.73 psf	58,400
	AC	2,100 sf × $ 4.30 psf	9,030
	Ventilation	12 @ $1,125 ea.	13,500
	Office Heat/AC	13,514 sf × $ 3.20 psf	43,245
Electrical:		80,000 sf × $ 0.94 psf	75,200
Exterior Wall:	Concrete Tilt Wall	24,968 sf × $ 8.55 psf	213,476
	Glass/Concrete	3,320 sf × $15.75 psf	52,290
	Overhead Doors	25 @ $1,000 ea.	25,000
Roof Structure:	Steel Joists, Deck Concrete	80,000 sf × $ 4.22 psf	337,600
Roof Cover:		80,000 sf × $ 0.43 psf	34,400
Total Direct Costs			$1,872,762

INDIRECT COSTS

Architect's Fees	$ 90,000
Finance Fees	40,000
Other Fees, Closing Costs	35,000
Total Indirect Costs	$ 165,000
Reproduction Cost New	$2,037,762

Exhibit 6-4

	7/90	7/91	7/92	7/93	7/94	7/95	7/96	7/97	7/98	7/99
Tenant Rental Income										
Base Rents	200,000	206,000	212,180	218,545	225,102	231,855	238,810	245,975	253,354	260,955
Expense reimburs.	52,000	53,560	55,167	56,822	58,526	60,282	62,091	63,953	65,872	67,848
Vacancy	(13,000)	(13,390)	(13,792)	(14,205)	(14,632)	(15,071)	(15,523)	(15,988)	(16,468)	(16,962)
Total gross income	239,000	246,170	253,555	261,162	268,997	277,067	285,378	293,940	302,758	311,841
Operating expenses										
General expenses	12,000	12,360	12,731	13,113	13,506	13,911	14,329	14,758	15,201	15,657
Real estate taxes	30,000	30,900	31,827	32,782	33,765	34,778	35,822	36,896	38,003	39,143
Insurance	10,000	10,300	10,609	10,927	11,255	11,593	11,941	12,299	12,668	13,048
Total expenses	52,000	53,560	55,167	56,822	58,526	60,282	62,091	63,953	65,872	67,848
Net operating income	187,000	192,610	198,388	204,340	210,470	216,784	223,288	229,986	236,886	243,993
Releasing/Fixed Costs										
Tenant Finish	80,000				80,000					80,000
Leasing commissions	9,600				9,600					9,600
Deferred maintenance	50,000				50,000					50,000
Total Rlsg/Fixed Costs	139,600				139,600					139,600
Cash flow before debt	47,400	192,610	198,388	204,340	70,870	216,748	223,288	229,986	236,886	104,393
Cash flow from sale										2,439,926
NPV of cash flow before debt	851,111									
NPV of cash flow from sale	658,155									
NPV of all cash flows	1,509,266									

Assumptions: 14% discount rate
3% annual increase in revenues and expenses
5 year lease with 60% probability of renewal
10% capitalization rate assumed in year 10
Tax factors are not included

Exhibit 6-5 *Sales Summary Chart*

SALES NUMBER	SALES PRICE	LEASABLE AREA (SF)	PRICE PER SF	SALE DATE	OFFICE AREA %	YEAR BUILT	CEILING HEIGHT	SPRINKLER	RAIL SERVED
1	$ 963,865	50,998	$18.90	5/89	15%	1980	18 ft.	No	No
2	1,233,200	82,159	15.01	9/88	8%	1971	22 ft.	Yes	Yes
3	2,181,448	142,207	15.34	9/88	10%	1975	22 ft.	Yes	Yes
4	5,912,620	295,631	20.00	5/89	6%	1979	22 ft.	Yes	Yes
5	12,025,321	586,601	20.50	12/89	12%	1981	22 ft.	Yes	Yes
6	6,518,961	314,318	20.74	12/89	4%	1982	22 ft.	Yes	Yes
7	3,026,759	160,401	18.87	7/84	10%	1982	20 ft.	No	No
8	2,185,014	107,795	20.27	3/83	16%	1980	22 ft.	No	Yes
9	1,812,658	97,717	18.55	10/88	8%	1979	20 ft.	Yes	Yes
10	2,466,650	136,808	18.03	6/88	11%	1981	22 ft.	Yes	Yes

Exhibit 6-6 *Mortgage Payments*

	1990	1991	1992	1993	1994	1995	1999
Interest	$ 96,000	$ 95,152	$ 94,237	$ 93,249	$ 92,181	$ 91,028	$ 85,417
Principal	10,592	11,440	12,355	13,344	14,411	15,564	21,175
Mortgage balance	1,189,408	1,177,968	1,165,613	1,152,269	1,137,858	1,122,294	1,101,119

7

ANGUS CARTWRIGHT

In January, 1991, Martha and James DeRight, looking to diversify their investment portfolios, have retained Angus Cartwright to identify prospective real estate acquisitions. Mr. Cartwright has four potential properties which merit an in-depth analysis. The case provides an opportunity to examine the various components of real estate return—cash flow, tax benefits, and futures—and measure the profitability of a proposed investment through the calculation of net present value, internal rate of return, and capitalization rate. The class session permits discussion not only about techniques of financial analysis, and their usefulness, but adaptation of those methods to the needs of a particular investor.

Discussion Questions

1. Using the method for financial analysis employed by Cartwright for the Alison Green property, and assuming the figures given in the case, what are the financial returns for the other three properties?
2. What do the calculations in the various exhibits tell us? How valuable are they?
3. Which potential investment, if any, would you suggest for each of the investors?
4. Fill out all the exhibits in the case with backup analysis for **Exhibit 7-5** and **Exhibit 7-9**, and hand in one copy per group at the start of class. Students may work in groups of up to three people.

PEOPLE

Angus Cartwright, an investment advisor, was based in Arlington, Virginia, the home of many members of the DeRight family. In January 1991 his attention focused on the needs of two cousins at different stages of their lives. James DeRight had recently sold his business to a medium-sized public company in exchange for $3.2 million of the company's stock. He then retired and expected to live comfortably on the $100,000 dividends paid on the stock. He felt the need to diversify his investments, however, and planned to sell up to half of his stock and reinvest the money from the sale in real estate or some other investment.

Martha DeRight was President and sole stockholder of a small sized chemical company that had earned in excess of $800,000 before taxes and $550,000 after taxes in each of the previous five years. She had received many offers to sell her company in exchange for the stock of a public company; but she enjoyed the independence of running her own business. On the other hand, she did feel it was wise for her to diversify her company's activities. Her company had accumulated over $2,500,000 in short term securities which she considered unnecessary for her present operations and thus available for outside investment. She had determined that her chemical business could best grow through internal expansion rather than by acquisition. Yet, she did not want the management headaches of an investment in another less familiar manufacturing field.

James DeRight felt that real estate would give him the benefits of diversity and protection from inflation. He also felt that if his income from real estate investments was sheltered for income tax purposes, his overall cash flow would increase substantially. Each DeRight wanted to purchase a property large enough to attract the interest of a professional real estate management company to relieve them of the burden of day-to-day management, and they wanted a minimum return on their investments of 12% after tax.

PROPERTIES

Angus Cartwright had dealt with the DeRight family for many years and had located four properties which he felt might be suitable investments for his two clients. He had brokers show the properties to the two DeRights and the DeRights

This case was prepared as the basis for class discussion rather than to illustrate either effective or ineffective handling of an administrative situation.

Copyright © 1975 by the President and Fellows of Harvard College. To order copies, call (617) 495-6117 or write the Publishing Division, Harvard Business School, Boston, MA 02163. No part of this publication may be reproduced, stored in a retrieval system, used in a spreadsheet, or transmitted in any form or by any means—electronic, mechanical, photocopying, recording, or otherwise—without the permission of Harvard Business School.

were enthusiastic about them. One property was Alison Green, a 100-unit garden apartment project located in Montgomery County, Maryland. This property had been completed in 1984 and had been operating at a 97% occupancy level since the initial rentup. There was a sewer moratorium in the county, preventing much short term competition. The asking price for Alison Green was $3.3 million, but the broker had received indications that a price of $3.2 million would probably be acceptable. The gross rental income from the property was $600,000 with cash flow before financing of $340,000[1]. Real estate taxes in Montgomery County were generally about 14% of the gross rent roll. A new $2.4 million mortgage at an 11% interest rate had recently been arranged. The term was 20 years, but the amortization period was very favorable, 40 years. The land value of the property, for purposes of depreciation, was estimated at $200,000 and the depreciation period (cost recovery period) for the building would be 27.5 years. The method of depreciation since the enactment of the 1986 Tax Act would have to be straight line rather than an accelerated method.

Close by was the second property, a five-story, 40,000 square foot office building, 900 Stony Walk, with 33,500 square feet of rentable space. 900 Stony Walk was rented to lawyers, accountants and small service companies each of which rented between 2,000 and 5,000 square feet. 900 Stony Walk was completed in 1978 and had been operating at a 97% occupancy level since its initial rentup. The asking price was $2.7 million, but the broker believed a price of $2.65 million would be accepted. The gross rentals for 900 Stony Walk were $469,000 with cash flow before financing of $310,000. A new $2.25 million mortgage at an 11% interest rate had been arranged. The term was 20 years with amortization over 20 years. The land value for purposes of depreciation was estimated at $250,000. 900 Stony Walk, being a non-residential building, would have to be depreciated on a straight line basis over 31.5 years. Like Alison Green, real estate taxes at a rate of 14% of gross rent would be paid.

The third property was Ivy Terrace, an 80-unit garden apartment project under construction near Arlington, Virginia. The property was for sale for $2.9 million, but the broker was certain it could be purchased for $2.8 million. A 30-year, fully amortizing $2.3 million mortgage at an 11% interest rate had been arranged. The land was leased for 99 years with annual payments for $20,000. The buyer would take title upon completion of the construction. For depreciation purposes, the owner would be able to depreciate the full $2.8 million purchase price using a straight line method over 27.5 years. The gross rentals for the property were estimated at $560,000. The net income before financing and leasehold payments would be about $322,000. Cartwright knew that property taxes in Arlington were about 12% of the gross rent roll. Living nearby, Cartwright and the DeRights had checked the area closely and concluded that the rental and expense projections were reasonable.

[1]Cash flow before financing = cash flow from operations, or net operating income. It is also referred to as free and clear cash flow.

Also under construction in Arlington was The Fowler Building, a two-story, 45,000 square foot office building with 38,000 square feet of rentable space. Leasing for the building had already begun with 80% of the space rented, mostly to small computer and consulting companies. The Fowler Building was for sale for $3.8 million, but the broker was sure it could be purchased for $3.6 million. A 30-year, fully amortizing $2.6 million mortgage at an 11% interest rate had been arranged. The land was leased for 99 years with annual payments of $55,000. As with 900 Stony Walk, the person who purchased The Fowler Building would undoubtedly depreciate it using straight-line depreciation over 31.5 years. The gross rentals for The Fowler Building were estimated at $551,000 and the cash flow before financing and leasehold payments was projected at about $380,000 once the building reached 95% occupancy. These figures also seemed reasonable, but because a number of new properties were on the market in the Arlington area, Cartwright was able to negotiate a guaranteed return on both Ivy Terrace and The Fowler Building during the first three years until rentals reached projected levels, 95% occupancy.

Although Cartwright expected income from these properties to keep up with inflation, he made what he thought was a conservative assumption that the cash flow from operations would only increase at a rate of 5% per year. After talking with the DeRights, Cartwright also felt that it was unlikely that either of them would hold any property longer than seven years. He therefore assumed a sale in year seven and projected a sales price for all four properties based on projected cash flows and trends in the suburban Washington, D.C. apartment and office markets. For Alison Green he projected a sales price, net to the seller in year seven, of $4,700,000. For 900 Stony Walk he projected a sales price of $3,400,000. Ivy Terrace he estimated would sell for $3,700,000, and The Fowler Building would sell for about $6,000,000. He predicted the highest appreciation rate on that building since he felt that the present leases had been written at below market rent to facilitate leaseup.

PRELIMINARY ANALYSIS

Time was valuable to Cartwright but he had always found a preliminary analysis worthwhile. It enabled him to identify quickly those properties where detailed financial analysis and a more careful physical inspection and examination of day-to-day operations were warranted. He knew from experience that he would then have to spend considerable time studying comparable projects if he were to validate the reasonableness of the purchase prices, operating expenses, rent levels and the amenities provided in the properties he felt were worth purchasing.

Cartwright first noted the assumptions underlying his analysis. He assumed that:

1. There would be a 5% annual increase in the return from operations in any property until the time of sale and that the projected resale price was as shown earlier;
2. His clients would supply the necessary equity investment;
3. In spite of uncertainties as to future changes in income tax laws, for purposes of initial calculations an ordinary tax rate of 31% and a capital gain tax rate of 28% would apply (State income taxes would not be taken into account at this time);
4. His clients could fully use any tax losses as they occurred against other income[2] and tax laws would not change again during the holding period.

Then, being methodical, he developed a list of the salient facts he would need in his analysis (see **Exhibit 7-1**).

Cartwright's next step was to develop the property set ups for each property. Once again he returned to the original brochures given to him by the brokers for each property. In general, the data was not in the form he found most useful. The setup Mr. Cartwright developed for Alison Green follows (**Exhibit 7-2**).

Cartwright then calculated the major comparable statistics for each property (**Exhibit 7-3**).

To validate the reasonableness of the asking price Cartwright would have to compare the capitalization rates and per unit costs of recent sales elsewhere in Arlington and Montgomery County. He would also attempt to establish the replacement costs of each project. Unit cost and operating expenses were usually related items.

Operating expenses for similar properties in the same general areas should be close to average, Cartwright believed. Good management could move them down a little, but very deviant expenses were typically signals of trouble and deserved detailed inquiries. Rents were affected by competition, both present and near-term future. What would have to be done to raise rents? What could be done to cut expenses? Basically, how could he increase the cash flow from operations while maintaining or enhancing future value? What would the owners' operating policies be? He felt the DeRights would want to keep their properties well-maintained rather than run them down, but this was a decision each would have to make. Then there were taxes to consider.

Real estate taxes are an important expense of property ownership. Cartwright believed it was worth examining current property taxes and local tax practices, because, over time, tax increases could materially affect net operating income. Property taxes varied widely throughout the country; for example, in southern New England and New York City property taxes were often higher than elsewhere in the U.S.

[2]The 1986 Tax Act permits the deduction of losses from real estate which is considered a passive investment only from other investments generating passive income. Although the De Rights in this case do not have other passive income, for the purpose of learning the mechanics, it is assumed that they can utilize their losses, if any. In practice, investors now attempt to balance their real estate portfolio to take advantage of any losses.

Exhibit 7-1

	ALISON GREEN	900 STONY WALK	IVY TERRACE	THE FOWLER BUILDING
Number of units/or square feet of rentable space	100	33,500		
A) Gross Purchase Price	$3,200,000			
B) Depreciable Base	$3,000,000			
C) Depreciable Life (Capital Recovery Period)	27.5			
D) Method of Depreciation	straight line			
E) Estimated Sales Price	$4,700,000			
F) Expected Year of Sale	7			
G) Net Operating Income	$ 340,000			
H) Annual Increase in Operating Income	5%			
I) Leasehold Payments	$ 0			
J) Equity Investment	$ 800,000			
K) Amount of 1st Mortgage	$2,400,000			
1) Interest Rate	11%			
2) Term	20 years			
3) Amortization Period	40 years			
4) Constant Loan Payments*	11.172%	12.557%	11.502%	11.502%

Note: Here an annual payment schedule including principal and interest is used to limit the calculations necessary for class preparation. Normally, mortgages like those in the case would be repaid monthly.

RISK ANALYSIS

Cartwright had noted (see **Exhibit 7-1**) that the use of financial leverage in each situation differed. Alison Green was offered on a 3:1 debt to equity ratio, while Ivy Terrace, for example, was offered at a ratio of 4.6:1. Cartwright felt the return on Ivy Terrace might be obtained at a slightly higher risk premium.

His next step was to assess the nature of the operating risks attached to each property. He realized his later financial analysis would rest on the assumption that his clients could maintain the occupancy levels now prevailing. Cartwright referred to the set-ups he developed in **Exhibit 7-2**.

With this information, Cartwright could complete a rough first year breakeven analysis for each property. It was apparent to him, for example, that every 1% increase in occupancy added $6,000 to the BTCF of Alison Green. This meant that an 11.98% decrease in occupancy would wipe out the BTCF of the property (see **Exhibit 7-4**).

Exhibit 7-2 *First Year Project Setups (000's)*

	ALISON GREEN	900 STONY WALK	IVY TERRACE	THE FOWLER BUILDING
Gross Rents	$600.00			
− Vacancies	18.00			
Net Rents	582.00			
− Operating Expenses	158.00			
− Real Estate Taxes	84.00			
Net Operating Income ("Free and Clear")	340.00			
− Finance Payments	268.12			
− Lease Payments	0			
BEFORE TAX CASH FLOW	71.88			

Cartwright then calculated the major comparable statistics for each property (**Exhibit 7-3**).

Cartwright could envisage problems which might necessitate additional cash investments in the Alison property. The break-even analysis suggested that risk might be related to reward in the set of properties he was examining.

Financial Analysis

Since each of his clients was anxious to invest in real estate and because he felt that the four properties were potentially attractive investments, Cartwright decided to expand his analysis. Two simple measures of return are widely used in the real estate industry: the free and clear capitalization rate or return on assets and the cash-on-cash return. The capitalization rate is determined by

Exhibit 7-3 *Purchase and Operating Comparables*

Price/Unit or Price/ Rentable Square Foot	$32,000	79.10		
Total Operating Expense/ Unit or Operating Exp./Rentable Square Foot	1,580			
Operating Exp./Gross Revenue	26.33%			
Real Estate Taxes/Gross Revenue	14%			
Average Monthly Rents for the apartments or yearly dollars per rentable sq. ft. of office space	$ 500	14.00		
Actual or Projected Occupancy	97%			

Exhibit 7-4   *Break-Even Analysis*

	ALISON GREEN	900 STONY WALK	IVY TERRACE	THE FOWLER BUILDING
Current or Projected Occupancy	97%			
Break-even Occupancy	85.02%			
Added Margin	11.98%			

dividing the net operating income by the purchase price. Cartwright calculated that Alison Green had a capitalization rate of 10.63%. The cash-on-cash return is derived by dividing the cash flow before taxes by the equity investment. Alison Green's cash-on-cash return was 8.98%. Cartwright felt, however, that these simple measures of return did not take into account income tax or future value considerations. Additional steps were necessary.

Cartwright had been given a method for analyzing income producing real estate that he considered appropriate for the type of comparative analysis he wanted to make in this case (See **Appendix A**.) For the purpose of the calculations, he decided (as already noted) even though there were uncertainties as to future income tax laws, to assume a 31% tax rate for ordinary income, and a 28% capital gains tax rate.

Because he had already assembled the critical facts about Alison Green in **Exhibit 7-1**, it was easy for him to determine the Before Tax Cash Flow, the Tax Payable and the After Tax Cash Flow associated with the project over his projected seven year ownership period. The steps are outlined in **Appendix A**. Having determined the potential cash flow after taxes, including the computation of net cash from sale (see **Exhibit 7-5**), Cartwright calculated the Internal Rate of Return and the Net Present Value of the Project (NPV) at 12%.[3] He felt this last figure could be useful in setting a maximum price for any subsequent negotiations. His calculations are summarized in **Exhibit 7-6**.

It was obvious that Alison Green more than met the DeRights' minimum return requirements of 12% but Cartwright was intrigued. He wondered how the other projects would measure up to Alison Green in **Exhibit 7-6**. Cartwright wanted to determine the rank of each project on each measure in **Exhibit 7-7**.

Offsetting these returns were the risk factors the Break-Even Analysis (**Exhibit 7-4**) had revealed. Cartwright wondered to what tax liabilities his clients might be exposed if they had to default on the mortgages for some reason. Since he had already calculated the annual amortization and depreciation schedules, he proceeded quickly. The tax payable would be based on the "gain" on foreclosure. The IRS considers the unamortized mortgage balance as the sales price. The tax basis is the net book value of the property. When the tax basis is less than the unamortized loan balance, a taxable gain results from foreclosure

[3]See **Appendix B** for a summarized set of Present Value Tables.

Exhibit 7-5 *Alison Green Projected Cash Flow ($000's)*

	0	1	2	3	4	5	6	7
Free and Clear		340.00	357.00	374.85	393.59	413.27	433.94	455.63
− Lease Payments		0.00	0.00	0.00	0.00	0.00	0.00	0.00
− Finance Charge		268.12	268.12	268.12	268.12	268.12	268.12	268.12
BEFORE TAX CASH FLOW		71.88	88.88	106.73	125.47	145.15	165.82	187.51
+ Amortization		4.12	4.57	5.08	5.64	6.26	6.95	7.71
− Depreciation		109.09	109.09	109.09	109.09	109.09	109.09	109.09
Taxable Income		(33.09)	(15.64)	2.72	22.02	42.32	63.67	86.13
Tax Shelter Benefit @ 31%		10.25	4.85	(0.84)	(6.82)	(13.11)	(19.74)	(26.70)
AFTER TAX CASH FLOW		82.14	93.73	105.89	118.65	132.04	146.08	160.81
− Equity in	(800.00)							
+ Net Cash from Sale								1,707.00
TOTAL RETURN	(800.00)	82.14	93.73	105.89	118.65	132.04	146.08	1,868.00

Sales Price	$4,700,000	Sales Price	$4,700,000
Net Book Value	2,436,364	− Income Tax	633,818
Gain on Sale	$2,263,636	− Mortgage Balance	2,359,670
Tax Liability at 28%	$ 633,818	Net Cash from Sale	$1,706,511

NET PRESENT VALUE AT 12%: $492,746
INTERNAL RATE OF RETURN: 21.99%

although the investor is without cash proceeds from the property. In the case of Alison Green, **Exhibit 7-8**, a foreclosure would not result in a taxable gain.

Next, Cartwright wanted to examine the cash flows from the Alison Green project to see whether the source of return suggested an appropriate match of people to property. There are three sources of cash from a real property investment:

Before Tax Cash Flow
Tax Effects
Future Value

He separately listed the annual cash flows from each source for Alison Green and discounted them at the project's internal rate of return of 21.99%. This allowed him to look at the present values of each cash stream and compare

Exhibit 7-6 *Financial Analysis*

	ALISON GREEN	900 STONY WALK	IVY TERRACE	THE FOWLER BUILDING
Equity Required	$800.00			
Simple Return Measures				
Capitalization Rate— Purchase	10.63%			
Capitalization Rate—Sale	9.69%			
Cash-on-Cash Return (year 1)	8.98%			
Increase in Value =	46.9%			
$\left(\dfrac{Sales\ Price\ -\ Purchase\ Price}{Purchase\ Price}\right)$				
Discounted Return Measures				
Net Present Value @ 12%	$492,746			
Internal Rate of Return	21.99%			
Profitability Index[1]	61.59%			

[1]$\dfrac{\text{Net present value}}{\text{Initial equity}}$

the separate streams to one another and the initial investment. Since the internal rate of return can be found by discounting the cash flows at a rate which makes the net present value of the project zero, i.e., discounted costs equal discounted benefits, each separate discounted income stream could be compared with the total initial investment to identify the proportionate sources of benefits. **Exhibit**

Exhibit 7-7 *Investment Ranking* [2]

	ALISON GREEN	900 STONY WALK	IVY TERRACE	THE FOWLER BUILDING
Simple Return Measures				
Capitalization Rate—Purchase				
Capitalization Rate—Sale				
Cash-on-Cash Return				
Discounted Return Measures				
Net Present Value				
Profitability Index[1]				
Internal Rate of Return				

[1]$\dfrac{\text{Net present value}}{\text{Initial equity}}$

[2]All investment rankings reflect the perspective of the DeRights as prospective purchasers in year 1, sellers in year 7.

Exhibit 7-8 *Tax Consequences of Foreclosure (000's) Alison Green*

YEAR	0	1	2	3	4	5	6	7
Unpaid Mortgage Balance	2400	2396	2391	2386	2381	2374	2376	2360
Net Book Value	3200	3091	2983	2873	2764	2655	2545	2436
Taxable Gain on Foreclosure	*	*	*	*	*	*	*	*

7-9 illustrates his analysis for Alison Green. The results are summarized in **Exhibit 7-10**.

Cartwright felt that the "Breakdown of Futures" gave him information which would be useful in advising his clients. It highlighted the impact of taxation on the sale. He believed that by forcefully bringing the impact of taxation to his clients' attention he could help them avoid decisions which could be costly later. The breakdown suggested the need for careful planning of the eventual sale.

Angus Cartwright had some additional analysis and some hard thinking to do. He decided to repeat his analysis for 900 Stony Walk, Ivy Terrace, and The Fowler Building. He wanted to match the needs of his clients with the characteristics of the properties and the returns they offered. He felt this was the best way to select an investment for each of the DeRights. Cartwright wished to test his intuitive perceptions of the properties against the ranking of each project, although he knew that differences in rankings could be due to differences in the implicit assumptions underlying each measure and the size of the original investment in each project.

Cartwright was not about to make a purchase without additional field work and analysis. However, his analysis would allow him to establish sensible priorities upon which he could efficiently allocate his time.

Exhibit 7-9 *Breakdown of 21.99% Internal Rate of Return*

Year	CASH FLOW BEFORE TAX Actual	Discounted	TAX SHELTER BENEFIT Actual	Discounted	FUTURES Actual	Discounted	TOTAL Actual	Discounted
1	$71,880	$58,924	$10,258	$8,409	0	0	$82,138	$67,334
2	88,880	59,729	4,848	3,258	0	0	93,728	62,987
3	106,730	58,797	(843)	(464)	0	0	105,887	58,332
4	125,470	56,663	(6,826)	(3,083)	0	0	118,644	53,580
5	145,150	53,736	(13,119)	(4,856)	0	0	132,031	48,879
6	165,810	50,321	(19,738)	(5,990)	0	0	146,072	44,331
7	187,510	46,650	(26,700)	(6,642)	1,706,511	424,560	1,868,321	464,567
Total	891,430	384,821	(52,120)	(9,369)	1,706,511	424,560	2,546,820	800,000
Percent		48.10%		−1.17%		53.07%		100.00%

Exhibit 7-10 *Percent of Total Benefits (At Internal Rate of Return)*

	ALISON GREEN	900 STONY WALK	IVY TERRACE	THE FOWLER BUILDING
Before Tax Cash Flow	48.10%			
Tax Benefits	− 1.17%			
Future Value	53.07%			

To ensure that he correctly assessed the worth of the tax shelter components of the total returns to his clients, Angus Cartwright carefully noted the range of the taxable income of each property (**Exhibit 7-11**).

Mr. Cartwright then examined the breakdown of Alison Green's "Futures" into components on a simple proportionate basis, **Exhibit 7-12**. It was apparent that the increase in sales price over time was an important part of the total "future" cash flows, but capital gains taxes substantially reduced the net cash flow to the seller.

Exhibit 7-11 *Range of Taxable Income ($000's)*

	ALISON GREEN	900 STONY WALK	IVY TERRACE	THE FOWLER BUILDING
Maximum Income	+ 86			
Minimum Income	− 33			
Positive in Year	3			

Exhibit 7-12 *Breakdown of Futures*

	ALISON GREEN	900 STONY WALK	IVY TERRACE	THE FOWLER BUILDING
	Actual $	Actual $	Actual $	Actual $
Return of Initial Cash	800.0			
Recapture Mtg. Amortization	40.4			
Increase in Sales Price	1500.0			
Capital Gains Tax on Depreciation	(213.8)			
Capital Gains Tax on Increased Sales Price	(420.0)			
Total[1]	1706.5			

[1]Future $ return from **Exhibit 7-9**.

APPENDIX A   METHOD FOR FINANCIAL ANALYSIS OF INCOME PRODUCING REAL ESTATE

1. Establish the following variables:
    A. *Gross Purchase Price* or construction cost.
    B. *Depreciable base* which is gross purchase price less land value (Land value is either actual value of land or is proportionate to the amount of real estate tax attributable to land.)
    C. *Depreciable life* of building (capital cost recovery period).
    D. Method of *Depreciation*.
    E. Estimated *Sales Price*.
    F. Estimated *Year of Sale*.
    G. *Net Operating Income* (Free & Clear) for each year of ownership. (Gross — Vacancies, Operating Expenses and Real Estate Taxes).
    H. Annual Increase or Decrease in Operating Income (% or $).
    I. *Leasehold Payments* (if any).
    J. *Equity Investment* Required.
    K. Amount of *Mortgage* or *Mortgages*.
    L. *Interest Rate, Term, Amortization Period* and *Annual Carrying Cost of Mortgage or Mortgages*.
    M. *Income Tax Bracket* of Owner (if unknown, use 31% rate.)
2. *Determine Cash Flow Before Income Taxes* by deducting all leasehold expenses and financing charges (interest and principal) from cash flow from operations. The ratio of cash flow before income taxes to cash investment gives simple return on investment, sometimes known as the cash on cash return. The ratio of cash flow from operations to total cost of investment is the free and clear return or the capitalization rate.
3. Determine *Taxable Income* by deducting leasehold expenses (if any), interest charges, and depreciation from cash flow from operations for each year. Annual depreciation is calculated by dividing the depreciable base by the total economic life if the straight line method is used. Prior to the 1986 Tax Act, accelerated depreciation methods were permitted for certain types of properties. For example, if a double declining balance method was used, the approach would be to multiply for each year the portion of the base still undepreciated by a percentage found by the product of 1/ economic life times 200%.
4. Determine *Income Tax Payable* by multiplying taxable income by the income tax bracket of the owner.
5. Determine *Cash Flow After Income Taxes* by deducting income tax payable from either cash flow before income taxes or from taxable income plus depreciation less amortization.
6. Determine *Gain on Sale* from the future sale of property by deducting from net sales price, the book value of the property (original purchase price less depreciation taken).
7. Determine the *Capital Gains Tax* payable on sale by applying the appropriate capital gains tax to the capital gain. If an installment sale, the tax paid each year is generally based on the ratio that the cash received bears to the total consideration for the equity of the property.
8. Determine *Net Cash Flow from Sale* by subtracting from the net sales price any mortgage balances and any taxes payable.
9. Determine *Internal Rate of Return* by applying the appropriate discount rate from the present value tables to the net after tax cash flow for each year, until the sum of these figures approximates the initial cash investment.
10. If the internal rate of return is known, the relative importance of each of the component cash flow streams can be ascertained by discounting the net after tax cash flows of each stream at the internal rate of return.

APPENDIX B

Present Value of $1.00 (Received in a single payment on the 1st day of the year)

YEAR	10%	12%	15%	20%	25%	30%	YEARS
1	.909	.893	.870	.833	.800	.769	1
2	.826	.797	.756	.694	.640	.592	2
3	.751	.712	.658	.578	.512	.455	3
4	.683	.636	.572	.482	.410	.350	4
5	.621	.567	.497	.401	.328	.269	5
6	.564	.507	.432	.335	.262	.207	6
7	.513	.452	.376	.279	.210	.159	7
Present Value of 7 Year Annuity	4.868	4.564	4.160	3.605	3.161	2.802	

8

KING'S PARK

In January, 1982, Wolff, Morgan and Company have assembled a 400 acre tract of raw industrial land on the outskirts of Houston. Intending to subdivide the property and market development-ready parcels, Wolff, Morgan evaluates possible financial structures with joint venture partners. The case also discusses the effect of the absence of zoning or other land use regulation on the development climate, and on the valuation of land.

Discussion Questions:

1. How do you evaluate King's Park as an industrial park? To whom would you market the site?
2. How does the fact that Houston has no zoning controls affect your attitude toward investment? What land use planning controls would you advocate?
3. How does the financial structure of King's Park differ from Reddway and Granville? What are the potential risks and returns to the promoter and investor of each project?
4. Evaluate the growth of Wolff, Morgan as a firm. What is its role as manager for this land development investment?

In late January 1982, the two partners of Wolff, Morgan and Company, David Wolff and Niel Morgan were reviewing the package of material which they had prepared for prospective investors in their latest land development project, King's Park. They hoped to find a financial joint venture partner for King's Park and to structure an agreement even more advantageous than those which they had negotiated with the investor in their previous ventures, Reddway and Granville. They believed that the project performance and the preliminary financial returns of these past two projects added credibility to their presentation now.

They were aiming their presentation at a widely varied group. Among those to whom it would be presented were a large insurance company with a major Houston office, a local mortgage company, and a large industrial firm. They wanted to make certain that the material would be sufficiently clear to explain the project, its economics, their own expertise, and the dynamic Houston environment. They knew that financial institutions had been very bullish on Houston and were anxious to finance new projects.

THE PARTNERS

Since graduation from the Harvard Business School, Messrs. Wolff and Morgan had been working in the real estate development field. Both had been employed by the Brookhollow Corporation, a publicly owned real estate corporation and subsidiary of Texas Industries, Inc. David Wolff was vice president and development manager for the company's office and industrial parks in Houston and New Orleans and responsible for all marketing activities including land sales, building leasing, advertising and public relations. In addition, he headed Brookhollow's land acquisition and property management programs. Niel C. Morgan, also a vice president, was development manager for the company's 1,200-acre office/industrial park and high-rise office complex in Dallas. He was responsible for all corporate financial activities and administrative matters including the negotiation of interim and long-term project financing, financial planning, and economic feasibility analysis.

Research Associate Elizabeth McLoughlin prepared this case under the supervision of Adjunct Professor William J. Poorvu as the basis for class discussion rather than to illustrate either effective or ineffective handling of an administrative situation.

HISTORY

Prior to beginning Reddway and Granville, Wolff and Morgan saw substantial opportunity for more development in the southwest Houston area. Houston had emerged as one of the preeminent cities of the Western Hemisphere. It was a world leader in medicine, space, oil, chemicals and metals, the third largest seaport in the country, and the sixth largest city in the United States (the largest south of Philadelphia and east of Los Angeles) with a growth record second to none. It had become a corporate headquarters city with a population whose average age was younger than any other major metropolitan area.

The southwest quadrant of Houston contains a concentration of the city's wealth and its most dramatic growth. The Astrodome, the $200 million Texas Medical Center, the city's most desirable residential areas, the "Magic Circle" (called in *Business Week*, "the best merchandising corner in the World") where 30-story buildings are rising from what was raw land-- all are in southwest Houston.

Wolff's and Morgan's plan was to combine their real estate talents and "sweat equity" with the substantial dollars of large corporations to create large, master-planned professionally controlled industrial parks. Individual building sites would then be sold to developers. With this game plan in mind, they formed an independent partnership—Wolff, Morgan and Co.

Many developers were glad to have Wolff, Morgan take care of the complex predevelopment issues associated with site acquisition and facility construction. Unanticipated off-site development costs were virtually eliminated, street and utility system requirements were provided for, and the immediate environment was professionally planned and controlled.

Houston was the largest city in the United States without zoning. This made it particularly important to select a site where there was some measure of internal control of contiguous parcels. Wolff, Morgan envisioned a master-planned development scheme where protective covenants would control land uses, construction standards, building setbacks, landscaping, and the use of signs, and require screened, off-street parking and careful maintenance. For the builder these covenants would provide the assurance of standards that would eliminate the need to acquire additional land as a buffer area. For the investor, it was hoped that such standards would contribute to a more rapid increase in land value.

The two partners felt that a joint venture with a financial institution would provide Wolff, Morgan with the capital they needed to fund their ambitious development programs and investment management services and would enable major companies to make successful equity investments in real estate.

From a developer's point of view, they were aware that many seemingly successful real estate groups had gotten into serious financial trouble by staking all their equity on a development effort which, in the long run, their financial resources were not fully capable of funding. A joint venture partner with deep pockets would substantially alleviate this risk. And from a financial partner's standpoint, the arguments for the involvement of a large corporation in a joint venture real estate partnership were persuasive.

It was generally acknowledged that the return on invested capital for many institutions was the product of a relatively passive investment strategy, and often measured less than 10%. And yet the opportunity for these firms to participate in the extraordinary profits generated by successful land developers in the '70s was limited. A joint venture with a professional land development team allowed the large corporation to achieve a very attractive rate of return without undue risk.

REDDWAY—THE FIRST PROJECT

When the 400-acre parcel of land known as Reddway first came to Wolff, Morgan's attention in early 1979, it was a portion of the most substantial private landholdings of any metropolitan area of the United States—the 3,200-acre James ranch. Wolff and Morgan estimated that Reddway would in seven years represent an investment of $800 million in land and improvements. By the end of the first year however, sales velocity put Reddway more than two years ahead of schedule with 43% of the project sold to ten companies. The total value of announced developments reached $440 million.

Reddway was announced as a joint venture with Diversified Resources Corporation, and represented a commitment to develop the 400-acre multi-purpose project. Diversified Resources, the financial partner, is a publicly owned financial holding company with savings and loan associations throughout Texas.

Diversified Resources had originally owned a 530-acre parcel which they had purchased from the James Ranch for $72,800 per acre. They had, however, already sold 130 acres from the tract at $120,000 per acre. This was to be dedicated to residential use. The implicit valuation for the remaining 400 acres for purposes of the joint venture agreement was thus $120,000 per acre or $48,000,000, even though that was greater than the financial partner's actual cost. The financial partner agreed to fund all budgeted project costs excluding any developer's overhead allowance. The development partner was to be responsible for all aspects of project management and 50% of any cost overruns. In return, they would share equally (50/50) in the profits which were defined as the sale price, less commission, less $120,000, less a pro rata allocation for development costs and developer's out of pocket expenses. Afterwards cash flow would be split 50/50.

Completed sites in Reddway sold in the $320,000-per-acre range. Profit was net of the imputed land valuation of $120,000, approximately $48,000 per acre for construction of street and utility systems, and about $8,000 per acre for general and administrative expenses. Of the per-acre profit of $144,000, each partner would ultimately receive $72,000 in profits.

Reddway was located near the intersection of the West Belt Freeway, and

Bellaire Boulevard, a major thoroughfare leading to the Southwest Freeway and across the southern part of the city (see **Exhibit 8-1**). It was felt that Reddway's excellent location and accessibility would save valuable travel time for service and distribution companies and minimize the commuting time for executives and employees alike.

Because of its accessibility to roadways, Wolff, Morgan and Co. marketed the site as a professionally developed business park, where street and utility system requirements had been anticipated and provided in ample quantities and where all off-site development costs had been absorbed. The parcel ultimately encompassed a 200-acre business park for office and light industrial use, 100 acres of garden apartments and townhouses, and 100 acres devoted to retail-commercial development. Southern Pacific Railway tracks paralleled the northern boundary of the project, and a section of the business park had been reserved for rail users.

The development partners created a preliminary design/marketing scheme, and carried out initial feasibility studies and financial projections of all anticipated project costs, cash requirements, and probable timing of sales revenue. They hired an engineering firm to do soil borings, an environmental survey, and a site plan of the property—information on which the planner's subdivisions and master plan for electric utilities, storm drainage, sewer, and water lines, and heavy-duty street systems would be based. They coordinated the site preparation process and the submission of plans and permit applications through the numerous governmental agencies required for final approval. They put the project out to bid, and acted as general contractors throughout the land development process. They supervised the preparation of all legal documents pursuant to the construction loan, partnership agreements, and final transfers of title. And finally, they kept in continuous contact with real estate brokers in an effort to maintain a high level of excitement about marketing the project.

The development community showed an early and strong endorsement. George M. Shaw, president of the Greater Houston Rental Housing Association and one of the largest apartment builders in the southern United States was the first to break ground in Reddway. Shaw purchased 50 acres of land in Reddway; his village of garden apartments and landscaped greens ultimately involved 1250 units and an estimated investment of $120 million. The west side of Houston had much of the area's expensive housing.

Another major purchase of Reddway land, twenty-seven acres with 750 feet of West Belt frontage, was made by the Viscount company, a development firm active in the Houston and Dallas areas. Viscount planned immediate construction of commercial/light industrial buildings, and, at a later date, a series of high-rise office buildings and a motor hotel for the freeway frontage. The projected total investment would be in the $96-120 million range.

Approximately 25 additional acres were purchased by other investors for such uses as a health and fitness facility, a two story Health Maintenance Organization (H.M.O.) structure, office-warehouse units, retail projects, an industrial complex, and a full service bank. When completed, Reddway was to house more than 8000 residents and include an office/industrial tenancy of approximately 12,000.

GRANVILLE—THE SECOND PROJECT

As Reddway attracted some of the finest developers in Houston, the project was running ahead of its projections both as to pace and volume of sales. As a result, Wolff, Morgan and Co. and Diversified Resources Corporation launched Granville in mid-1980, another multi- use project involving 630 acres of land, and representing an ultimate investment of $1.2 billion. Granville was one of the few undeveloped freeway parcels in West Houston, and a five-minute distance from Reddway, located at the intersection of West Belt and Clay Road. The total land cost was $63 million or $100,000 per acre. The sellers gave a purchase money mortgage for $57 million at 8% interest repayable in 5 years.

Because Wolff, Morgan felt that the strong growth trends to the west and south of Houston were likely to continue, they saw Granville as a logical, master-planned extension of Houston's expansion. The plans for Granville consisted of a 188-acre office park, a l74-acre industrial park, 96 acres of retail and commercial facilities, and 140 acres of apartments and townhouses.

Again, the developers selected the property with multi-use development in mind. With this plan, they were not dependent on any one market. Each land use, they felt, enhanced the others, and created an increased momentum of sales and development potential.

Wolff, Morgan took the initiative in assembling the 630-acre property at a price which it considered to be approximately $3.2 million under its appraised value. The total acreage involved three separate tracts with 15 separate owner-ship interests.

Diversified Resources agreed to assume all the financial responsibility for the joint venture, including the $6 million down payment on purchase, interest on the $57 million promissory note plus all development and overhead costs. Profits were to be split on a 50/50 basis.

In this case, the investors were to receive all their cash back first before any profits were to be paid out. Wolff, Morgan had originally asked for the first $3.2 million of profit since they claimed that the land was being put into the transaction at their cost which was below market. It was compromised that Wolff, Morgan would get the $3.2 million but only after the first $16 million of profits had been split by the two parties.

With Reddway, the financial partner had retained title to the property. In this case, a new partnership company was created which owned the property subject to the financing provided by the sellers and which was in turn owned equally by each partner.

Because independent appraisals of this property had showed its market value to be considerably higher than its acquisition price, the level of exposure to the financial partner was considered to be minimal.

KING'S PARK—A NEW PROPOSAL

By January 1982, Wolff, Morgan was prepared to embark on a third venture. The company had negotiated the assemblage of eight parcels of land, comprising a total of 400 acres which they called King's Park. They thought this land could best be used for office, industrial and warehouse uses. The property had extensive frontage (almost two miles) on Interstate 10—Houston's most important freeway, a smaller distance on FM 60 the Katy Freeway and an additional 200 feet on both State Highway 6 and Barker Cypress Road, with several exit ramps and major entryways from frontage roads, and immediate access to and from both directions of travel via major thoroughfare interchanges (see **Exhibit 8-2**). Metro provided service from their Park and Ride lot adjacent to King's Park, and the Metro/AVL lanes were currently being extended beyond Highway 6, which has been improved to 8 lanes. Rail service was available from the MKT Railroad.

David Wolff, in correspondence with the Houston Chamber of Commerce, had received extremely favorable indications of the probable success of such a development program, and was assured of their support and promotion. Sumner, Clark, and Assoc., well-known consulting engineers in the Houston area, had performed extensive engineering and development feasibility studies of the property. Their findings are excerpted in **Exhibit 8-3**. When fully developed, it was felt that sites could be profitably marketed at initial prices as low as $4.00 per square foot for interior land, and $6.00 for highway frontage.

The acquisition cost of the King's Park acreage was $88,000 per acre, or a total of $35.2 million, assuming a municipal utility district could be created as described in **Exhibit 8-3**. It was estimated that an additional $8.0 million in land improvement cost would be expended over a four-year period. The total capital requirement which the Investor Partner in the King's Park joint venture would be responsible for providing was thus $43.2 million.

To place this commitment in perspective, and to assess the downside risk involved, it should be noted that the assembled acreage—a corner tract on an interstate freeway and of sufficient size to enable the owner to create a Municipal Utility District to provide utilities—was now worth considerably more than its acquisition cost. Comparable tracts of between 5 and 20 acres immediately east of King's Park were priced on a retail basis at $156,000 per acre for interior sites and $256,000 per acre respectively for sites with freeway visibility. East of FM 1960, within five minutes of King's Park, prices ranged from $240,000 per acre on the north side of the freeway to $8.00-$16.00 per square foot on the south side.

Based on estimates by several reputable real estate appraisers, who arrived at their valuation by correlating such factors as the market activity in the area, comparable sales, and Wolff, Morgan's proposed development program, it was felt that the King's Park acreage, in its current state, was worth $108,000 to $116,000 per acre, or $20,000 to $28,000 per acre above its cost to the joint venture. Wolff, Morgan and Company would thus be making an "economic" equity investment equal to this excess value, or $8.0 million to $11.6 million. The partnership would bear all general, administrative, advertising and other overhead costs.

In this deal, Wolff, Morgan was again presenting to its prospective partner a 50/50 joint venture. The investor would put up the $35.2 million acquisition cost and $8 million for improvements. The investor could borrow a portion of these funds, but the interest would not be a project cost. Profits were to be split as each individual acre was sold deducting as cost $43.2 million divided by 370 saleable acres or approximately $117,000 per acre.

A projection of land sales revenues, and the resultant cash flow for distribution to the King's Park partners was made (see **Exhibit 8-4**). It was intended to indicate the minimum return on investment which might be expected by the Investor Partner, and to demonstrate the profitability of the venture even with extremely competitive beginning sales prices and a very conservative rate of both land sales and price increases.

The actual return on the Investor Partner's investment would, of course, depend on the degree to which it is leveraged. Were the total capital requirements invested as equity (an initial $35.2 million plus $8 million in equal annual increments) over a four-year period, the time-adjusted rate of return on the total capital investment would be approximately 21%. Assuming that 75% of this commitment is provided with borrowed funds, the time-adjusted rate of return to the Investor Partner on its equity investment would be significantly increased.

In evaluating this investment, other factors which would increase the potential rate of return should also be considered. The most important of these are the higher land sales prices which might be achieved and the faster rate at which the land might be sold.

Beginning sales prices of $6.00 per square foot for freeway frontage and $4.00 per square foot for interior sites are the basis of the projections shown. With an estimated breakdown of 60% frontage and 40% interior, the weighted average price projected for Year 1 is only $5.20 per square foot. Yet in Reddway today, interior, rail-served sites are priced at $8.80 per square foot, up from $6.00 eighteen months ago.

The initial sales prices were projected to hold steady through Year 1 and the first three quarters of Year 2, then to increase at the rate of 15%, compounded annually thereafter. In Reddway, however, prices were increased at an annual compounded rate of 24% and in Granville the rate of increase was 30% per annum. Forty-three percent of the Reddway was sold in the first 18 months. Here, only 5% of the developed acreage is projected to be sold in Year 1, and a cumulative total of 25% by the end of Year 2. Although they had confidence in the above assumptions, they were aware that investors would run their own numbers.

Obviously, either a higher volume of sales or more rapidly increasing prices in the early years of the venture would greatly improve the time-adjusted rate of return on the equity investment. The dynamics of the Houston market, and the results achieved by previous Wolff, Morgan and Company land development programs suggest that this will be the case.

For Wolff, Morgan, time was of the essence since the property was available because of a corporate distress situation—on a cash basis only. Though Wolff, Morgan had risked the $100,000 option money to tie up the land, they anticipated receiving all of that back from the financial partner. As a matter of policy, they would not further pledge either personal or partnership credit.

While they were aware that they were asking a lot, both partners felt that their firm had built up a significant reputation in the Houston community, and that this should afford them leverage in the discussions to follow. They were singularly optimistic about Houston's growth possibilities and their own abilities to perceive and package the most lucrative opportunities. It only remained for them to convince their potential investors.

Exhibit 8-1   *King's Park*

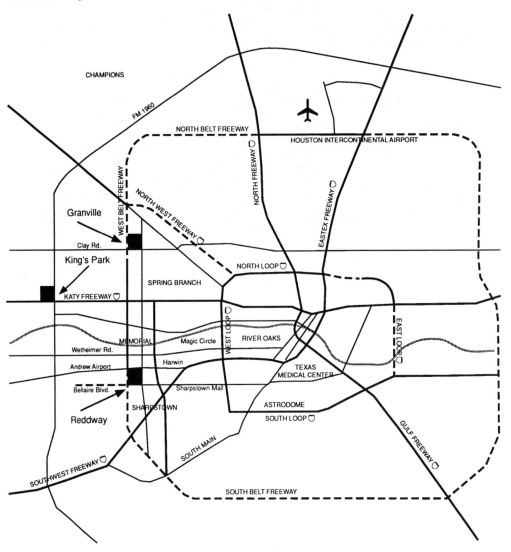

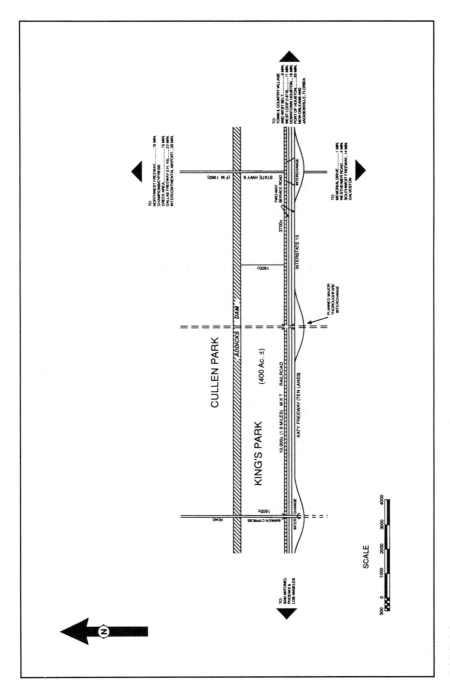

Exhibit 8-2

Exhibit 8-3

SUMNER, CLARK AND ASSOCIATES
1200 North Adams Street
Houston, Texas 77014

November 15, 1981

Wolff, Morgan and Company
1200 River Oaks Bank Building
Houston, Texas 77019

Re: 400-acre tract—Katy Freeway and Barker/Cypress Road
Job No. 555-7890

Gentlemen:

We have completed our preliminary studies of the above referenced tract. As instructed by you, our study assumed a flexible land use plan which could combine office, industrial, and/or commercial development, comparable to Brookhollow Business Park and Reddway, with heavy duty concrete streets and an underground storm sewer drainage system.

There are no apparent drainage, topographical, soil composition, or other problems which would restrict the accomplishment of your development plan. Of most importance, the internal drainage system could be achieved using existing outfall facilities. A sewage treatment plant and water supply for the property could be provided and development of the tract could commence immediately.

The property is located just beyond the present Houston City limits and therefore a Municipal Utility District, or "water district" could be created as you did for the development of Reddway and Granville. Such a district could pay for the cost of all drainage, sanitary sewer, and water facilities, and the related engineering and design fees, with the proceeds of the district bonds voted and sold for that purpose. These, of course, are costs which would otherwise have to be borne by the developer. At current cost levels, this would amount to a savings of approximately $32,000 per acre of the estimated $52,000 per acre development cost which would otherwise be entailed for the project you envision. A total of 26,000 acres adjacent to the property is owned by the U.S. government for flood control purposes. This should greatly add to the land value by restricting land availability and development in this corridor.

Assuming that the cost of storm drainage, sanitary sewage facilities, and water supply is borne by a Municipal Utility District, we estimate that the development cost of the project will not exceed $20,000 per acre.

Very Truly Yours,

John G. Sumner

Exhibit 8-4

Projected Land Sales & Distribution of Cash Proceeds ($000)

	YEAR 1 (1982)	YEAR 2 (1983)	YEAR 3 (1984)	YEAR 4 (1985)	YEAR 5 (1986)	YEAR 6 (1987)	TOTALS
Land Sold (net acres of sites)	18.5 ac.	74 ac.	74 ac.	74 ac.	74 ac.	55.5 ac.	370 ac.[1]
Average Price Per Square Foot	$5.20	$5.36	$6.16	$7.12	$8.24	$9.44	-
1. *Land Sales Revenue*	$4,192	$17,392	$20,000	$23,000	$26,448	$22,816	$113,848
Less:							
Realtor Commissions & Closing Costs	168	696	800	920	1,056	912	4,552
Ad Valorem Taxes	160	312	272	240	208	136	1,328
	328	1,008	1,072	1,160	1,264	1,048	5,880
2. *Cash Flow Available for Return of Investor Partner's Equity, and Profits*	$3,864	$16,384	$18,928	$21,840	$25,184	$21,768	$107,968
to be distributed as follows:							
3. *Proceeds to Investor Partner*							
(a) Return of Capital[2]	$2,160	$8,640	$8,640	$8,640	$8,640	$6,480	$43,200
(b) 50% Share of Profits[3]	848	3,872	5,144	6,600	8,272	7,648	32,392
(c) TOTAL	$3,016	$12,512	$13,784	$15,240	$16,912	$14,128	$75,592
4. *Proceeds to W/M & Company* 50% Share of Profits[4]	$848	$3,872	$5,144	$6,600	$8,272	$7,640	$32,376

[1] 400 ac. less 30 ac. of street r.o.w. and utility easements = 370 net saleable acres.
[2] To repay the $35,200,000 acquisition price plus $8,000,000 development costs.
[3] Available to pay interest charges on debt financing and for return on equity investment.
[4] Available to pay general & administrative; advertising, public relations and sales promotions; travel and entertainment expenses plus profit.

9

TYSONS CORNER

In July, 1989, the partnership owning the Tysons Corner Marriott is facing a cash flow deficit. The opening of a number of new hotels in the area, and the increased trend to product segmentation have resulted in lower occupancy rates and reduced cash flow. This case provides an overview of the hotel industry, the history of this particular hotel, and the dilemma of the general partners in attempting to deal with changes in the market environment.

Discussion Questions

1. Why is the partnership losing money? What will the cash flow look like in 1992? What are your assumptions?
2. What options and obligations does Green have? What should he do?
3. How successful has his partnership been? Was this a good partnership structure? What obligations does Green have?
4. How is hotel development different from commercial or residential development?

John Green, the managing general partner of Hollinswood Associates, casually inspected the lobby of the Tysons Corner Marriott. Green had been intimately involved in the development and operation of the hotel for the past eight years. Whenever he entered the hotel he felt a deep sense of pride. It was a Friday afternoon in July of 1989, and the hotel was busy with families and tour groups checking in and business men and women checking out. Green was pleased by what he saw but he also knew that the hotel faced a projected cash flow deficit of almost $700,000 for the year. The partnership meeting was set for the following Thursday, and Green knew that as the managing general partner he would be expected not only to explain the problems that the hotel faced but also to provide solutions.

THE HOTEL

The Tysons Corner Marriott was a 392-room, full-service hotel. The hotel complex consisted of a modern, 14-story concrete tower, and a two-story parking structure (see **Exhibits 9-1** and **9-2** for a rendering and floor plan for the project). Amenities at the hotel included the 200 seat Rumsford's Restaurant and Tavern, a state-of-the-art disco called Raffles, a 5,000 square foot grand ballroom, 10 meeting rooms, an indoor atrium swimming pool, an exercise room, and a gift shop. Overall the site covered approximately five acres. Surface and structured parking was available for up to 600 cars.

The site was located at the intersection of Route 7 and I-495 in Tysons Corner, Fairfax County, Virginia. The Northern Virginia area was experiencing rapid growth due to its geography, access to major highways, and proximity to a number of major markets including the Federal Government. As of 1989, there existed 16.6 million square feet of office space in the Tysons Corner area. Corporate residents of the market area included NEC, AT&T, Honeywell, McDonnell Douglas, Ford Aerospace, AAA, and TRW. Over 400,000 persons were employed in the area.

Adjacent to the hotel was Tysons Corner Center, a recently renovated major shopping mall offering 250 stores with Nordstrom's, Bloomingdale's, Woodward & Lothrop, and Hecht's as anchors, as well as restaurants and 12

Research Assistant Richard E. Crum prepared this case under the supervision of Adjunct Professor William J. Poorvu and Senior Lecturer Donald A. Brown as the basis for class discussion rather than to illustrate either effective or ineffective handling of an administrative situation.

movie theaters. Directly across the street from this mall was the Tysons II Galleria featuring Macy's, Saks Fifth Avenue, Neiman Marcus, and approximately 100 other specialty stores.

Washington, D.C. was approximately 10 miles from the hotel. Washington Dulles International was approximately 20 minutes away and Washington National Airport was 35 minutes away.

THE CONCEPTUAL STAGE

In the spring of 1979, Green and George Kettle, a local broker and developer, had formed Hollinswood Associates to build and own a proposed Marriott hotel in the Tysons Corner area. Kettle had been actively involved in the local real estate market as the Century 21 regional franchise holder, and he knew that Tysons Corner had been undergoing explosive demographic and commercial growth. Kettle had originally proposed that they build a 40,000 s.f. office building on a small piece of land that he controlled in Tysons Corner. The parcel was on a small knoll overlooking the rest of the Tysons Corner area and, although the area was zoned for commercial use, it was currently being used for Kettle's Century 21 office and single family housing.

Kettle had estimated that a 40,000 square foot class A office building could be built for an all in cost of $100 per square foot, and that it would yield triple net rents of $11 per square foot. The local area had an occupancy level of 99% and Kettle was confident that most of the space would prelease. He was also fairly sure that he could get an interest only, 30 year loan at 10% interest for 80% of the development costs. Since Kettle owned the land free and clear, no additional equity would be required.

Green had agreed with Kettle's assessment of the Tysons Corner area but he felt that they should acquire the rest of the block and build a 200 room hotel. He pointed to the limited competition in the area, the high occupancy levels and the rising average room rates in the area to support his position (see **Exhibit 9-3** for a summary of the original market study).

Green knew that hotels, as compared to residential, retail, and office projects were perhaps the riskiest and most complex form of real estate development and ownership. Hotels were generally characterized by large capital building costs, complicated design and construction, high fixed costs of operation, management intensity, and high levels of uncertainty relating to occupancy levels. Hotels, in effect, had to re-lease their entire facilities every night, a constraint which significantly increased operating risks, and which imposed a need for specialized management expertise and an ongoing refinement of market positioning.

The proposed hotel would be subject to not only internal management issues, but also to exogenous factors such as imbalances of supply and demand in the market, fluctuations in interest rates and building costs, and the availability of permanent financing, all of which would significantly affect the hotel's profitability.

Lenders typically required premium rates for hotel development loans because they were lending on a business, not a real estate venture. In fact, both Green and Kettle had seen surveys showing that lenders' hurdle rates for free standing hotels averaged two to three percentage points above office, retail, and industrial real estate projects. Most lenders also had strict selection criteria requiring affiliation with an established national chain.

Room rates were often used as a benchmark to determine the feasibility of new hotel construction or acquisition. One industry rule of thumb for full service hotels was that for every $1000 of project cost on a per room basis, a hotel must achieve $1.00 of average daily room rate. If, for example, total development costs of the hotel amounted to $100,000/room, an average daily rate of $100/room must be achieved.

THE HOTEL DEVELOPMENT PROCESS

After a brief discussion, Kettle and Green decided to form a joint venture partnership to develop a hotel on the site. Together they assembled the land, talked to lenders, and decided to pursue a Marriott management agreement. Green and Kettle had briefly considered other hotel operating companies but had quickly settled on Marriott due to their superior track record, national brand name, and high quality standards. Marriott would not come cheaply but Green believed that Marriott would be able to more than compensate for their high fees by increasing net operating income.

Green knew that expenses, commitments, and risk would all escalate rapidly as the development process progressed. In an attempt to disperse risk and gain professional experience for the project, Green invited a number of professionals that he had worked with in the past to join Hollinswood Associates as partners. The new partners included Jim Clark, a general contractor, Jim Beers, an accountant, Alex Jeffries, an architect, and Manuel Fernandez, a hotel owner. Each contributed cash except for Kettle who contributed cash and land. Green considered asking each to contribute their professional services in return for an interest in the project but then discarded the idea. The total amount raised was $2.5 million, which was expected to provide sufficient equity to fund a 200-room hotel.

During their initial talks, Marriott had urged the partnership to build a 400 room hotel in order to maximize the use of the site and to gain operating efficiencies. Marriott had recently identified Tysons Corner as the number one market that they wanted to enter and they were eager to strike a deal. Green was concerned, however, about the amount of risk Hollinswood Associates would be assuming. He briefly considered a two phase design in which a smaller hotel would be initially built and then expanded later. A proposed development budget and a stabilized pro forma operating budget were prepared for a full service, 400 room hotel (see **Exhibit 9-4** for a summary of both).

After a brief negotiation with Marriott, the partnership decided to build a 392 room full service hotel. The increase in size from the original plan, however, meant that the partnership now had to raise an additional $2.5 million in equity.

The partners decided to raise the additional equity by forming Tyman Associates, a limited partnership, which would receive a 50% share in Hollinswood Associates in return for $2.5 million. Clark, Kettle, and Green became general partners in Tyman Associates and they took a 20% subordinated interest in Tyman Associates in return for raising the money. The limited partners would get a 9% preferred return from Tyman Associates before the general partners received their distribution (see **Table 9-1** for a breakdown of each partnership). Green, as the managing general partner, had the option to "call" for an additional $500,000, allocated on a prorata basis amongst the Hollinswood Associates partners, in the event of cost overruns.

The management contract gave Marriott 3% of gross revenues and 20% of cash flow before debt service. Marriott's 20% fee would be subordinated, however, to the initial mortgage on the property. Marriott gave the partnership a non-compete clause for a three mile radius around the hotel.

Alex Jeffries, the partnership's architect, and Marriott quickly began design work on the proposed hotel. Site planning was somewhat complicated. The partnership had been unable to convince Marriott to sell their Roy Rodgers restaurant located on the front corner of the site. In addition, the County had established a height restriction of 145 feet and the hotel had to be set back behind a plane that started at the property line and rose at 28 degrees.

Inside, the hotel would represent Marriott's latest design and furnishing plans. The lobby would feature a two story atrium finished in red oak and quarry tile. A state of the art disco would be located to the right and immediately adjacent to the lobby. An all purpose restaurant would serve breakfast, lunch, and dinner to hotel guests. A grand ballroom and ten meeting rooms would be included so that the hotel could compete for banquet and meeting business. Behind the lobby, a 25-yard indoor pool would be located under another 40-

Table 9-1 The Partnerships

HOLLINSWOOD ASSOCIATES			TYMAN ASSOCIATES		
John Green	18%	$900,000	Limited Partners	80%	$2,500,000
George Kettle	14%	700,000	John Green	11%	10
Jim Clark	10%	500,000	George Kettle	5%	10
Manuel Fernandez	6%	300,000	Jim Clark	4%	10
Jim Beers	1%	50,000	**Total**	**100%**	**$2,500,030**
Alex Jeffries	1%	50,000			
Tyman Associates	50%	2,500,030			
Total	**100%**	**$5,000,030**			

foot atrium. Three floors of rooms would have walkways looking out over the pool. The rooms would be decorated in the traditional Marriott colors of orange, brown and yellow. The furnishings would be early colonial reproductions.

Based on the Marriott agreement and the construction drawings, the partnership obtained permanent financing in the form of a $20 million loan with a term of 20 years and an interest rate of 10.5%. The loan was non-recourse. A two year construction loan at the same interest rate but with a one point placement fee had previously been obtained from the National Bank of Washington.

The hotel was completed on time and on budget. On February 5, 1981, the partners invited all of their potential clients and many of their friends to the grand opening of the brand new Tysons Corner Marriott. The atmosphere was festive and everyone seemed pleased with the new hotel.

OPERATING THE HOTEL

The hotel almost immediately began to make money. Occupancy levels and average room rates were high; by 1985, the average daily room rate had climbed to $85.42 and the occupancy level was 75.9%. The Marriott name and high level of service, a good location, and an excellent design provided the strong results. During this time, regular quarterly cash disbursements were made to the partners.

Marriott considered average daily rates (ADR) and occupancy levels to be the key measures of the general strength of a hotel. While occupancy levels often reflected industry wide patterns, they were also a significant measure of a hotel's position within its local competitive market. As of 1985, the Tysons Corner Marriott was a leader in both market share and in ADR.

As the operating results continued to improve, Green began to consider refinancing the project. Connecticut General Life Insurance Company, the original lender on the project, agreed to provide a $10 million second mortgage in 1985. The loan was interest only at a rate of 12% and it had a term of 7 years with an option to extend for 3 additional years. The loan closed on October 4, 1985. The cash, once obtained, was distributed to the partners. Because this was a refinancing the partners incurred no tax liability.

In 1985, Marriott recommended that the partnership authorize a major renovation plan for the hotel rooms and public spaces. A capital expenditure budget and schedule was prepared and approved. Some of the guest rooms were completely renovated in 1986 at a cost of $1.8 million. Subsequently, the Raffles lounge, the lobby, the ballroom, the gift shop, and the mezzanine level were all renovated. The total cost of all renovations and capital expenditures was approximately $2.5 million. Some of the funds had come from a capital budget escrow account that was required by the Marriott management contract and funded from operations, and the rest had come from funds that would otherwise have been used for partnership distributions.

MARRIOTT

The Marriott Corporation was a diversified company involved in lodging, food service, and entertainment. Founded in 1927 by J. Willard Marriott, the company began as a small root beer stand in Washington, D.C.. As of 1988, the company had revenues of almost $7.4 billion and net income of approximately $232 million. Marriott owned or managed 121,000 rooms and it ran nearly 1,100 restaurants. The company had consistently finished first in customer surveys conducted by Business Travel News. The company's occupancy level was proclaimed to be ten points higher than the industry average of 63%. Between 1978 and 1988, Marriott averaged an ROE of 21.7%.

In 1988, Marriott developed over $1 billion in hotel properties. During the mid eighties, the company began to pursue a strategy of concentrating on hotel management and development, and as a result almost all of the new hotels were sold off or syndicated, subject to a management contract to Marriott, as they were developed. At the same time, Marriott began a program of rapid product expansion as the company pushed into the extended stay, budget, economy, suites, and elderly care markets through its Courtyard, Fairfield Inn, Residence Inn, and Brighton Gardens chains. Marriott's position as a market leader allowed the company to command profit sharing of 20% of operating cash flow versus an estimated industry average of 20-30% of cash flow after debt service.

THE CURRENT SITUATION

By 1989, the operating results had begun to deteriorate for the Tysons Corner Marriott. Average room rates had leveled off and occupancy levels had fallen slightly. Intense competition in the area had developed; four new hotels had been built in the area since 1985 and six more were planned for the next two years. Food and beverage profits had also fallen precipitously. Expenses had risen slowly but with the flattening of revenues even modest increases had had a negative impact on the operating profits (see **Exhibit 9-5** for a summary of operating results). During 1987 and 1988, the general partners had personally guaranteed $900,000 of third mortgage loans to cover the cash flow deficit.

At the national level, hotel operating performance had also begun to decline. A sharp downturn in hotel construction in the mid-seventies had been followed by strong industry operating performance in the early eighties. This led to increased interest on the part of developers and investors in building new hotels, and, combined with an influx of funds, caused a tremendous oversupply of hotel rooms.

At the industry level, profitability had been declining since the early eighties. Overbuilding, declining occupancy, increased competition, an inflationary cost spiral, soaring labor costs, and huge increases in insurance premiums had all had a negative impact on the bottom line. The 1986 tax reform bill further

Net Change in Hotel Room Supply versus Demand, Occupancy Rates and Average Daily Rates, 1972-89E (Hotel Room in Thousands)

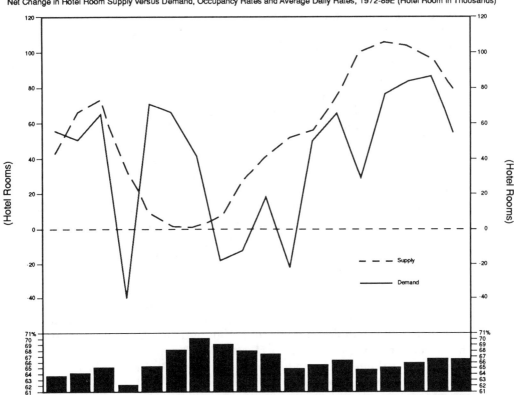

ADR $20.26 $22.05 $22.10 $23.98 $26.44 $29.99 $33.49 $37.50 $42.10 $44.75 $48.41 $51.90 $56.59 $59.78 $61.95 $65.45 $70.02 $73.60

Source: Solomon Brothers, June 29, 1989

increased pressure on the industry by eliminating accelerated depreciation, reducing the value of interest deductions, and limiting allowable passive investment losses.

Within the Tysons Corner area, competing hotels had begun to use sophisticated marketing programs to segment the market and selectively attack for market share. This trend was particularly troubling to Green since many of the new hotels were using newer designs and additional amenities to selectively target the most profitable segments (see **Exhibit 9-6** for a summary of the competitive situation.) Was the Tysons Corner Marriott correctly positioned for the 1990s?

Green believed that it would cost $140,000 per room to build a hotel comparable to the Tysons Corner Marriott. This seemed to imply that the Tysons Corner Marriott, with a debt level of only $75,000 per room, should be able to compete based on its low cost position, and yet as new hotels continued to enter the market room rates remained flat. Budget hotels, such as Rodeway Inns, which could be built for as little as $25,000 per room, were also entering the market, albeit in less desirable locations. Conversely, Green knew that his net operating income could not support the debt level of $75,000 per room. How could the new hotels be making money, he wondered? He knew that comparable hotels were selling with cap rates of 10% but this also did not seem to make sense. How should the Marriott rooms be valued? Was this the right time to sell the hotel? What would the tax consequences be? Should they hang on until operating results improved?

Immediately behind the hotel, the JTL Tyson Towers I office building had recently opened with almost 500,000 square feet of office space. Two additional towers, each with 500,000 square feet of space, were planned for 1991 and 1993. Overall, experts were estimating that almost a million square feet of office space would be delivered to the Tysons Corner market in 1990 and that an additional eight million square feet would be completed by 1999.

Marriott had assigned five managers to the property over the eight years that the property had been in operation. The managers had all seemed to be extremely professional, and the hotel and staff had received consistently strong marks in customer surveys. The Marriott reputation for attention to customer service, commitment to its employees, and excellence in operations appeared to be warranted. And yet, Green still wondered if they were getting all of the cash flow that they could out of the property. How should he assess Marriott's performance in keeping costs down and rates up? How should he manage them?

Green also wondered how the design and the physical condition of the hotel were affecting the hotel's performance. The newer hotels "felt" different and many of them offered additional amenities and services. Which amenities and services should the hotel offer? How much would it cost to offer them? Should additional funds be committed to the seemingly endless rounds of renovation?

However, Green was sure of two things: he would have to come up with a way to fund the deficit and he would also have to come up with a solution to the underlying problem. Green knew that the raising of any new, outside equity would require a vote of the partners. Local lenders had offered to lend against the property but only if the general partners guaranteed the loan. Green wondered if the other general partners would be willing to give a personal guarantee. What about the limited partners? Where else could he raise some cash?

In addition, the second mortgage would initially come due in three years. Green could extend the loan for 3 years but this would only delay the problem. Would operating results improve enough in the next six years to allow the partnership to roll over the loan or should they cut their losses and sell now? How much would operating results have to improve in order to breakeven? Would it be a mistake to commit more capital since they had no personal liability? What were his other options?

Over the past eight years, Green had acted as the managing partner of Hollinswood Associates, and he had often acted alone to make day to day operating decisions for the partnership. He wondered now what his obligations were to his friends, investors, partners, and employees? How should he weigh their different interests and rights? How should he go about implementing a solution?

Many things had changed since his first meeting with Kettle back in 1979. Green was proud of the hotel and proud of what the partnership had accomplished. The complex development process had been successfully completed. The hotel, with close to 400 employees, was a major employer in the local community and the existence of the hotel had helped to spur local development. His partners had all earned handsome profits. Now however, the hotel was struggling, and Green wondered how the various partners would react to the changes which threatened the project. What should he recommend to them?

Exhibit 9-1 *Rendering of Tysons Corner Marriott*

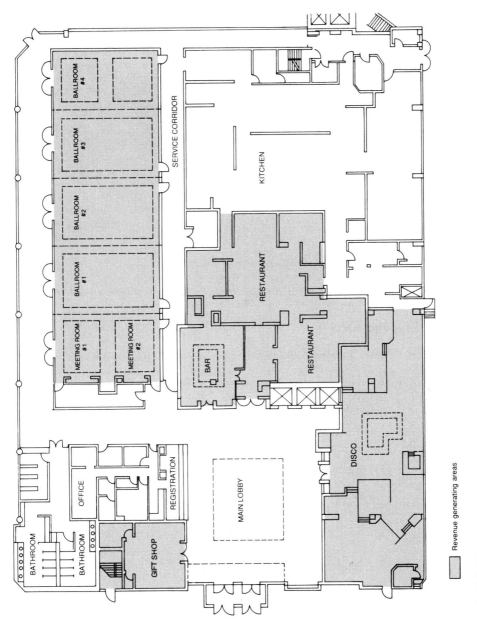

Exhibit 9-2

☐ Revenue generating areas

Exhibit 9-3 *Summary of Market Analysis—June 1979*

Fairfax County and Tysons Corner Data

Fairfax County, a 406 square mile area, is located in Northern Virginia. It lies at the confluence of three major interstate highways and the region's primary circumferential artery, the Capital Beltway. As of January 1978, there were 578,300 persons residing in Fairfax County. This represents an increase of 11,300 persons or 2% over the estimated 1977 population of 567,000. The County's population is expected to increase by approximately 47,700 persons by January 1980. The average family income after taxes is more than $22,300, the highest in the United States.

In June 1978, there were 221,304 persons employed in Fairfax County. Major categories of employment include industrial (16%), Federal, State and Local Government (23%), Retail (19.2%), Finance and Real Estate (5.8%), Services (19.7%), and Other (15.5%).

Tysons Corner is the center of the most active transportation corridor in Fairfax County. According to County figures, the daily traffic count through this area is 48,570 cars on Route 7, 46,400 cars on Route 123, and 74,830 cars on I-495. The new Tysons II regional mall is expected to attract an additional 30,000 cars.

Tysons Corner is presently the largest and fastest growing office concentration in suburban Metropolitan Washington. Almost half of the 7.5 million square feet of office space in the County is located here. Demand for office space has been strong and developers currently report an occupancy rate of 99% for the area's nearly 4 million square feet. Developers currently have plans for an additional 2.4 million square feet of new office space.

Two major office parks, Westgate and Westpark, represent almost 60% of the existing office space. The corporate group and transient business generated by the corporate base in these two parks will be the dominant midweek market at the proposed hotel.

Competitive Information

The Tysons Corner area is presently served only by a Holiday Inn on Route 123 and a Ramada Inn on Route 7. The Ramada Inn is newer and is in better condition than the Holiday Inn. Both hotels will be competitive with the Marriott; however, neither facility can be considered first class. A proposed 300 room Best Western Hotel at Route 7 and Westpark drive should open in 1979. Its level of quality will be close to that of the Ramada.

FACILITY	ROOMS	AVERAGE RATE	OCCUPANCY	TRANSIENT	GROUP
Holiday Inn	240	$33.00	80%	75%	25%
Ramada Inn	209	35.00	80%	85%	15%
Best Western	301	NA	NA	NA	NA

Exhibit 9-3   (*continued*)

Tyson's Corner Area Map: LOCATION ANALYSIS

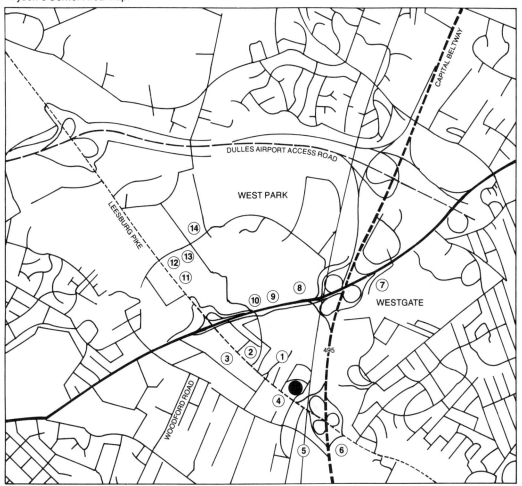

- ● Subject Site
- ① Tysons Corner Mall
- ② Dominion National Bank
- ③ Rozansky & Kay Site
- ④ Telcom Building
- ⑤ Boeing
- ⑥ Ramada Inn

- ⑦ T-Cas Building
- ⑧ Proposed Tysons II
- ⑨ Holiday Inn
- ⑩ 1st American Bank
- ⑪ Prudential Building
- ⑫ Best Western

- ⑬ Honeywell
- ⑭ The Rotunda
- ------- Route 7
- ▬ ▬ ▬ I-495
- ———— Route 123
- ▬ ▬ ▬ Dulles Airport
  Access Road

Exhibit 9-4   Stabilized Pro Forma Operating Statement—June 1979 ($000s)

	KEY BRIDGE MARRIOTT				TYSONS CORNER MARRIOT	
	1977		1978		1980	
Sales						
Rooms	$4,671	46.8%	$ 5,311	48.8%	$ 6,658	51.2%
Food and beverage	4,027	40.3	4,158	37.2	4,000	30.8
Banquet	694	6.9	852	7.8	1,600	12.3
Other	599	7.0	558	6.2	748	5.7
Total Sales	9,991	100.0	10,879	100.0	13,006	100.0
Department Profit						
Rooms	3,718	37.2	4,331	39.8	5,193	39.9
Food and Beverage	1,032	10.3	1,037	9.5	984	7.6
Banquet	312	3.1	384	3.5	928	7.1
Other	64	0.1	65	0.1	250	1.9
Total dept. profit	5,126	51.3	5,817	53.5	7,355	56.6
Expenses						
On-site management	694	6.9	483	4.4	715	5.5
Heat, light and power	324	3.2	317	2.9	468	3.6
Repairs and main.	292	2.9	320	2.9	507	3.9
Corporate overhead	300	3.0	310	2.8	390	3.0
Advertising and sales	313	3.1	336	3.1	429	3.3
Capital reserve	300	3.0	327	3.0	390	3.0
Taxes	234	2.3	275	2.5	325	2.5
Other	323	3.2	379	3.5	390	3.0
Total expenses	2,845	28.5	2,812	25.8	3,614	27.8
Profit for Dist.	**2,281**	**22.8**	**3,005**	**27.6**	**3,741**	**28.8**
MARRIOTT FEE	**456**	**4.6**	**601**	**5.5**	**748**	**5.8**
NOI	**1,825**	**18.3**	**2,404**	**22.1**	**2,993**	**23.0**
Number of rooms	372		372		400	
Average occupancy	85%		85%		80%	
Average room rate	$40.60		$46.75		$57.00	

Proposed Development Budget—June 1979

Land		$ 1,400,000
Real Estate Taxes and Insurance		35,000
Architect and Engineering		820,000
Civil Engineering	37,000	
Architectural	430,000	
Marriott Design and Review Fees	257,000	
Miscellaneous Consultants	6,000	
Construction Inspection	90,000	
General Overhead		690,000
Office and On-Site Personnel	110,000	
Preliminary and Feasibility	11,000	
Marriott Purchasing Fee	150,000	
Developer Fee	420,000	

Exhibit 9-4 *(continued)*

Legal Fees		100,000
Zoning	30,000	
Syndication	30,000	
Loan Closing	30,000	
Reimbursables	10,000	
Hotel Pre-opening		800,000
Wages–Sales, Marketing, and Management	95,000	
Hourly Wages and Benefits	160,000	
Moving	150,000	
Media	150,000	
Sales Non-Wages	70,000	
Miscellaneous	150,000	
Opening Party and Other PR	25,000	
General Contract		14,000,000
Hotel Furniture and Fixtures		3,000,000
Other		693,000
Caissons	100,000	
Sound and Audio-Visual Equipment	45,000	
Telephone System	270,000	
Wall Vinyl	150,000	
Miscellaneous	128,000	
Contingencies		492,000
Interest Expense		2,720,000
Operating Deficit Allowance		250,000
Total Development Budget		25,000,000

Exhibit 9-5 *Summary of Operating Results 1981-1988 ($000s)*

	1981	1982	1983	1984	1985	1986	1987	1988
Sales								
Rooms	$5,437	$6,688	$7,740	$9,052	$9,455	$9,747	$9,453	$9,754
Food and beverage	2,052	2,559	2,925	2,860	2,806	2,778	2,554	2,148
Banquet	1,254	1,543	1,912	2,030	1,850	1,963	2,112	2,531
Other	506	629	673	770	732	769	786	739
Total	9,249	11,419	13,250	14,712	14,843	15,257	14,905	15,172
Department Profit								
Rooms	4,631	5,708	6,651	7,813	7,989	8,261	8,021	8,165
Food and beverage	696	892	1,051	958	848	718	587	340
Banquet	594	721	851	971	863	927	865	809
Other	80	106	95	181	198	186	181	209
Total	6,001	7,427	8,648	9,923	9,898	10,092	9,654	9,523
Expenses								
On-site management	890	934	985	1,111	1,221	1,255	1,317	1,383
Heat, light, and power	420	432	535	523	509	439	434	515
Repairs and maintenance	360	383	445	458	501	542	608	665
General and administrative	335	334	388	430	435	450	475	482
Advertising and sales	517	453	495	611	757	751	768	794
Capital renovation allowance	90	167	291	430	435	490	508	515
Taxes	239	317	313	346	314	470	482	506
Other	118	129	142	150	152	206	277	317
Total expenses	2,969	3,149	3,594	4,059	4,324	4,063	4,869	5,177
Cash Flow from Operations	**3,032**	**4,278**	**5,054**	**5,864**	**5,574**	**5,489**	**4,785**	**4,346**
First mortgage @ 10.5% interest	2,430	2,430	2,430	2,430	2,430	2,430	2,430	2,420
Marriott fee (3% of gross + 20% CFO)	884	1,198	1,408	1,614	1,560	1,556	1,404	1,325
Second mortgage	0	0	0	0	0	1,200	1,200	1,200
Third mortgage	0	0	0	0	0	0	12	55
Capital expenditures in excess of allowance	0	0	0	0	1,584	0	0	0
Free Cash Flow	**(282)**	**650**	**1,216**	**1,820**	**0**	**303**	**(261)**	**(663)**
Depreciation	(1,447)	(1,888)	(1,917)	(1,971)	(2,027)	(1,659)	(1,320)	(1,486)
Add back: Amortization	300	362	400	442	488	549	597	659
Capital expenses	213	0	107	210	1,423	357	930	197
Taxable income	(1,216)	(876)	(194)	501	(116)	(450)	(54)	(1,292)
Occupancy	**75.8**	**79.6**	**80.3**	**80.1**	**75.9**	**77.5**	**74.3**	**74.7**
Average daily rate	**$50.13**	**$58.67**	**$67.34**	**$79.00**	**$85.42**	**$87.87**	**$88.93**	**$91.48**

Exhibit 9-6 Property Positioning and Planning, February 9, 1989

I. TCM Property Definition

We are a suburban corporate transient hotel in a highly competitive market. We are a well established, full service facility. In addition, we are accessible to Dulles and National Airports, Washington, D.C., Tysons Corner Mall and many local defense, commercial, and high tech companies in the Tysons Corner area.

II. Marketplace Considerations

A. Market Segments

1. Mid-Week Transient—This segment makes up 78% of our Sunday-Thursday business. The largest segment within this segment is corporate. We continue to experience a decline in corporate to special corporate and mid-week super saver. This segment is the most profitable at a rate of $104.24.

2. Mid-Week Group—This segment makes up 18% of our Sunday-Thursday business. The average rate is around $84.52. Most of this business is made up of short term, corporate business of (30) rooms or less, which we have two executive meeting managers covering. We have contracted one large producer (ICS) which produces 5,000 Sunday-Thursday room nights. This is the second most profitable segment.

3. Weekend Transient—Weekend transient (Friday and Saturday) makes up 67% of the weekend business. We continue to book between 80-100 for breakfast (TFB) per Friday and Saturday. This average rate is around $69.00. Our proximity to the Tysons Corner Mall is a big advantage. This is the third most profitable segment.

4. Weekend Group—This segment makes up 29% of our weekend business. Most of this business is in conjunction with an in house catering event, i.e., weddings, bar/bat mitzvah, reunions, etc. Also we host (4) large soccer tournaments per year in addition to many bus tours in April, May, and June. The average rate is around $61.74.

5. Contract—We presently enjoy the pleasure of Saudi Arabian Airways (15) rooms on Thursdays and Sundays with a rate of $64.00. We are presently negotiating an agreement with British Airways and have concluded a deal with Mobil Oil for (6) rooms at $75.00 each for approximately (4) months.

B. Competition

1. Hilton—The Hilton has (456) rooms and is considered a suburban, luxury hotel with over 30,000 square feet of convention meeting space. They are relatively new in the market place (approx. one year) and they compete in all segments, in addition to large local catering events. We feel that their accessibility is a disadvantage.

2. Marriott Fairview—The Marriott Fairview is a (400) room suburban, luxury hotel located within a major office park complex. Although they will not be completed until late 1989, we feel that because they are a Marriott and only 5.1 miles from Tysons Corner, they will be a major competitor. Their business will primarily be corporate, although they feature over 13,000 square feet of meeting space for conventions. They are accessible to Mobil Oil's headquarters in addition to Dulles and National Airports.

3. Sheraton—They are a (455) room suburban, full service, luxury hotel with over 27,000 square feet of meeting space. They compete in all segments especially corporate. Most of the growth is heading west and we feel in the coming years that their location will improve.

4. Ramada—The Ramada is a (404) room full service hotel with over 10,000 square feet of meeting space. They appeal to the government sector on weekdays and tour groups and travel on weekends. They have had a recent upgrade. However, the service continues to suffer.

5. Embassy Suites—The Embassy Suites is a (232) all suite limited service hotel with very limited meeting space. It is accessible to many of the local businesses and restaurants. In addition to a (2) room suite, you receive a buffet breakfast for up to five along with two hours of complimentary cocktails. They compete in the business transient segment and weekend pleasure segment.

6. Hyatt Dulles—Opens May 1989—We may feel the impact with AT&T (headquarters located next to Dulles), catering, and social business. They have approximately 8,000 square feet of meeting space and (317) suites.

Exhibit 9-6 (*continued*)

C. **Relative Position within Customer Segments**—Although it is difficult to determine who the leader is in market share within each segment, the following was determined from our data:
1. Weekday Transient—Our honored guest award (HGA) program continues to make TCM the market share leader in this segment. This program is represented by 53% of our weekday transient business. We continue to see our competitors improve in this segment in that we are fighting for the same customer. The Embassy Suites is probably second in this segment because of their superb price/value. This segment continues to decline by over 8.2% compared to 1987. The shift continues to fall into special corporate which has increased by over 10% compared to 1987. The remainder is shifting into the government segment.
2. Weekday Group—Because of meeting space capacity, the Hilton and Sheraton are the leaders within this market. The Embassy Suites presents no threat because they have no meeting space. However, we believe that because of Marriott's high standards and executive meeting manager (EMM) that we are the first hotel called.
3. Weekend Transient—The Embassy Suites is the market share leader in this segment because of their excellent price value. Our two for breakfast program continues to make us the second choice. In addition, our location is the best in the Tysons Corner area. The Hilton and Sheraton are third and fourth choice and the fifth is the Ramada.
4. Weekend Group—We believe that TCM is the leader in this segment. We do host kids groups which the Hilton and Sheraton do not. In addition, our social segment is very strong because of our reputation and name recognition. However, the Sheraton and Hilton feature a distinct advantage with large conventions because of meeting space size and capacity.
5. Contract—We presently have Saudi Arabian Airlines as contract rooms. They chose us because of reputation, location, competitive pricing, and excellent past experience. The Embassy Suites does not pursue this business and because of the location and size of the Hilton and Sheraton, it is difficult for them to book contract business. We continue to be the leader in this segment.

D. **Competitive Information**

HOTEL	YEAR BUILT	INITIAL COST	# ROOMS	1988 OCCUPANCY	WEEKDAY RATE	WEEKEND RATE
Tysons Marriott	1981	$25MM	392	74.7	$126	$82
Embassy Suites	1985	30MM	232	79.6	124	87
Hilton	1987	67MM	456	67.1	130	81
Sheraton	1986	70MM	455	65.7	132	81
Holiday Inn[1]	1974	13MM	314	67.6	92	81
Ramada Inn[2]	1975	10MM	404	62.1	85	81
Residence Inn	1988	12MM	96	NA	113	59

[1]The Holiday Inn was renovated and expanded to 314 rooms in 1986 at a total cost of $6 million.
[2]The Ramada Inn was renovated and expanded to 404 rooms in 1987 at a total cost of $20 million.

III. **Future Projections**
A. **Aggregate Share and Demand**—In 1989 we see that the demand for the TCM and the marketplace is relatively flat. In 1989/90 with the opening of the Marriott Fairview, we expect demand to decrease. Office buildings continue to be built yet occupancies for them are down. 1988 office building occupancies compared to 1987 are down by 3%. Office building occupancies are projected to be flat for 1990.
B. **Occupancies**—In 1988 year to date (YTD) occupancy is better than last year and close to budget '88. However, overall average rate is down. We expect occupancies to remain flat. 1988 YTD 74.7%—ACT budget 74.5%—LYTD 74.3%.
C. **Market Shares**—We see that TCM is maintaining itself as the leader in the market. However, with continued hotel openings our overall market share will decrease, particularly in the weekday segments.

Exhibit 9-6 *(continued)*

D. **Targets**—We must continue to focus in on our major advantages over the competition, i.e., service, location, and HGA. The continued use of yield management will help us maximize our revenue in relation to price and mix. Finally, we must target in on the shortage of labor and enhance our overall service.

E. **New Competition**

April 1989	Hyatt Dulles	350 rooms
June 1989	Hyatt Fair Lakes	350 rooms
September 1989	Marriott Fairview	420 rooms
November 1989	Marriott All Suite	250 rooms
November 1990	Ritz Carlton Tysons	380 rooms
June 1991	Hyatt Reston	550 rooms

The above projected hotel openings are going to impact the supply of rooms in the marketplace in that they are all within a 5-8 mile radius of the Tysons Corner Marriott.

10

GRAYBAR SYNDICATIONS

In March, 1958, the Graybar Building, a one million square foot older office structure in midtown Manhattan, is facing competition from a new generation of buildings. Its proposed acquisition by a syndicate is predicated on a tiered structure of financing and returns to a complex array of participants. The challenge for the student is to wade through the legal documentation of the offering, decipher the priority and breakdown of the cash flow from the property, and decide who gets what return and when. The case deals with many of the issues relating to financial deal structuring.

Discussion Questions:

1. What are the key factors to consider when analyzing the rental income from this property? How would you evaluate operations?
2. What is the value of the property both in 1958 and 1977 to the various participants?
3. What are the potential advantages and disadvantages of investing in a real estate syndication? What has determined the form of ownership chosen for the Graybar Building?

In March 1958, Mr. Harold Morse was trying to decide whether to recommend an investment in a real estate syndication, "Graybar Building Associates." (See **Exhibit 10-1**.) At the time the Graybar Building was built in 1927, it was one of the largest office structures ever completed. In 1953, the controlling ownership of Graybar was sold in a package that included the acquisition of the 77-story Chrysler Building, the second tallest building in the world, and its 32-story annex, the Chrysler Building East. This $52 million deal, the largest real estate transaction in the city's history, followed by two years the landmark purchase of the Empire State Building, the world's tallest skyscraper, for $51 million.

Mr. Morse was a Long Island attorney whose many clients looked to him for financial advice. Most of these clients lived comfortably and were in tax brackets of about 50%. One of these clients, Dr. Planter, had sent Mr. Morse the Graybar prospectus. He had received it from friends who were planning to invest. Dr. Planter asked Mr. Morse to read it and advise him as to what he should do. The total capital being raised was $4.2 million, which was subject to an $18 million leasehold position simultaneously being acquired by Metropolitan Life and to a ground lease held by New York Central.

Mr. Morse reviewed the advantages of investing in real estate. He knew that real estate prices were rising sharply. He had read of the "big killings" many had made. The field was supposed to be an excellent hedge against inflation while providing a high annual cash return substantially above the 3.2% return currently obtained from dividends of stocks listed on the S&P 500 index. Depreciation allowances also permitted much of the income to be tax sheltered. Further equity was being built up through mortgage amortization. The New York area, where the property being syndicated was located, was supposed to be especially desirable. Since most of his clients' funds were invested in their own businesses, and in the stock market, real estate appeared to be a sound means of diversification.

Mr. Morse had heard a number of favorable reports recommending syndications as the correct vehicle for owning and investing in real estate. Before large-scale real estate syndication developed, investment in high-priced real estate was confined almost exclusively to the large real estate firms and to wealthy individuals. During the 1950s, however, there was a rapidly growing tendency for some properties to be owned by small investors, who pooled their cash in real estate syndicates. The idea of high guaranteed returns paid out in monthly checks was

Adjunct Professor William J. Poorvu prepared this case as the basis for class discussion rather than to illustrate either effective or ineffective handling of an administrative situation.

appealing. An investor not only could diversify holdings into another field, but diversify within the field by buying units in several properties of various types. Small investors would also benefit from experienced property management.

Syndications appeared to cure the prime drawback to real estate for the small investor, the lack of liquidity. The syndicators were sometimes providing markets for the resale of the units they had sold, often at higher than original prices. They appeared to be attempting to institutionalize their operations in the same manner as stock brokerage firms had. People said that the field was taking on a more professional character. He knew that during the depression many real estate syndications failed, but at this time in 1957 Mr. Morse felt that the economy was basically sound.

The decision then revolved around the soundness of this particular offering. Mr. Morse tried to list the questions he would want answered after he had completed his analysis. He first wanted to examine both the projected cash and after-tax returns offered to the investors, and the opportunities for higher returns through mortgage refinancing, appreciation in value, increase in rentals and income. How secure were these returns? How was leverage used in each case, and what bearing did it have upon the risks involved? How did the uses to which the properties were being put affect the risk factor?

He was interested in the role of the promoters. What risks were they taking, and what were they getting in return? Was there an equitable relationship between the two? Based upon the merchandising techniques used by the promoters in their prospectus, what type of investors should be attracted? Do the promoters appear reputable from their background, and the way they are presenting the investments? What protection is there from mismanagement by the promoters? Is there any government protection, and if not, should there be?

The Graybar offering was set up as a joint venture, with each of two partners acting as agent for one half of the investors (a one half interest). This created potential liability for each investor, as the participants would share proportionately in all profits and losses realized by the senior venturer from whom they purchased their partnerships. Any one participant could be liable to a person outside the venture for the full amount of any obligation to which the senior venturer might be subject by reason of his ownership in the property.

As a protection, tenant leases and debt financing agreements would have specific clauses exculpating the joint venturers from personal liability. General liability insurance would cover many property-related risks. Still, he wondered if there were any other areas uncovered that he should worry about. As an alternative he inquired about the limited partnership format, but was told that it created a danger of double taxation since in 1958 the IRS had certain provisions under which some partnerships were liable to be taxed as corporations.

Lastly, he was concerned about the adequacy and reliability of the information presented. What other information would he want? Can any real estate offering be evaluated solely from the figures?

Exhibit 10-1 *Prospectus*

PROSPECTUS

Graybar Building
420 Lexington Avenue
New York City

$4,180,000 of Participations in Partnership Interests in
GRAYBAR BUILDING ASSOCIATES

PRICE PER PARTICIPATION: $10,000 MINIMUM

THESE SECURITIES HAVE NOT BEEN APPROVED OR DISAPPROVED BY THE SECUR-
ITIES AND EXCHANGE COMMISSION NOR HAS THE COMMISSION PASSED UPON THE
ACCURACY OR ADEQUACY OF THIS PROSPECTUS. ANY REPRESENTATION TO THE
CONTRARY IS A CRIMINAL OFFENSE.

	Price to Public	Underwriting Commissions*	Proceeds to Issuer
Total	$4,180,000	None	$4,180,000
Per unit	10,000	None	10,000

*As to the remuneration and interest of the members of Associates in the
transactions described herein, see page 12.

The date of this Prospectus is March 10, 1958

Exhibit 10-1 (*continued*)

No person has been authorized to give any information or to make any representations other than those contained in this Prospectus, and, if given or made, such information and representations must not be relied upon as having been authorized by Graybar Building Associates or by any of the members thereof.

CONTENTS

		Page
I.	General Nature of the Offering	3
II.	Terms of the Offering	3
III.	The Graybar Building	4
	1. Description	4
	2. Rental Statistics as of January 1, 1958	4
	3. Summary of Operations	5
IV.	Proposed Acquisition of the Leasehold by Associates	5
V.	Description of the Leasehold	6
	1. General	6
	2. Important Provisions	6
VI.	Operation of the Graybar Building Under the Sublease	7
	1. Provisions of the Sublease	7
	2. The Sublessees	8
	3. Physical Inspections	8
VII.	Formation of Associates	8
VIII.	Status of Purchasers of Participations	9
	1. Participating Agreements	9
	2. Tax Status of Associates and Joint Ventures	10
	3. Tax Treatment of Cash Distributions to Participants	10
IX.	Information as to Partners in Associates	11
	1. Biographical	11
	2. Remuneration and Interest in Transactions described herein	12
X.	Legal Opinions	12
XI.	Financial Statements	13

A Registration Statement has been filed with the Securities and Exchange Commission, Washington, D. C., by Graybar Building Associates and the individual partners therein, as Co-Registrants, for the Participations offered hereunder.

This Prospectus does not contain all of the information set forth in the Registration Statement, certain items of which are omitted or included in condensed form as permitted by the Rules and Regulations of the Commission. Statements contained herein as to the contents of any contract or other document are not necessarily complete, and in each instance reference is hereby made to the copy of such contract or other document filed as an Exhibit to the Registration Statement, each such statement being qualified in all respects by such reference.

Copies of the Registration Statement may be obtained from the Commission on payment of the prescribed charges.

Exhibit 10-1 (*continued*)

I.

GENERAL NATURE OF THE OFFERING

1. GRAYBAR BUILDING ASSOCIATES ("Associates") is a partnership consisting of Lawrence A. Wien and William F. Purcell. It has contracted to purchase a net lease of the Graybar Building, 420 Lexington Avenue, New York City, for $4,000,000 in cash.

The net lease to be purchased by Associates is referred to as the "Leasehold" in this Prospectus.

2. The Metropolitan Life Insurance Company is the Lessor under the Leasehold, and Associates will be its Lessee. The Metropolitan recently paid $18,000,000 for its position as Lessor.

3. The term of the Leasehold extends to May 30, 1976, but Associates has renewal options to the year 2030. Renewal of the Leasehold is automatic upon the giving of appropriate notice by Associates and does not require the payment of any additional consideration. The Leasehold requires the payment of certain rents, which are described at page 6.

4. Associates will not operate the property. It will purchase the Leasehold subject to an existing Sublease under which Webb & Knapp, Inc., and its wholly-owned subsidiary, Graysler Corporation, operate the premises.

5. The Sublease has a term and renewal options similar to the Leasehold. It provides for the payment by the Sublessees to Associates of an annual net rent in an amount sufficient to enable Associates

 (a) to pay all rents called for in the Leasehold;

 (b) to defray administrative costs; and

 (c) to make a monthly cash distribution to each participant equal to $1200 per year on each $10,000 Participation during the initial term of the Sublease.

 In the event of renewal of the Sublease at the end of the initial term in 1976, the rent payable by the Sublessees is rearranged so that thereafter the cash distribution to participants will be increased to $1900 per year.

An analysis of such cash distribution and a discussion of the assumptions on which it is calculated appear at pages 10 and 11.

6. The Sublessees pay all expenses connected with the operation of the Graybar Building. The rent payable to Associates will be a net rental, subject only to the expenses listed above. The Sublessees, however, may assign the Sublease under certain conditions, as set forth on page 8, and may then be relieved of further liability. The investment offered hereby should therefore be judged primarily on the basis of the income-producing capacity of the property itself. A summary of operations for the property appears at pages 9 and 10.

7. Each of the two partners in Associates will himself contribute $10,000 to the partnership capital, and is offering Participations of $2,090,000 in his partnership interest through this Prospectus. The total partnership capital will thus be $4,200,000, which will be used to purchase the Leasehold ($4,000,000), to defray costs incident to the acquisition ($175,000), and to pay the expenses of this offering ($25,000). Purchasers of Participations will share proportionately in the ownership of the partnership interests in Associates, under Participating Agreements with the partners (see page 9).

II.

TERMS OF THE OFFERING

1. The offering is being made by the partners in Associates.

2. Offers to purchase Participations will be accepted only from individuals of full age.

Exhibit 10-1 (*continued*)

3. Each offer to purchase shall be for a minimum of $10,000 or a multiple thereof.

4. A deposit of up to 25 per cent of the price may be required for any Participation. All deposits will be held in Special Account by counsel for Associates, Wien, Lane, Klein & Purcell, 60 East 42d Street, New York, New York.

5. The title closing is scheduled for April 30, 1958, with rights of adjournment to May 31 or June 30, 1958. If offers totaling $4,180,000 have not been accepted by June 30, 1958, all deposits will be repaid without interest. This amount, together with the $20,000 contribution of the two partners, is the sum required to make the payment under the purchase contract and defray the costs and expenses noted above.

6. The balance of each Participation will be payable at the office of Wien, Lane, Klein & Purcell, upon demand, at any time after the required amount of offers has been accepted.

III.

THE GRAYBAR BUILDING

1. Description. The Graybar Building is one of the largest and best known office buildings in New York City. It occupies the entire city block on the westerly side of Lexington Avenue between 43rd and 44th Streets, in the heart of New York's business center.

The building forms the eastern entrance to the Grand Central Station and provides a broad concourse leading directly to the Main Hall (upper level) of the terminal. It also affords connections to various subway lines and other transit facilities.

Completed in 1927, the Graybar Building is of fireproof, concrete and steel construction and contains 30 stories and penthouse, with ground floor stores and interior shops. It covers a ground area of some 68,400 square feet, has a volume of approximately 16 million cubic feet and a gross floor area of about 1,250,000 square feet. The net rentable area is approximately 971,163 square feet, including store space.

The building is serviced by 32 Otis, signal control, micro-leveling passenger elevators and 2 Otis freight elevators. About 74 per cent of the tenant areas in the building are air-conditioned through 2060 tons of water-cooled and air-cooled units, of which 315¼ tons are landlord owned. All units utilize permanent electric and water facilities installed by the landlord. Construction of a water cooling system sufficient for the entire building is planned. All requisite piping from the roof down to the second floor has been installed, and one 750 ton cell of the cooling tower has been erected on the roof.

The 406 tenants of the building are of widely diversified types, and include the Great Atlantic and Pacific Tea Company (executive offices), Conde Nast Publications, Inc., the J. Walter Thompson Advertising agency, the Chase Manhattan Bank, the Dictaphone Corporation, American Gas Company and Sun Oil Company.

2. Rental Statistics as of January 1, 1958. Associates is advised that on this date, the building was 99.86 per cent occupied. For the past ten years occupancy percentages were as follows:

1957 — 99.8%; 1956 — 99.7%; 1955 — 99.6%; 1954 — 99.9%;
1953 — 99.4%; 1952 — 99.8%; 1951 — 99.4%; 1950 — 98.9%;
1949 — 98.9%; 1948 — 98.9%.

On January 1, 1958, the average rate per square foot for the building was $4.61. The total annual rent roll was $4,474,160, exclusive of percentage rentals and tax escalator increases. In addition, leases already executed provide for annual increases amounting to $18,254 beginning in 1958, $5,910 in 1959, and $150,407 in 1960, or a total of $174,571.

Exhibit 10-1 *(continued)*

On January 1, 1958, the following lease expiration schedule applied:

Year	Square Ft. Area	% of Gross Rental Value
1958	102,446	11.06
1959	93,907	11.24
1960	250,447	22.13
1961	153,680	17.88
1962	67,386	6.79
1963	3,539	.41
1964	8,382	1.17
1965	100,535	11.35
1966	44,174	4.06
1967	29,019	3.66
1970	1,620	.21
1976	51,082	5.01
Statutory	62,594	4.96
Monthly	1,016	.07
TOTAL	969,827	100%
VACANT	1,336	
	971,163	

The Graybar Building competes with office structures in the Grand Central area and other sections of New York City. In the past five years, new construction has accounted for some 5,800,500 square feet of rentable space in the Grand Central area, which comprises the district between 38th and 50th Street, and Sixth and Second Avenues. Associates is advised that virtually all of this new space is rented, and for the most part is occupied by large tenants under long term leases. At present, other new buildings under construction are expected to result in approximately 3,500,000 square feet of additional space in this area. The greater portion of this space also is reported to be rented at this time.

3. Summary of Operations. A summary, showing the results of operations of the Graybar Building for the five year period ended December 31, 1957, is set forth at Page 15 of this Prospectus.

The total rent payable by the Sublessees to Associates under the Sublease will be $2,540,000 per year during the initial term. As shown in the summary of operations, the net operating revenue from the building in the year 1957 was sufficient to cover this rent, although the net operating revenues for the years prior to 1957 were not. However, neither the 1957 net operating revenues nor those for the previous years are indicative of the present net operating revenue.

For example, the rent roll as of January 1, 1958 was $70,726 more than the total rent collections shown for the year 1957, which in turn were substantially higher than those shown in the summary for prior years. In addition, based upon previous experience, it is expected that approximately $20,000 will be received during the current year for percentage rents and under tax escalator clauses. Also, as indicated above, future rent increases contained in leases already executed, will add approximately $174,571 annually to the rent roll over the next three years.

The present net operating revenues from the building are more than sufficient to cover the rent provided for in the Sublease. Of course, no representation can be made that such net operating revenues necessarily will continue without change in the future since that will depend upon competition and the general state of the economy.

IV.
PROPOSED ACQUISITION OF THE LEASEHOLD BY ASSOCIATES

(1) On December 30, 1957, Lawrence A. Wien purchased the Leasehold on the Graybar Building, subject to the Sublease. The purchase was made from Webb & Knapp, Inc., and Graysler Corporation.

Exhibit 10-1 (*continued*)

(2) The purchase price was $4,000,000, of which Mr. Wien paid $400,000 in cash and the balance by a 6 per cent Mortgage on the Leasehold, maturing July 1, 1958 and prepayable at any time.

(3) On January 22, 1958, Mr. Wien contracted to sell the Leasehold to Associates for $4,000,000 in cash. In addition to the purchase price, Associates will incur expenses of $200,000 in connection with the transactions described in this Prospectus. Thus, its total cost for the Leasehold will be $4,200,000.

(4) The $3,600,000 Leasehold Mortgage will be prepaid and discharged by Mr. Wien on the closing date of the sale to Associates.

(5) The sale is scheduled to close on April 30, 1958, but Associates has the right to adjourn the closing to May 31, 1958, or June 30, 1958.

(6) Until such closing, Mr. Wien will receive on his own behalf the rents paid under the Sublease and will discharge the obligations of the Leasehold and the Leasehold Mortgage. The net return on Mr. Wien's $400,000 investment during the period of his ownership will be $4,167 a month.

V.

DESCRIPTION OF THE LEASEHOLD

1. General. (a) The land under the Graybar Building is owned by the New York Central Railroad. Acting through a subsidiary real estate corporation, the railroad created a Ground Lease on the property to May 31, 1976, with renewal options to the year 2030. The original tenant under the Ground Lease built the Graybar Building in 1927.

(b) On December 30, 1957, the then tenant under the Ground Lease created the Leasehold as a net lease of the entire premises for the same term and renewal periods as it had under the Ground Lease, less one day.

(c) Immediately thereafter, Metropolitan Life Insurance Company purchased the position of tenant under the Ground Lease for $18,000,000, and Lawrence A. Wien purchased the position of Lessee of the Leasehold for $4,000,000.

(d) The Leasehold was purchased by Mr. Wien subject to a Sublease, also created on December. 30, 1957, under which Webb & Knapp and its wholly-owned subsidiary, Graysler Corporation now operate the Graybar Building as Mr. Wien's Sublessees.

(e) When Associates acquires Mr. Wien's position it will become entitled to receive the rent payable by the Sublessees; the Metropolitan Life Insurance Company will receive the rent called for in the Leasehold; and the New York Central Railroad subsidiary will receive the annual Ground Rent.

2. Important Provisions. The important provisions of the Leasehold are:

(a) The initial term runs to May 30, 1976. By giving written notice, Associates may renew the Leasehold for three additional terms extending to the year 2030.

(b) Upon such notice, renewal of the Leasehold term is automatic. Renewal of the Leasehold also results in a like renewal of the Ground Lease.

(c) The Leasehold Rent payable by Associates to Metropolitan Life Insurance Company is $1,620,000 during the initial term. During all renewal periods the Leasehold Rent is $540,000 annually, or a reduction of $1,080,000.

(d) Associates, as Lessee, also will be required to pay the Ground Rent to the New York Central Railroad subsidiary. The Ground Rent is $390,000 per year during the initial term of the Leasehold and

Exhibit 10-1   (continued)

for each renewal year until 1988. During renewal years from 1988 to 2009, the Ground Rent will be a sum agreed upon by the parties to the Ground Lease or, failing agreement, a sum equal to 5 per cent of the value of the land (considered vacant and unimproved), but not less than $390,000. For the remaining period from 2009 to 2030, the Ground Rent shall be determined by the same formula, but shall not be less than that paid in the prior period.

(e)   Upon renewal of the Leasehold at the end of the initial term, the total rent payable by Associates (i.e., Leasehold Rent and Ground Rent) will be $930,000 per year.

(f)   Associates, as Lessee, will be obligated to pay all operating and maintenance expenses, including real estate taxes, make all necessary repairs, maintain insurance coverage of various types and rebuild or replace the building in the event of fire or other casualty.

(g)   The Lessee also is required to perform all obligations contained in the Ground Lease. Such obligations are the same in all material respects as those contained in the Leasehold itself. The Sublease described below, under which the premises are being operated, imposes upon the Sublessees obligations which are equivalent in all respects to those of Associates under the Leasehold and Ground Lease. The rent payable by the Sublessees includes the funds necessary to meet the Leasehold and Ground Lease rents. The Sublessees also pay all of the operating and maintenance expenses.

(h)   Associates may assign the Leasehold at any time, without consent of its Lessor, Metropolitan Life Insurance Company, provided the assignment is to a corporation the stock of which is owned equally by its two partners. Consent of the Metropolitan is required for any other type of assignment. In all cases, upon assumption by the assignee of the Leasehold, Associates will be relieved of any further obligation thereunder.

VI.

OPERATION OF THE GRAYBAR BUILDING UNDER THE SUBLEASE

1.   Provisions of the Sublease.

(a)   The Sublease is for the same initial term as the Leasehold, less one day and, therefore, extends to May 29, 1976. It has co-extensive renewal privileges.

(b)   The total annual rent payable to Associates by the Sublessees is $2,540,000 per year to December 31, 1972; $2,530,000 thereafter per year to May 29, 1976; and $1,774,000 per year in the event of renewal at the end of the initial term. This annual rent consists of three parts:

    i.   a sum sufficient to pay the Leasehold Rent to the Metropolitan Life Insurance Company;

    ii.   a sum sufficient to pay the Ground Rent to the New York Central subsidiary; and

    iii.   a basic rent which Associates will use to defray administrative costs and make its cash distributions to participants. This portion of the annual rent payable by the Sublessees will be $530,000 per year to December 31, 1972, $520,000 per year to May 29, 1976, and $844,000 annually during any renewal periods.

(c)   As previously stated, the annual Leasehold Rent payable to the Metropolitan Life Insurance Company reduces by $1,080,000 at the end of the initial term on May 30, 1976. In the event of a renewal of the Sublease at that time, both Associates and the Sublessees will share in the benefit resulting from this reduction as follows:

Upon any such renewal, the Sublessees will pay an additional $324,000 annually to Associates as basic rent under the Sublease, thus increasing Associates' portion of the total rent from $520,000 to $844,000.

Exhibit 10-1 (*continued*)

The Sublessees will have the benefit of the remaining $756,000 reduction in the annual Leasehold Rent. Thus, their overall rent obligation, upon a renewal at the end of the initial term, will be reduced from $2,530,000 to $1,774,000.

(d) As additional rent, the Sublessees shall pay to Associates one-third of the amount by which the Sublessees' net income derived from the operation of the premises, after payment of operating and maintenance expenses, real estate taxes and all rents, but before amortization of the cost of the Sublease and before income taxes, exceeds $600,000 in any year up to May 31, 1976 and $1,356,000 in any year thereafter.

(e) The Sublessees are obligated to pay all operating and maintenance costs and real estate taxes, keep the property in good repair, maintain full insurance coverage, rebuild in case of fire or other casualty, and satisfy all other obligations of Associates under the Leasehold.

(f) Consent of the Metropolitan Life Insurance Company is required for any assignment of the Sublease, except where the assignment is to a corporation or corporations each stockholder of which owns the same proportionate amount of stock in the Sublessees. Upon compliance with these provisions and the assumption by the assignee of the obligations of the Sublease, the present Sublessees would be relieved of any further obligation thereunder.

2. The Sublessees. In addition to the Graybar Building, Webb & Knapp, Inc., and/or its subsidiary, Graysler Corporation, operate such large New York City office structures, having the following net rentable areas, as: The Equitable Building at 120 Broadway (40 stories—1,215,270 sq. ft.); the Chrysler Building (75 stories—827,724 sq. ft.); Chrysler Building East (32 stories—401,620 sq. ft.); and 1407 Broadway (42 stories—982,000 sq. ft.).

3. Physical Inspections. Helmsley-Spear, Inc., one of New York City's leading real estate management firms, will be retained by Associates to make periodic physical inspections of the building and its equipment, to render reports thereon, and to act as consultant to Associates with respect to any matters arising out of the ownership of the Leasehold. Helmsley-Spear, Inc., will receive $10,000 annually for these services for the period ending December 31, 1972, and $4,000 per annum during the remainder of the initial term and during any renewals of the Leasehold.

VII.

FORMATION OF ASSOCIATES

1. Associates was formed in New York, by a written agreement dated January 20, 1958, to purchase the Leasehold on the Graybar Building, subject to the Sublease.

2. Under the partnership agreement, the partners will share equally in all profits and losses of the partnership.

3. The partnership will continue until it shall have disposed of all of its assets. The partnership is not to be interrupted by any other cause, including the death of a partner or assignment of his interest. Provision is made for succession to the interest of a deceased partner by a designee.

4. The consent of both partners is required for any sale, or other transfer of the Leasehold, the modification or renewal of the Leasehold, the making or modification of any mortgage thereon, the making or revision of any lease of the property by the partnership, or the disposal of any partnership asset.

5. Wien, Lane, Klein & Purcell will supervise the operation of the partnership agreement, and will maintain the requisite books and records for the partnership.

Exhibit 10-1 (*continued*)

VIII.

STATUS OF PURCHASERS OF PARTICIPATIONS

1. Participating Agreements. Each of the two partners in Associates will enter into a Participating Agreement with investors contributing $2,090,000 toward the $4,200,000 total required to acquire the property. Each partner also will contribute $10,000 toward the partnership capital.

Each Participating Agreement will create a joint venture among the parties thereto, who will own the particular partner's one-half interest in Associates in proportion to their respective contributions to its total cost. The Agreements will contain the following provisions:

(a) The partner will act as "Agent" for the participants in his one-half partnership interest.

(b) The participants will share proportionately in all profits or losses realized by the Agent as a partner in Associates. Under New York law, one participant may be liable to a person outside the venture for the full amount of any obligation of the Agent as a partner in Associates or any liability of the partnership. However, in such event he would be entitled to demand and receive pro-rata contributions from his co-participants. As stated previously at page 7, Associates may assign the Leasehold and thereafter be relieved of any further liability thereunder.

(c) The Agent may not agree to sell, or transfer the partnership interest or the Leasehold, to make or modify any mortgage thereon, to modify or renew the Leasehold, to make or modify any sublease of the premises, or to dispose of any partnership asset, without the consent of all his participants. However, if participants owning 80 per cent of the Agent's interest consent to any such action, the Agent or his designee shall have the right to purchase the interest of any non-consenting participant at its original cost, less any capital repaid thereon.

(d) The Agent will incur no personal liability for any action taken by him, except for wilful misconduct, gross negligence or any liabilities under the Securities Act of 1933.

(e) Except as above limited, the Agent may bind his participants, and the participants will agree to indemnify him proportionately against any liability arising by reason of his acting as Agent.

(f) The Agent may resign upon accounting to his successor for all funds he has received. He may be removed by the written direction of participants owning at least three-fourths of the Agent's interest.

(g) If the Agent dies, is removed, resigns or is unable to act, he will be succeeded by one of five persons named as successors in each agreement. If no such designee qualifies, the owners of at least three-fourths of the interest shall select the new Agent.

(h) Each joint venture shall continue until it shall have disposed of the entire interest which it owns in Associates. It will not be interrupted by any other cause, including the death of a participant or any transfer of his Participation.

(i) A participant may transfer his Participation in the joint venture to any individual of full age. Any transfer must be of the full Participation owned, unless such Participation exceeds $10,000. In the latter case, the transfer must be in multiples of $5,000, with a minimum transfer of a $10,000 Participation. The transferee must accept the transfer in writing, and duplicate originals of the transfer instruments must be filed with the Agent, before the transfer shall be effective.

(j) Upon the death of a participant, any individual of full age, designated in the decedent's will or by his executor or administrator, may succeed to his Participation. If no such individual

Exhibit 10-1   (*continued*)

qualifies within eight months after date of death, the surviving parties to the joint venture may purchase proportionately the Participation of the decedent, at its original cost, less any capital repaid thereon.

(k) The Agent shall receive no compensation for acting in that capacity.

2. Tax Status of Associates and the Joint Ventures. The status for Federal income tax purposes of Associates and the joint ventures described in this Prospectus has been passed upon by Roswell Magill, Esq., of Cravath, Swaine & Moore, 15 Broad Street, New York City, and by the firm of Stevenson, Paul, Rifkind, Wharton & Garrison, 1614 Eye Street, N.W., Washington, D.C., tax counsel.

Both such counsel have furnished Associates with separate opinions that the members of Associates and of the joint ventures to be formed under the Participating Agreements will qualify as partners for Federal income tax purposes. Therefore, each individual member of Associates and each participant will be taxed on his distributive share of the net income, but the net incomes of Associates and the joint ventures will not be taxable as such.

Both opinions note that the Treasury Regulations contain provisions under which partnerships or joint ventures may be taxed on their net income in the same manner as corporations and the members thereof may be taxed as shareholders. Each opinion, however, concludes that Associates and the joint ventures involved herein do not fall within the said provisions, and therefore should not be taxable as corporations.

3. Tax Treatment of Cash Distributions to Participants.

The following table, which assumes that Associates and the joint ventures will be taxable as partnerships, estimates the aggregate cash income to Associates in each year during the initial term of the Leasehold on the Graybar Building. It also shows the portion of such income distributable to participants under the Participating Agreements.

The rent income shown is based upon the minimum annual net rent provided for in the Sublease to Webb & Knapp, Inc., and Graysler Corporation. The table and the accompanying text below assume that the Sublease will continue in accordance with its terms over all of the years discussed. There is no assurance that the foregoing assumptions necessarily will hold true, but if such rent is paid and Associates and the joint ventures are taxable as partnerships, the following information is applicable:

Rent Income		$2,540,000.00
Expenses:		
Rent Expense (consisting of $1,620,000 Leasehold Rent and $390,000 Ground Rent)	$2,010,000.00	
Legal, accounting and consultant's fees	26,000.00	
		$2,036,000.00
Net Receipts, Before Leasehold Amortization		$ 504,000.00
Leasehold Amortization, write-off over 18 years and one month, 5.53% of $4,200,000		$ 232,258.00
Net Receipts allocable to Participants for Federal income tax purposes		$ 271,742.00

CASH AVAILABLE FOR DISTRIBUTION

Total (Net Receipts, before Leasehold Amortization, as above)	$ 504,000.00
Per $10,000 Participation	1,200.00

Exhibit 10-1 (*continued*)

The cash available for distribution, shown immediately above, will represent both income, and to the extent of annual Leasehold amortization, a return of capital. That portion which represents a return of capital will not be reportable as income for Federal income tax purposes. On this basis, each $1200 cash distribution will consist of $647 which constitutes reportable income, and $553 representing a non-taxable return of capital. Although each such return of capital constitutes a partial reduction of the cost of the investment, it does not in any way change the proportionate interest of each participant in Associates.

Deducting the return of capital from the original cost, the rate of income on the remaining invested capital increases each year. The average invested capital over the initial term of the Sublease is $2,100,000, or $5,000 per minimum Participation. The rate of income on the average invested capital over the initial term is 12.94%. Of course, these calculations are based on the assumption that the Sublease will continue and that the rent provided for will be paid throughout the initial term of 18 years and one month.

At the end of the initial term on May 30, 1976, the cost of the Leasehold will have been fully amortized and, thereafter, the entire amount of cash distributed annually in the event of any renewal of the Leasehold will be reportable as income. It should be noted that renewal of the Leasehold by Associates is automatic upon the giving of appropriate notice and does not require the payment of additional consideration.

As heretofore stated, the rent requirements of both the Leasehold and Sublease will change in the event of their renewal at the end of the initial term. In such case, Associates' Rent Income will be $1,774,000 and its Rent Expense will be $930,000. Legal, accounting and consultants' fees will be $46,000 per year during any renewal terms. Thus, upon any such renewal, the cash available for annual distribution to each $10,000 participant will be increased to $1900, all of which will constitute income.

In the above discussion, amortization has been calculated in accordance with present tax law. On January 20, 1958, the House of Representatives passed a bill which would change the law and could require that the cost of a renewable lease be amortized over both the original and renewal terms. This bill has not yet been enacted into law, but is pending before a Senate Committee for its consideration. If enacted, the bill would in no way change the amount of the yearly cash distributions described above. The only effect of the bill could be to decrease the amounts treated as nontaxable return of capital and increase the amounts treated as taxable income during the initial term. However, if this occurred, a portion of the cash distributions received during renewal periods would be treated as a return of capital, which is not the case under the amortization schedule which Associates presently plan to use. Thus, the total amount treated as a return of capital would not be affected by the proposed legislation. At this time, no prediction can be made as to whether or when the bill may become law.

IX.
INFORMATION AS TO PARTNERS IN ASSOCIATES

1. Biographical.

Lawrence A. Wien, Newtown Turnpike, Weston, Connecticut, is a graduate of Columbia College and Columbia Law School, and has been practicing law in New York City since 1928. He is the senior partner in the firm of Wien, Lane, Klein & Purcell. He has specialized in the field of real estate law for over twenty-six years and has been particularly active in creating investments in real property. Such investments include the Hotel Taft at Seventh Avenue and 50th Street, the Equitable Building at 120 Broadway, the Lincoln Building at 60 East 42nd Street, the Garment Center Capitol Buildings at 498, 500 and 512 Seventh Avenue, the Fisk Building at 250 West 57th Street, and the Broad-Exchange Building at 25 Broad Street, all in New York City, and the Warwick Hotel in Philadelphia.

William F. Purcell, 930 Fifth Avenue, New York City, is a graduate of Manhattan College and Fordham Law School, has been a member of the Bar of the State of New York since 1935 and is a partner in the firm of Wien, Lane, Klein & Purcell.

Exhibit 10-1   (*continued*)

2. Remuneration and Interest in Transactions Described Herein.

Wien, Lane, Klein & Purcell, as counsel for Associates, will be paid an annual fee to supervise the operation of the partnership agreement, from which sum they must defray all regular accounting costs and disbursements. Such fee will be $16,000 per year until December 31, 1972, $12,000 per year from January 1, 1973 to May 31, 1976, and $42,000 per year during all renewal periods.

Of the $200,000 to be used by Associates to defray expenses in connection with the transactions described herein, the firm will receive a legal fee now estimated at approximately $125,000.

As more fully set forth at page 6, Associates will purchase the Leasehold from Mr. Wien.

X.

LEGAL OPINIONS

The legality of the Participations, and other matters of New York State law relating to this offering, have been passed upon by Wien, Lane, Klein & Purcell, 60 East 42nd Street, New York, New York. Legal matters in connection with the Securities Act of 1933 have been passed upon by Milton P. Kroll, Esq., Cafritz Building, Washington, D. C. Questions relating to the status for federal income tax purposes of Associates and the joint ventures created under the Participating Agreements have been passed upon by Roswell Magill, Esq., of Cravath, Swaine & Moore, New York, New York, and by the firm of Stevenson, Paul, Rifkind, Wharton & Garrison, Washington, D. C.

CERTIFICATE OF INDEPENDENT PUBLIC ACCOUNTANTS

We have examined the summary of operations of the Graybar Building, New York, New York, for the five years ended December 31, 1957, during which years the property was leased by Eastern Offices, Inc. for the period from January 1, 1953 to October 9, 1953 and thereafter to the extent of an undivided 75% interest by Webb & Knapp, Inc., or its wholly-owned subsidiary, 65039 Corporation, and to the extent of an undivided 25% interest by Graysler Corporation. Our examinations were made in accordance with generally accepted auditing standards, and accordingly included such tests of the accounting records and such other auditing procedures as we considered necessary in the circumstances.

In our opinion, the summary of operations presents fairly the income from property operations of the Graybar Building, New York, New York, for the five years ended December 31, 1957, before deducting mortgage interest, depreciation and amortization, Federal income and State franchise taxes and other expenses, as noted thereon, in conformity with generally accepted accounting principles applied on a consistent basis.

HARRIS, KERR, FORSTER & COMPANY

New York, New York
March 6, 1958

Exhibit 10-1 (*continued*)

GRAYBAR BUILDING, NEW YORK, N. Y.

SUMMARY OF OPERATIONS

YEARS ENDED

	December 31, 1953	December 31, 1954	December 31, 1955	December 31, 1956	December 31, 1957
INCOME FROM PROPERTY OPERATIONS:					
Rental Income (Including Percentage Rents)	$3,326,820.36	$3,479,537.07	$3,725,469.52	$4,087,447.83	$4,403,434.34
Other Charges to Tenants and Other Income (Note B)	438,427.09	471,452.85	407,816.25	775,400.19	1,012,526.39
Total income	$3,765,247.45	$3,950,989.92	$4,133,285.77	$4,862,848.02	$5,415,960.73
DEDUCT:					
Operating Expenses Exclusive of Items Below (Note C)	$1,673,346.87	$1,638,861.55	$1,550,019.88	$1,988,192.70	$2,319,425.79
Payroll Taxes	26,885.66	25,718.21	25,845.12	26,766.62	39,415.07
Maintenance and Repairs (Note D)	—	—	—	—	—
Real Estate Taxes	420,323.69	477,603.98	476,591.86	498,124.88	508,438.22
Total	$2,120,556.22	$2,142,183.74	$2,052,456.86	$2,513,084.20	$2,867,279.08
Operating Income Before Mortgage Interest, Depreciation and Amortization, Federal Income and State Franchise Taxes, Corporate Expenses and Rental under Basic Ground Lease or Leases Effective December 30, 1957	$1,644,691.23	$1,808,806.18	$2,080,828.91	$2,349,763.82	$2,548,681.65

NOTES:

A. The above statement has been prepared from income statements of the present and prior lessees for the applicable periods which have been restated to reflect a net refund of real estate taxes of $12,122.70 applicable to the year 1954 which was received in 1955.

B. Other Charges To Tenants And Other Income include gross billings for electricity, supplies and work orders chargeable to tenants and also commissions on towel service, telephone booths, etc. The fluctuations in "Other Charges To Tenants And Other Income" reflected in the above summary are due primarily to billings on tenant work orders. Prior to 1954 no separate record of such billings or the costs pertaining thereto were maintained, nor are they readily determinable. Gross billings on tenants' work orders amounted to $182,206 in 1954, $74,966 in 1955, $357,350 in 1956 and $597,399 in 1957.

The costs applicable to such tenants' work orders were in large measure responsible for the fluctuations in "Operating Expenses" shown in the summary. These costs were $106,940 in 1954, $38,087 in 1955, $240,975 in 1956 and $453,733 in 1957. The only other major variation was in salaries and wages which increased $139,104 in 1956 when compared with 1955.

C. Operations for the period from January 1, 1953 to October 9, 1953 include a fee based on collections which covered both management and renting services. Operations after October 9, 1953 include management fees and leasing commissions, computed at standard New York City Real Estate Board rates for commercial properties. The leasing commissions are charged into operations on a pro-rata basis over the term of the individual tenants' leases.

D. Maintenance and repairs are reflected in wages and other building expenses and are not separately classified as such in the accounts or readily determinable.

11

THE COOLIDGE BLOCK

In November, 1990, William Jeffries and Eric Gilliland of Chestnut Hill Limited Partners (CHLP) were evaluating their prospective acquisition of the Coolidge Block, a 60,000 S.F. Class B office building in Springfield, Mass. Commonwealth Bank was scheduled to foreclose on the property at auction two weeks hence. The case takes us through a discussion of the factors which will impact their determination of the ultimate value of the property in the context of a rapidly declining market both in Springfield in particular and in the industry in general.

Discussion Questions

1. As a potential investor, what price would you propose paying for this property?
2. What are your assumptions?
3. What is your acquisition strategy and how would you structure the negotiations?

William Jeffries and Eric Gilliland, the Managing Partners of Chestnut Hill Limited Partnership (CHLP), had just met with Sumner Lester, Senior Vice President of the Bank of the Commonwealth's Restructured Loan Department. They had discussed CHLP's interest in purchasing the Coolidge Block from the bank. The property was a 60,000 gross square foot, class B, office building located in the heart of the office district in Springfield, MA. The owner had stopped paying interest on its loans earlier in the year. The lender, Commonwealth Bank, had given a $4.5 million, 9% interest only loan on the property and was scheduled to foreclose at an auction on the site in two weeks on November 27, 1990. Terms of the sale were all cash.

Jeffries could either bid at the auction, or try to buy the loan privately from the bank before or after the auction. The bank could bid up to $4.5 million to wipe out the junior creditors and acquire clear title to the property without a cash outlay. It also had the option to accept the proceeds in cash of a lower bid but would have no further rights to the property since there were no personal guarantees or additional security attached to the loan. Commonwealth was most anxious to dispose of the property since it was under pressure to reduce its real estate portfolio. The bank knew that other lenders in the area were foreclosing on a number of similar type properties.

THE HISTORY

CHLP was formed in 1987 with $5,000,000 of equity from approximately 100 limited partner investors. The purpose of the partnership was to invest money in income producing properties. The investors were looking for properties where the full potential income had not been achieved. It was hoped that the cash from operations would improve, and the properties would be sold in three to five years. The after tax hurdle rate for CHLP was 16%.

St. Paul's Properties (SPP), the general partner of the partnership that owned the 103 year old Coolidge Block, had approached the bank in 1985 for a loan. SPP had purchased the property the prior year for $1.3 million and spent another $6.5 million for renovation and soft costs. The improvements were financed partially through the $4.5 million loan from the Bank of Commonwealth. Gene Feller (the prior owner of Coolidge Block) held a five year $450,000

Lecturer Jeffrey A. Libert and Adjunct Professor William J. Poorvu wrote this case as the basis for class discussion rather than to illustrate either effective or ineffective handling of an administrative situation.

Copyright © 1990 by the President and Fellows of Harvard College. To order copies, call (617) 495-6117 or write the Publishing Division, Harvard Business School, Boston, MA 02163. No part of this publication may be reproduced, stored in a retrieval system, used in a spreadsheet, or transmitted in any form or by any means—electronic, mechanical, photocopying, recording, or otherwise—without the permission of Harvard Business School.

10% interest only second mortgage note, and there was a $600,000 five year 15% interest only third mortgage given by a private lender to St. Paul. The latter two loans were given at the time of initial purchase. SPP's investors had put up the remaining cash to complete the project.

The bank felt that its loan would be a secure one. SPP's Properties had a very good track record. The property's projected income from operations was $569,000 (see **Exhibit 11-1**). Although the property was only about 60% leased at the time, the state agencies were negotiating with the owner for significant space in the building. The pro forma at that time indicated that all the debt would be serviced from cash flow.

THE PROPERTY

CHLP and its management/advisory firm Chestnut Hill Properties (CHP), which was owned by Jeffries, began investigating the Coolidge Block in September of 1990. During the next six weeks a lot was learned:

1. Many of the tenants were unhappy. Management of the building had begun to suffer as the cash flow of the property was insufficient to meet the needs of the tenants and the mortgages.
2. The boiler and the common area were in need of significant repairs estimated at about $20,000.
3. The vacant space was partially fitted with dropped ceilings, carpet, and lighting. It was estimated that these spaces and other spaces that became vacant could be built to a tenant's specification for $10 per square foot average.
4. Marketing expenses of $5 per square foot were incurred when space was leased to new tenants.
5. The Department of Social Services wanted another 3,300 square feet. Other tenants expressed interest for 1,500 square feet.
6. Many contractors including those who maintained the elevator and heating and cooling system had not been paid for months.
7. The city's assessed value for real estate tax purpose based on 100% of market value was $5,541,400. The tax rate was $11.19 per thousand dollars of assessed value.
8. A lease synopsis was generated as well as an estimate of operating expenses (see **Exhibits 11-2** and **11-3**). The synopsis shows 1991 rents under existing leases, which totals $729,000. It also shows the value of those leases if they were to be renegotiated today at market rents, which were on average ten percent less, for a total of $656,000.
9. Copies of a typical floor plan without interior partitions were obtained from SPP (see an example of the floor plans in **Exhibit 11-4**).

THE APPRAISAL AND FINANCING

In meetings and discussions with Lester from the Bank of Commonwealth, Jeffries had learned that an all cash purchase would be much more favorable to the bank. Were the bank required to give financing, the price would be considered less attractive than an outright purchase. However, Lester had indicated that in no event would the bank "give away" the property. Jeffries knew that the holders of the second and third mortgages which were also in default could bid at the auction, but unless they were able to repay the first mortgage they would have no advantage over CHLP.

With the New England economy in a tailspin, Jeffries was at first discouraged in his efforts to find a mortgage for the property. After knocking on about 20 doors, Jeffries found that Scollay Square Bank would lend $2,000,000 for five years at 11% interest only. Other terms required CHLP to guarantee the loan, which in effect would allow the lender in case of default to look to the partnership's other assets. As the bank required an appraisal which showed significant value over the first mortgage, an appraisal was ordered by Jeffries from Jones and Daniels, the most respected appraisal firm in the City of Springfield (see **Exhibit 11-5**).

CHLP'S DELIBERATIONS

At CHLP, Eric Gilliland, William Jeffries, and Pat Beene (the Senior Property Manager of CHP) were concerned with a number of factors beyond the economics of this property. CHLP only had about $700,000 in cash, and its lenders were not likely to advance funds for a work out. The only additional sources of funds for CHLP would be from its investments. At best only $150,000 additional could be expected within three months.

Beene pointed out that besides the deferred maintenance of the building, tenant requests for additional space would require capital of about $15 per square foot ($10 for buildout and $5 for marketing expenses). However, she felt confident that if occupancy achieved 90%, the property could be sold at a 10% capitalization rate after five years. Jeffries alternatively was nervous that real estate would be further depressed by that time because the economic and financial crisis in Massachusetts may have just begun. He wondered if in the future equity and debt would be available for real estate.

Jeffries was concerned about the State leases. They could be terminated by the State with a 30-day notice if funding was not available. A new governor was about to take office committed to reducing State expenditures. He also was concerned about the management of the property. In the past, he, along with Beene and a local property manager would become actively involved with the tenant leasing efforts, management and renovations. Although CHLP managed three similar properties, they were closer to Boston than Springfield. An apartment complex that CHP managed was only 15 minutes away from Springfield in Connecticut. Beene argued that the property manager on that site was underutilized and could spend 1/3rd of her time at Coolidge Block. She also argued that the income from the management fee would be beneficial to CHP (Beene was compensated based on CHP's earnings.)

Jeffries did not have much time. Lester called him frequently, and he knew that the Scollay Square commitment might be lost if he did not act soon. His main questions were what, if anything, to pay for the property, how should he structure the deal and how should he conduct the negotiation with the bank. Should he bid at the auction? He knew that the bank had solicited offers from others, and likely had written down the property on its books. Still, the officers of the bank were nervous about selling at a price that would open them to criticism if the property later proved successful. He wondered what might be the bank's bottom line?

Jeffries remembered his days as a student at business school. After he finished an exam, he could move on to new courses--not so this time. He could not even ask for more information. He would have to make the best assumptions he could and after evaluating the property, come up with a decision on how best to proceed.

Exhibit 11-1 *1985 Projected Pro Forma Income and Expense Statement*

Rental income 54,000 S.F. @ $15	$810,000
Vacancy allowance at 3%	25,000
Net rental income	785,000
Operating expenses @ $4.00	216,000
Cash flow from operations	569,000
First mortgage expense	405,000
Cash flow after financing	$164,000

Exhibit 11-2 *Lease Synopsis: The Coolidge Block October 1990*

TENANT	FLOOR	SQ. FOOTAGE	% OF SPACE	LEASE EXP.	CURRENT RENT/SF	1991 RENTS	MARKET RENTS
American Discount	1	4,700	8.7	12-31-90	$14.50	$68,150	$61,335
Pagoda East	1	2,500	4.6	12-31-91	11.44	28,600	25,740
Plymouth Optical	1	1,845	3.4	12-31-92	18.50	34.133	30,719
Vacant	1	2,500	4.6	0-0-0	14.00	35,000	31,500
United Temps	2	5,131	9.5	12-31-91	12.50	64,138	57,724
FBI	2	1,650	3.1	12-31-94	13.15	21,698	19,528
Dennis Group	2	4,492	8.3	12-31-92	12.25	55,027	49,525
Department Mental Retardation	3	7,573	14.0	12-31-93	13.00	98,449	88,604
Vacant	3	3,000	5.6	0-0-0	13.50	40,500	36,450
Mass. Drug Enforcement Agency	4	5,141	9.5	12-31-93	13.50	69,403	62,463
Vacant	4	5,300	9.8	0-0-0	13.50	71,550	64,395
Department Social Services	5	10.168	18.8	12-31-93	14.00	142,352	128,117
Total		54,000	100.0			729,000	656,100
Average					13.50 PSF		12.15 PSF

Market Rents represent 90% of 1991 rents, for an average rent per square foot of $12.15. Rental rates for individual leases range from $10.29 PSF to $16.64.

Exhibit 11-3 *Operating Expenses: The Coolidge Block—October 1990*

ADMINISTRATIVE EXPENSES	$	$/S.F.
Management Fee	23,000	0.43
Legal, Accounting, Miscellaneous	12,000	0.22
Total	$35,000	$0.65
Taxes, Insurance, Utilities		
Gas Heat	12,000	0.22
Electricity Common Area	11,000	0.20
Electricity State Agencies	30,000	0.56
Real Estate Taxes (1990 Tax Bill)	62,000	1.15
Property Insurance	12,000	0.22
Water and Sewer	4,000	0.07
Total	$131,000	$2.42
Repairs and Maintenance		
Salaries	20,000	0.37
Cleaning, HVAC, Security Contract	31,000	0.57
Trash Removal	2,000	0.04
Elevator Repairs	4,000	0.07
Misc. Building Repairs	38,000	0.71
Total	$95,000	$1.76
All Expenses Total	$261,000	$4.83

Exhibit 11-4   *Typical Floor Plan Without Interior Partitions*

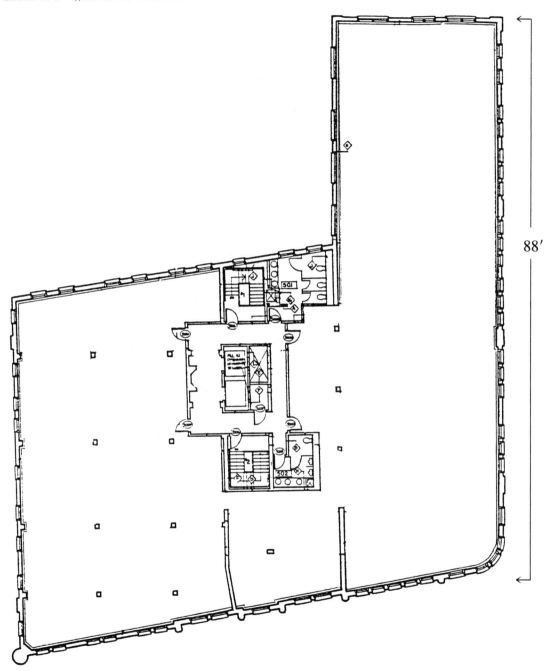

88'

Exhibit 11-5

October 27, 1990

Mr. William Jeffries
Chestnut Hill Companies
222 Newton Street
Boston, MA 02116

    RE: The Coolidge Block
       Springfield, MA
       S & R 8472

Dear Mr. Jeffries:

    In accordance with your request, I have personally inspected and made an appraisal of property in Springfield, Massachusetts, known and designated as The Coolidge Block. The purpose of this inspection and subsequent analysis is to provide a brief or preliminary estimate of the subject property's market value.

    Various data has been assembled and analyzed and it is my opinion that the market value of the subject property as of September 25, 1990 was:

$3,250,000

    The attached report represents a review of the appraisal process together with any analysis of the data collected and certain materials upon which the estimate of value is predicated.

    If you have any questions, please call me at (413) 753-1000.

Respectfully submitted,

                 E. Brookfield, III
                 Jones and Daniels, Inc.

EB/lek

Exhibit 11-5 (*continued*)

Summary of Salient Facts and Conclusions

Property Name:	Coolidge Block
Location	Main Street Springfield, MA
Improvements:	5-story office building with first floor retail and basement storage
Building Area:	60,000 s.f.—Gross Area
	54,000 s.f.—Net Rentable
Year Built:	1887
Condition:	Good—renovated in 1985
HVAC:	Heat pump
Elevators:	Two (2), 2,000# capacity
Windows:	Thermopane, aluminum (upper floors)
Roof:	Rubber membrane
Sprinklered:	100%, wet system
Parking:	Off-site garages and parking lots
Assessment & Taxes:	
Land:	$1,541,400.00
Improvements:	$4,000,000.00
Total:	$5,541,400.00
Real Estate Taxes	$ 62,000.53
Land:	17,690 s.f., corner lot
Zoning:	Business C—Central Business District
Highest and Best Use:	Commercial
Interest Considered:	Free and Clear Ownership
Date of Valuation:	October 25, 1990
Value Estimate:	$3,250,000

Market Analysis

The Springfield office market could be described as being generally weaker in 1989 then in years just prior, and tended to favor tenants rather than landlords. It was a year of delayed decisions. As the regions' major tenants reviewed growth plans and facility options, developers delayed the construction of significant office developments. Preleasing requirements were stiffened as the appetite for financing and developing new speculative projects decreased.

The result was a drop in the region's vacancy rates. The annual absorption of 235,000 s.f. of office space, down 20% from 1988's 260,000 s.f. occurred largely in existing inventory. The chief benefactors of this growth were the suburbs of Springfield, where nearly two thirds of the area's total absorption took place.

Parking continues to be a major issue in downtown Springfield. However, while in past years the concern centered primarily on availability, the focus has now shifted to pricing and policy. Tenants continue to voice concern over how rates are determined and the overall effect of parking on their occupancy costs.

In light of these concerns, it is not surprising that Springfield trailed its satellite towns in the performance of its office market. In fact, Springfield was the only municipality to experience a net increase in vacancy rate. The only improving market was Class A office buildings. Availability rates of Class A inventory continued a three year improvement trend as Monarch Place completed its initial leasing program.

The strong performance of Class A space came largely at the expense of Class B and C buildings. Tenants vacating these buildings to upgrade to Class A availabilities, together with the addition of 114,000 s.f. of additional inventory account for the 12% increase in the vacancy rates of Class B and C properties. Class A space offered much needed parking and excellent views of western Massachusetts.

Exhibit 11-5 *(continued)*

Office Space—Greater Springfield 1989

TYPE	TOTAL S.F.	% VACANCY	NO. BUILDINGS	RENT RANGE
Class A	1,186,000	9.6%	6	$16.00-22.00
Class B	1,345,000	30.7%	42	11.50-15.50
Class C	419,000	25.4%	21	8.00-12.00
Total	2,950,000	21.6%	69	8.00-22.00

In the downtown market area, vacancies range from 10% to 25% (generally 25% for Class B), and rents are generally being quoted from $11.50 to $15.50 per square foot (gross) for Class B space. Operating expenses, including maintenance and utilities are typically paid by landlords (average: $4.00-$5.00 per square foot). Landlords have generally been successful in obtaining leases that are indexed to a national consumer price index; however, work letters for tenant buildouts were significantly more generous than the $10 that tends to prevail in this market and tenants were given substantial "free rent" concessions. Significant sales of office buildings in both the downtown and close-in suburban market generally tended to be in the $55.00 to $60.00 per gross square foot range. However, most recently a number of office buildings are in the process of being foreclosed on. The impact of these foreclosures on the market will be adverse.

The retail market was also weaker, vacancy rates generally being in the 15% range. Rents in the downtown market area are generally quoted between $12.00 and $25.00 per square foot (gross). Baystate West Shopping Center located nearly opposite the subject property reported sales of $174.00 per square foot.

12

THE TEXTILE CORPORATION BUILDING

In March, 1987, Martin Donwill hopes to submit the winning offer in a sealed bid auction for a 350,000 square foot Boston office complex. Although he feels his skills in management and rehabilitation give him an economic advantage over his competitors, he has to quantify the ways in which he can create value, and profitably outbid his competitors. This case offers an opportunity to compare the risk and rewards of new construction with rehabilitation. It also introduces students to the art of bidding, within the greater context of theories of negotiation.

Discussion Questions

1. How much should Donwill bid for the Textile Corporation Building and why?
2. How has Donwill planned to increase the cash flow from operations for this property? What do you think of his approach?
3. What are the problems of improving or rehabilitating an existing building? How do they differ from the problems of new construction?
4. Has Textile Corporation picked the best method for selling the property?

In March 1987, Martin E. Donwill was trying to decide how much to offer for the properties owned and 50% occupied by the Textile Corporation. Textile had issued an invitation on February 21, 1987, for sealed bids for the four parcels comprising: a 12-story building with 300,000 total square feet of space; a 6-story office building, with 50,000 square feet of space; a 3-story garage with parking space for 355 vehicles; and an adjoining vacant parcel of approximately 8,400 square feet, used as a parking lot for approximately 40 additional vehicles.

The minimum acceptable bid price was announced by Textile to be $16,000,000, and because of the size and prominence of the properties and their location in a rapidly improving area only a few blocks from Boston's financial district, there was considerable interest in the bidding on the part of local and out-of-town realtors.

DESCRIPTION OF PROPERTY

The buildings were completed in the 1920s and were solidly constructed. A broad arched entrance in the main building led into a magnificent brick, high-ceilinged lobby and large arched entrances. From the upper floors, there were views of the harbor. The Textile Company had originally used the property for its offices and manufacturing facilities. Over the years, its manufacturing operations were moved out of the area, and approximately half of the 12-story building and all of the six-story building was converted for use by other firms, primarily distributors who liked the location, and were willing to accept class C minimally modernized space. The buildings had been well-maintained, serviced by eight recently installed passenger elevators that replaced the manually operated ones. Each floor was air-conditioned with individual package units.

Approximately 80% of the gross footage was usable. The remainder was for public space such as stairways, elevators, utility rooms, public corridors and bathrooms on multi-tenanted floors. Gross rents for tenants other than Textile averaged $15 per rentable square foot in the larger building and $12 in the smaller including electricity. Occupancy had traditionally been about 97%.

Adjunct Professor William J. Poorvu prepared this case as the basis for class discussion rather than to illustrate either effective or ineffective handling of an administrative situation.

Copyright © 1987 by the President and Fellows of Harvard College. To order copies, call (617) 495-6117 or write the Publishing Division, Harvard Business School, Boston, MA 02163. No part of this publication may be reproduced, stored in a retrieval system, used in a spreadsheet, or transmitted in any form or by any means—electronic, mechanical, photocopying, recording, or otherwise—without the permission of Harvard Business School.

COMPANY HISTORY

The Martin E. Donwill Company, a sole proprietorship real estate investment company, was one of the largest private property owners in the area. Since 1970, Mr. Donwill had accumulated approximately 10,000 apartment units and over 1,200,000 square feet of office space in the area. He specialized in modernizing older apartment houses and office buildings, and felt that he should invest exclusively in this area of real estate as opposed to constructing new buildings in which he had no experience. According to Mr. Donwill, each area of real estate required its own special talents and his talents were in this area.

He saw the risks of developing new properties as being considerable because of the uncertainties of predicting five to seven years ahead the costs of construction, financing charges, tenant rentals, and completion dates. He felt that he was making a positive contribution to society, and the preservation of urban values, by rehabilitating areas that were not yet fully recognized. He was able to do this without government subsidies or without destroying or demolishing neighborhoods. Also, the pricing of his rental or condominium units enabled middle-class residents to live and work in the city. One had to know what was worth rehabilitating, and how much one should spend to still make a profit.

He prided himself on his ability to control costs. A continuous and large volume of work was one factor that enabled him to achieve this efficiency. He was able to develop a full-time, year-round, experienced staff of construction and maintenance personnel. He attained economies through large-scale purchasing, often of manufacturer's closeouts. He closely supervised all phases of his operation, from maintenance to the negotiation of most office leases. His imagination was important in solving many difficult problems. Because of his attention to detail, he considered it desirable to concentrate his real estate investments in the Boston area.

Mr. Donwill managed his real estate operations from his office, consisting of four rooms and a small secretarial area in an older office building he had renovated. This office handled the bookkeeping for all of his properties and the rental and management for the office buildings. The apartments were managed from local offices and maintenance was handled by full-time maintenance personnel operating from company-owned, radio-controlled trucks dispatched from a central supply warehouse.

He had begun by acquiring apartment buildings in one area close to and accessible by public transportation. Rents for older one-bedroom apartments then ran from $300 to $400 per month. He looked for stable neighborhoods with middle class residents capable of paying higher rents if their apartments were renovated. The increase to $450 or $550 per month seemed substantial but still produced a market rental well below that of new construction.

As an example of the economies of his operation, Mr. Donwill would spend $9,000 to modernize the kitchen and bathroom and to redecorate a one-bedroom apartment. By increasing the rents by $150 a month or $1,800 per year, he could recapture his investment in five years. Immediately, his $9,000 investment was worth $18,000 since apartment buildings in the area were being valued at ten times their annual cash flow. The value of his investment was increased still further since the modernization program resulted in the reduction of maintenance costs and in the elimination of the substantial vacancies in the buildings he bought. Because most of the operating costs of a property do not relate to the level of occupancy, a difference of 5% in vacancies can have a major impact on the owner's return on investment.

Donwill next started to acquire warehouse buildings in neighborhoods close to downtown for conversion to commercial space. He felt that market conditions at that time were ideal. The high cost of new construction, the growth in service industries and the interest of many firms in attractively renovated older space provided him with an opportunity. He was imaginative in his approach. In one building, he added 9% to the building's rentable floor area by building an extra floor between the old first and second floors, exploiting a ceiling height of 20 feet on the first floor. At another, he enclosed an interior court and added 10% to the rentable floor area. The additional space was quickly rented since the modernization of the building made the interior space, now air-conditioned and properly lit, desirable.

PROPOSED SALE OF PROPERTY

Mr. Donwill first heard of the proposed sale of the Textile Corporation Building in February 1987. The thought of owning this building was very appealing to him. He had always regarded the building as one of the best and largest of the existing buildings near downtown. He doubted whether he would again have an opportunity to purchase this building. Textile Corporation owned and had been the major tenant of the building since its completion in 1926. It had fully depreciated the property on its balance sheet and as a result decided that its investment in the building could better be used in other areas of its business. An earlier purchase offer was almost accepted, but the company was uncertain about the optimum price available. As a result, the company decided to have a sealed-bid auction for the property with the prospective bidders prescreened as to their financial responsibility. Bids had to be received by March 30, 1987, and would be acted on by April 15. To ensure that any bids submitted would be serious, a $1 million deposit was required with each submission. An offering circular was printed describing the terms and conditions of the proposed sale with the current income and expense figures. A floor plan was also shown (see **Exhibit 12-1**).

Textile decided to utilize the services of six local established real estate brokerage firms to offer the property. The broker of the successful bidder was to receive a commission, to be paid by the seller, of $250,000 plus 2% of the amount that the successful bid exceeded the minimum price of $16,000,000.

EVALUATION OF PROPERTY

Based upon the income and expense figures supplied to him by the seller (see **Exhibit 12-2**), Mr. Donwill attempted to evaluate the property. He saw that the gross income figure of $4,400,000 was based on a new lease for $1,650,000 entered into by the Textile Corporation for 12 years. Textile had also retained rights to extend the lease for two 5-year periods at an annual rent of $2,200,000 including electricity. The space covered by the lease was 139,000 gross square feet or 46% of the gross rentable area in the 12-story building. Although the rental averaging $11.87 per square foot at first seemed low to him, Mr. Donwill was satisfied when he saw that the area rented included a considerable amount of basement space, was calculated on a gross square footage basis and included public areas. This made the effective office rent on a net usable basis about $14 per square foot. Also, Textile was taking the space in its present condition. There also was a tax clause which specified that Textile would pay 46% of any property tax increase over the 1986 level, and an operations clause covering a similar portion of increased cleaning expenses and all utilities. The operating expenses for the building were based on the actual experience of the Textile Corporation with the building and totalled $2,950,000. This left a net before financing of $1,450,000. Mr. Donwill then took an allowance for vacancies of 3% of gross income and a management expense figure of 2% which reduced this net figure to $1,230,000.

Mr. Donwill estimated that he would probably be able to get an institutional first mortgage equal to 75% of the price paid for the property. The mortgage term would be for 26 years with interest at 10%, requiring a constant annual payment of 10.9%. He had recently placed another mortgage at this level. On this basis, if he made the minimum bid of $16,000,000 he could obtain a $12,000,000 first mortgage costing $1,308,000 per year. This left a negative cash flow of $78,000 based upon Textile's numbers with only minor adjustments.

Cash Flow from Operations (see **Exhibit 12-2**)	$1,450,000
Less: 3% Vacancy	132,000
2% Management	88,000
First mortgage: Interest & Principal	1,308,000
Net Cash Flow	($ 78,000)

There was a possibility of obtaining an interest-only first mortgage for the first three years with an annual cost of $1.2 million. This would put his cash flow in the black, yielding $30,000 per year.

Mr. Donwill, obviously, was not satisfied with such a low return on his investment. Yet, he felt that competitive bids would be in excess of the minimum as indicated by the high level of public interest.

INCOME

There was a considerable amount of new office space downtown under construction at rents in excess of $30 per square foot. Published figures showed a two to three year absorption period. It was difficult to calculate the size of the demand for Class C space or Class B space if he improved the Textile Building. How many professional firms would move from downtown to save money? Moreover, he was not sure how many of the present tenants would remain, first, because Textile Corporation was no longer the landlord and second, because he had a reputation for upgrading and raising rents.

He began to analyze those factors that affected the income of the property. He first considered the general market area. He next considered the amount of space available for rent. He knew from his past experience that although a building was fixed in size, there were several approaches to measuring rentable square footage. He saw that there were about 25,000 square feet of non-income-producing yet potential rentable space. Of the 25,000 feet on each floor of the 12-story building, approximately 2,200 square feet were used for elevators, the elevator lobby, and stairs and would always be public and unrentable. But some of the corridor space and the toilet and storage spaces might become rentable if used by a single tenant. By rearranging certain areas and by attempting to lease individual floors to only one or two tenants, he thought it was reasonable to expect that he could increase his rentable space by at least 15,000 square feet which, at $15 per square foot, could increase his income by $225,000. Another 5,000 square feet with income potential of $75,000 per year could be "created" by measuring space from the window or glass line of the building to the glass line of the entrance door. In the past, measurements were taken from the inside walls of the space. In an older building with 18-inch masonry walls, the 9 inches included in rentable area could add up. The periphery of many of the floors was as much as 750 feet.

Mr. Donwill also had an idea which he thought could add to the total fixed space of the property. Between the two buildups was an open area of approximately 600 square feet. By filling this area with a new structure, he could not only create 500 square feet of rentable space at each level but make it possible for the floors of the 6-story building to be entered off the elevator lobby of the building with the greater prestige and the higher rental levels. The 3,000 rentable square feet created could be rented at $15 per square foot or $45,000 per year. In addition, the 40,000 square feet now renting at a lower level could then be worth as much as $2.00 per square foot more or $80,000 per year, merely because of the change in entrance.

Another means of increasing income was to increase the quality of the space offered through modernization. He estimated that he could increase rentals by $325,000 by improving 110,000 square feet of space for both existing tenants and new tenants coming into the building.

He analyzed whether rental income could be increased by offering additional services to the tenants. Although Mr. Donwill intended to clean, operate and maintain the building in a first-rate manner, he knew that Textile had also done so. Therefore, he concluded that he would probably not be able to increase income in this manner. Mr. Donwill felt, though, that his active promotional efforts, his encouragement of local rental brokers, and his existing institutional advertising might give him a broader choice of tenants and since the building was not yet well known, he felt that this advantage might be substantial. The more property he owned, the more likely it was that tenants would come to him for space either in this property or other buildings he owned.

In summary, through renovation, the building of new space, and the remeasuring of old, Mr. Donwill expected to increase rents by $750,000. Mr. Donwill knew that this increase would not be achieved immediately but would probably take about three years. A reasonable estimate would be that the income would increase over the $4,400,000 by $100,000 in Year 1, $300,000 in Year 2, $500,000 in Year 3, and $750,000 in Year 4. In addition, parking and other miscellaneous income generated $470,000 annually.

CAPITAL EXPENSES

To remodel space and to build the new addition involved substantial capital expenses. Also, additional vacancy must be expected since a tenant could not occupy space until the work was complete. In addition to the 3% for vacancy already included in his expense statement, Mr. Donwill allowed for an additional $150,000 in vacancy the first year, $300,000 the second year and $150,000 the third year. Then the present over-all allowance of 3% should again be adequate. The major capital expense would come from the renovation of 110,000 space feet of presently leased space and approximately 15,000 square feet of public space to permit its inclusion as rentable area. Mr. Donwill felt that this renovation would cost the normal property owner $25 per square foot or $3,125,000 but that because of his expertise he could probably do the work for $20.00 per square foot or $2,500,000.

For this $20.00 per square foot, he could remodel a typical office to include carpeting, dropped acoustic ceilings, recessed fluorescent lighting, air-conditioning, the enclosure of all pipes and radiators, partitioning finished at the tenant's option with prefinished wood paneling, paint, or vinyl wall covering, overhead storage cabinets, shelving, new entrance doors, counters, closets. The layout was designed to the tenant's particular specifications, prepared by an architect selected and paid for by Mr. Donwill. Yet, Mr. Donwill chose materials that he expected would reduce the landlord's future maintenance responsibilities.

There were many reasons why Mr. Donwill's costs were lower than average, none of which he felt affected the quality of his finished product. First of all, because of the amount of work he was doing, he could effect large economies through mass purchasing. As an example, he bought his own lumber direct from Oregon with carload deliveries. Walnut paneling bought in quantity cost 25% less. The vinyl wall covering was bought direct from manufacturers' closeouts at 60% off. Rather than buy 8-foot long, four-tube lighting fixtures from a manufacturer, he bent and painted the metal troffers himself and then separately purchased and added the ballast, socket, tube and plastic cover. In renovating one major building, he had taken out the old-fashioned marble dividing partitions in the toilet areas and replaced them with new metal partitions. Then he had the marble repolished and reused to create an elegant marble entrance lobby. Imagination was an important factor in remodeling.

Besides savings on material, Mr. Donwill's labor costs were well below average. In an industry noted for its cyclical employment practices, Mr. Donwill had experienced, non-union work crews whom he employed on a year-round basis. He was able to take non-skilled workers at $8 per hour and teach them to do tasks that normally were done by employees receiving $12 per hour. Each individual was expected to do work in more than one trade. By subcontracting only ceiling, floor tile, and air-conditioning installation, he was able to reduce the number of outside trades involved, saving both time and money.

The six-story addition of 600 square feet per floor would cost $200,000 to complete. The cost of this was high because of the difficulty of installing steel and materials in such a small enclosed space. Few outside contractors would even attempt the job. Mr. Donwill expected to install two new boilers costing $100,000. Presently the heat was purchased from Edison Steam, a method Mr. Donwill, from his experience in other buildings, knew to be very expensive. Mr. Donwill also put in an allowance for $200,000 to cover contingencies for the whole project.

These capital costs totalling $3,000,000 would be spent equally over the three year period. The increased vacancies over the three-year period totalled $600,000. Mr. Donwill expected to finance this $3,600,000 partially through reinvesting any money received from operating the property over the three-year period and the remainder through a second mortgage from a private source. Until he knew his actual mortgage cost based on the amount of his bid to Textile, he could not estimate exactly how much would be available from operations. But by Year 4, the $30,000 profit should rise to $1,052,000.

OPERATING EXPENSES

Mr. Donwill then examined the various operating expense figures submitted to him by Textile to see whether or not through more efficient operation he could increase his return. He knew that in any building that had been owned by the same owner for a long period of time inefficiencies in operation would be bound to occur. This was especially apt to be true in a company such as Textile where the property was being operated not for its real estate return but for the service of the office and executive employees of the company. He expected to reduce the building payroll figure of $810,000 to $530,000 (not including payroll taxes). This reduction was accomplished in three ways. First, since the buildings had been recently converted to automatic elevators, 12 operators could be released immediately, saving $180,000. Second, another major cost of building payroll was office cleaning. His cost in other buildings was $.60 per square foot and he expected his cost to be the same here, resulting in another saving of $60,000. Third, the permanent maintenance staff would consist of an engineer and three helpers at a cost of $80,000 per year as compared with Textile's cost of $120,000. In addition to the direct wage cost savings, he expected to save an additional $40,000 for payroll and FICA taxes. He realized that his costs were below that of published national average figures. Yet, because of his efficiencies and because the building would be easier to maintain and clean as it was modernized, he felt the $320,000 figure of savings for payroll and related taxes was appropriate. Also, he knew that in the early years of owning a property, the owner normally pays more attention to details and is more efficient. Then it was natural even in his own properties for a certain degree of inefficiency to creep in.

Mr. Donwill knew that he was not expected to retain any of the present building employees or be responsible for their severance, vacation or unemployment pay when they were discharged. Textile was prepared to assume these costs. As payroll costs were reduced, there would be a corresponding percentage decrease in payroll taxes.

Heating costs could be expected to drop from $280,000 to $200,000 for two reasons. He was installing his own boiler system, probably in the summer of the third year when the present Edison contract expired. In addition, as the ceilings in the offices were dropped, less area was required to be heated.

He checked with his insurance agent who told him that because of a special package policy written by the Factory Mutual Insurance Company for all his properties, his insurance costs would be reduced by $10,000.

Electricity, which cost $500,000 per year, was a large expense and was a service included in the basic rent. In other buildings he owned, each tenant had a meter and paid the utility company directly. On a rent-inclusion basis, the landlord could make money since electricity was purchased on one meter at a bulk rate. A disadvantage was that a tenant, even though it was more expensive, might be inclined to rent space at $13.50 per foot without electricity rather than at $15.00 with electricity. In any case, Mr. Donwill knew that it would be a very expensive electrical job to change over the system to individual meters, and Textile had recently put in a new modern electric service to the building capable of handling all the foreseeable needs of the tenants based upon the rent inclusion principle. The electricity charge also included the usage for air conditioning. He would have to wait for more experience before deciding if there were any savings in electricity. Besides, he thought it would be safer to have the tenants share in increases and decreases in electricity costs rather than predict future energy prices.

Mr. Donwill next analyzed the repairs and decorating figure. Historically, this figure had been $260,000. This seemed high to him. He thought it might represent some unusual expenditures because of the impending sale of the property. Furthermore, as the building was modernized, repairs should decrease. He calculated that $200,000, approximately 4% of income, was reasonable especially since Mr. Donwill's staff was accustomed to doing most repair work themselves.

Real estate taxes were the largest operating expense item, and it was in this area that Mr. Donwill was especially sensitive. Mr. Donwill had a special problem with the local assessors since his business was modernizing and increasing the rent rolls of older buildings. The assessors kept careful watch of his operations and continually tried to raise his assessments. In this case, he anticipated an increase of $100,000. Over that initial rise, the tenants would pay their share of further increases. Still, Textile's tax clause would result in their paying 46% of any initial increase in the 12-story building or 40% of the bill for the whole project. Therefore, he adjusted his own cost by the net amount, $60,000.

A management figure of 2% seemed fair to him for this property even though this percentage was higher than his cost in other areas. He knew that this high-grade property would require special attention. The $103,000 figure would include the salary of a manager and secretary plus office expenses and professional fees.

In any case, he knew that a potential mortgagee always put a figure for management in an expense set-up to determine the net income of the property for appraisal purposes. The reason for this is that a potential mortgagee must consider the fact that if it comes into ownership of the property through foreclosure, it would have to hire an outside management firm.

Mr. Donwill now made a new income and expense statement which he expected to achieve by year 4 based upon his adjustments of the figures submitted to him (see **Exhibit 12-3**). His income after vacancy on a stabilized basis was increased to $4,996,000 and his expenses on an adjusted basis were reduced to $2,643,000. This left a figure of $2,353,000 before financing after deducting 3% for vacancy and 2% for management.

BIDDING STRATEGY

The question now became how much to bid for the property. He wanted to win the auction. The prestige of owning the property was worth $500,000 to $1,000,000 to him both in pride and in the fact that this building would upgrade his whole portfolio of properties. The more property he owned, the more flexibility he would have in satisfying space needs of new or existing tenants. Mr. Donwill, however, did not want to pay any more for the property than he had to. He knew that all the other bidders as well would use the income method for determining value. Replacement cost produced a value far higher than the actual market value of the property. The 67,771 square feet of land for all the parcels was worth at least $3 million as raw land. He would use that figure as a deduction from his purchase price to determine his depreciable base. To be conservative, he decided not to depreciate the payments until Year 4. In accordance with the new 1986 Tax Act, depreciation would have to be taken on a straight line basis over a 31.5 year life. The income tax rate he estimated at 28% for ordinary income and capital gains.

Normally, Mr. Donwill expected a cash return after federal income taxes of 15% on his invested capital even though he knew other bidders might be satisfied with a 12% return. Yet, he doubted whether other bidders would see as many areas to increase net income as he did, especially with regard to the connection between the two buildings. The $200,000 expenditure increased income by $125,000. Another bidder might be willing to modernize 110,000 square feet to obtain the extra $325,000 income, but it might cost $625,000 more. Other bidders, if experienced in the area, would also plan on converting from steam and would know of the elimination of the elevator operators. They would also make an effort to reduce public areas and would try to use the revised measurement standard. Whether they could be as persuasive as Mr. Donwill in obtaining tenants, he did not know.

His prospective mortgage lender had informed him that as long as his purchase price was within reason, he could still expect a 75% mortgage at 10% interest. The term of the mortgage would be ten years and amortization would not start until the fourth year and then would be on a 26 year basis. Based upon his personal reputation and guaranty and the prestige of the property, he was able to secure the pledge of a three-year $3 million second mortgage at 12% annual interest with interest only payments during the three-year period. At that time, he felt he could increase his first mortgage by an amount adequate to repay the second, on the same terms as his present mortgage. In the meantime, he would have to put in any cash flow deficits personally. He also had enough passive income from other properties to offset any losses from this project.

The number of competitors he would have in this bidding was another question. He knew that virtually all the outstanding real estate firms in the area and a few from New York City were analyzing the property, but he expected only five or six to put up the $1,000,000 deposit and actually make a bid. Mr. Donwill sat down to weigh all these factors and prepare his bid.

Exhibit 12-1   *The Textile Corporation Building*

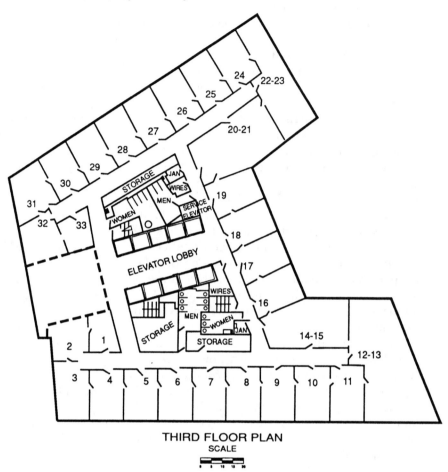

THIRD FLOOR PLAN
SCALE

Exhibit 12-2   *1986 Operating Income and Expenses*

INCOME

Textile Corporation	$1,650,000
Other Tenants: 12 Story Building	1,800,000
6 Story Building	480,000
Parking	320,000
Miscellaneous	150,000
Gross Revenues	4,400,000

Exhibit 12-2 (continued)

OPERATING EXPENSES

Building Payroll	810,000
Payroll Taxes	140,000
Window Cleaning	20,000
Elevator Maintenance	30,000
Insurance	40,000
Water	20,000
Heat	280,000
Electricity	500,000
Decorating and Repairs	260,000
Miscellaneous	50,000
Building Operations	2,150,000
Real Estate Tax	800,000
Total Operating Expenses	2,950,000
Cash Flow from Operations	1,450,000

Exhibit 12-3 Projected Income and Expenses (as of Year 4)

INCOME

Textile Corporation	$1,650,000
Other Tenants	3,030,000
Parking	320,000
Miscellaneous	150,000
Gross Revenues	5,150,000
Vacancies	154,000
Net Revenues	4,996,000

OPERATING EXPENSES

Building Payroll	530,000
Payroll Tax	100,000
Window Cleaning	20,000
Elevator Maintenance	30,000
Insurance	30,000
Water	20,000
Heat	200,000
Electricity	500,000
Decorating and Repair	200,000
Miscellaneous	50,000
Management	103,000
Building Operations	1,783,000
Real Estate Taxes	860,000
Total Operating Expenses	2,643,000
Cash Flow from Operations	$2,353,000

Exhibit 12-4

Syndications/John Brown

Boston Business Journal/February 23, 1987

Looking at leases: It takes two to tango

When we're talking investment property, we're talking leases. Most appraisers will agree that the value of investment property is primarily determined by its income, and income is determined by the leases that are in place.

Leasing has to be looked at from two vantage points: that of the lessor (landlord or owner) and that of the lessee (tenant). The relationship is an adversarial one—but it needn't be unfriendly. After all, the tenant needs space, and the owner must have tenants in order to survive and prosper.

The relationship is shaped by the existing market and the type of property that's being leased. For the purposes of this discussion, let's focus upon office leasing, from the viewpoint of both the owner and the prospective tenant.

The discussion that follows is for nonprofessionals who occasionally get involved with the leasing process for their company or for other reasons. It may also be helpful for prospective investors in investment real estate or real estate limited partnerships, who have some understanding of leasing but could use further knowledge in order for them to evaluate potential investments or offerings.

If the office-space market (or retail or industrial markets) is soft, the tenant will have more space to choose from and will be in a better position to get "concessions" or "incentives," whether they be lower rental charges, a period of free or reduced rent, higher quality buildout allowances (interior finishes) or even a possible equity position in the property. The latter would apply only to a long-term, large-space user.

Space measurement

The measurement of space is part of the adversarial relationship we mentioned above. The tenant thinks in terms of usable space, while the owner usually thinks in terms of gross area. Let's pause for a moment and sort out some terms, such as "gross," "gross rentable," "net rentable," "leasable" and "usable," among others.

The Institute of Real Estate Management (IREM) defines "gross rentable" as all area within outside walls minus stairs, elevator shafts, flues, pipe shafts, vertical ducts and balconies. It defines "net rentable" as the above minus utility rooms, restrooms, corridors and other areas not available to the tenants for their furnishings and personnel.

In years past, the Boston area largely rented on a "usable" basis, which was the actual space available to the tenant. Most areas of the country followed this pattern except for New York City. The so-called "New York system" was what we would now call "gross area" or "gross rentable" and included all area of the building (and sometimes part of the thickness of the walls), prorated to each tenant.

For example, you might lease 10,000 square feet but find that only 8200 square feet usable. The rest is scattered throughout the building in the form of restrooms, corridors, stairways, utility closets, etc. The lost space is called the "waste" or "efficiency" factor and is expressed as a percentage (in this case, 18 percent).

Boston started moving toward the New York system in the early '60s and has been pursuing it with a vengeance in the past eight to 10 years. Most buildings are now leased on what is called a "leasable space" basis (the terms net and gross are dropped entirely). Leasable space is usually the space actually occupied by the tenant plus a proportionate share of the waste factor (except stairways and elevator shafts).

This can vary from building to building.

If you are contemplating leasing space, the important thing to have is a floor plan (to scale) of the space being offered. Actually measure it to determine how much space you will have to use. This is important for space-planning purposes, but it will also allow you to calculate the waste factor by comparing your usable space to the leasable space figure in your lease. Waste factors range from less than 5 percent to about 20 percent depending upon the type of building and tenancy, and the size of individual tenant spaces. Usually, the lower the waste factor, the better deal you will be getting, but you will have to do the calculations.

Tenant buildout

When you bought your first tract home, the builder probably had allowances for this and allowances for that, things such as electrical and plumbing fixtures or wall coverings. Any upgrades over the standard allowances were "extras." The same is usually true for the office developer. The standard tenant improvements (buildout) might include two coats of off-white paint, medium-grade carpeting, acoustical ceiling with fluorescent lighting and a specific length of interior ceiling-to-floor partitioning, depending upon the number of square feet being rented.

The longer the term of the lease, the longer the period for amortization of these costs, and the less impact on per-square-foot annual rent rates. If, for example, extras come to $60,000 on 10,000 square feet of space, the increase in the rental rate might be about $2 per square foot on a five-year lease. On a three-year lease the increased rate would be about $3 per square foot.

Some space is advertised with no buildout allowance included and obviously sounds like a bargain. Once buildout is added, the rate could increase by as much as $6-10 per square foot.

Tenant charges

The terms "gross" and "net" above refer to the way space is measured. Just to confuse things, the same terms apply to the way certain charges are made to the tenant: gross leases, net leases and triple net leases, to name a few.

All leases charge what is called "base rent." This is the rent that is due without regard to any backcharges for operating costs or real estate taxes. If only base rent is charged, it is termed a "gross lease." This means that the landlord provides services such as cleaning, utilities, security, maintenance and repair and pays all real estate taxes. In today's market, this is rare. The usual type of gross lease establishes a base year (usually the first year of occupancy) and then charges for any increases in operating costs or real estate taxes.

Such a gross lease, with operating cost and real estate tax "escalators," usually requires that electricity the tenant uses for lighting, air conditioning and other purposes be separately metered and paid for by the tenant. This is sometimes called a "single net" lease or a gross lease "net of electricity."

At one time, we had single, double and triple net leases. Today, if we say "net lease" we normally mean what once was called "triple net."

As you can see, it will pay to read the fine print in a lease proposal and have your calculator handy. You may also find it appropriate to be represented by a real estate consultant or broker who will both advise you on options available and help you negotiate the best deal.

John A. Brown is president of John Brown Associates of Cambridge, a city planning and real estate firm.

13

THE MIDWEST CORPORATE FUND

In January, 1992, Donna Jones, the Director of Portfolio Investments for the Midwest Corporate Fund was preparing to hear the presentations of those three firms which MCF, one of the larger corporate pension plans in the country, had shortlisted as potential real estate advisors. Given the softness of the real estate markets nationally, many pension funds were reassessing their investment positions. With a little over 3% of its $3.5 billion in assets currently invested in limited term real estate assets, MCF was hoping to restructure and perhaps add to its real estate portfolio. Jones knew that each firm was aware of the tremendous investment capacity of a pension fund such as MCF and that each was aggressively looking to grow its client capital under management.

Discussion Questions

1. Should MCF increase its investments in real estate? What are the risk/reward tradeoffs?

2. How should MCF make its investment decisions? What are the investment criteria which are most important to MCF? As MCF, what kind of information would you require, both now, and over the life of a fund?

3. How do the three potential managers differ in the investment products they are offering? What are the stategic issues each firm faces in the marketplace? If you were making a decision tomorrow, what firm or firms would you decide to invest with?

4. As one of the firms applying to MCF, how would you structure a brief presentation? What are the major issues you would want to address?

MIDWEST CORPORATE FUND

MCF was a tax exempt corporate fund with approximately $3.5 billion in pension fund assets to invest. Approximately 2/3 of the $100 million value of its real estate assets owned were in an open end commingled fund managed by a major insurance company. The remainder was in a closed end fund, which was scheduled to be liquidated this year.

MCF had a number of concerns about its current portfolio structure. Many of the properties in both funds were concentrated in the office sector. Due to recent devaluations, the estimated worth of MCF's properties owned was almost 20% lower than that of appraisals conducted in December 1988. Though its investments had done better than many, the Russell/NCREIF index had measured mediocre returns for the real estate portfolios of institutional investors since the mid-1980s (See **Exhibit 13-1**).[1]

Some members of the Finance Committee to which Jones reported were beginning to question the fund's real estate investment strategy, and were inclined to think about possible real estate disposition programs before even greater portfolio markdowns ensued. Others were bullish that this economy created unique investment opportunities.

Jones herself felt that it might be an opportune time to increase MCF's portfolio allocation to real estate, possibly up to 6% of invested assets, slightly higher than current industry averages. The new capital, combined with the proceeds from the liquidating fund, would give her investment committee approximately $135 million to invest. One caveat to her strategy was the possibility that the closed end fund would not be liquidated as planned, but extended until the market improved. On balance, however, she felt that developers, property owners, or other portfolio managers—particularly those from the banking sector—were likely to be in a much less liquid position than pension funds, and that there existed strong buying opportunities at favorable prices for those with the leverage and the staying power to negotiate profitable deals.

---

[1]The Russell/NCREIF Index is compiled quarterly by the National Council of Real Estate Investment Fiduciaries, a non-profit research organization, and the Frank Russell Company as part of its larger data base which tracks the performance of institutionally owned real estate over time.

Research Associate Elizabeth McLoughlin prepared this case under the supervision of Adjunct Professor William J. Poorvu as the basis for class discussion rather than to illustrate either effective or ineffective handling of an administrative situation.

THE REAL ESTATE CAPITAL MARKETS 1992

During the 1980s the supply of capital into the real estate arena had significantly outstripped the demand for real estate space, as lending institutions ignored market indicators and continued to finance construction activity at record levels. Approximately 60% of all the bank loans added during the period 1985-1989 were for real estate. By the late 1980s as vacancies soared, the extent of overbuilding became known, many speculative projects were in default, and the faucet of money was rather dramatically shut off.

As project cash flows proved inadequate to fund the debt service owed to the banks, the artificially sustained levels of capital plummeted. Congressional legislation dramatically limited the availability of real estate credit by tightening capital requirements within the banking system, and requiring lending institutions to re-evaluate existing loan and mortgage portfolios to better reflect market conditions. Banks whose loan loss reserves were inadequate to satisfy increasingly strict regulatory levels were forced to liquidate assets at substantial discounts to book value. Nonperforming loans dragged down the banking system, and resulted in a severe contraction of liquid funds for even well conceived ventures. For example, the 10 largest U.S. commercial banks held more than $7 billion in foreclosed property, and $10 billion of nonperforming loans as of March 31, 1991.

Real Estate: For Sale
Largest Banks' Portfolio of Problem Real Estate
As of March 31, 1991 (in Billions)

	NON-PERFORMING REAL ESTATE LOANS	FORECLOSED PROPERTIES	TOTAL
Citicorp	$3.04	$1.43	$4.47
Chase Manhattan	2.07	0.76	2.83
Security Pacific	0.87	0.93	1.80
Chemical Banking	1.15	0.63	1.78
First Interstate	0.38	0.96	1.34
Bank of Boston	0.49	0.60	1.09
BankAmerica	0.75	0.23	0.98
Fleet/Norstar	0.61	0.36	0.97
Wells Fargo	0.44	0.48	0.92
First Chicago	0.34	0.54	0.88
TOTAL	$10.14	$6.92	$17.06

Source: Salomon Brothers

By the end of 1991, the process of damage control irrevocably shifted the flow of capital away from what had been mainstream sources of financing. The dominance of the thrifts in real estate lending had become a condition of the past; many commercial banks were unwilling or unable to underwrite new real estate ventures. Offshore investors, particularly the Japanese, were experiencing problems of their own, and were severely restricting their real estate investments. (By 1991 Japanese investment in U.S. real estate was less than a third of 1988 levels.) And the Tax Reform Act of 1986 had reduced the attractiveness of most commercial real estate investments for individual investors.

By 1991, as well, the severe capital shortage forced developers and project owners to look for alternatives to traditional sources of real estate financing. Faced with the need of selling off their short term loans and foreclosed properties, both the government (as the receiver for many projects in default of their loan obligations), and other private lending institutions were actively marketing the real estate they owned. Jones agreed with many industry analysts who felt that pension funds, with their enormous resources and liability structures which stretched out far into the future, were one of the few potential large scale purchasers who could provide vital liquidity to the fractured real estate capital markets over the long term. She felt that pension funds such as MCF had the opportunity to become the dominant players in the real estate investment community in the 1990s.

PENSION FUND INVESTMENT INTO REAL ESTATE

Pension funds are the fastest growing source of savings in the domestic economy, and one of the largest pools of private capital in the world. In 1950, U.S. private pension fund assets totalled $12 billion. Forty years later, in 1991, those same assets exceeded $2.3 trillion, representing a doubling almost every five years.

Prior to 1950, pension fund assets were invested primarily in fixed income products, government bonds, and other conservative investments. By the 1950s and 1960s, however, an increasing percentage of fund assets were invested in common stocks. Today, institutional trading of stock by pension funds represents about 70% of all transactions. By the early 1970s, pension funds were considering adding another major asset class to their investment portfolios—real estate equities, or the ownership of income producing property.

In 1974, the enactment of ERISA (Employee Retirement Income Security Act) guidelines imposed fiduciary standards for managing the invested portfolios of pension funds, and encouraged the distribution of resources across a diversified range of asset categories. Within these guidelines, what became known as the "prudent man" definition of investment stressed that a fiduciary of trusteed funds should make portfolio decisions, acting with the "care, skill, prudence, and diligence under the circumstances then prevailing that a prudent man, acting in like capacity and familiar with such matters would use in the conduct of an enterprise of a like character and with like aims; by diversifying the investments of the plan so as to minimize the risk of large losses, unless under the circumstances its is clearly prudent not to do so."

This one legislative act had a significant effect on the investment strategies of funds looking for an optimal combination of assets, as for the first time real estate was targeted as a viable investment vehicle. Up until that time real estate

PENSION FUND ASSETS AS LISTED IN THE *MONEY MARKET DIRECTORY Of PENSION FUNDS AND THEIR INVESTMENT MANAGERS* 1971-1991 ($ in billions)

YEAR	CORPORATE AND ELEEMOSYNARY BENEFIT FUNDS	UNION MEMBER BENEFIT FUNDS	GOVERNMENT EMPLOYEE BENEFIT FUNDS	TOTALS
1971	$ 80	$ 5	$ 50	$ 135
1972	90	10	60	160
1973	105	10	60	175
1974	124	13	90	227
1975	125	15	97	237
1976	135	15	107	257
1977	155	15	115	285
1978	186	16	132	334
1979	224	22	147	393
1980	265	27	167	459
1981	318	34	186	538
1982	398	38	210	646
1983	439	55	233	727
1984	571	63	290	924
1985	616	72	325	1,013
1986	685	88	391	1,164
1987	912	121	486	1,519
1988	1,053	131	576	1,760
1989	1,050	146	618	1,814
1990	1,188	156	706	2,050
1991	1,319	192	806	2,317

Source: Money Market Directory

had been perceived as largely illiquid, management intensive, and dominated by local market specific firms. It had performance that was difficult to measure, no reliable data base for evaluation, pricing which was non-standard, and transactional costs which were burdensome. Though national tax policy, development regulations, and other government intervention can affect real estate returns, the "real" pricing of unique properties was difficult to assess, unlike the more easily measurable shares of common stock or bonds whose value was set through numerous market transactions.

However, as high rates of inflation eroded the performance of stocks and bonds, institutional investors found that real estate offered favorable risk adjusted returns relative to other assets, offered a hedge against inflation, and provided diversification insofar as it was found that positive real estate returns did not seem to move in tandem with those of other asset classes (See **Exhibits 13-2 and 13-3**).

There were other structural factors which argued for a presence by pension funds into the real estate markets. One of the oft cited contributors of the monetary crisis in the late 1980s had been the mismatch of funds in the real estate capital markets, beginning as early as the 1970s with the savings and

Varying Risk/Return Characteristics of Five Asset Classes
Quarterly Returns 1979-1991

ASSET	MEAN RETURN	MEDIAN RETURN	STD. DEV.	MAX. RETURN	MIN. RETURN	RISK-ADJ. RETURN
Property	2.83	2.47	1.41	6.43	0.20	2.65
Stocks	4.22	5.73	7.99	21.31	-22.67	2.46
Bonds	2.70	2.09	6.09	22.38	-12.16	2.29
T-Bills	2.21	2.07	0.66	3.82	1.38	—
Inflation	1.49	1.25	1.05	4.31	-0.43	—

Though the mean quarterly return of property over a 12 year period appears to be significantly less than that of stocks (2.83% vs 4.22%), the standard deviation (level of volatility, or risk) of common stocks is five times that of property.

Source: AEW Research

loan institutions who funded their long term credit obligations with short term depositor savings. At that time when yields on alternative investments (i.e., T- bills) surpassed those allowable by thrift regulations, savers withdrew funds from passbook accounts in favor of other investment options. S & L's were unable to satisfy the increased demand for real estate credit nor fund their existing long term mortgage obligations. By contrast, it was felt that the long term nature of real estate holdings was a more appropriate matching of maturities with the payout structure of pension funds. Many felt that a closer alignment of the sources and uses of funds targeted to real estate could provide greater capital stability over time.

Lacking the industry knowledge, or the in-house information and management systems to perform their own due diligence and make direct real estate investments, fiduciaries of tax exempt funds turned to other industry players for management and advisory services. As their demand for the hard asset heated up, an increasing supply of investment vehicles were developed and dedicated to the needs of pension fund managers. Thus began the engines which drove the potential investment of billions of new dollars into the real estate industry.

INSTITUTIONAL INVESTMENT AND ADVISORY FIRMS

Life insurance companies were one of the first institutions to act as financial intermediaries to trusteed funds. Pension funds invested a small percentage of their assets in large open end commingled funds which were set up to acquire and manage real estate investments. The purchase of shares in these pooled trusts allowed fiduciaries of tax exempt assets to make equity investments in a diversified portfolio of properties—typically unmortgaged, investment grade real estate in major domestic markets. Unlike direct equity investment in real estate, there was some measure of liquidity in that, within limits, and given normal market conditions, provision was made for the regular redemption or repurchase of the invested shares, and the acquisition of additional shares. Life insurance companies managed these funds on behalf of their clients for fees which approximated 1% of invested assets.

The first account aggressively marketed to pension funds was Prudential Insurance Company of America's PRISA (Prudential Real Estate Investment Separate Account), begun in 1970. It was copied by others, but still commanded nearly 70% of the $1.3 billion market in 1975. By 1990 PRISA had $5 billion of assets under management for a client base of over 200 investors. In 1991, Equitable, then the largest pension fund manager, managed $11 billion in real estate assets for pension funds, out of a total real estate portfolio of $35 billion.

Ten Largest Tax Exempt Managers Ranked by Total Real Estate Assets
September, 1991

FIRM	$ MILLIONS
Equitable Real Estate	11,455
JMB Institutional	9,981
Copley Real Estate Advisors	9,225
Heitman Advisory	6,870
Prudential Asset	5,634
LaSalle Advisors	5,120
GE Investments	4,998
Yarmouth Group	4,700
Aetna Life & Casualty	4,464
AEW	4,450

Source: Pensions & Investment Age, September 1991

As pension funds demanded increasingly diversified investment options, the field of competitors and product offerings became more complex. Large syndication firms who had been heavy suppliers of real estate credit on behalf of individual investors courted pension fund clients. Bank trust departments and other intermediaries established commingled accounts, limited partnerships, REITS, and provided real estate advisory services to funds. Full service real estate companies such as Coldwell Banker entered the field with specialized offerings, mortgage products, and other equity investment options. Rosenberg Capital Management introduced one of the first and largest closed end funds, RREEF (Rosenberg Real Estate Equity Fund), which was specifically created and managed for pension funds.[2] Life insurance companies broadened their product offerings as well. Aetna, for example, introduced a participating mortgage fund as a new investment vehicle. In 1976, the Boston Company developed a Private

[2]Closed end funds were typically smaller than open end funds, with a predetermined investment life, and a cap on invested capital. Income was generally distributed on an annual basis, though appreciation returns were generally paid out only upon the dissolution of the fund.

Direct Investment Account which allowed for its various pension fund clients to participate in specific deals.

By 1991, approximately 4-5% of pension funds assets were invested in real estate, amounting to slightly under $100 billion (See **Exhibits 13-4 and 13-5**). As managers of tax exempt assets achieved greater understanding of the investment performance characteristics of real estate, and as they came closer to reaching targeted asset allocation goals, pension fund managers developed increasingly specific requirements, looking for the optimal asset mix to balance their real estate portfolios. Managers were aware that investment grade real estate trading at reasonable rates had become difficult to find, as the overflow of capital, decreased demand for high dollar space, declining absorption, and overbuilding—particularly of office space—had driven returns down. Funds began to look at those properties or market areas which in the past might have been perceived as riskier investments, i.e., smaller retail centers, apartments, industrial properties, or even raw land, rather than the "trophy" office buildings and major shopping malls which were the institutional investment staple of the eighties. Some, as well, were willing to invest at the development stage as they sought to achieve higher returns.

Sophisticated decision making tools developed oftentimes for use in financial markets were used to support the construction of optimal investment models. Insofar as pension funds were used to hiring managers to evaluate the performance of their portfolios of stocks and bonds, these models were readily understandable to fund managers. Not all firms, however, were convinced of their usefulness.

For example, some firms felt that the constructs of Modern Portfolio Theory (MPT) provided an appropriate device for making investment evaluations. MPT looked at any given portfolio as a collective pool of assets rather than as individual properties, with a goal of maximizing asset returns for a given level of risk. In the same manner that the inclusion of real estate as a fourth asset class provided diversification to early pension fund investment portfolios, so diversified properties whose returns do not move in tandem with each other lower the systematic risk of the collective mixed asset unit. The goal is to make the most "efficient" investment choices with a combination of assets which exhibit different performance characteristics, where the year to year weighted sum of the **returns** of the portfolio compares most favorably against the weighted sum of the **variation in returns** (risk). In other words, the most efficient portfolio exhibits the lowest level of risk for the highest level of return.

MPT suggested that diversification was attained by investing in a combination of property types which exhibited different performance characteristics—a balance of geographically diverse properties of different types, sizes, or ages, with varying lease structures, with tenants of different industries, or locations in cities whose economies depended on fundamentally different bases. For example, the investment in property in both Las Vegas, Nevada or Atlantic City, New Jersey does not really eliminate systematic portfolio risk if the economies of both cities are dependent on the entertainment/gambling industry.

Property Type Efficient Frontier

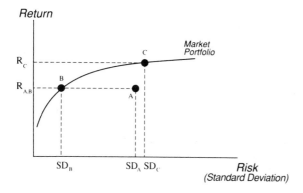

In comparing two groups of assets with identical average returns, portfolio B has a much lower level of risk. Therefore, on a risk adjusted basis, portfolio B is said to outperform portfolio A. Source: Prudential Real Estate Investors, The Portfolio Construction Process, Charles H. Wurtzebach. © 1988 Prudential Realty Group—Institutional Investment Management.

Institutional advisory and investment players looked for strategic niches, and supplied products to satisfy the increasingly specific needs of funds. Their portfolio offerings differed by *types of properties*—industrial, retail, office; or *stage of investment*—raw land, developmental joint ventures, or fully leased completed buildings; *diversification strategy*—by geography, market, length of leases, degree of risk within each fund; *investment forms*—limited partnerships, commingled funds, separate accounts, or *type of financing*—equity, straight debt, or debt with equity kickers.

THE DECISION

Three very different firms—Zell/Equity, Aldrich, Eastman, and Waltch, and Drever Partners—had been identified by Jones as potential property fund managers. Each had found extremely profitable opportunities in what others perceived to be a difficult investment market. Though Jones had had impressive meetings with each over the past several months, she wondered whether their presentations would be persuasive enough to convince her committee to release new funds for real estate investment. She was aware that many felt that the current climate was not one where pioneering investment strategies were likely to be looked favorably upon. Members of her committee and other trustees of the corporation were increasingly calling upon her to justify even current levels of real estate allocations. Out of weeks of discussions, Jones had distilled some of their major concerns, and had developed some guidelines for evaluating further investments. She had also prepared an RFP detailing a range of items which she expected each firm to address in its presentations. A brief synopsis follows.

Investment Concerns

1. Why should we invest, or allocate more dollars into real estate? Is this a good time to be in real estate?
2. How can we attain our real estate investment objectives—a 5-6% yield over inflation? What part, if any, should real estate assets play in our overall portfolio mix?
3. How can your firm achieve greater balance within our portfolio? How would you provide appropriate investment vehicles, product types, or markets for MCF? What form should investments take—closed end funds, separate accounts, limited partnership interests?
4. How can you help us more closely measure and monitor the performance of our invested funds in real estate? How do you implement control and reporting strategies to evaluate performance objectives?

Real Estate Manager Selection Criteria

Background of Firm/Individuals
Philosophy/strategy
Organizational structure
Financial strength
Real estate expertise
Major activities of firm to date
Investment performance
Ability to work with clients
Conflicts of interest

Investment Vehicle
Number of investors/properties
Ownership form
Funding procedures
Financial structuring
Partnership structure
Investment horizon
Target return/risk
Fee structure/reimbursements

Investment Strategy
Property/market types
Diversification/asset mix
Other real estate products
Investment Stage

Acquisition Ability
Due diligence capability
Sources of deal flow
Negotiations/Pricing

Asset/Property Management
In house services
Marketing/exit strategy
Tenant relations
MIS/reporting format
Value creation plan
Valuation procedures
Investor Communications

Each of the three finalists were asked to make presentations to the Finance Committee detailing its firm's investment approach, and how it could address the needs of MCF. Jones felt pressured to make a strong recommendation to the larger corporate board this month as to the direction MCF would pursue in its portfolio investments, and hoped that this meeting would be instrumental in helping her make a decision. Though her compensation was not directly related to the performance of MCF's investment portfolio, her quarterly review was not far off, and the Mazda Miata she had her eye on depended on a sizable bonus.

ZELL/EQUITY

Founded by real estate entrepreneur Sam Zell, Equity Financial and Management Company is a Chicago-based real estate organization which owns and operates a national portfolio of residential and commercial properties. Zell/Equity has been engaged in the acquisition, development, ownership, management, financing, and disposition of real estate since 1968. It currently has controlling interests in more than 275 real estate projects nationwide, which are valued at approximately $5 billion, making the firm one of the largest owner/operators of real estate in the country. This portfolio includes approximately 14 million square feet of office space, more than 20 million square feet of retail space, approximately 34,000 apartment units, and 44 mobile home communities.

Acquisition decisions are made in Chicago by a group of 17 people supported by 117 professionals. Property development, management, and leasing functions are organized on a more decentralized basis from 18 regional offices consisting of 401 professionals and a property management staff of more than 1600.

In 1988, the firm teamed up with Merrill Lynch Capital Markets to form a limited partnership for real estate investment. Merrill Lynch is a preeminent global securities firm and is a leader in real estate investment banking. During 1989 Merrill Lynch completed 57 real estate related transactions globally, totalling more than $11 billion in value. It was agreed that the vast brokerage network of Merrill Lynch combined with Zell/Equity's own strengths in real estate acquisition and management would allow them to successfully market a large, national investment fund. By August 1988 Opportunity Partners I was formed with equity capital commitments of $408 million.

Following its success, Zell/Equity and Merrill Lynch again pooled their resources to sponsor a new limited partnership, Opportunity Partners II, in 1990-91. As with OP I, the fund was formed to take advantage of investment opportunities in the troubled real estate market, primarily by acquiring properties owned by entities seeking to redeploy capital or experiencing financial difficulties.

For the 22 years of its existence, Zell/Equity's investment focus has been enhancing the value of underperforming real estate assets. Its investment philosophy has been based on a combination of "replacement cost" theory and risk analysis. The firm considered replacement cost to be the ultimate determining factor of real estate value. According to the firm, " As excess supply of space is absorbed, market rents must eventually generate investment returns sufficient to justify new construction. When this occurs, existing buildings of comparable quality will command similar rents. In addition, purchasing a real estate asset at a discount to replacement costs permits a building owner to offer tenants lower effective rents while providing comparable services. Occupancy increases and the achievement of market rents will generate above market returns."

In addition to identifying and acquiring "opportunistic" real estate assets with significant long term appreciation potential, properties were enhanced through intensive asset management, capital restructuring, repositioning, redevelopment, expansion, and capital infusions. In 1992, Zell/Equity believed that strategic portfolio acquisitions would be available on increasingly favorable terms, as financial institutions continued to accelerate and simplify their divestitures of real estate.

Opportunity Partners II was formed to invest in office, residential, retail, and industrial properties. Its primary objective is to realize an internal rate of return for investors of 15% to 20% during an investment period of at least ten years. One limited partner of Opportunity Partners II is a private (not publicly traded) real estate investment trust (REIT).[3] Taxable partners can invest in OP II directly as limited partners, or indirectly through the REIT. All tax-exempt entities will invest in Opportunity Partners II by purchasing shares in the REIT.

Upon a sale or refinancing, Opportunity Partners II will provide the owners of invested shares (the capital partners) with a cumulative compounded return of 9%. If inflation exceeds 4%, the 9% return will go up. After the preferred return, the managing partner will then be paid 15% of the excess cash proceeds, and the capital partners will be entitled to the 85% balance until they have received an aggregate cumulative compounded preferred return of 13% (again adjusted by increases in the CPI over 4%). Thereafter, the capital partners will receive about 75% of any additional excess cash flow.

Equity capital commitment from limited partners will be a minimum of $250 million. Zell/Equity and Merrill Lynch agreed to commit the greater of $25 million or 2.5% of the limited partners' equity capital commitments. The general partner's back end share is expected to average 25% of profits, after the capital partners have received back their original invested capital and their preferred return.

Affiliates of Zell/ Equity will receive an acquisition fee of 1.5% of the purchase price of each property, and an annual asset management fee of .75%, based on the original purchase price of each asset. The firm expects to create significant value over the long term by aggressive asset management. Zell/Equity and Merrill Lynch agree to actively pursue opportunities to sell the properties as appropriate, but no later than the tenth year.

OP II's investment criteria for acquisitions is as follows:

Properties which have a history of poor management, are in need of rehabilitation and/or are experiencing occupancy and financial problems.

Properties whose owners are experiencing significant financial difficulties or regulatory restrictions which adversely affect their ability to own and operate the property.

Properties owned by financial institutions seeking to return capital to other uses.

---

[3] Real Estate Investment Trusts are business trusts, normally managed by professional independent advisors for a fee, which invest in a pool of properties or mortgages, and distribute the income annually to shareholders. Some are publicly traded, and act in effect as a mutual fund for the small investor.

Properties located in regions where geography or governmental policies restrict current or future competition.

Properties located in economically depressed regions.

Founder Sam Zell was confident that his organization possessed the talent, experience, and sufficient capital to successfully execute OP II's distinctive investment strategy. Zell's orientation was entrepreneurial and opportunistic. His success in what many perceived to be high risk investment strategies was undisputed. His turnaround strategy was applied to acquisitions ranging from troubled apartment buildings to undervalued companies, bought and sold at tremendous profits to investors. Zell's net worth was recently estimated by Forbes Magazine at over $400 million; his ability to profit from the instability of troubled markets in a number of investment areas was legendary.

But, Jones wondered, were these the right investments for her firm? She knew that the ownership of shares in REITs by any individual is subject to a cap, according to the "Five Person Rule" which stated that no fewer than five stockholders could control 50% of a REIT's stock. Pension funds, which were currently treated by law as a single person, were restricted in their ownership position to less than 10% of a REIT's stock. Though there was some industry lobbying to remove that restriction for institutional investors, it was not clear if and when the legislative restrictions would change. How would that affect her buy/sell position? Would investment in multiple REITs require extensive monitoring/administration/her own management time?

Should MCF be in the workout investment realm? Though Jones knew that many, if not most of Zell's acquisitions were institutional quality assets less than five years old, there was a large disparity between Zell/Equity's typical portfolio, and what her committee might consider to be conservative investments. And, though very intrigued by the potential profits to be made from distressed properties, she knew it was extremely difficult to predict the timing of market recovery, and the performance of assets over time.

ALDRICH, EASTMAN AND WALTCH

Aldrich, Eastman, and Waltch of Boston has created and managed real estate portfolios for pension plans, endowments, and other large investors for over 10 years. In that time it has become a significant player in the U.S. market, employing over 190 people, and having over $4 billion in institutional equity assets under management in both separate accounts (which currently account for over 90% of AEW's assets under management) and commingled investment funds. Of the 190 employees, approximately 140 were real estate and related professionals, over 40 of whom participated in the ownership and profit sharing of the firm.

The rapid growth of the firm was attributed in part to the depth of its research and advisory services, which allowed it to work in collaboration with

AEW Investment Performance 1985-1990

	1985	1986	1987	1988	1989	1990
Income	11.8%	11.3%	10.3%	8.8%	8.1%	7.8%
Apprec.	0.5%	2.6%	3.7%	3.2%	1.0%	(6.0%)
Total	**12.3%**	**13.9%**	**14.0%**	**12.3%**	**9.3%**	**1.5%**
FRC Prop. Index	9.8%	6.3%	5.3%	7.1%	6.0%	1.2%
CPI	3.8%	1.1%	4.4%	4.4%	4.8%	6.1%

Source: Aldrich, Eastman, and Waltch

each prospective client in developing long term portfolio objectives, identifying acquisition opportunities, and structuring appropriate investment vehicles to maximize those opportunities. Over time a range of product offerings and investment tools were developed to respond to changing market needs, changing capital circumstances, and changing investor preferences. This creativity led to impressive relative returns, and, the firm felt, well managed risk.

AEW felt that optimal performance depended on three key factors—strategic property selection, sound deal structuring, and pro-active asset management. Toward that end, AEW was organized into four functional groups—Clients, Portfolios, Investments, and Operations.

Within each functional area, various subgroups performed specific responsibilities. Asset management, for example, was one of them. With increasing controls on development, and demographics that argued for limited revenue growth nationwide, AEW felt strongly that asset management was the key to profitable property performance, particularly in a mature market where growth was minimal and competition for market share intense. The firm felt that tremendous value could be added over the life of a property through aggressive monitoring of project performance. Its asset management approach was threefold:

> On-site *facilities management* teams from the locality who implemented operating, leasing, and capital improvement programs designed by AEW;
> *Financial management* which dealt with capital and ownership structuring, acquisitions and disposition;
> Focused *marketing management*—market research, strategy, positioning and implementation.

Working with a number of brokers, developer/partners, and owners nationwide, AEW invested directly in the real estate private markets on behalf of its clients. In 1991 its asset management portfolio was valued at $11 billion (including equity plus debt), with 206 properties in 36 states—35% office, 42% retail, 12% industrial, 8% multifamily, and 2% hotels. New business initiatives had targeted an increased presence in multifamily rental properties in selected regional markets, and single tenant commercial properties.

Business Overview Portfolio Composition

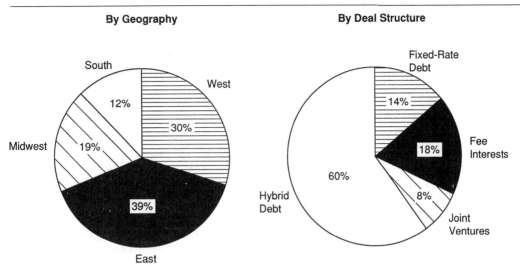

By Geography

South 12%
West 30%
Midwest 19%
39%
East

By Deal Structure

Fixed-Rate Debt 14%
Fee Interests 18%
Hybrid Debt 60%
Joint Ventures 8%

Source: Aldrich, Eastman, and Waltch

Throughout the 1980s AEW focused on highly structured deals. Not all acquisitions were all equity, and leverage was often used to create larger and more diverse portfolios. The firm offered investment programs that utilized hybrid debt and equity vehicles (participating mortgages, convertible debentures or shared appreciation products, to name a few) as well as joint ventures, straight fee ownership, limited partnerships, or other pooled interests. The firm felt that the financial products they offered ensured that its clients could earn a competitive return under varying market scenarios. As there was a large upfront management commitment by AEW in structuring these offerings, the firm typically charged an acquisition fee, an asset management fee, and a disposition fee upon sale. Industry-wide competition for pension fund dollars had put downward pressure on fees; with each new product offering AEW expected to negotiate the firm's compensation.

By 1991, AEW knew that the market dynamics that had favored their strategy during the past decade had changed dramatically. Moreover, AEW saw opportunities in the changing real estate climate that it felt would grow to be major sources of pension fund returns in the future. Though some initiatives were in their infancy, the firm felt that these new investment vehicles would give it a competitive edge over other industry players.

While the firm was aware that there was a vast segment of its clients who were unlikely to allocate more dollars into real estate, AEW felt that it had a strong case for pension funds to increase their presence in the real estate markets. When clients called, anxious about the markdowns of their existing portfolios, they were invariably answered, " For a long term saver, for retirement savings, the key to wealth isn't the investment decision today. The value of a property today is less important than the capacity of an asset to produce income and wealth *over time*, and the ability of the recipient of that to *reinvest* at any point in time." As a result of strategic new business initiatives, AEW had received over a half billion dollars in new allocations from both existing and new clients in 1991.

AEW was exploring a number of new investment options. One was the entrance into the over $1 trillion commercial and multifamily mortgage market through the acquisition of existing portfolios of mortgages. In 1991 the flow of funds into commercial and multifamily mortgages was less than any in the previous forty years. Though pension funds had been heavy investors in the $1.3 trillion corporate bond market, they had participated only minimally in the commercial mortgage market. By contrast, life insurance companies, whose investment profiles were not significantly different from those of pension funds, had invested over $200 billion in the commercial mortgage market.

To capitalize on what the firm felt to be an extraordinary market opportunity, AEW acquired Secured Capital of Los Angeles in 1990, a firm specializing in the underwriting and marketing of pools of mortgages. AEW felt that pools of commercial mortgages offered excellent investment opportunities with pricing and yield characteristics which would be of great appeal to fund managers (See **Exhibit 13-6.**). As the majority of AEW's capital under management was for clients who invested in excess of $100 million with the firm, typically in separate accounts, a pool of mortgages in its entirety could be acquired on behalf of any one client. Net yields on pools of small commercial loans obtained through secondary market offerings were expected to be 90-130 basis points higher than the large commercial loans which had formed much of the basis for mortgage investment over the last decade. With their predictable cash flow patterns, relatively long term maturity, and underlying security characteristics they could provide an appropriate match for pension funds whose contingent liabilities stretched far into the future.

In addition, AEW felt that the involuntary downsizing of commercial banks, and the loan and asset portfolios of the RTC and FDIC[4] as lenders of last resort created opportunities to acquire portfolios in the secondary market at a sizeable discount to value. AEW had taken the time to explain how this worked to Jones in one of their past meetings. For example, the head of the Portfolio Management team said, flipping to his chart, " Let's take a look at a simple case. The RTC holds a $750,000 portfolio of performing commercial mortgages secured by properties initially valued at $1,000,000. These mortgages are currently performing, and the RTC is receiving 10% annually in debt service, or $75,000. New appraisals have placed property values closer to $800,000. However, AEW as the highest bidder, may be able to procure this pool of mortgages for $600,000 from the RTC, who is anxious to inject needed capital into the banking system.

AEW receives on an annual cash basis the debt service payments of $75,000

---

[4]The Resolution Trust Company (RTC) and the Federal Deposit Insurance Corporation (FDIC) were charged with the resolution of the problems of the nation's insolvent banks through recapitalization, asset disposition, and restructuring.

on a capital outlay of $600,000, garnering a 12.5% return on what we feel to be a very conservatively underwritten investment. In fact, to divide the financing even further, AEW, might borrow $200,000 against the properties from a third party at 10%, for which the third party receives $20,000 annually. AEW's clients, however, would then receive a $55,000 current yield on an investment of $400,000, or 13.8%."

Though she was very intrigued by the firm's analysis, Jones knew that no investment was without risk. It seemed to her that valuation of these numerous small mortgages would be difficult, particularly for those mortgages which included floating rate obligations, that shares were relatively illiquid, and that the possibility of default and delinquency affected the guarantee of high yields.

Another avenue was to buy portfolios of the foreclosed properties themselves. As of March 1991, the RTC owned more than $160 billion in assets, and was beginning an aggressive disposition program. AEW felt that the plethora of distressed properties on the market created lucrative investment opportunities for institutional investors to acquire properties at significantly below book value. AEW knew it would have to overcome some investor reluctance. Many fund managers perceived these properties to be extremely risky, and to require enormous due diligence. The vast majority of RTC properties were not of institutional quality, and were poorly located or concentrated in specific areas of the country. As future values were heavily dependent on expectations of inflating rents and extremely uncertain future economics, strict performance control and intensive property management would likely be required.

There were some legislative obstacles to the firm's strategies. Current legislation discouraged pension funds from acquiring real estate assets which utilized seller financing, which, in the case of RTC properties, was often available at extremely advantageous borrowing rates. Domestic pension funds, whose earnings were otherwise tax exempt, were taxed on the income from investments which included seller financing or contingent purchase prices. With a range of nontaxable investment alternatives, attracting pension fund dollars might be difficult without more favorable legislative treatment.

The firm was lobbying on the industry level for legislative reform which would facilitate pension fund investment into these areas. For example, one effort was directed at lessening the restrictions for tax exempt institutions to invest in REITS. It was felt that publicly traded REITs offered a number of advantages for institutional investors. The current economic climate had taught many fund managers the value of an ability to restructure their portfolio emphasis to respond to market conditions. Investment in a REIT, a publicly traded security, offered the opportunity to purchase a measurable fee interest, with easy valuation and liquidity, and to have an in-place exit structure. AEW felt that if banks were able to shift their liquid assets into a REIT, or diminish the size of their mortgage portfolios, the ability of pension funds to recapitalize the market would be enormous.

The firm, in these and other lobbying efforts, knew it had behind it the resources of the powerful Pension Real Estate Association, and the support of many significant industry players. AEW hoped that it was just a question of time.

DREVER PARTNERS

Drever Partners was formed in 1985 and since that time has specialized in the acquisition of multi-unit rental housing. Prior to that time the predecessor organization to Drever Partners—Drever, McIntosh, and Co., Inc.—had invested approximately $100 million in properties in Denver, Columbus, Tampa, Dallas, and Memphis in the period from 1971-1981, all of which were sold by 1985. The compound annual return to investors was approximately 23%.

As a hands-on entrepreneurial firm, Drever looked for depressed but rebounding markets where the firm could buy at favorable acquisition prices, and where the potential for value added management was high. Typically, in such a market, the firm was one of the few investors with sufficient capital to both acquire *and* improve properties. Its acquisitions, therefore, enjoyed a competitive position in the marketplace. The firm looked for properties which would benefit from new product positioning, enhancements, and active property management. Each of the firm's seven principals and other key people participated in the profits of the firm.

Maxwell Drever, the president, had identified a number of promising markets, where he felt there was a supply of undervalued multifamily real estate that could be significantly enhanced. Through an analysis of industrial and office leasing activity (both gross and net), employment indicators, and measurements of economic growth, the firm identified those markets where properties could be purchased at a substantial discount to replacement cost, and where rents were expected to rise rapidly. It then targeted specific properties of interest to the firm. In 1991, Drever concentrated its acquisitions primarily in Austin, Phoenix, Dallas and Houston. As the economies within those cities rebounded, housing demand was expected to escalate, and occupancy levels to rise. This, combined with a limited supply of new housing and construction invariably put upward pressure on rental rates. In Houston, for example, Drever Partners had acquired almost 7,700 units in 36 apartment projects since 1987. In the words of Mike Masterson, SVP, "The linchpins of this system are identifying the right time in a market's down cycle to begin buying, selecting sound properties in affluent areas, and then negotiating favorable terms of purchase to produce acquisitions at a fraction of replacement cost."

Within those markets, specific acquisition criteria were outlined. The firm targeted upscale developments less than twelve years old in good locations which would benefit by physical upgrading, corrections to deferred maintenance, and new product positioning. Drever expected that acquisitions would be made primarily from distressed sellers. Once a property was acquired, the firm's in-house construction arm spent from $1,250 to $10,000 per unit in redevelopment, averaging $7,000 per unit in 1991. It was Drever's experience that enhancements to the properties and hands-on property management were extremely cost effective, and could dramatically alter the revenue structure of the project. From a competitive standpoint, the projects were perceived favorably by consumers who were impressed by the new capital investments being made. Rental collection increases in their previous projects averaged 17%, with a corresponding increase in investment value. In Houston, averages were closer to 25%. It was expected, though, that as the projects and submarkets stabilized the rate of increase would naturally moderate.

The new more marketable apartment complexes offered specialized property management which emphasized customized attention—concierge and maintenance services, discounts at local businesses, laundry pickup, car washes, evening concert series, or door to door trash pickup, to name a few. Jones was impressed with the firm's long term commitment to its properties. She felt that those firms which played the dual role of in house asset/property management brought to the table an ownership perspective which resulted in a more timely flow of information, allowing them to pre-empt potential erosions in rental income, insulate the project from tenant loss, and focus on the long term value of the property, not the short term cash flows.

Since February 1987 Drever had acquired thirty six properties in the Houston area and five others in Austin, Dallas and Phoenix, for a total of 8,908 units and $230 million in total investment. Per unit purchase prices ranged from $17,970 to slightly over $25,000. In the Houston area, in 1991 it was estimated that replacement costs for comparable apartment complexes would reach slightly over $40,000 per unit.

In 1991, Drever created the Apartment Opportunity Fund, a limited partnership formed to invest a minimum of $50 million and a maximum of $100 million of equity capital over a two year period on behalf of tax exempt institutional and selected private investors, in a number of targeted markets. The fund would carry a seven year investment term (with a three year extension contingent upon the approval of a majority of limited partners). As General Partner, Drever Partners would acquire properties for the fund until all capital was fully invested, and would improve, manage, and ultimately sell them for the fund's investors. Drever had also committed to invest its own capital in the fund, in this case a minimum of $1 million. It felt that maximum leverage of 50% of the total capitalization of the fund was prudent, and that capitalization of up to $100 million provided excellent market presence for negotiating acquisitions.

The key features of the fund are:

Diversification into four or more targeted markets
Conservative leverage with portfolio debt no greater than 50% of acquisition costs
A targeted internal rate of return of 18% net to investors over a 4-7 year time frame
Fee structure based primarily on back end participation in profits and an annual asset management fee covering only portfolio overhead cost (amounting to approximately 2% of invested capital), with no acquisition or disposition fees

Yale University was the lead investor in the fund. Yale's investment team had a reputation for seeking out innovative firms in the industry, a strategy which had been well rewarded by the yields it had obtained over the last decade. In August, 1991 it offered to provide interim financing of $10 million, which would allow Drever to acquire several representative properties prior to marketing the fund. Additional institutional and private investors would contribute the balance of the equity capital. At that point Yale's capital would be converted into an ownership position proportional to its interest in the total capital raised.

Yale felt that regional discontinuities within the larger U.S. economic climate of 1991 created many opportunities for advantageous purchases of multifamily housing developments. With its market knowledge, existing purchase contracts at locked in prices, and experience in the industry, it appeared that Drever had a jump start on much of the competition.

SUMMARY

Jones knew that there were members of her committee who still harbored fundamental objections to the addition of real estate assets to MCF's investment portfolio, and, she had to admit, some of their reasons were valid. She was concerned about the availability of investment capital from the fund, particularly if the closed end fund in which they had invested was not liquidated this year as planned. What happens as a closed end fund reaches maturity in a weak market? Jones knew that the dissolution date was likely to be extended, with the expectation that portfolio properties would regain some of their lost value in the next three years and permit a more orderly liquidation at better prices. And, though she felt it unlikely, it was possible that a capital call would be asked of current investors. What should be her response? What is an appropriate exit strategy for her current funds? How would that affect MCF's decision to allocate new funds?

The current investment climate had underscored one of the fundamental concerns which recurred at committee meetings with some frequency—the evaluation of portfolio worth of both current properties and prospective acquisitions. Jones was repeatedly asked to justify the performance of her real estate investments. She asked herself, how can pension funds evaluate the comparative returns of real estate versus those of other asset classes? In the absence of a perfect exchange of buy and sell, how can one determine the true value of property? Even in those funds which provide some provision for the redemption of invested shares, real estate is still largely illiquid. Given a projected return, should some discount be taken to reflect the lack of liquidity relative to other investments? Or is the question of liquidity even relevant to pension fund investment? In the evaluation of existing portfolios, or potential property acquisitions, appraisers looked at the current income, and made adjustments based on their expectation of market—in a market undergoing uncertainties such as those in the 1990s how subjective are those appraisals? At the macro level, will the 1990s be a period of low inflation, an economic scenario in which real estate values do less well?

Many committee members felt that funds should have a greater stake in the decision making and investment process, or greater control over the performance of their property funds. Jones knew that some of her counterparts in the industry were being more pro-active in managing their portfolios, insisting on appraisals updated monthly, reports on individual properties, or rights of approval over major leases, capital improvements, and refinancing or sale. What level of involvement is appropriate for her committee? With currently only 3% of assets invested in real estate, is that a meaningful amount sufficient for Jones to justify management time—in terms of generating the in-house expertise to thoroughly understand a complex and fragmented industry?

And, more immediately, what advisory firm(s) would provide the best fit for MCF? On what criteria should she base her determination? While product and portfolio considerations were certainly key, Jones knew that in a collaborative endeavor such as this the people issues were equally important. The size of the firm, its organizational structure, its ability to be responsive to MCF would all be critical to her deicision making.

Jones knew that this meeting would be pivotal in informing and advising MCF of current opportunities for real estate investment. It would then be up to a vote as to whether any or all of the presenters would have a stake in MCF's investment future, and if so, how much, and in what form?

Exhibit 13-1   *Russell-NCREIF Index Property Type Returns*

		INDEX	APTMNT	OFFICE	RETAIL	R&D/ OFFICE	W'HSE
	Income	6.6	7.1	6.0	6.3	7.4	7.3
	Appreciation	−1.2	0.1	−4.0	2.9	−2.5	1.4
1990	Total	5.3	7.2	1.9	9.4	4.7	8.7
	Income	6.9	6.8	6.5	6.9	7.4	7.6
	Appreciation	−0.2	−1.3	−2.5	6.3	−2.9	2.0
1989	Total	6.7	5.4	3.8	13.5	4.3	9.7
	Income	7.1		6.5	7.1	7.5	7.9
	Appreciation	−0.1		−3.9	5.8	0.0	3.8
1988	Total	7.0		2.4	13.1	7.5	11.9
	Income	7.0		6.7	6.9	7.5	7.9
	Appreciation	−2.2		−5.6	4.0	−1.2	0.7
1987	Total	4.7		0.8	11.1	6.2	8.6
	Income	7.5		7.2	7.5	7.9	7.9
	Appreciation	1.4		0.3	3.4	1.5	3.7
1986	Total	9.0		7.6	11.1	9.5	11.8
	Income	7.4		7.0	8.0	8.1	8.0
	Appreciation	3.0		2.0	5.3	3.3	4.0
1985	Total	10.6		9.1	13.7	11.7	12.3
	Income	7.4		6.7	8.5	8.2	7.6
	Appreciation	7.8		8.2	8.1	14.4	3.9
1984	Total	15.7		15.3	17.1	23.4	11.7

Exhibit 13-2

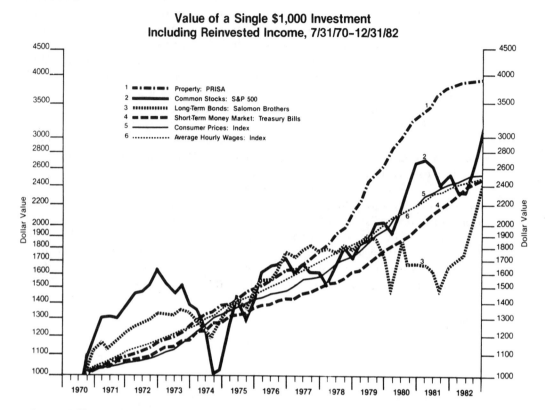

Value of a Single $1,000 Investment
Including Reinvested Income, 7/31/70–12/31/82

Source: Goldman Sachs, Our Expanding Universe, June 1983.

Exhibit 13-3 *Lowry Fund Return Indexes Annual Returns*

YEAR	REAL ESTATE OPEN END FUNDS	REAL ESTATE CLOSED END FUNDS	REAL ESTATE COMBINED FUNDS	U.S. EQUITY FUNDS	FIXED INCOME FUNDS	MONEY MARKET FUNDS
1980	14.17%		14.17%	31.96%	2.38%	12.72%
1981	16.84%		16.84%	−0.82%	5.18%	17.25%
1982	9.43%		9.43%	25.11%	29.81%	12.57%
1983	13.50%	14.18%	13.79%	20.31%	11.43%	8.66%
1984	12.38%	14.50%	13.28%	−1.60%	10.01%	10.00%
1985	9.62%	10.18%	9.84%	26.80%	20.47%	7.69%
1986	7.90%	9.90%	8.67%	13.13%	12.05%	6.21%
1987	5.31%	8.08%	6.38%	0.90%	1.09%	6.04%
1988	4.69%	10.93%	7.07%	14.02%	8.94%	7.11%
1989	1.37%	6.71%	3.04%	23.45%	7.63%	8.53%
1987-89 Three Years	3.79%	8.57%	5.50%	12.70%	5.89%	7.23%
1980-89 Ten Years	9.52%		10.25%	15.33%	10.90%	9.68%

Source: The Lowry Fund. Copyright © 1991, Communication Channels, Inc., Atlanta, GA USA.

Exhibit 13-4 *Pension Fund Asset Mix December, 1991*

TYPE OF INVESTMENT	CORPORATE FUNDS	PUBLIC FUNDS	ENDOWMENTS AND FOUNDATIONS
Common Stocks	46.7%	49.1%	49.1%
Marketable Bonds	27.2	43.0	34.5
Cash and other Short Term Investments	8.3	9.0	8.0
Equity Real Estate	5.4	4.5	3.7
International Stocks	5.8	2.9	4.6
Guaranteed Investment Contracts	6.7	.5	.1

Source: Greenwich Associates, Greenwich, Conn. Copyright © 1991.

Exhibit 13-5   *Total Real Estate Capital by Source (Billions)*

Distribution of Real
Estate Capital, 1989

Pensions	2.6%
Financial Institutions	19.4
Foreign Investors	1.2
Securities	2.5
Corporations	74.3
TOTAL	100.0%

Pension funds, with almost $100 billion invested, have overtaken the weakening real estate securities sector as a source of real estate capital.

	1980	1981	1982	1983	1984	1985	1986	1987	1988	1989
Pension Funds	$ 19.0	30.2	40.1	49.5	56.1	63.7	73.3	87.8	89.8	99.6
Financial Institutions	238.8	262.3	287.7	335.6	402.5	466.8	546.4	652.0	702.2	755.7
Foreign Investors	7.3	10.7	13.5	17.2	20.7	22.8	26.2	31.8	40.0	45.9
Real Estate Securities	15.2	19.4	24.9	34.2	49.4	64.3	77.7	90.4	98.4	98.8
Corporations	1,514	1,748	1,871	2,054	2,281	2,460	2,556	2,629	2,766	2,890
TOTAL	$ 1,795	2,071	2,238	2,490	2,810	3,078	3,281	3,491	3,697	3,890

Corporate real estate almost doubled between 1980 and 1990, increasing by nearly $1.4 trillion.

The $6 billion growth in direct foreign investment was $2 billion less than in 1988, but higher than in any prior year.

Change from 1988 in Total Real Estate Capital

	Billions	Share of Change
Pensions	$ 9.8	5.1%
Financial Institutions	53.5	27.6
Foreign Inv.	5.9	3.1
Securities	0.4	0.2
Corporations	124.0	64.0
TOTAL	193.6	100.0

Source: The Roulac Group of Deloitte and Touche, in *Real Estate Capital Flows, 1990*, Equitable Real Estate Investment Management, Inc.

Exhibit 13-6   *Gross Spreads of Various Debt Obligations and Treasury Bonds*

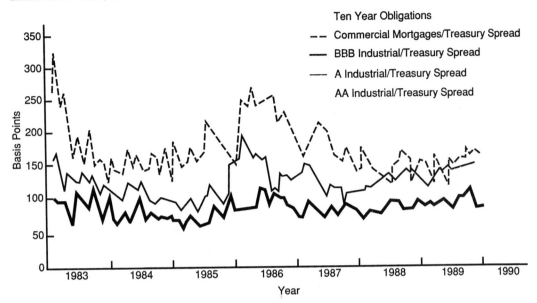

Commercial mortgage yields have consistently exceeded investment grade corporate bond yields from 1983-1989. *Source:* Reprinted from *Real Estate Review* (New York, Warren, Gorham, and Lamont), © 1991 Research Institute of America, Inc. Used with permission.

14

THE GLOBAL FUND

In January, 1989, Bob Riley, the new Chairman of the Prudential Realty Group, has to decide if Prudential should proceed with the creation of a $2-3 billion global real estate investment fund. Both domestic and international real estate markets are changing rapidly. Does it make sense to invest globally? If it does make sense, what types of properties and locations should Prudential target, and how should it structure and manage the fund?

Discussion Questions:

1. Does global real estate investment make sense for major institutional investors? For Prudential?
2. Where should the fund be invested? What types of properties should the fund invest in? What guidelines should be established?
3. How should the fund be structured? What are the issues? Who should make the decisions? What role should Prudential itself play?
4. Who are the logical investors for this fund? What marketing strategy should be used to attract their participation?
5. Should Prudential attempt to manage this fund alone or should it co-venture the management?

Bob Riley, the new Chairman of the Prudential Realty Group, was clearly intrigued by the concept of a global real estate investment fund. It was early in 1989, and Riley had just finished reading a memo from outgoing Chairman Don Knab that recommended that Prudential either aggressively pursue the Global Fund concept or abandon it. It was time for a decision.

THE GLOBAL FUND

The first discussions about the Global Fund had taken place in early 1985 when Don Knab, the then chairman of the Prudential Realty Group (PRG), had met informally with an Australian institutional investor. Over dinner, they had discussed the increasing globalization of real estate and the desire of many institutional real estate investors for a vehicle through which the institutions could invest in international properties. At that time, no such fund existed.

Throughout 1985, the senior managers at the Prudential Realty Group had met to discuss the creation of a $2-3 billion global real estate investment fund. Knab believed that changes in both the domestic and international real estate markets had created a situation in which Prudential could obtain higher yields and lower total portfolio risk by investing in international real estate markets. By creating a $2-3 billion fund as an investment vehicle, Prudential could also obtain economies of scale, diversification, and an extension of its fee based asset management business. As the fund's manager and lead investor, Prudential realized that it would be expected to invest a substantial amount from its own General Account funds.

The group's initial enthusiasm for the project had become tempered by the end of 1985 by the breadth and depth of the issues that had been identified during their discussions. The concept for the Global Fund was powerful and innovative. However, Prudential had no previous experience in international real estate. The senior managers knew that any General Account investment had to be justified on the basis of its own investment merits to Prudential's Finance Committee. They also knew that the Finance Committee would be concerned about how this new fund would affect Prudential's existing asset management business.

Research Assistant Richard E. Crum prepared this case under the supervision of Adjunct Professor William J. Poorvu as the basis for class discussion rather than to illustrate either effective or ineffective handling of an administrative situation.

Five major areas that would require additional research had been identified:

1. Does global real estate investment make sense for Prudential as an investor?
2. Who are the logical investors for this fund? What marketing strategy should be used to attract their participation?
3. Where should the fund be invested? What types of properties should the fund invest in? What guidelines should be established?
4. How should the fund be structured? What are the issues? Who should make what decisions? What role should Prudential itself play?
5. Should Prudential attempt to manage this fund alone or should it structure a management co-venture?

During 1986, Knab began conceptual discussions with an international real estate firm about becoming a co-sponsor of the Global Fund. At the same time, he met with a number of potential investors. The investors were interested in the concept but wanted to hear more details. It quickly became apparent to Knab that Prudential would have to advance funding for substantial feasibility studies and marketing costs in order to maintain control of the project. It also became clear that Prudential would have to make its own investment commitment to the project before discussions continued too much further or Prudential risked jeopardizing the credibility of the investment product it was sponsoring.

THE PRUDENTIAL REALTY GROUP

The Prudential Realty Group is a subsidiary of the Prudential Investment Corporation (PIC). PIC was formed in 1984 to transform a relatively traditional, functionally structured insurance investment operation into a federation of semiautonomous, client-driven investment management units. Between 1984 and 1987, PIC's assets under management grew from $100 billion to over $160 billion and net investment income grew at a compound annual rate of more than 10 percent.

As the real estate arm of PIC, the Prudential Realty Group manages a portfolio of equity real estate and mortgages that totals $48 billion. The Group is a substantial participant in all aspects of real estate investment, including property development, acquisitions and sales, leasing and property management, mortgage lending, and agricultural investing. It manages property and mortgage portfolios for both the General Account of the Prudential and a wide variety of outside clients. These include domestic pension plans, foreign institutions, and individual investors.

Collectively, the Prudential Realty Group includes Prudential Real Estate Investors (PREI), the Prudential Property Company (PPC), and the Prudential Mortgage Capital Company, Inc. (PMCC). These three business units work closely in providing its clients with a coordinated, full range of real estate services. Approximately 450 Realty Group professionals operate through a network of offices located in 35 different cities across the country. They are supported by in-house attorneys, accountants, architects, engineers, and marketing specialists.

Within the Prudential Realty Group, Prudential Real Estate Investors combines real estate acquisitions, sales, investment research, portfolio management, and marketing. PREI focuses on three areas: (1) acquiring outstanding properties in highly competitive markets; (2) developing new real estate investment products to sell through Prudential's marketing branches to the domestic and foreign, private and public, equity markets; (3) providing research and investment strategy recommendations on its existing portfolios.

PREI's acquisition and sales expertise is nationally recognized. Recent transactions have included the $551 million May Center Inc. corporate acquisition and the $268 million sale of the Hyatt Regency Chicago.

The largest real estate portfolio that Prudential manages for outside clients is the Prudential Property Investment Separate Account or PRISA. PRISA is a $4 billion open-end, commingled real estate equity fund that is invested in completed, well leased, income producing properties. The account is broadly diversified among the traditional types of investment grade real estate and across geographic locations and industries. Tenant lease terms vary considerably. It is considered to be a "core" portfolio of high quality properties around which an investor could build a broader real estate portfolio.

For the ten year period ending December 31, 1987, PRISA had realized an income return of 8.5% and an appreciation return of 5.13% for a total return of 13.63%. Inflation during this period was 6.37%. Prudential charges a management fee of approximately 1% of the assets in the fund. There are 219 investors in PRISA. In general, properties in the PRISA fund are wholly owned by the fund with only $220 million in debt on the properties in the portfolio.

The Prudential Property Company (PPC) develops, leases and manages the Prudential's and its clients' portfolios of properties. With an inventory of about 284 office buildings, 224 office/warehouse/R&D facilities, 309 distribution centers, 49 retail malls, and 70 hotels under management, the PPC's breadth and depth of asset management and property development is extensive.

Through its Prudential Mortgage Capital Company (PMCC) subsidiary, Prudential offers commercial real estate mortgage loans. PMCC offers loans ranging in size from $10 million to over $500 million to developers, real estate investors, and major corporations. PMCC originated over $3.5 billion in new loans in 1986 and it manages and services a $23 billion loan portfolio. Recent loans have ranged from a $430 million loan to a major corporation on a portfolio of existing properties to a $100 million construction loan to a nationally known real estate developer for the development of a trophy office building in downtown Washington, D.C. PMCC often uses complex financial structures.

THE INVESTMENT MANAGEMENT PROCESS

In order to invest globally, Riley believed that PRG had to develop or acquire the ability to do four things extremely well: (1) research; (2) portfolio management; (3) investment origination; and (4) asset management. The Global Fund's staff would have to be able to perform the necessary research to determine the investment climate in each target country. The research would encompass analyses of national and local economic conditions, currency trends, political, legislative and regulatory events, and real estate market conditions.

Portfolio management would entail having the capability to both acquire and dispose of assets in an environment of restricted market information and in the absence of long standing personal and business relationships. The solicitation of investable funds and the management of the assets at both the property and investor levels were other key capabilities that the staff would need to successfully implement the fund.

The Prudential had been active in North American real estate markets for over a hundred years and these capabilities had been carefully refined within the domestic market. Could these skills be transferred to international markets?

The parent company had offices in most major countries and had good contacts with the key financial players but it had little direct real estate investment experience overseas. The legal side of foreign ownership was complicated and he knew that his legal advisers were unlikely to give him a simple solution. Should Prudential go it alone or should it recruit a co-sponsor who was more experienced in the international arena?

Riley's staff had collected a variety of information for him. He had to decide which information to use in making his decision as well as what types of information should be collected by the fund to use in its decision making process (see **Exhibits 14-1 through 14-3** for examples).

Riley was also faced with the issue of how the PRG's international activities would impact its existing domestic business. How should he allocate the group's limited resources? How should the new organization be staffed and structured?

SUMMARY

The decision on whether or not to proceed with the Global Fund was one of the first major decisions that Riley had to face since becoming Chairman. He knew that it represented an opportunity for him to express a vision that might transform the Prudential Realty Group from a major player in the domestic real estate market into an innovative leader in the global real estate community. Even though economic growth rates of many non U.S. countries were rising faster than at home, did it make sense to invest globally? Should Prudential take the risk of promoting an innovative product in an area in which it had little previous experience? If it did decide to proceed, how should the fund be structured and managed? Which steps should Riley take?

Exhibit 14-1

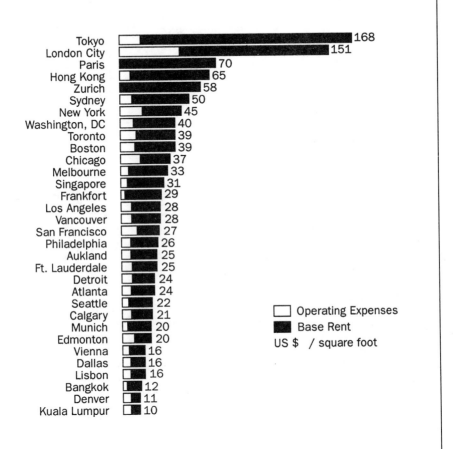

COLLIERS INTERNATIONAL GLOBAL OFFICE MARKET RENTS 1988

City	Value
Tokyo	168
London City	151
Paris	70
Hong Kong	65
Zurich	58
Sydney	50
New York	45
Washington, DC	40
Toronto	39
Boston	39
Chicago	37
Melbourne	33
Singapore	31
Frankfort	29
Los Angeles	28
Vancouver	28
San Francisco	27
Philadelphia	26
Aukland	25
Ft. Lauderdale	25
Detroit	24
Atlanta	24
Seattle	22
Calgary	21
Munich	20
Edmonton	20
Vienna	16
Dallas	16
Lisbon	16
Bangkok	12
Denver	11
Kuala Lumpur	10

☐ Operating Expenses
■ Base Rent
US $ / square foot

SOURCE; Compiled from Colliers Macaulay Nicolls Canadian Office Market Survey, p. 24, 1988.

Exhibit 14-2 *1988 Historical Perspective*

	CAPITALIZATION RATES (OFFICE)	RENTAL GROWTH (5 YEARS)	IRRs (LAST 5 YEARS)
U.S.	7%	(2)%	7%
U.K.	6	11	15
Spain	5.5	11	30
France	4.5	8	20
Germany	4	11	25
Japan	2	39	40

Source: Goldman Sachs

Exhibit 14-3 *The EC'92: Major Economic Indicators*

	POPULATION (MILLIONS)	GDP (BILLIONS)	UNEMPLOYMENT	INFLATION RATE
U.K.	56.8	$ 670	8.7%	6.8%
Portugal	10.2	37	5.9	11.7
Ireland	3.5	29	17.6	2.7
Belgium	9.9	139	10.8	1.9
W. Germany	60.1	1,118	6.4	1.6
Luxembourg	0.4	6	2.5	1.9
Netherlands	14.7	213	10.0	1.0
Italy	57.3	758	12.4	5.4
France	55.6	880	10.4	3.7
Spain	38.7	289	19.8	5.9
Denmark	5.1	101	6.5	4.5
Greece	10.0	47	8.0	14.0

Source: Organization for Economic Cooperation and Development

15

503 RUGBY ROAD

In 1970, Mason Sexton, a young, inexperienced developer, made plans to replace a rooming house he had inherited next to the University of Virginia campus in Charlottesville with a new 14 unit, 5 story apartment house. His attempts throughout 1970 and 1971 to assemble the information, approvals, and resources necessary to go ahead point up the steps and risks inherent in the development process. Using the example of a small scale residential project, the case illustrates development lessons applicable to projects of any scale.

Discussion Questions:

1. How well does Sexton carry out the conceptual, investigative, and planning stages of this development?
2. How and why does Sexton change his initial plan over time?
3. How does Sexton's return compare with his investment as the setup is revised over time?
4. Which problems that Sexton incurred were avoidable and which were beyond his control?

In September 1971, Mason Speed Sexton was evaluating how he should proceed with his property at 503 Rugby Road, Charlottesville, Virginia. In 1961, he had inherited the stucco house. It was located on a 14,000 sq. ft. lot approximately one block from the main campus of the University of Virginia. Four years later he attended that institution as a freshman and immediately took over the management of the property. This was his first exposure to real estate management and to the benefits and problems of rental property.

Even before he took control, the house had been divided into individual rooms which were rented to students. There were 7 double bedrooms, 6 large single bedrooms, 2 kitchens, a large living room, and 5 1/2 bathrooms. He spent two summers with a local handyman cleaning, painting, refurnishing and generally improving the property which had been long neglected. After this remodeling, he was able to raise the rents by percentages that varied from 25% to 100% and operated the property at a profit for the first time (see **Exhibit 15-1**). His experience enabled him to understand certain crucial factors. He realized that its location (as shown in **Exhibit 15-2**) made it possible to demand rents out of proportion to the space and the facilities provided. He also understood that the age of the current structure and the amount of upkeep and repairs required to maintain it were consuming the little profit there was. As the building continued to age and deteriorate, he thought that the situation would only get worse.

During the period of his management, he filled the house with his undergraduate friends. As a precaution he required his tenants to sign a formal lease drawn by his lawyer and to get their parents' signatures if they were under twenty-one. Among these friends were two architecture students who came to him three years later in the spring of 1970 proposing to build an apartment house at 503 Rugby Road. Their original concept was to design an "architectural commune" under the supervision of one of the professors in their graduate program. The idea seemed logical to Mr. Sexton since many of the tenants had always been architecture students and since architect friends had managed the property for him after he had left Charlottesville to work in New York City.

PLANNING A NEW BUILDING

In mid-1970, Sexton was planning to start the first year at the Harvard Business School. At that time he sought the advice of his mother on tearing down the old house and erecting an apartment building. In his opinion, her 20 years of real estate experience as a successful broker on Long Island combined with her interest in the property made her a source of sound judgment and invaluable aid. After the first set of plans had been submitted by five different groups of architecture students, he and his mother were able to visualize a feasible design which would provide the best use of the property. They had learned that under Charlottesville zoning laws for this location, which was zoned R-3, they were restricted to building one housing unit per thousand square feet of available land. This meant that they could put a maximum of 14 units, but these were unrestricted as to the size or number of rooms in each unit as long as the required setbacks from the property line and the 5-story height limitation were respected. At this point, he made the decision to try to optimize the value of the property with any project that might be built, since it was his only inheritance and he wanted to make the most of it both in terms of current cash flow and cash to be realized at the time of sale.

After choosing the design and architect which he liked best, Mr. Sexton spent many hours with his mother and the architect constantly revising the sketches and the floor plans until he was satisfied that he had met his maximum use criteria and had an esthetically pleasing and economically feasible set of plans. Among the decisions which were made at this time which determined the final shape of the project were: (1) to provide 14 units each with its own kitchen and bath; (2) to use concrete decking planks and brick bearing walls as the primary means of construction because of their cost advantages over other building systems and their long durability and maintenance-free characteristics; (3) to build all bedrooms large enough and with enough closet space for at least two people; (4) to build all bathrooms, kitchens, and facilities to withstand maximum wear and tear while requiring the least possible amount of maintenance; (5) within the constraints above, to make the apartments as attractive, airy, convenient, luxurious as possible. The major goal of this early planning phase was to build something of lasting value that would require a minimum of time and expense to maintain.

In conjunction with the design phase, Sexton became concerned about property management and the marketing of his property. Since his mother was sixty-five, he decided to suggest that she retire, move to Charlottesville, and take over the management of the building. Due to the location of the property, he determined that his prime rental market was going to have to be the more affluent students which was a departure from his original concept of a luxury, high-rise for young marrieds. In order to make this proposal attractive to his mother, who was divorced, he promised her a "penthouse, designed to her specifications" and a comfortable management fee on which to live. He did not know whether he could afford this offer, or if he could, whether his mother would regard it as desirable for her.

Concurrently, he surveyed the list of available contractors in Charlottesville who were willing and able to undertake this kind of job. To his great chagrin he discovered that only one person had ever built a high-rise apartment house before and that project had been in Richmond, 90 miles away. The problem was that because his project was to be one of the first high-rise apartment buildings in Charlottesville most local contractors were hesitant even to bid on it. He explained his concept to the one general contractor with some experience and showed him his plans and sketches asking for an estimate of what he thought it would cost to build. Within a day the contractor produced the construction cost estimate of $300,000 and Mr. Sexton had estimated his total development costs from that base. Next, based on his knowledge of the local rental market and some preliminary research he had conducted with the help of the general contractor, he projected the rents that he could get for each apartment, estimated his operating expenses and debt service, and derived his expected cash flow. On the basis of these very rough numbers he decided that the project was economically feasible and that he should go ahead with it. This was an important decision since up to this point he had invested a relatively small amount of time and money in the project. His architect friend had done the sketches and designs on speculation with the understanding that if and when the project was built he would receive either fair compensation for his work or a small share in the building.

MARKET RESEARCH

Before making any major dollar commitment to the project, Sexton wanted to do a more in-depth survey of the local rental housing market and, if possible, get a verbal commitment for permanent financing on the basis of the plans and numbers he had at that time. He spent two full days talking to local real estate brokers to determine what the demand might be for luxury apartments and whether or not he could get the rents he was projecting. Reactions were mixed with most agreeing that such rents were too high for young families, professionals, and nonstudents in general—especially for the three-bedroom penthouse units. A visit to the Off-Grounds Housing Bureau was much more encouraging. There he learned that the off-grounds housing situation was critical. Students would pay almost anything for good, clean housing that was within walking distance of the university. The director informed him that in the last two years, available apartments had been given out by lottery. More recently, they had done away with even that system as unworkable and the current situation was described as a "free-for-all" with local landlords responding with sharply increasing rents.

During this same trip to Charlottesville, Sexton got a break in the form of a tip from his contractor that a "Special Report" from the Housing Guidance

Council had recently been released and that he might get a copy from one of the largest builder-developers in central Virginia. He called the developer's office and a secretary told him that he could read the report while he was there, but that it couldn't leave the office. He therefore took a small tape recorder and recorded the parts he felt to be important to his project, while he was in an empty conference room.

In general the report indicated that there was a strong market for rental property within walking distance of the university and that demand would remain strong through 1975 even without further expansion by the University of Virginia.

A major problem had arisen in getting information on apartment and rent comparables for the immediate neighborhood and the Charlottesville area in general. He was not able to identify comparable buildings or apartments. There were no high-rise apartments, no luxury apartments, and no three-bedroom apartments within easy walking distance of the university. Therefore, when he compared a small two-bedroom unit with tiny kitchen, living room, and small bath which rented for $225 to $245 one block away to his projected rents, he had an unfavorable and distorted comparison. In addition, since he planned to rent to students who were willing and able to live two to a bedroom, he had to make rent comparisons on a per-student basis.

The large rooms in the existing 85-year-old, deteriorating structure have rented during the last three to five years for over $100 per month per bedroom with four or five people sharing the same bathroom and kitchenette. Occupancy levels have been virtually at the 100% level for the entire period of his ownership with long waiting lists for any available rooms. Many students seem to be quite willing and able to pay this price for housing that is conveniently located despite its run-down condition and lack of amenities. Bedrooms in the new structure would rent for an average of $120 per month and could easily accommodate two persons, resulting in a per-person cost of $60 per month.

AVAILABILITY OF CREDIT

Armed with his new market data, the "Special Report" excerpts, and a pro forma income and expense statement as shown in **Exhibit 15-3**, Sexton visited the Charlottesville Savings and Loan Association where, after presenting his proposal, he got a verbal commitment for $18,500 per unit or a $260,000 first mortgage with a mortgage constant of 9.37%. This was some $40,000 below the loan he was hoping for. He was told that the bank had never lent more than $16,500 per unit before and that they were stretching themselves even at that level. Other visits to the Shenandoah Life Insurance Company, the local savings bank, etc., had produced similar results with the general feeling that this project was "too rich for our blood." In his opinion, his experience pointed up the problem of dealing with small town, local financial institutions. First, since this was a pioneering effort in the sense that it was to be the first high-rise in the town and since it was aimed at students, most lenders approached it cautiously and, in his opinion, with undue conservatism. Secondly, he believed that the size of the loan was, in some cases, "too heavy" for the institution, although that was never stated.

Seeking additional sources he sought out the most reputable mortgage broker in town. He couldn't spend any more time in Charlottesville and was not getting very encouraging results. The gentleman to whom he was referred turned out to be the executive vice president of the commercial bank where he kept a house account. He was very helpful in suggesting sources of mortgage money and assured Sexton that for 2% of the loan he could secure financing of $300,000 with a carrying cost of $29,000 quickly and easily. Unfortunately, he would have to get final bids on the project to determine the construction costs more exactly against which a commitment could be made. This, in turn, required that a complete set of working drawings and specifications by an architect certified in Virginia be procured. The architect that had done all the work up to this point was with a New York firm. In addition, a local engineer had to take test borings on the land to determine what kind of foundation would be needed. To proceed further would require a commitment of almost $15,000 in architect's, engineer's and landscape architect's fees. These would have to be paid whether the building was built or not. On the basis of Sexton's mother's credit, they would be able to delay payment of these bills until they got financing or the project was shelved.

PROBLEMS WITH THE PLANNING COMMISSION

In late August 1970, a disturbing piece of news arrived which caused Sexton added expense and worry through the fall. As of October 1, all plans for multi-family housing, office, and industrial buildings had to be approved by a new City Planning Commission. His project was the first to seek approval and it was being treated somewhat as a test case. The young planning director was very "tough" in his meetings with Sexton and insisted that he didn't disturb a single tree or bush in putting up the buildings or he wouldn't receive his certificate of occupancy. In addition, Sexton had to present detailed landscaping plans and elevations of the building to get his project approved. He therefore hired a local landscape architect at a cost of $1,500 to do the plans and appear before the commission in his behalf. The outcome of all this was that his plans were not only approved, but were "hailed" by the Planning Commission which asked if they could use the project as a model for future development in Charlottesville.

NEW COST ESTIMATES

Once the working drawings were completed, the general contractor sent out invitations to local subcontractors to bid on the property. By March 1971, when the bids were returned, the building market had taken a dramatic turn from what it had been a year earlier. The previous year, in a lethargic economy, the biggest developer in Charlottesville had gone bankrupt leaving debts of $17 million. The contractors, architects, and other subcontractors who had worked for this developer were out of jobs and hungry for work. By the following year, however, the economy was heating up and construction in Charlottesville, especially in single-family homes and townhouses on the outskirts of the city, was booming. These reasons combined with the contractors' inexperience with high-rise construction and the fact that this was Sexton's first project, made it difficult just to get people to bid on the project. When he got bids, his worst fears were realized. As can be seen in **Exhibit 15-4**, the original bids of $429,700 were approximately $125,000 over his estimates.

There were a number of factors behind this huge difference which required a great deal of time and effort to discover and, in some cases, eliminate. A major reason for the high construction costs was the fact that the test borings showed the need for reinforced spread footings which had to go down 40 feet for the foundation. This, including the cost of the underground garage, cost $50,000 extra. To get around this problem, Sexton attempted to swap his piece of land for a similarly sized, but less attractively located piece owned by the university. Unfortunately, the Board of Overseers was not interested in his proposal and he was stuck with the extra cost.

During this period, his general contractor, architects, and his mother were of tremendous help in finding ways to save money and cut costs. Ultimately, the original bids were reduced almost $50,000 which was absolutely critical to keeping the project economically viable and saleable to investors. For instance, he quickly discovered that he could save $9,400 on the masonry (see **Exhibit 15-4**) by changing from the 8'4" ceilings called for in the plans to 8 ft. ceilings and by using oversized instead of standard brick. This meant that precut, regulation 8 ft. wallboard could now be installed without the extra labor it would require to patch every piece and use extenders. It also meant a 10% saving on the cost of the cheaper bricks and correspondingly less mortar and labor. Some other ways in which he cut costs (see **Exhibit 15-4**) were to: (1) eliminate all the ceramic tile work; (2) take out all dishwashers and garbage disposal units making them optional on a rental basis; (3) change from the $2.50 electric switches called for in the specifications to ones costing $.69 and move the position of the boxes while using cheaper electrical cable; (4) make kitchens smaller by 1½ feet and switch to inferior-grade cabinets. Fortunately, he was not the only one in Charlottesville facing high buildings costs. A recent article in the local paper showed that at an average cost of $19.92 per square foot Charlottesville has among the highest building costs in the nation. Even at these costs levels, Sexton expected a return on his investment. The total development budget, based on a 12-month construction period, is shown in **Exhibit 15-5**.

PRO FORMA INCOME STATEMENT

A major reservation which he had to confront on the part of potential lenders was centered around his pro forma income statements. His rental income schedule is shown in **Exhibit 15-6**; a pro forma income statement is shown in **Exhibit 15-7**. Specifically, bankers believed that his operating expenses of $11,758 and management fee of $2,836 were too low since they totalled less than 25% of the net rent of $56,715. They wanted to see operating expenses, including real estate taxes, in the neighborhood of 34% of net rental income since their experience had shown that this is what it would cost them to run the building should there be a default on the mortgage. His case was further complicated by the fact that the owner/developer, his mother, was also the manager of the property. The question arose as to whether the management fee was an expense or part of profit. For this reason, the pro forma income statement was drawn up showing net income before and after the management fee. **Exhibit 15-7** also shows net profit before a vacancy factor given the negligible vacancy rate of less than 1% for Charlottesville as a whole. The return on investment using the net profit, without a vacancy allowance, of $11,520 with the same equity basis of $117,000 was projected to be an acceptable 9.85%. This was better than average for a project of this size according to studies done by the Institute of Real Estate Management.

If the income statement projects expenses at 34% of net income of $56,715 after taking out a 5% vacancy rate Sexton would be left with a very small cash flow and correspondingly poor return on investment as can be seen in **Exhibit 15-8**. These calculations raised in the banker's mind questions about the economic feasibility of the entire project, especially if they assumed that rents were overstated by, for example, 10% and expenses were even higher than 34%. The project was disastrous.

Naturally, the primary source of the problems which arose in regard to rates of return, expense ratios, interest coverage, etc., was the high cost of construction which was projected at $27,071 per apartment unit. This created the need for a large mortgage with correspondingly high fixed interest and amortization charges which severely reduced the cash flow from the project. In spite of these adverse factors, there were factors which Sexton believed made the project an attractive investment. These were the hedge against inflation and the tax shelter available.

TAX SHIELD AND DISCOUNTED CASH FLOW—ANALYSIS OF RETURN

Exhibit 15-9 was prepared by Sexton to illustrate potential investor returns. A percentage of the after-tax net cash flow from the development was projected to come from the tax shield created by the large depreciation and interest deductions taken. The actual savings in tax that these "losses" would produce for an investor were treated as cash income, since the investor was assumed to be able to apply the losses against other income. The amount of savings would decline each year as both the interest payments and depreciation deduction were reduced. The other major element of return for the investor was the potential equity appreciation.

Sexton had decided to use the discounted cash flow analysis of return format in the pro forma, because he believed it was the only method which would relate the estimated value of a project with its cash flow over time. He knew that real estate investors establish value and base their investment decisions on four sources of entrepreneurial reward: (1) possible appreciation, (2) possible loan amortization, (3) possible income tax savings, and (4) possible cash flow or dividend. He believed that the method used in the analysis integrated these elements and told "The Rugby Road Story" in what he felt was the best way. The 22% after-tax projected return was, he thought, impressive and would awaken the interest of most investors.

CURRENT SITUATION

By September 1971, when Sexton returned to the second-year MBA program, the project was in limbo. He had not been able to obtain the permanent financing on acceptable terms. He had almost completely ceased to deal with his original mortgage broker because he had not lived up to his promise to secure a take-out loan. At this point his architects had become very helpful in arranging meetings with interested potential lender/investors. On his own, he had spoken to a number of REITs to which he had sent proposals. These were still being evaluated and reviewed. Unfortunately, he had thus far no favorable responses. Moreover, as time passed, it became less and less likely that the building could be completed before the original target date of January 1, 1973. This meant that he would miss the change in semesters at the university when a new influx of students would be looking for housing. Consequently, he would have a difficult time renting the property until the following September which would mean large additional carrying costs. He was left wondering about his next steps.

APPENDIX A

Charlottesville and Albermarle County are situated in central Virginia along the eastern slope of the Blue Ridge Mountains just 30 minutes away from the Skyline Drive. Charlottesville is 67 miles west of Richmond and 115 miles southwest of Washington, D.C. Albermarle County had an estimated population of 41,000 in 1970 while the city had a population of 39,000. This represented an increase of 30% over the 1960 levels and 50% over the 1950 levels. Census projections indicated that the populations would continue to grow at an average rate of 3% per year, and that growth was expected to come in spurts rather than as a single smooth trend. The average income per household for both the city and the county was $9,371 in 1970 with a total estimated purchasing power of $224,000,000.

Housing construction in the Charlottesville-Albermarle area had kept pace with the increase in population. The level of completed housing was 70 units in 1954, 690 in 1960 but only 532 in 1971. The level of construction was expected to rise dramatically to the level of 1,000 per year for the years 1972 through 1975.

Manufacturers in many different industries provided a payroll in excess of $65 million. There were nine electronics firms in the immediate area including General Electric, Sperry Marine Systems, and Stromberg-Carlson. Morton's Frozen Foods employed 1,500 people in a plant 12 miles to the west of the city. Three printing plants, the Allen Press, the Michie Press and the Lindsey Printing Company employing 400 persons in all were located in Albermarle County. Martin-Marietta operated a quarry to the north of the city. Two concrete manufacturers served the growing needs of the construction industry. Two clothing and textile firms had plants within the county. An office equipment manufacturer, the Acme Visible Record Co., and a tire plant for Uniroyal completed the list of major industrial installations.

Although there were indications that General Electric would locate another plant in the Charlottesville-Albermarle area, the prospect of further industry growth was limited by the diminished pool of available labor and the opposition of many local groups to any activity which might damage the local environment.

Charlottesville had many government jobs. The city served as a regional center for the state and as the county seat for Albermarle County. The federal government had a substantial payroll here on the staff of the Army Judge Advocate General's school and the Army Foreign Service Technological Center. Federal employment in the area was not considered likely to grow. It took substantial pressure from the local congressional delegation to bring in the Army Foreign Service Technological Center and even this did not replace all the jobs which had been lost when HEW vacated the federal office building several months earlier.

Albermarle County was still an active agricultural area. There were extensive apple and peach orchards within the county. Many large firms were still operating, specializing in cattle breeding, dairy products or horse raising.

The single most important influence upon the future of the county and the city was the University of Virginia. This was a prominent educational institution with schools of law, medicine and graduate business which ranked high among American professional schools. The university attracted to this area a well-educated and affluent group of professionals. It was also an important source of employment for unskilled workers in the county and city. The university served as the center of the cultural and much of the social life in the area by sponsoring concerts, lectures and exhibits. The university was playing a crucial role in the future of the city because it was thought by many to be a sure source of growth. Enrollment stood at slightly more than 10,000 and was scheduled to grow to about 18,000 by the year 1980.

The city's rich historical background, its natural scenic beauty and the remarkable examples of Jeffersonian architecture made it an important tourist center, drawing over 400,000 people a year.

The city and county were relatively well served in terms of transportation. Interstate 64 ran east-west through the city connecting it with Richmond and

Norfolk to the east, Roanoke and ultimately St. Louis to the west. Dual-lane Route 29 connected with Washington, D.C. Both the Chesapeake and Ohio and the Southern Railroads served the city which was still an important switching point for them. Charlottesville had a regional airport with daily scheduled flights to points as distant as New York and Atlanta.

Charlottesville and its surrounding area represented one of the fastest and most sustained small growth areas in the South. While many communities were dependent for their growth on a single source like commerce, recreation, politics, professionals, or education, Charlottesville was fortunate enough to have a strong base in many of these areas. This guaranteed to the community as a whole a more stable status than would fall to one without these advantages.

Exhibit 15-1 *Income and Expense Statement for Present Use*

Gross rental income[1]	$12,000	
Allowance for vacancies and bad debts	400	
Net rental income		**$11,600**
Operating Expenses		
Real estate taxes	1,021	
Water and sewer	271	
Heat and electricity	1,403	
Insurance	393	
Janitor	400	
Repairs	997	
Management fee	600	
Total operating expenses		**$5,085**
Income from operations		6,515

[1]13 rooms with 20 students paying $50 per room, per person, per month.

Exhibit 15-2

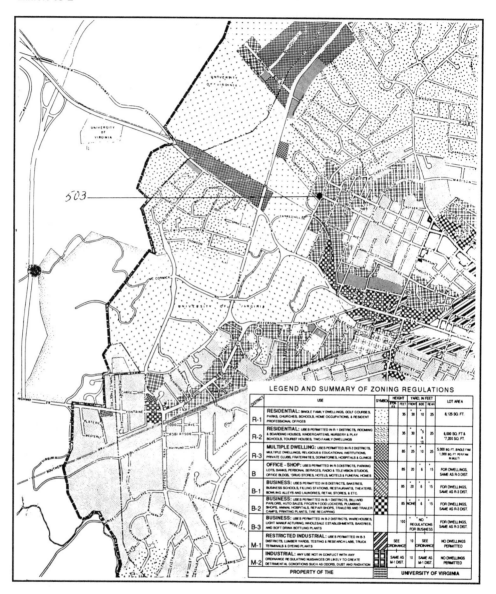

LEGEND AND SUMMARY OF ZONING REGULATIONS

DISTRICT	USE	SYMBOL	HEIGHT STOR IES	HEIGHT FEET	YARD, IN FEET FRONT	YARD, IN FEET SIDE	YARD, IN FEET REAR	LOT AREA
R-1	**RESIDENTIAL:** SINGLE FAMILY DWELLINGS, GOLF COURSES, PARKS, CHURCHES, SCHOOLS, HOME OCCUPATIONS, & RESIDENT PROFESSIONAL OFFICES			35	30	10	25	8,125 SQ. FT.
R-2	**RESIDENTIAL:** USES PERMITTED IN R-1 DISTRICTS, ROOMING & BOARDING HOUSES, KINDERGARTENS, NURSERY & PLAY SCHOOLS, TOURIST HOUSES, TWO FAMILY DWELLINGS			35	30	5	25	6,000 SQ. FT & 7,200 SQ. FT.
R-3	**MULTIPLE DWELLING:** USES PERMITTED IN R-2 DISTRICTS, MULTIPLE DWELLINGS, RELIGIOUS & EDUCATIONAL INSTITUTIONS, PRIVATE CLUBS, FRATERNITIES, DORMITORIES, HOSPITALS & CLINICS			85	25	10	25	5,000 SQ. FT. SINGLE FAM 1,000 SQ. FT. PER FAM IN MULTI
B	**OFFICE - SHOP:** USES PERMITTED IN R-3 DISTRICTS, PARKING LOTS, BANKS, PERSONAL SERVICES, RADIO & TELEVISION STUDIOS, OFFICE BLDGS, DRUG STORES, HOTELS, MOTELS & FUNERAL HOMES			85	20	6	15	FOR DWELLINGS, SAME AS R-3 DIST.
B-1	**BUSINESS:** USES PERMITTED IN B DISTRICTS, BAKERIES, BUSINESS SCHOOLS, FILLING STATIONS, RESTAURANTS, THEATERS, BOWLING ALLEYS AND LAUNDRIES, RETAIL STORES, & ETC.			85	20	6	15	FOR DWELLINGS, SAME AS R-3 DIST.
B-2	**BUSINESS:** USES PERMITTED IN B-1 DISTRICTS, BILLIARD PARLORS, AUTO SALES, FROZEN FOOD LOCKERS, PLUMBING SHOPS, ANIMAL HOSPITALS, REPAIR SHOPS, TRAILERS AND TRAILER CAMPS, PRINTING PLANTS, TIRE RECAPPING			85	NONE	6	15	FOR DWELLINGS, SAME AS R-3 DIST.
B-3	**BUSINESS:** USES PERMITTED IN B-2 DISTRICTS, WAREHOUSES, AND SOFT DRINK BOTTLING PLANTS			100	NO REGULATIONS FOR BUSINESS	10		FOR DWELLINGS, SAME AS R-3 DIST.
M-1	**RESTRICTED INDUSTRIAL:** USES PERMITTED IN B-3 DISTRICTS, LUMBER YARDS, TESTING & RESEARCH LABS, TRUCK TERMINALS & DYEING PLANTS		SEE ORDINANCE		10	SEE ORDINANCE		NO DWELLINGS PERMITTED
M-2	**INDUSTRIAL:** ANY USE NOT IN CONFLICT WITH ANY ORDINANCE REGULATING NUISANCES OR LIKELY TO CREATE DETRIMENTAL CONDITIONS SUCH AS ODORS, DUST AND RADIATION		SAME AS M-1 DIST.		10	SAME AS M-1 DIST.		NO DWELLINGS PERMITTED
	PROPERTY OF THE					**UNIVERSITY OF VIRGINIA**		

Exhibit 15-3   *Preliminary Pro Forma Income and Expense Statement, Summer 1970*

Gross rental income	$58,920	
Vacancy allowance (5% of gross rent)	2,946	
Net rental income		**$55,974**
Operating Expenses:		
Real estate taxes	6,035	
Water and sewer	480	
Gas	2,400	
Insurance	893	
Janitor	750	
Reserve for general repairs	900	
Electricity	300	
Management fee (5% of net rent)	2,796	
Total operating expenses		**$14,554**
Income from operations[1]		**$41,420**

[1]Total development cost estimated at $388,000 including land at $65,000.

Exhibit 15-4   *Projected Construction Cost, Spring 1971*

	ORIGINAL	REVISED	DIFFERENCES
Demolition	$ 5,000	$ 5,000	-
Reinforcing & steel	0	1,350	+ 1,350
Concrete	24,715	24,315	− 400
Masonry	78,355	68,955	− 9,400
Structural steel	10,036	9,686	− 350
Steel stairs	6,231	6,231	-
Rough carpentry	11,983	11,383	− 600
Rough hardware	500	500	-
Finish carpentry	9,282	8,282	− 1,000
Finish hardware	1,150	1,150	-
Drainage	1,066	1,066	-
Roofing	6,115	6,115	-
Door A. Metal	1,804	1,804	-
Bi-Folding	1,040	1,040	-
Windows	9,954	6,454	− 3,500
Drywall	10,480	9,920	− 500
Tile work	219	-	− 219
Resilient tile	1,700	1,700	-
Painting	5,000	3,334	1,666
Special decoration	919	919	-
Kitchen cabinets	10,564	5,164	− 5,400
Appliances	7,700	5,672	− 2,028
Blinds & shades	888	888	-
Carpets	7,616	7,616	-
Metal shelving	905	905	-
Elevators	21,919	16,911	− 5,000
Plumbing	33,000	27,115	− 5,885

Exhibit 15-4   *(continued)*

	ORIGINAL	REVISED	DIFFERENCES
Tubs & showers, toilets, & basins	2,885	2,885	-
Termite protection	165	165	-
Precast slabs	33,400	33,400	-
Heating, ventilating, air conditioning	16,000	16,000	-
Electric	21,485	16,058	5,400
Fireplaces	850	425	− 425
Caulking	480	480	-
Earth moving	4,482	4,482	-
Site work	1,500	1,500	-
Walks, etc.	5,990	4,490	− 1,500
Lawns	3,000	-	3,000
General requirements	30,200	30,200	-
Tools	1,500	1,500	-
Total	**$390,498**	**$345,095**	**$44,403**
Taxes	11,090	9,812	1,278
Overhead & profits	28,112	24,154	3,955
Total	**$429,700**	**$379,164**	**$49,636**

Exhibit 15-5   *Total Development Cost Budget[1], Spring 1971*

Land at market value	$65,000	
Construction costs	379,000[2]	
Architectural	6,000	
Legal, builder's risk insurance, taxes	3,500	
Interest on construction loan	14,500	
Total development costs		**$468,000**
Less assumed loan of 75%	$351,000	
Equity investment required		117,000[3]
Less land	65,000	
Cash required		**$ 52,000**

[1]Based on plans and specifications included in *Proposal.*
[2]See *Projected Construction Costs* for a detailed breakdown.
[3]This figure used in following D.C.F.—*Analysis of Return Exhibit.*

Exhibit 15-6   *Rental Income Schedule, Spring 1971*

	ORIGINAL RENT SCHEDULE		NEW RENT SCHEDULE	
	Monthly	Annual	Monthly	Annual
1 penthouse apartment with fireplace	$400	$ 4,800	$425	$ 5,100
1 penthouse apartment	400	4,800	400	4,800
1 2-bedroom apartment 1st floor	250	3,000	265	3,180
1 2-bedroom apartment with 2 baths, 1st floor	275	3,300	300	3,600
3 2-bedroom apartments	275	9,900	275	9,900
7 3-bedroom apartments	360	30,240	360	30,240
12 indoor covered parking spaces	20	2,880	20	2,880
Total estimated income		**$58,920**		**$59,700**

Exhibit 15-7 *Pro Forma Income and Expense Statement, Spring 1971*

Gross rental income		$ 59,700
Vacancy allowance (5% gross rent)		2,985
Net rental income		**$ 56,715**
Real estate taxes	$6,035	
Water & sewer	480	
Gas	2,400	
Insurance	893	
Janitor	750	
Reserve for general repairs	900	
Electricity	300	
Total operating expenses		**−$11,758**
Management fee (5% net rent)		− 2,836
Cash flow before taxes		**42,121**
Debt service (9.57 constant. 75% financing;		
8.25%—25 years; $351,000 total mortgage)		− 33,586
Net profit after management fee and vacancy allowance		8,535
Net profit before management fee (additional risk $2,836)		11,371
Net profit before any vacancy allowance & after		
management fee		11,520

Exhibit 15-8 *Cash Flow Analysis*

	INCOME AND CASH FLOW	EXPENSES AS A PERCENTAGE OF NET RENTS
Gross rents	$59,700	
Less: 5% vacancy	2,985	
Net rental income	**$56,715**	**100.0%**
Total expenses	19,283	34.0%
Net cash flow—if free and clear		
of debt	37,432	66.0%
Debt service annually[1]	33,586	59.2%
Net cash flow after debt servicing	**3,846**	**6.8%**

[1]Assumes 75% financing as in Exhibit 15-7

$$\frac{\text{Cash flow after debt servicing}}{\text{Original Equity}} = \frac{\$\ 4,192}{\$117,000} = 3.29\% \text{ Return on investment}$$

Exhibit 15-9 *Discounted Cash Flow—Analysis of Return (Assumed Equity Investment Income of $117,000)*

A. Annual Cash Income—After Taxes—Assuming 50% Tax Rate (000s omitted)

	YEARS									
	1	2	3	4	5	6	7	8	9	10
Gross rent (+7%/year)	56.7	60.7	64.9	69.5	74.3	79.5	85.1	91.0	97.4	104.2
25% less: operating expenses	14.6	15.8	17.1	18.5	20.1	21.8	23.7	25.7	28.0	30.6
Free and clear return	**42.1**	**44.9**	**47.8**	**51.0**	**54.2**	**57.7**	**61.4**	**65.3**	**69.4**	**73.6**
Interest expense @ 8¼%	29.0	28.6	28.2	27.8	27.3	26.8	26.3	25.7	25.0	24.3
Depreciation expense[1]	26.9	25.1	23.4	21.8	20.4	19.0	17.7	16.6	15.5	14.4
Taxable income (loss)	**(13.8)**	**(8.8)**	**(3.8)**	**1.4**	**6.9**	**11.9**	**17.4**	**23.0**	**28.9**	**34.9**
Tax @ 50%	(6.9)	(4.4)	(1.9)	.7	3.5	6.0	8.7	11.5	14.5	17.5
Cash flow	**8.9**	**11.7**	**14.6**	**17.8**	**21.0**	**24.5**	**28.2**	**32.1**	**26.2**	**40.4**
Plus: Tax benefit above	6.9	4.4	1.9	(.7)	(3.5)	(6.0)	(8.7)	(11.5)	(14.5)	(17.5)
Net cash flow after taxes	**15.8**	**16.1**	**16.5**	**17.1**	**17.5**	**18.5**	**19.5**	**20.6**	**21.7**	**22.9**

[1]Uses double declining balance method, 30-year life on non-land cost of $403,000.

B. Net Proceeds From Sale

Sale price in Year 10 (73,000 capped at 8.25%)	$892,121
Less: brokerage commission @ 4%	26,764
Net sales price	**865,357**
Acquisition cost	468,000
Less: Depreciation	200,000
Net book value	**267,144**
Taxable gain	598,213
Tax on gain[2]	215,886
Net sales price	**865,357**
Less: Mortgage balance	285,357
Tax on gain	215,886
Net cash proceeds	**$363,934**

[2]Based on capital gains tax of 35% and recapture of a portion of accelerated depreciation.

Exhibit 15-9 (continued)

C. Present Value of Cash Flow Discounted at 22% (000s omitted)

PAYMENTS MADE END OF YEAR	FROM CASH FLOW AND TAX SHELTER	×	PRESENT VALUE OF $1 DISCOUNTED @ 22%	=	PRESENT VALUE OF CASH FLOW
1	$15.8		.820		12.96
2	16.1		.672		10.82
3	16.5		.551		9.09
4	17.1		.451		7.71
5	17.5		.370		6.48
6	18.5		.303		5.61
7	19.5		.249		4.86
8	20.6		.204		4.20
9	21.7		.167		3.62
10	22.9		.137		3.14

Net proceeds from sale and
  refinancing (after taxes)
  at end of 10th Year—
  from B above

	$363,934		.137		49.86
					118.35

Amount that an investor would have to invest today to get
  the above cash flow, assuming he was satisfied to receive an effective
  rate of return on his outstanding investment of 22% $118.35

Total equity investment required from first page $117,000

16

THE COSTA MESA PROJECT

In February, 1981, Copley Real Estate Advisors has to decide whether to proceed as a financial joint venture partner on a major, multi-phased office project in Orange County, California. While the $122 million project fits Copley's portfolio objectives well, the market is uncertain, interest rates are high, and the development partner is new. The case illustrates how the structure of a joint venture arrangement must take into account the players, the property, and projected economics.

Discussion Questions:

1. How would you evaluate Copley's overall strategy for involvement in real estate? How does it differ from other institutional investors?
2. What is your evaluation of the market?
3. Should O'Connor proceed with an investment in this office park in Orange County? What are the potential risks and rewards?
4. If so, how should he attempt to structure the joint venture with the developer?

Joe O'Connor took one last look at the pile of papers on his desk, loaded a bunch of them into his briefcase and decided it was time to go home. It was already 6:30, and he had the long Washington's Birthday weekend ahead of him. This February 1981 weekend, however, would not be much of a holiday for him. He would in fact be working most of the time as he tried to come to grips with whether to proceed as a joint venture partner on a major, multi-phased office project in Orange County, California.

O'Connor was president and chief executive officer of Copley Real Estate Advisors, the real estate equity investment arm of New England Life. Armed with a Harvard MBA, O'Connor had steadily climbed through the ranks of New England Life's real estate hierarchy and had gained a reputation for shrewd and aggressive investment strategies. He thrived on tough decisions, and he had one to make now. Last month O'Connor had received preliminary information about a 50-acre development project near Irvine, California and last week his correspondent in California, a Los Angeles mortgage company, sent him the details of the project with the recommendation that he act quickly. "It's one of the last big undeveloped parcels in the county," his contact told him, "and one of the best." Joe remembered how often he had heard that and how the graveyard of real estate was strewn with "last undeveloped parcels." Still, he had reason to believe that this was a pretty good site and he liked what his correspondent had told him about the developer and proposed joint venture partner, Shurl Curci (pronounced Kursee). O'Connor was sufficiently interested in the project to tack on to a trip to Texas a visit to Los Angeles to see the site and meet Mr. Curci. He was impressed with what he saw.

O'Connor also knew that the Orange County office market was weakening and Copley would be making a big commitment with this project. The total project cost was $122 million. While Copley's initial investment would be small, he knew that Copley might be required to put in more money as the project progressed. Still, even with these caveats, O'Connor was leaning toward the deal. He knew there was no time to lose. Another major financial institution was also looking at the project and had ordered an appraisal which would take a week or two. His Finance Committee was meeting on Wednesday. Over the weekend, O'Connor had to decide whether he should write up this investment and propose it to the Finance Committee. He had arranged to make one more phone call to Curci on Monday to discuss the final structure of the venture.

John H. Vogel, Jr. prepared this case under the supervision of Adjunct Professor William J. Poorvu as the basis for class discussion rather than to illustrate either effective or ineffective handling of an administrative situation.

COPLEY REAL ESTATE ADVISORS

Copley Real Estate Advisors was started in 1981 to make real estate investments and manage New England Life's $1.9 billion real estate portfolio. The firm was staffed by key personnel from the parent company. The idea behind the spin-off was to create an investment group that could take advantage of many of the opportunities becoming available such as working as an investment advisor to large pension funds and creating limited partnerships to be sold by New England Life agents. Copley Real Estate Advisors would have the best of both worlds: the flexibility and decision-making structure of a small company, and the staff, resources and credit of New England Life.

Whereas most institutional investors tended to buy existing, fully leased properties, Copley generally invested earlier in the development cycle, while the land was being prepared for development and before final decisions about the layout and design of the project were completed.

By getting in at an early stage of development, Copley generally assumed greater leasing and construction risks. Copley felt, however, that these risks could be quantified and made manageable especially if one worked with high quality developers. On the other hand, by getting closer to the source and the manufacture of real estate investments, Copley gained access to higher quality projects at a lower cost. With fewer competitors willing to invest in developmental real estate, Copley's experience was that the risk/reward tradeoff was extremely favorable.

In a typical Copley joint venture, a developer would bring to the table a site which he controlled and assurances that most of the requisite permits and zoning approvals were obtainable. The developer would be looking for an investor/partner with the financial staying power to support a project over time and ability to bear the risks that are often incurred with development projects. Copley, in return, would put up cash and guarantees to cover the cost of developing the project. In the usual investment, Copley would seek a 50-70% ownership

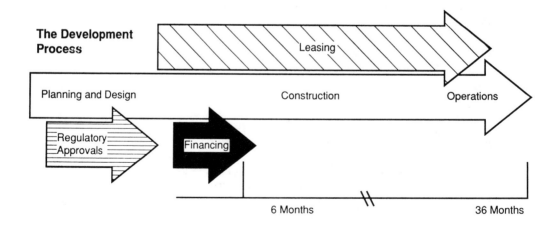

The Development Process

Leasing

Planning and Design   Construction   Operations

Regulatory Approvals   Financing

6 Months   36 Months

interest, a 12-13% cash on cash return on its investment and an active voice in the development and management of the project. Copley generally structured its investments so that a developer got a share of the tax benefits in proportion to its ownership position, though occasionally Copley traded off some additional tax benefits for more of the cash flow and appreciation. This ability to allocate tax benefits in a joint venture was, however, becoming more difficult to do with the newly proposed IRS guidelines.

Copley would not hesitate to get involved in long-term, multi-phase projects, where the payoff might not be achieved for several years, but they would parcel out their investment in increments to minimize the exposure.

Copley would specialize in a dozen or so markets which they knew well and then team up with local or regional developers. Copley would hear about good projects and potential partners through their extensive network of correspondents.

SHURL CURCI

Copley tried to minimize some of the risks of developmental joint ventures by getting involved with partners with good reputations and track records. Shurl Curci, the partner on the Costa Mesa site, had been a principal in Barclay Hollander Curci, Inc., a large West Coast condominium developer and homebuilder. The firm was sold to Castle and Cook in 1969 and Curci stayed on for a few years as a senior executive. In 1973, Curci left the company to set up his own partnerships to develop commercial properties in Southern California. Curci had put together an impressive roster of office buildings, shopping centers and hotels, many of which had been joint ventured with institutional partners.

For the Costa Mesa project, Curci had assembled an impressive team including a prominent leasing company, a well-respected local architect, and a top site planning and engineering firm. He had not yet selected a contractor or a property manager. O'Connor knew that the construction team would be key in keeping such a large scale project within budget.

THE PROPERTY

The Costa Mesa site had been farmed for many years by a Japanese truck farmer. In 1978, Curci successfully negotiated a 50-year ground lease for 50 acres of the farmstead. The terms included an initial ground rent of $800,000 per year and future rental increases every five years pegged at 50% of the CPI. In addition, Curci had rights of first refusal for the remaining 115 acres of the property. Curci was able to get his 50 acre parcel rezoned from agricultural to commercial use and by 1981 had obtained most of the necessary approvals for the property. As a result, the site was now in a PDC zone which permitted a variety of commercial and professional uses, so long as a conditional use permit was obtained in accordance with the general plan. The City had tentatively approved a 1.3 million square foot office complex to be constructed in phases. Curci's one hang-up with the city of Costa Mesa was compliance with their inclusionary zoning law which required that a certain number of housing units be provided as part of any new commercial development. By the time Curci brought his proposal to Copley, however, he had gotten approval in principle to start developing the first phase of his office project without having to build housing and felt that he could probably get approvals to build all the commercial development before he started the housing. He had also solved most of the traffic and circulation issues of the site to the satisfaction of the municipality.

The site itself was located in a prime office and commercial area about 26 miles southeast of downtown Los Angeles and 4 miles northeast of Newport Beach, a popular residential and office area. The site had substantial frontage on the San Diego Freeway and was near the cloverleaf intersection with the Newport Freeway. It was within minutes of the John Wayne Airport (see **Exhibit 16-1**). Near the property were two very successful commercial projects, South Coast Plaza and Two Town Center, both of which had been developed by the Segerstrom family. The 1,645,000 square foot South Coast Plaza was the second largest regional shopping center in both size and sales in the Los Angeles area. The Town Center project already included a hotel, twin 15-story towers, restaurants, and a major cultural center. The next phase, slated to commence in the fall of 1983, was to include a 21-story, 462,000 square foot office tower. The Segerstrom family was planning more than 2 million additional square feet of office space in Costa Mesa over the next few years (see **Exhibit 16-3, Table 16-5**).

As was his style, Curci planned a good solid project—nothing flamboyant or flashy, but nevertheless a project of high quality and class. The basic concept called for a six building complex, interspersed with plazas and parking facilities. The buildings would be a combination of low rise office structures, typical of southern California, and a few 12-story high rise focal point buildings. A careful landscaping scheme would tie the complex together (see **Exhibit 16-5**). Overall, Curci expected to build about 1,400,000 gross or 1,190,000 net rentable square feet of office space at a total estimated project cost of about $122 million (see **Exhibit 16-3**). The estimated build-out period was 3-5 years.

As a start, Curci proposed to build a 12-story 258,000 net rentable square foot speculative office building and 1,000 spaces of parking as the centerpiece of the project. The total construction cost for this first phase was to be $32 million.

THE MARKET

The Orange County office market had grown rapidly during the last five years, doubling in size from 8.27 million square feet in 1976 to 17.54 million square feet in 1980. Despite this level of construction, leasing had kept pace until 1980, when the market began to soften and vacancy rates climbed. A market study prepared by a consultant to the developer projected, however, that vacancy rates would be back down to 5% by late 1983 when the first building in the Costa Mesa project was scheduled to be completed (see **Exhibit 16-3**).

The market study also pointed out that the current vacancy problem in Orange County was not uniformly distributed, but concentrated in the less developed northwest section which recently had a 15.5% vacancy rate. In contrast the Newport-Airport-Costa Mesa area had only a 5.8% vacancy rate, and Costa Mesa itself had only a 2.8% vacancy rate.

What concerned Joe O'Connor most, though, was the number of new projects currently under construction. The market study projected that leasing activity would keep up with this new construction, but Joe wanted to think long and hard about the absorption rates projected in the market study and the implications of using a more conservative space absorption assumption.

One other gauge of market conditions that O'Connor felt was important was the amount of land being sold in the area and the prices developers were paying. He had received a letter from a local mortgage banker who served as a New England Life correspondent giving him some information on comparable land sales for the area. Both he and the mortgage banker were, however, aware of the difficulty of making such comparisons (see **Exhibit 16-4**).

THE SITUATION

Shurl Curci was now at the stage where he wanted to proceed with the first building in Phase I of his project. That meant proceeding on the initial development and construction of a 258,000 square foot office building at an estimated cost of $32 million. Curci's pro forma showed annual rental rates for the completed office space of $19.00/square foot (see **Exhibit 16-2**).

Curci knew that most insurance companies were not equipped to make construction loans, and therefore he had begun talking with a major West Coast bank about getting a $25-$30 million construction loan. Many construction lenders insisted that before they would loan any money the developer had to secure a commitment for a long term mortgage. This was so that when the construction was completed, money would be available to repay the bank. In some joint ventures, Copley would either commit to make the mortgage loan itself or, at least, commit to step up as a lender of last resort. In this case, however, Curci thought the construction lender would make an open-ended construction loan and not insist on a prior mortgage commitment. He knew that O'Connor would prefer this situation, and it would give the joint venture flexibility in securing long-term financing at the optimum time.

Curci expected that it would take at least a year and a half to get started on construction with Phase I and he was looking for a money partner with deep pockets who could stick with him during the 3-5 year development stage for the total project. At the moment he was looking for an initial infusion of equity to help him carry the land, prepare site plans, complete road work, and cover other development costs, such as legal fees and permits. This would probably come to about $3-4 million.

Curci knew that no lender would lend on raw land, but 3-5 year funds for commercial development projects were beginning to open up. Rates were in the 14% range for 3-4 year funds and long-term lenders were looking for returns of 15-17%. Longer loan terms tended to include kickers and periodic rate adjustments (see **Exhibit 16-3**).

THE DEAL

Most of Curci's recent deals had been structured as joint ventures and he was comfortable with this sort of arrangement. Furthermore, in this case, he felt he was bringing substantial value to the table in addition to his own experience as a developer. He had spent three years working with the municipality to get building approvals and had a leasehold position on what he thought was an extremely good site.

O'Connor was aware that the site had potential and that the leasehold interest had value, although Copley did not normally allow imputed land appreciation as a factor in its investments. In this case, he felt that the short-term prospects for the project might be difficult but that the site probably had good long-term potential for growth in value.

Even with these substantial market risks, O'Connor was leaning toward making the commitment. He thought Curci's estimates of a $3-4 million need for equity were low, since it was always difficult to estimate development costs. He felt there might be unforeseen delays in the project. Actual construction of the project was not expected to begin for a year and a half from this initial equity investment. O'Connor thought Copley's initial investment ought to be more like $6 million, should they go ahead with the deal. This would give Copley more leverage in the project and would help cushion possible increases in costs. He also wondered if he should work out in advance an arrangement if, for example, $9 million of equity was eventually needed.

O'Connor knew that, in addition to the economic factors, there would be some tough issues involved in structuring the joint venture document. These included:

1. *Control* What should be the division of responsibility and decision-making between the money partner and the developer? Who should have authority for the major decisions (e.g. refinancing, leasing) and who should have authority for the day-to-day decisions? How should Copley exercise control over the project yet not stifle the developer's entrepreneurial spirit? How much control should Copley exert over other professionals and contractors involved in the project? Basically, all major decisions would be made jointly, and hopefully amicably. But as a last resort, O'Connor always insisted on a provision in the joint venture agreement allowing either partner to buy out the other if they reached an irreconcilable conflict.

2. ***Funding***   Should Copley's participation be in the form of a capital contribution or a loan? Should funding be staged and under what conditions? What will be the source of additional funds to defray cost overruns and other contingencies?

3. ***Allocation of benefits and risks***   Who gets dollars out of the project and in what order? How are benefits allocated and in what form? How are losses allocated?

4. ***Dissolution***   How does one partner get rid of the other if things do not work out? How would Curci be compensated for the value he had created in this project, especially if it were sold before it was built out? What provisions should be included in case the development partner dies? What provisions would there be for resolving disputes short of dissolution of the partnership?

This weekend, O'Connor would have to make two decisions. The first was whether he should proceed with the investment at all. If the answer to that question was yes, how should he structure the venture to protect Copley but give Curci incentives to stick with the project and make it successful.

Exhibit 16-1

COSTA MESA
Orange County, California

 NORTH

1. Costa Mesa
2. San Diego Freeway
3. Newport Freeway
4. American Bank
5. Great Western Savings
6. Downey Savings
7. South Coast Plaza Hotel
8. Imperial Bank
9. Bristol Street
10. South Coast Plaza Shopping Center

MORGAN STANLEY

Exhibit 16-2 *Development Budget—February 15, 1981*

The following development budget is based on both current construction costs and current market rentals. It assumes the buildout of this land over a period of 3-5 years with all of the development consisting of mid-rise office space totaling approximately 1,190,000 s.f. of net rentable area.

I. Land: (under long-term ground lease)		N/A
II. Building Development Costs:		
Shell costs:		
1,400,000 s.f. @ $46.00	$64,400,000	
Parking		
Structured: 509,000 s.f. @ $17.00/s.f.	8,650,000	
Surface: 700,000 s.f. @ $ 2.00/s.f.	1,400,000	
Interior tenant improvement finish:		
1,190,000 s.f. @ $10.00/s.f.	11,900,000	
Site work	4,100,000	
Total estimated building costs		**$90,450,000**
III. Indirect Costs:		
Architectural and engineering	$ 2,500,000	
Ground lease payments	4,000,000	
Interest and indirect costs	20,000,000	
Lease commissions	5,000,000	
Total indirect costs		**31,500,000**
Total estimated project costs		**$121,950,000**

Income Projections (on a stabilized basis, $ in thousands)

	FIRST BUILDING IN PHASE I	TOTAL PROJECT
Gross rent at $19.00 per sq. ft.		
(Phase I: 258,000 sq. ft.:		
Total: 1,190,000 sq. ft.)	$4,902	$22,610
Parking spaces at $25 net per month		
(Phase I: 1,000 spaces, total 3,900 spaces)	300	1,170
Gross revenue:	**$5,202**	**$23,780**
Vacancy (5%)	260	1,189
Net revenue	**$4,942**	**$22,591**
Operating expenses ($4.50)[1]	1,161	5,355
Net operating income	**$3,781**	**$17,236**
Ground rent	200	800
Net operating income	**$3,581**	**$16,436**
Unleveraged return on investment		
(Phase I: $32 million, total, $122 million)	11.23%	13.52%

[1]Operating costs in excess of $4.50 will be passed through to the tenants.

Exhibit 16-3

Excerpts from
THE OFFICE MARKETS OF ORANGE COUNTY

Prepared for

CURCI DEVELOPMENT PROJECT

February 1981

COOK, MERCER AND DESIMONE
Economics Consultants
300 California Federal Building
707 Silver Lake Road
Laguna Hills, California 90274

SECTION I

Summary of Conclusions

The essential conclusions of the study are summarized briefly as follows:

1. The proposed Southcoast Metro Center should commence construction on a schedule that will insure ability to lease and deliver space by late 1983 or early 1984. Market conditions by that time should be favorable for a fairly rapid absorption of space, and the projected vacancy rate by that time should be in the neighborhood of 5 percent, since the heavy volume of current construction should have been absorbed.

2. In the near term, however (i.e., 1981 through early 1983), the Newport-Airport-Costa Mesa sub-market will be overbuilt, since the volume of current construction of 2.5 million sq. ft. represents about a 2-year supply of space at projected absorption rates. Thus, the vacancy rate will rise rather sharply this year and next, but should begin falling late in 1982, and should continue to decline to about 5 percent by early 1984.

3. The Newport-Airport-Costa Mesa sub-market is second only in size and importance to the Downtown Los Angeles office market.

Further, it is the most dynamic and rapidly developing office center in Southern California. Over the last 5 years, for example, the average annual absorption rate in Newport-Airport-Costa Mesa has been 20 percent greater than the long-term average for downtown Los Angeles, and about equal to the combined long-term absorption rate in Beverly Hills, Century City, Westwood, Brentwood, Santa Mon-

Exhibit 16-3 (*continued*)

ica, and Culver City. Moreover, the absorption rate in Newport-Airport-Costa Mesa and throughout Orange County, has been steadily rising over time.

4. Throughout the sub-market, project scale and quality are on the rise, and the long term outlook for the ownership of investment real estate here appears very bright. The area enjoys premium rents compared with other sub-markets of Orange County, and low cost competition from less well developed neighboring markets has not inhibited growth and rent escalation in the past.

   In both high and low rise buildings in Costa Mesa, Newport Beach, and Irvine, the rental rate typically is 10 to 20 percent higher than elsewhere in Orange County. Today, most of the space in high and mid-rise buildings is going for $1.65 to $1.85 per square foot, per month and in 1982-83, leasing agents anticipate a rent structure of from $1.85 to $2.25 per square foot.

5. For the remainder of Orange County, the outlook is less bright, and a seriously overbuilt condition may emerge—particularly in the Northwest and South sub-markets. In these two sub-markets, vacancies already are high (±15%), and scheduled and planned construction is substantially in excess of probable absorption. Thus, there is a real possibility that in these less well developed sub-markets of Orange County a level of market distress will become evident fairly soon, and given the limited absorptive capacities, it could persist for some time to come.

Table 16-1 Comparative Office Space Vacancy Rates in the Cities of Orange County

	JANUARY 1981	AUGUST 1980	JANUARY 1980
Northwest County			
Anaheim	21.0%	13.1%	12.6%
Fullerton	9.2	8.3	3.9
Garden Grove	22.6	23.7	22.0
Huntington Beach	10.2	3.0	0.9
Fountain Valley	5.2	12.8	–
Brea	17.1	17.4	–
Other	18.8	32.5	–
Average	**15.5%**	**12.4%**	**8.0%**
Central County			
Santa Ana	7.4%	8.4%	7.2%
Orange	3.3	4.3	7.6
Tustin	8.5	10.1	3.3
Average	**6.5%**	**7.6%**	**6.7%**
Newport-Airport-Costa Mesa			
Newport Beach	7.7%	4.6%	3.0%
Airport	5.5	3.8	6.0
Costa Mesa	2.8	2.6	7.1
Other	17.1	44.8	–
Average	**5.8%**	**4.3%**	**5.4%**

Exhibit 16-3 (*continued*)

	JANUARY 1981	AUGUST 1980	JANUARY 1980
South County			
Laguna Beach-Hills-Niguel	23.2%	17.9%	10.2%
El Toro	20.1	9.1	12.9
Mission Viejo	7.6	10.7	7.9
Other	5.2	6.2	6.3
Average	**16.1%**	**12.4%**	**9.0%**
Total Orange County	**8.3%**	**7.0%**	**6.3%**

Table 16-2 Distribution of the Office Space Inventory in Orange County—January 1981

	JANUARY 1981 TOTAL	JANUARY 1981 VACANT	% VACANT
Northwest County			
Anaheim	986,600	207,700	21.0
Fullerton	679,300	62,500	9.2
Garden Grove	169,400	38,300	22.6
Huntington Beach	230,700	23,600	10.2
Fountain Valley	191,600	10,000	5.2
Brea	299,600	51,400	17.1
Other	75,200	14,100	18.8
Total	**2,632,400**	**407,600**	**15.5**
Central County			
Santa Ana	3,310,600	244,800	7.4
Orange	1,500,700	49,700	3.3
Tustin	926,100	78,300	8.5
Total	**5,737,400**	**372,800**	**6.5**
Newport-Airport-Costa Mesa			
Newport Beach	1,945,600	150,300	7.7
Airport	4,901,900	268,100	5.5
Costa Mesa	900,400	25,300	2.8
Other	78,700	13,500	17.1
Total	**7,826,700**	**457,200**	**5.8**
South County			
Laguna Beach-Hills-Niguel	575,600	133,500	23.2
El Toro	246,700	51,300	20.1
Mission Viejo	332,100	25,300	7.6
Other	224,000	11,600	5.2
Total	**1,377,400**	**221,700**	**16.1**
Total Orange County	**17,573,900**	**1,459,200**	**8.3**

Exhibit 16-3 (continued)

Table 16-3 Comparative Rental Rates in Modern Orange County Office Buildings (rates quoted in dollars per square foot, per month)

	JANUARY 1980	JANUARY 1981	% GAIN
Northwest County			
Low rise	$ .85	$1.02	+ 20.0
High rise	–	–	–
Central County			
Santa Ana			
Low rise	1.00	1.13	+ 15.0
High rise	1.20	1.38	+ 15.0
Orange-Tustin			
Low rise	1.08	1.08	± 0.0
High rise	1.25	–	–
Newport-Airport-Costa Mesa			
Newport-Airport			
Low rise	1.25	1.26	+ 0.1
High rise	1.42	1.70	+ 19.7
Costa Mesa			
Low rise	1.33	1.25	− 6.1
High rise	1.23	1.50	+ 22.0
South Coast			
Low rise	.91	1.01	+ 11.0
High rise	–	1.33	–

Table 16-4 Office Space Absorption Rate, Orange County, 1973-1980, with Projections for 1981-1983

	NORTH COUNTY	CENTRAL COUNTY	S.F. LEASED PER YEAR NEWPORT AIRPORT COSTA MESA	SOUTH COUNTY	TOTAL ORANGE COUNTY
1973	44,500	206,300	296,100	113,500	860,400
1974	129,000	179,400	298,300	57,500	764,200
1975	70,400	133,100	340,600	30,600	574,700
1976	177,000	251,100	589,000	71,800	1,097,900
1977	198,100	624,000	629,300	71,300	1,522,700
1978	42,700	692,600	945,800	180,800	1,861,900
1979	176,300	621,500	1,946,100	193,300	2,937,200
1980	775,700	737,000	312,200	168,100	1,993,000
Projected[1]					
1981	373,600	798,300	1,311,800	204,300	2,688,000
1982	411,900	880,000	1,445,900	225,200	2,963,000
1983	450,100	961,700	1,580,100	246,100	3,238,000

[1]Based on a 1973-1980 regression analysis of the total county. The projected values for the county then were pro-rated to the submarkets based on submarket share of total county absorption.

Exhibit 16-3 (continued)

Table 16-5 Projection of Current Development Trends, Orange County and the Newport-Airport-Costa Mesa Submarket

	1980	1981	1982	1983	1984
Orange County Total					
Inventory (S.F.)					
Beginning of year	14,925,300	17,573,900	21,181,500	25,489,500	
New construction[1]	2,648,600	3,607,600	4,944,600	3,897,200	
End of year	**17,573,900**	**21,181,500**	**26,126,100**	**29,386,700**	
Vacant Space (S.F.)					
Beginning of year	941,500	1,597,100	2,516,700	4,498,300	
New construction[1]	2,648,600	3,607,600	4,944,600	3,897,200	
Absorption	−1,993,000	−2,688,000	2,963,000	−3,238,000	
End of year	**1,597,100**	**2,516,700**	**4,498,300**	**4,157,500**	
Vacancy Rate					
Beginning of year	6.3	9.1	11.9	17.2	17.6
Newport-Airport-Costa Mesa					
Inventory (S.F.)					
Beginning of year	7,458,300	7,826,800	9,991,900	11,262,100	
New construction[1]	368,500	2,165,000	1,270,200	1,072,200	
End of year	**7,826,800**	**9,991,900**	**11,262,100**	**12,334,300**	
Vacant Space (S.F.)					
Beginning of year	400,900	457,200	1,310,500	1,134,800	
New construction[1]	368,500	2,165,000	1,270,200	1,072,200	
Absorption	−312,300	−1,311,800	−1,445,900	−1,580,100	
End of year	**457,200**	**1,310,500**	**1,134,800**	**626,900**	
Vacancy Rate					
Beginning of year	5.4	5.8	13.1	10.1	5.1

[1]1980 values based on published differences in inventory. Subsequent years based on 85% delivery of volume during the year construction begins.

Exhibit 16-4 *Letter from New England Life Correspondent*

TEX MORTGAGE BANKERS
1200 Avenue of the Stars
Los Angeles, California 90067

February 1, 1981

Mr. Joseph W. O'Connor
President
Copley Real Estate Advisors, Inc.
535 Boylston Street
Boston, Massachusetts 02116

Dear Joe:

Pursuant to your request, I have asked Gerard to use his MAI contacts to provide you with an overview of land values of properties comparable to your proposed South Coast Metro project in Costa Mesa.

As you will see, Gerard found very few land sales the size of the 50-acre Costa Mesa site in Orange County in the last two years. None of the comparables were precisely identical to the subject property, and all need adjustments. I would also point out to you that your fifty acre site is divided into five legal parcels which could be developed or sold separately.

With this in mind, I am forwarding the following list of comparables to you. I hope this information will be useful to you in making your decision.

Please feel free to contact me if I can be of any further assistance.

Very truly yours,

Tex Jones

Land Sale of Comparable Properties

	LOCATION	SIZE (ACRES)	DATE OF SALE	TOTAL PRICE ($000)	PRICE PER SQ. FT.	COMMENT
1.	San Diego Freeway and Lake Forest Drive	4.7	12/1980	$ 3,888	$19.03	Good highway exposure and access, inferior location.
2.	Jamboree Boulevard and Kelvin Avenue, Irvine	8.6	1/1981	7,335	19.50	Inferior in location. Also Irvine imposes a $2.50 to $5.00 per square foot development fee.
3.	Kelvin Avenue, Irvine	2.9	1/1981	2,500	20.36	Inferior in location and faces the Irvine development fee. Currently on the market at $25 per square foot.

Exhibit 16-4 (continued)

LOCATION	SIZE (ACRES)	DATE OF SALE	TOTAL PRICE ($000)	PRICE PER SQ. FT.	COMMENT
4. San Diego Freeway and Von Karmen Avenue, Irvine	34.0	For sale	27,444	18.53	The price is listed at $47 million but we feel it can be bought for $40 million. We also subtracted from the price an existing structure which we valued at $12 million. Inferior location plus the Irvine development fee.
5. Anton Boulevard, East of Bristol Street, Costa Mesa	14.7	6/1979	11,500	18.00	Value at which the property was contributed in a joint venture between Prudential and the Segerstrom family.
6. San Diego Freeway and Harbor Boulevard	100.0	For sale	100,000	23.00	This property is slightly inferior in location.

Exhibit 16-5 The Costa Mesa Project

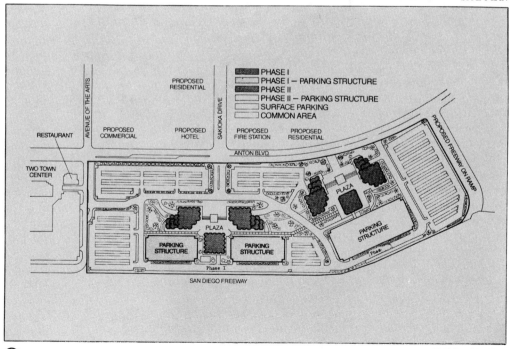

COSTA MESA
Orange County, California
SITE PLAN

● NORTH

MORGAN STANLEY

Exhibit 16-5 (*continued*)

Exhibit 16-5 (continued)

TYPICAL FLOOR PLAN

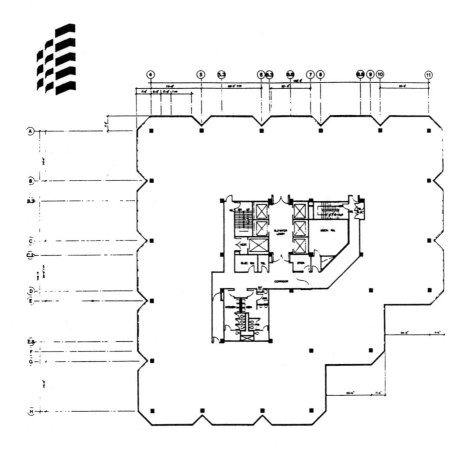

Exhibit 16-6 Benchmark Real Estate, Inc.

Benchmark Real Estate Rates, Apartment Mortgages—2/12/81

	FEBRUARY 10, 1981	JANUARY 13, 1981	DECEMBER 10, 1980
Interest rate	Proposed—not available Immediate—15¼ (FHLMC)	Not available	Not available
Fee	1½-2		
Terms (years)	Immediate 30 years		

Benchmark Real Estate Rates, Commercial Real Estate Projects (medium-size shopping centers, office buildings, industrial buildings)

	FEBRUARY 10, 1981	JANUARY 13, 1981	DECEMBER 10, 1980
Interest rate	Mortgage rate + participation or equity adding up to 14½-15	Mortgage rate + participation or equity adding up to 15-17	Mortgage rate and participation or equity adding up to 15-17
Fee	1 point	1 point	1 point
Terms (years)	25-30 year amortization	25-30 year amortization	25-30 year amortization

Benchmark Real Estate Rates, Credit Projects (all types)

	FEBRUARY 10, 1981	JANUARY 13, 1981	DECEMBER 10, 1980
Interest rate	Mortgage rate + participation or equity adding up to 14½-15	Mortgage rate + participation or equity adding up to 15-16½	Mortgage rate + participation or equity adding up to 15-16½
Fee	0	0	0
Terms (years)	30-35 year amortization	30-35 year amortization	30-35 year amortization

- There is an improving tone in the market. At least some lenders are interested in locking in current high yields. Lenders' target for total rate of return (including kickers) has leveled off to 15% or under. They're willing to go as low as 12% for the initial rate of return.
- Funds are becoming available for straight mortgages with no kickers. Current rate is 14½-14 with five-year and ten-year call provisions. One lender has allocated $100 million through 1983, $20 million this year. He will trade piece of rate for piece of participation if package adds up to 14% within two years.

17

LAKESIDE CENTER

In November, 1989, Maria Sanchez, the leasing agent for a 95,000 s.f. class A office building in Boca Raton, Florida, has to prepare and negotiate lease proposals with three prospective tenants. The building is only 38% occupied, and has fallen behind the project's proforma operating projections. This case is designed to expose students to the leasing process, the strategy and tactics of lease negotiations, and the impact of rental rates and concessions on financial and partnership structures.

Discussion Questions:

1. How would you assess the current situation at Lakeside Center? What leasing strategy should Sanchez propose to Martin?
2. What lease rates and terms should Sanchez offer to the prospective tenants: SFS, A&G, and BCI? How should she structure her presentation? How should she handle the negotiations?
3. What are the financial implications of your lease proposals? How should Southern handle the deficit?
4. What options does the financial partner CREA have? How might CREA respond to your lease proposals and your solution to reducing the deficit?

Maria Sanchez, the leasing agent for Lakeside Center, stared intently at her computer monitor as she tried to prepare for a breakfast meeting with John Clark, the CFO of SouthEast Financial Services (SFS). SFS was actively seeking to lease 13,000 s.f. of office space. Clark had called the previous afternoon and told her that two competing projects, Financial Place and 700 Glades Road, had beaten her initial offer by almost $5 p.s.f. If she wanted her project to stay on his short list of potential sites, she would have to come up with a better proposal. She also had to prepare proposals for Anderson & Gray (A&G) and BCI Marketing, two other potential tenants for Lakeside Center.

It was early November in 1989, and the once hot Boca Raton market had cooled considerably. Potential tenants had become increasingly elusive. Even though Sanchez's building, Lakeside Center, had been ready for occupancy for almost a year, the building was only 38% filled and it had been almost three months since the last tenant had signed on. As a result, the project had fallen behind its lease up schedule and it was not meeting its pro forma projections. On a more personal level, Sanchez was working on a commission basis and she was struggling to pay off a mountain of student loans from her MBA education. She needed to sign a tenant.

MARIA SANCHEZ

Sanchez had quickly become one of Southern Tier Development's top leasing agents after she joined Southern in July of 1987. A year later, she had been given responsibility for the leasing of Lakeside Center, a 95,372 s.f. office building in Boca Raton, Florida. Sanchez had grown up in southern Florida, and she wanted to pursue a career in real estate development. Completing the leasing of Lakeside Center would be a tough, high profile job; it was the type of challenge that she had thrived on in the past.

The last year and a half had been filled with cold calls, presentations, and negotiations. At times it had been tough. Sanchez had encountered repeated rejections as she tried to fight her way into the close knit leasing community. The Southern name and organization had helped but she had found that she was being judged, both personally and professionally, as an individual. Leasing

Research Assistant Richard E. Crum prepared this case under the supervision of Adjunct Professor William J. Poorvu as the basis for class discussion rather than to illustrate either effective or ineffective handling of an administrative situation.

was a profession where the successful were highly compensated and the unsuccessful were quickly let go. She had to perform.

Sanchez's job description was simple: find and sign strong tenants that were willing and able to pay market rents. Her first step was to locate and contact prospective tenants. This entailed making cold calls, working her list of contacts within the business and brokerage communities, and developing a marketing program to advertise the project. Her second step was to contact the prospective tenant and make a presentation to the executive in charge of real estate decisions. Her third step was to analyze that tenant's specific needs, determine the tenant's credit worthiness and overall attractiveness to her project, and then to formulate a detailed lease proposal. The fourth step was to negotiate with the tenant and close the deal. Finally, after the deal was closed and Sanchez's formal responsibilities were over, she would work informally with Southern's in-house property management team to follow the tenant fit up and move in process.

Southern had established a commission plan that was competitive with the commission plans of competing projects. Outside leasing agents would receive 3% of the value of the lease. In this case, the lease value was defined as the total gross rent that would be paid over the life of the lease. The commission would be paid as a lump sum when the tenant moved in. In addition, Sanchez would receive 25% of the amount that the outside broker was receiving as an "override." She would receive 1.5% of the lease value if she located a tenant directly and no outside leasing agent was involved.

She had found that she had to sell her abilities not only to prospective tenants but also to the other leasing agents in the area. Contacts and market information were critical ingredients for success as a leasing agent. Access to both had only become available after she had established herself with the other leasing agents. In return, they expected her to generate business, contacts, and market information for them.

Sanchez had found herself working from early morning breakfast meetings through late night receptions and parties. What kept her going was the brief, euphoric high of closing a deal and the substantial commission check that followed. Experienced leasing agents in a strong market could easily make upwards of $100,000 per year if they had a good reputation, a strong project, and the tenacity to chase every potential tenant that they encountered. Of course, she had also had quite a few doors slammed in her face.

LAKESIDE CENTER

Lakeside Center was a six story, 95,372 s.f. office building (see **Exhibit 17-1** for the Southern marketing material that describes the project). The building was part of a larger "business community" that Southern had developed on a 25 acre site. In addition to the office building, there was a 202 room hotel, a 34,000 s.f. retail structure, a fitness club, a bank, and four restaurants. There were 500 parking spots dedicated to the office building. The entire complex was centered on a small lake which served as a focal point for the development. The project was heavily landscaped and it had a pleasant, campus like atmosphere.

The building was 38.4% occupied. The tenants and their lease terms are summarized below in **Table 17-1**. The building had a gross area of 95,372 s.f. and an efficiency ratio of 86% which translated into a rentable area of 82,020 s.f.. The rentable area listed below would be applied to the lease rate quoted below in order to calculate the lease payment for each tenant. In this case, the lease rate is the gross rental rate including operating expenses. Free rent was the length of time during which the tenant could occupy the space for free before it was required to pay rent. It was customary in the area for parking to be offered at no extra charge.

TI was the tenant improvement allowance that Southern was giving to the tenant in order to offset the costs of customizing the space to the tenant's needs. Generally, in new office construction, the office space was not finished and the TI allowance was used for such items as carpeting, ceiling tiles, lighting, wall coverings, and interior partitions. Typically, the budgeted TI allowance would be held back by the lender and only disbursed when a tenant had signed a lease and was ready to begin the finish work. Often, a tenant spent more than the TI allowance to finish its space in which case the tenant was responsible for the additional cost. $18 per s.f. had been budgeted for TI allowances at Lakeside Center.

Construction on Lakeside Center had started in December of 1987. The certificate of occupancy was received twelve months later on January 2, 1989. Total development costs had initially been estimated at $14,500,000 or $152 per s.f. (see **Exhibit 17-2**). As the market had begun to soften in early 1988, the project manager had worked with the project's architect to "value engineer" the design. The resulting $550,000 in savings had come almost exclusively from downgrading the heating, ventilating, and air conditioning (HVAC) systems and simplifying the entry lobby. The $550,000 in savings had been added to the $450,000 allowance for operating losses that was already incorporated in the development budget.

Original gross income projections for 1990 were $1,968 million (82,020 x

Table 17-1 Lakeside Center Lease Terms

TENANT	S.F.	LEASE RATE	TERM	TI	FREE RENT	SIGN DATE	OCCUPANCY DATE
Southern	13,700	24.00	12	18.00	—	8/88	1/89
Workman & Rhine	2,910	23.00	5	18.00	—	8/88	1/89
Verten	4,094	23.00	10	18.00	6 months	9/88	1/89
Sache, Halsey & Witt	4,856	23.00	8	18.00	6 months	12/88	4/89
Centex Marketing	3,130	23.00	5	19.00	6 months	7/89	9/89
Sullivan & O'Brien	2,790	23.00	5	21.00	6 months	8/89	11/89
Totals/Average	31,480	23.44	10	18.37	3 months		

$24.00 p.s.f.). Operating expenses for the building at 100% occupancy were budgeted to be $410,000 per year (see **Exhibit 17-3**). This budget amount provided a base stop of $5 per s.f. for operating expenses as part of the initial rental rate quoted above. The tenant would be required, however, to pay its pro rata share of any future increases in operating expenses. This additional charge would be calculated by multiplying the increase in operating costs by the tenant's rentable area and then dividing by the building's rentable area. In this case, the net rent that the owner would receive was the gross rate quoted in **Table 17-1** minus the operating stop of $5 per s.f. The $5 per s.f. in operating expenses was considered to be in line with expenses at competing buildings.

Southern had formed Lakeside Associates, a limited partnership, to own and develop the complex. Southern, as the managing general partner, would make all day to day operating decisions for the project as well as be responsible for lease up. In addition, in the event of cost overruns or unbudgeted operating deficits, Southern would be required to fund these deficits in the form of a 10% interest only, subordinated loan to Lakeside Associates.

If the operating deficit exceeded the $1 million that had been budgeted, Southern had guaranteed that it would fund the next $1.2 million in unbudgeted operating deficits. If the total deficit exceeded $2.2 million and Southern decided not to fund the excess, Cambridge Real Estate Advisors (CREA) had the option to purchase Southern's position for $1. Southern was well capitalized and it had access to significant amounts of additional capital. Raising the cash to cover an operating deficit would not be difficult for the company. Any requests for additional funds, however, would have to be approved by Southern's Executive Committee.

CREA, which was the real estate subsidiary of a large insurance firm, had provided a $14,500,000, seven-year, 10% interest only, non-recourse, first mortgage loan to Lakeside Associates in return for the right to convert the loan into a limited partnership interest at any time. After conversion, CREA would receive an 8% cumulative, preferred return, and then any remaining cash flow would be split 50/50 with Southern. If CREA did not convert, the loan would come due in full in January of 1995.

In practice, this meant that CREA would receive either $1,450,000 per year as interest on its loan or, after conversion, $1,160,000 per year as its preferred return plus a 50% share in any excess cash flow. Upon the sale or refinancing of the project, CREA would first receive either its outstanding loan balance or its invested capital. Southern would then receive the outstanding balance of any loans that it had made. Finally, any remaining proceeds would be split 50/50. CREA had the right to approve all leases, asset sales, and refinancings.

THE COMPETITION

700 Glades Road was a 240,000 s.f., four story office building located at the corner of Glades and Powerline roads. The building had a serpentine floor plan, an interior atrium, and structured parking for 850 cars (see **Exhibit 17-4**). There

were 180,000 s.f. of rentable space in the building. This corner site was considered by many brokers to be the prime location in Boca Raton. Across the street was Boca Center, a super regional shopping mall with over 200 shops. Gary Stamfel, the local entrepreneur who owned 700 Glades Road, had been extremely aggressive in matching his asking rents to the current market conditions.

Still, occupancy at 700 Glades Road was only 29%. The first tenants had moved into 700 Glades Road during May of 1989. A listing of the tenants and a summary of what Sanchez had been able to learn about their rents and lease terms are listed below in **Table 17-2**.

Financial Place was a 66,000 s.f., six story, office building located at the corner of Glades Road and I-95 (see Exhibit 17-5 for a typical floor plan). The building had 52,800 s.f. of rentable space. Access was complicated, however by the fact that Glades Road was divided and elevated at this point. As a result, even though the building enjoyed visibility from I-95, tenants would have to exit I-95 at Glades Road, loop onto Military Trail, and finally enter the project from the northeastern corner. The building was five years old and there was parking for 350 cars.

Occupancy at Financial Place was 62%. Eight tenants had left Financial Place during 1989 after their initial leases had expired. The institutional owner of Financial Place had been aggressive in offering free rent and generous tenant improvements in an effort to lease the vacant space. The project was plagued, however, by a reputation for having poor maintenance and difficult management. The tenants and their lease terms are summarized below in **Table 17-3**.

THE MARKETING PROGRAM

Sanchez had a marketing budget of $350,000. She used that money to create and fund a marketing program that targeted prospective tenants at three levels: national, state, and local. At the national level, she made a contribution of $50,000

Table 17-2 700 Glades Road Lease Terms

TENANT	S.F.	RATE	TERM	TI	FREE RENT	SIGN DATE	OCCUPANCY DATE
The BTF Corporation	14,000	22.00	5	18.00	6 months	10/88	5/89
Simpson & Post	3,000	21.50	5	18.00	6 months	10/88	5/89
Greyrock Financial	6,000	21.50	10	18.00	6 months	10/88	5/89
The Matte Group	12,000	21.00	10	18.00	6 months	10/88	5/89
Boca Medical Group	4,000	21.00	5	18.00	6 months	1/89	6/89
Mizner Securities	4,000	21.50	5	18.00	6 months	3/89	8/89
Morton Diskin Inc.	3,000	20.50	10	18.00	6 months	4/89	8/89
Winniker Investments	2,000	20.00	5	18.00	6 months	6/89	10/89
Tobias Enterprises	4,200	20.00	5	18.00	6 months	8/89	1/90
Totals/Averages	52,200	21.25	7	18.00	6 months		

Table 17-3 Financial Place Lease Terms

TENANT	S.F.	RATE	TERM	TI	FREE RENT	SIGN DATE	OCCUPANCY DATE
MLR	4,200	16.00	10	15.00	—	3/83	2/84
Laflor	1,680	16.00	7	15.00	—	3/83	2/84
ManTech	1,680	15.50	10	16.00	—	3/83	2/84
Cannif Industries	2,520	17.00	7	16.00	—	6/83	5/84
Carlstrom Metals	5,040	16.50	10	16.00	—	9/83	7/84
Olympis Services	3,360	16.50	7	16.00	—	12/83	11/84
CDL Associates	4,200	17.50	5	16.00	—	4/84	12/84
AFC Corp.	2,520	23.00	5	20.00	1 year	11/88	2/89
Boca Index Fund	2,520	23.00	10	22.00	1 year	1/89	4/89
Fiske & Mel	1,680	23.00	5	23.00	1 year	4/89	8/89
Clunan & Cocco	1,680	23.00	5	23.00	1 year	7/89	11/89
Belden Insurance	1,680	23.00	5	23.00	1 year	9/89	1/90
Totals/Averages	32,760	18.53	8	17.06	4 months		

to the Southern Commercial Industrial Division's national advertising campaign. At the state level, she had allocated $80,000 for print advertisements in the Miami and Fort Lauderdale newspapers as well as listings in the Southeast Real Estate Journal and an office leasing guide. At the local level, she had invested $75,000 in a new brochure and mailing packet. $50,000 had been allocated for promotional events. Signage was also placed at the front of the site in order to generate interest.

Sanchez had positioned the project in the marketing campaign to exploit the project's high quality standards, its Boca Raton address, the convenience of a mixed use development, the pleasant ambience of a master planned community, and the Southern name and reputation.

THE WEST BOCA MARKET

During the late sixties, Southern had responded to an anti-growth movement within the city of Boca Raton by moving the focus of its activities to the unincorporated area due west of the city. In this area, which later came to be called West Boca, Southern had started by creating the 850 acre Southern Corporate Park and the 1000 acre Glades West residential community. When first IBM, and then Siemens, Mitel, Microtel, Allstate Insurance, Burroughs, AT&T, Castle & Cooke and a host of other companies built facilities in the area, the white collar, high tech, Fortune 500 nature of the real estate market was established.

The growth which transformed West Boca from an unpopulated tract of scrub pines, sand, and rattlesnakes to a densely populated suburban center of corporate headquarters, golf courses, and luxury homes, was dramatic. Growth in West Boca had been centered on the area surrounding Glades Road but by

1988 almost all of the land in this area had been developed and many developers had started to develop on secondary sites along I-95.

During the eighties, both supply and demand for office space had been strong. The figures for all of Boca Raton, including both the city of Boca Raton and West Boca, are listed below in **Table 17-4**. The figures for 1989 and 1990 are estimates for the full year.

THE PROSPECTIVE TENANTS

Sanchez had three prospective tenants who were currently considering lease proposals that she had prepared. All three were also considering both 700 Glades Road and Financial Place. A summary of Sanchez's previous contact with each firm along with the lease terms are detailed below.

SouthEast Financial Services

Sanchez had arranged to meet John Clark, the CFO of SouthEast Financial Services, at the Boca Raton Chamber of Commerce monthly luncheon series. She had heard from a friend that SFS's lease was expiring. They currently occupied 10,000 s.f. in an older building in downtown Boca Raton. Clark had brushed off Sanchez's initial attempts to talk about their space needs and had suggested instead that they talk over drinks or dinner. Sanchez had followed up by arranging for dinner at one of Boca Raton's better restaurants.

At the dinner, Sanchez had presented her proposal. Southern would lease the entire sixth floor of Lakeside Center, over 13,000 s.f. of space, to SFS at $24 per s.f.. Southern would also provide $18 per s.f. for tenant improvements plus six months of free rent. By taking an entire floor, SFS would not only have a

Table 17-4 Greater Boca Raton Supply and Absorption Figures

YEAR	OFFICE SPACE	NEW SUPPLY	ABSORPTION	OCCUPANCY
1980	647,000	130,000	140,000	98.9%
1981	980,000	333,000	220,000	87.8
1982	1,200,000	220,000	180,000	86.7
1983	1,625,000	425,000	250,000	79.4
1984	2,150,000	525,000	380,000	77.7
1985	3,000,000	850,000	560,000	74.3
1986	4,350,000	1,350,000	625,000	65.6
1987	4,600,000	250,000	290,000	68.4
1988	5,200,000	600,000	260,000	65.6
1989E	5,500,000	300,000	310,000	67.5
1990E	5,550,000	50,000	450,000	75.0

prestigious space but it would gain by having a more efficient floor layout. Clark had been pleasant but noncommittal. "These items," he had said, "were all negotiable anyway." He would be, however, interested in an "equity kicker" with the lease if that could be worked out. This would be an equity position in the project that would allow SFS to participate in any future appreciation in value of the project. Clark had toured the project later in the week and had been impressed by the building.

SFS was a regional discount brokerage house for financial securities. The firm had aggressively expanded throughout the bull markets of the 1980s. Its current lease was due to expire on March 31, 1990 so Sanchez was confident that it would sign a deal within the next thirty days. SFS wanted a five year lease with an option to renew for an additional five years at its discretion. Clark had insisted that the space had to be ready by March 15, 1990. Sanchez had checked with Southern's construction division and had been told that they would be hard pressed to complete the tenant improvements in less than 10 weeks. Work could only start after the design drawings had been completed and these drawings would take between two weeks and two months to complete depending on the tenant and the architect.

Anderson & Gray

Sanchez had been contacted by Paul Nolan, a local broker, who had been hired by Anderson & Gray, a local law firm, to represent it in its lease negotiations. In October, Nolan had asked Sanchez to submit a proposal for Anderson & Gray to take 8,000 s.f. for 10 years. He had explained that a number of projects were also submitting proposals and that Anderson & Gray would, after evaluating the leases, enter into negotiations with the top three projects.

Nolan had also explained the basic criteria by which the leases would be evaluated:

1. Net effective rent. This was defined as all charges minus all concessions divided by the term of the lease.
2. Location
3. Layout and design of the building
4. Amenities
5. Parking
6. Reputation of the owner and quality of the management team.
7. Tenant Improvement Allowance of $20 per s.f.

Anderson & Gray would also need to have 500 s.f. of the space reinforced to support the high loads associated with their law library. The cost of this work was assumed to be $20,000 and this amount could be either included as a higher base rent or charged directly to Anderson & Gray.

Sanchez had submitted a proposal of $24 per s.f. for ten years. She had also offered $18 per s.f. in tenant improvements, six months in free rent, and no charge for the reinforcement of the library floor slab. Nolan had called later that week to tell her that her offer had been on the high side but that the partners wanted to include Lakeside Center in the final group. Nolan had asked her to prepare a second proposal for Anderson & Gray for the following week.

BCI Marketing

Sanchez had cold called Gail Mahoney, the CEO of BCI Marketing, late in October. BCI was a small firm which sold low priced gifts and other marketing materials to financial institutions to give to their customers. Another leasing agent at Southern had heard that BCI's lease was expiring and Sanchez had simply walked in through the front door early one morning and caught Mahoney alone at her desk. The two had hit it off almost immediately and Sanchez felt that she had the inside track in signing BCI. She had considered asking for $26 per s.f. but had ultimately decided to offer $24 per s.f., $18 per s.f. in TI, and six months free rent. BCI was looking for 3,000 s.f. and a four year lease. BCI was currently in an older building located in a secondary location. The current asking rate in this building was $18 per s.f.. Mahoney had called recently and asked Sanchez why she should pay more than $18 per s.f. in rent. Could Southern improve its offer?

Unfortunately, these were Sanchez's only prospects at the moment. This did not mean, however, that additional prospects weren't just around the corner.

LEASING STRATEGY AND NEGOTIATING TACTICS

In preparing for her meeting with Clark, Sanchez had to make a number of decisions. First, she had to decide what type of leasing strategy she would pursue. Second, she had to decide what combination of lease rate per s.f., TI per s.f., and amount of free rent to offer. Third, she had to prepare a presentation and decide on her negotiating tactics.

Her decisions would rest, at least in part, on her assessment of the market and on how important signing SFS was for the project. How aggressive should she be in cutting her rental rate? Was SFS willing to pay a premium for space at Lakeside Center? What would the competition offer? What was the current market rate? How should she structure her presentation? How should she handle Clark?

In order to estimate the current market rental rate, Sanchez decided to calculate the net present value for the last lease that had been signed at each of the three competing projects. As an example, for the Sullivan & O'Brien lease at Lakeside Center, a five year lease with no unusual expenses, a net rent of $18 ($23 gross rent less a $5 expense stop), six months free rent, and $21 in TI allowance, the cash flows for Lakeside Associates would be as follows:

Cash Flow to Lakeside Associates

	1	2	3	4	5
Net rent	$18	$18	$18	$18	$18
− Free rent	(11.5)	—	—	—	—
− Extra TI	(3)	—	—	—	—
Cash flow	$3.5	$18	$18	$18	$18

For simplicity, Sanchez had assumed that all cash flows occurred at the beginning of the year and that $18 had been budgeted for TI at all three properties. Using this method and a 12% discount rate, Sanchez calculated NPVs of $58.17, $50.56, and $44.67 for Lakeside Center, 700 Glades Road, and Financial Place.

From an owner's standpoint, these calculations were often valuable in evaluating alternative lease proposals. Sometimes an owner would compare the cash flows or net present value of a lease proposal with a building standard. In some cases, an owner might not take free rent allowances into account if he or she felt that the space would remain vacant anyway.

It was also appropriate in some situations to do an analysis from the tenant's standpoint. In this case, the cash flows from the tenant's perspective for the Sullivan & O'Brien lease at Lakeside Center would be as follows:

Cash Flow from Sullivan & O'Brien

	1	2	3	4	5
Gross rent	$23	$23	$23	$23	$23
− Free rent	(11.5)	—	—	—	—
− Extra TI	(3)	—	—	—	—
Cash flow	8.5	$23	$23	$23	$23

From the tenant's perspective, Sanchez calculated NPVs of $78.36, $70.75, and $64.86 for Lakeside Center, 700 Glades Road, and Financial Place.

Finally, Sanchez decided to calculate the rent in a simpler way for the three leases. She added the cash flows and divided by the number of years of the lease to arrive at an average rent.[1]

From these cash flows, she calculated average rents of $20.10, $18.00, and $17.40 for Lakeside Center, 700 Glades Road, and Financial Place. Sanchez knew that many real estate professionals and many tenants did not bother with

[1] In this case, Sanchez only took into account those tenant improvement and leasing costs above or below the amount included in the development budget. After the initial development period, to calculate the net effective rent over the lease period, she would deduct the total costs.

discounted cash flow analyses of leases. The simplified rent calculation neglected the time value of money but it was easy to do and the final number was easy to understand.

It was not that the numbers alone would dictate a tenant's decision, but it was certainly the first ingredient. Sanchez had to decide on what basis she was going to make her lease recommendations.

After deciding on her base offer, Sanchez still had to prepare a presentation and decide on her negotiating tactics. What should she stress in her presentation? Where should she make it? What other information should she include?

Sanchez believed that Clark would still want to negotiate, even after she had made her second offer. She knew that there was no way to predict exactly how the meeting would go but she knew that she had to be prepared for a variety of contingencies. She felt that momentum was important in some deals and that she might have to make a series of quick decisions in order to keep the deal alive. What should her final position be?

Sanchez was not sure what to make of Clark. He seemed to enjoy pushing her. She had heard from a personal friend at SFS that 700 Glades Road and Financial Place had offered lease terms that were only two to three dollars lower than her offer and yet Clark had told her that her offer was five dollars too high. She knew that Clark had been on elaborate fishing and golfing trips with the other two leasing agents. She wasn't sure how or if she should use her information about the other offers in her negotiations. This was an important deal. She didn't want to hurt the project, but she also didn't want to compromise her principles.

Sanchez also had to prepare responses for both Anderson & Gray and BCI Marketing as well as performing her ordinary marketing and leasing duties. As always, she was short on time and had to set some priorities for the coming week.

SOUTHERN TIER DEVELOPMENT

Her boss, Bill Martin, had asked her to meet with him that afternoon in order to update him on the status of the leasing program and to help him prepare for the partnership meeting with CREA the following week. The leasing program would be, as always, the initial item on the agenda.

The problem, however, was more than the lease proposals themselves. At the current 38% occupancy level, the project had already exhausted the initial $450,000 carried for operating losses and it would consume by the end of 1989 the additional $550,000 that had been saved during construction. Southern had guaranteed that it would fund the next $1.2 million in operating losses. Martin was considering three strategies for dealing with the impending cash flow deficit: (1) fund the deficit from Southern's other resources; (2) attempt to bring in a second financial partner; or (3) begin negotiations with CREA to get CREA to loan additional funds to the partnership on the same basis. In order to assess these strategies, he knew that he would have to come up with a revised income and expense projection for the project as well as an estimate of the carrying costs. Sanchez knew that Martin would rely heavily on her in making his decision.

Sanchez also knew that senior management at Southern was currently reviewing the company's strategy, organization, and human resources at the annual management conference. She was concerned about a number of the issues that would be raised. How important was it for Southern to have in-house leasing versus hiring an outside leasing company? Should it compensate the leasing agents with commissions or salaries or a mixture of both? Why was Lakeside Center not performing as projected? What should the company do to improve returns?

Sanchez would not attend the management conference but she knew that both her performance in leasing Lakeside Center and her assessment of the current situation would go a long way towards making or breaking her career at Southern.

Exhibit 17-1 *Lakeside Center Site Plan*

Site Plan

Not only are a shady park setting and shimmering lake part of your working environment, nestled amid all the beauty are a variety of retail shops, professional services, fitness center and lakeside restaurants. And, with a Radisson Suite Hotel, you and your clients may enjoy a jogging/exercise trail, conference rooms and 202 beautifully appointed suites. Plans for banking facilities will round out the myriad of conveniences.

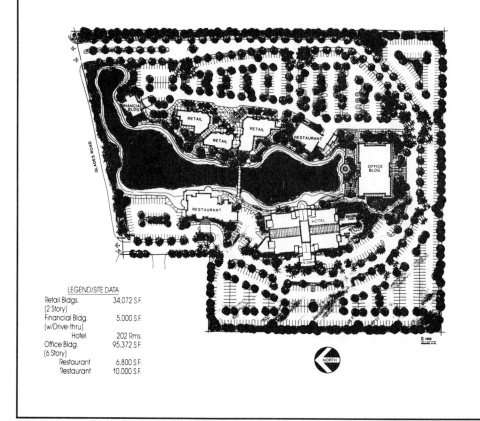

LEGEND/SITE DATA

Retail Bldgs. (2 Story)	34,072 S.F.
Financial Bldg. (w/Drive-thru)	5,000 S.F.
Hotel	202 Rms.
Office Bldg. (6 Story)	95,372 S.F.
Restaurant	6,800 S.F.
Restaurant	10,000 S.F.

SIXTH FLOOR

Grid Module = 4'8"

Approx 13,692 usable SQ. FT.

Exhibit 17-1 (continued)

Exhibit 17-2 *Pro Forma Development Cost Analysis, January 14, 1988*

Project Description
Acreage   5.1
F.A.R.   0.43
Building Area   95,372
Efficiency   86%
Rentable Area   82,020

Development Cost Analysis

I. Planning and Professional				
Architectural			$	295,000
Engineering				120,000
Landscape architect				50,000
Graphics consultant				40,000
Legal				80,000
		Subtotal:		585,000
II. Development				
Site work				0
Hardscape feature				250,000
Shell construction	$59 per sq. ft.			5,627,000
Tenant improvements	$18 per sq. ft.			1,476,000
Landscaping	$40,000 per acre			204,000
Fees, bonds, and taxes				189,000
General conditions				100,000
Graphics				60,000
Contingency				387,000
Project management				262,000
		Subtotal:		8,555,000
III. Marketing				
Leasing commissions				350,000
Brochures and displays				50,000
Advertising				200,000
Promotion				100,000
		Subtotal:		700,000
IV. Land 5.1 acres @ $653,400 per acre				3,332,000
$15.00 per sq. ft.				
V. Interest 10% for 12 months				725,000
VI. Financing Cost				153,000
VII. Future Operating Losses During Leaseup				450,000
VIII. Total Development Cost				$14,500,000

Exhibit 17-3

Pro Forma Income Statement

	1990
Projected gross income	$1,968,480
Less 5% vacancy	98,424
Effective gross income	$1,870,056
Less operating expense	410,000
Net operating income	$1,460,056

Pro Forma Full-Year Operating Budget

	ANNUAL BUDGET	VARIABLE PORTION
Repairs and Maintenance		
General	$15,000	
Structural	5,000	
HVAC	5,000	
Elevator	8,000	
Janitorial		
Janitorial service	45,000	$30,000
Pest control	4,000	
Window washing	5,000	
Utilities		
Electric	100,000	79,000
Water/sewer	10,000	8,000
Trash	7,000	5,000
Security	18,000	
Insurance	14,000	
Landscape and Parking Lot Maintenance		
Landscape and irrigation maintenance	23,000	
Parking lot sweeping	6,000	
Real estate taxes	90,000	
Contribution for roads and maintenance	15,000	
Management fee	40,000	40,000
Total operating budget	$410,000	$164,000

700 GLADES ROAD

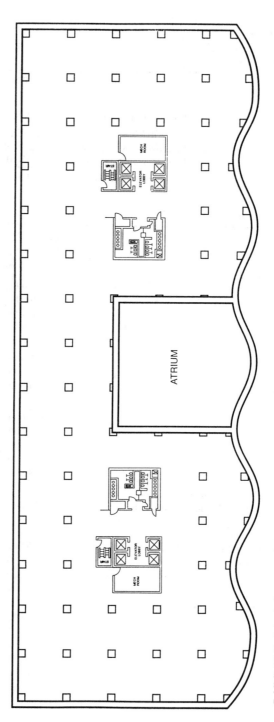

ATRIUM

Exhibit 17-4 *Lakeside Center 700 Glades Road*

Exhibit 17-5 *Lakeside Center Financial Plaza*

FINANCIAL PLAZA

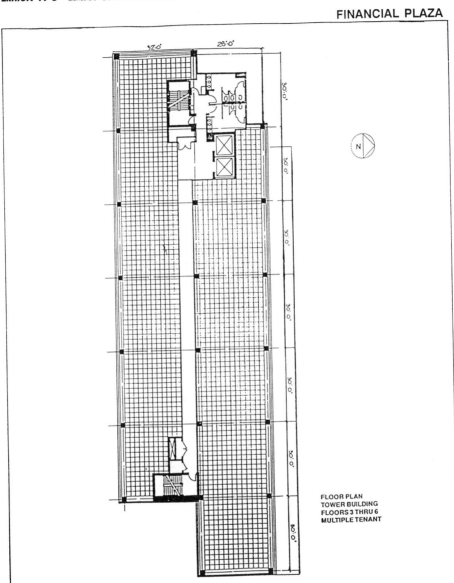

FLOOR PLAN
TOWER BUILDING
FLOORS 3 THRU 6
MULTIPLE TENANT

18

ONE LEATHER STREET

In October, 1987, the Smith brothers, seeking a new real estate niche, elect to rehabilitate a small Boston office building. They run into difficulty with their architect, contractor, regulatory officials and their lenders. The case discusses the issues raised by their development problems, economic projections, as well as their highly leveraged financial structure.

Discussion Questions:

1. What should the Smiths do now? What actions should they take with regard to contractors, architects, bankers, investors, and the Inspectional Services department?

2. Evaluate the Smiths' business strategy. Was One Leather Street an appropriate investment for the brothers? In particular, were the risks worth the anticipated returns? What do you think of their marketing and design decisions?

3. How might you have proceeded differently?

On a sunny Saturday morning in early October of 1987, Harry and Eric Smith were discussing recent developments at One Leather Street. Harry had just returned to work having recovered from back surgery. He was interested in the progress of the property since his admittance into the hospital. Eric was eager to share with his brother the problems he was facing on the project.

One Leather Street was the Smiths' most ambitious project to date. It was a six-story commercial and retail building located in Laclede's Landing, an older area near the river and adjacent to St. Louis's downtown, blocks from the financial district. It contained 49,000 gross square feet and 45,710 net rentable feet. Substantial renovation to the exterior and common area interiors was underway. Although 75% full, additional vacancies were anticipated when rents were increased. The new occupants would require substantial tenant improvements.

PRIOR PERFORMANCE OF THE SMITHS

In 1981, while attending Harvard Business School, Eric Smith bought several three-family houses in Somerville, Massachusetts. By improving the properties cosmetically, he discovered that he could raise rents often as much as 50%. By the end of the school year, he had acquired six of these frame, multiple-family houses and had put together a small renovating team of carpenters, plumbers, and painters.

After graduating from Business School, Eric persuaded his brother to leave his job at a prestigious consulting company and move to St. Louis. They agreed that Harry would sell their existing projects and identify future projects for acquisition in St. Louis, while Eric would enter the consulting field there. In Eric's free time, he was expected to participate in the business, primarily in raising capital for growth. They would share equally in Eric's salary, the business, and the real estate. They named the business Redstone Associates.

Redstone's business philosophy was simple. The objective was to purchase property at prices below the cost of replacement and then to improve the property primarily through cosmetics. Often, improvements included new roofs, windows, electrical service and heating systems. These improvements cost approximately $2,000 to $5,000 per unit. Gut rehabs and new construction were

Research Associate Jeffrey A. Libert prepared this case under the supervision of Adjunct Professor William J. Poorvu as the basis for class discussion rather than to illustrate either effective or ineffective handling of an administrative situation.

avoided. On completion, Redstone's projects were described as clean B + properties. Harry and Eric applied this philosophy primarily to apartment houses, but also used the strategy successfully on small strip centers.

On the management side, they took pride in providing efficient and prompt service to their tenants. A solid management team included cleaners, painters, service personnel and property managers. Redstone's motto was to be the best landlord in the middle-income market segment.

By the end of 1986, the Smiths had raised $3,015,000 from friends, relatives, and business associates for 10 real estate limited partnerships. These partnerships had purchased for $5,763,000 seven St. Louis residential projects consisting of 400 apartments and for $3,063,000 three shopping centers with 87,000 square feet.

The success of the Smiths' strategy was reflected in Redstone's returns to investors. The following two partnerships are examples of the types of returns investors had become accustomed to and were indicative of the deals in which Redstone excelled.

South Huntington Courts Associates, a limited partnership, was formed by Redstone in the summer of 1984. The property consisted of 56 residential units in four buildings. Most units required painting, floor sanding, storm windows, and minor repairs to the plumbing and electrical systems. In addition, the boilers and the roofs were replaced. Total capital improvements to the property in the first six months totalled $125,000. During this period 60% of the leases were terminated and released to tenants paying as much as 75% higher than the original occupants.

The investors in South Huntington Courts contributed $300,000 to the deal, which had a mortgage of $700,000. The cash flow to the limited partners in the first three years was 6%, 8%, and 13.3% respectively on their investment. In the fourth year, 85% of the original capital contribution was returned through a refinancing.

Hemenway Courts Associates, a limited partnership, was formed in January, 1985. The property consisted of two apartment houses that together contained 62 apartments. The properties were in terrible condition and were infested with vermin. Upon purchase, common areas were redone, apartments were repainted, floors sanded, roofs and heating systems were replaced and the steel supporting structures in the basements were reinforced to stop settling. Most of the tenancies were terminated during the improvement period. New leases were signed at rents nearly 100% above the prior ones.

The purchase price of the buildings was $584,000. With improvements of $100,000, the deal was capitalized for $700,000, of which $200,000 was equity and the rest was debt. Just over one year from acquisition the properties were refinanced, and the investors received $160,000 from the refinancing proceeds.

The Smiths preferred cosmetically renovating projects to new construction and gut rehabs. They believed that they could a) turn projects around within 6 to 9 months from acquisition, b) provide substantial returns to investors, c) avoid the aggravation of dealing with building departments, architects, and City Hall and d) lower their business risk by staying in the middle market that served the bulk of the population. Most importantly, the Smiths believed they had a competitive advantage: their projects on completion were averaging about 35% of the cost of new construction, and yet their rents were only about 25% less than rents being collected on new projects.

However, at the end of 1986, the Smiths were forced to reevaluate their business strategy. They felt that residential units would come under increased regulatory controls and that commercial properties were a better buy.

IMPLEMENTING THEIR NEW STRATEGY

At the end of 1986, Eric had decided to work full time at Redstone. He had had back troubles of his own the prior year. The travelling schedule at his consulting job only served to worsen his condition. More importantly, 1986 had been a watershed year for Redstone in terms of profitability. Eric's salary had been dwarfed by the returns from Redstone.

Harry's and Eric's responsibilities were simply split. Harry as President of Redstone Properties Corp. would supervise property acquisition, management, construction and disposition. Eric would raise equity and debt capital in his position as President of Redstone Equities Corp. Together they would review all investment decisions.

To facilitate apartment house acquisitions, the Smiths decided to raise $2,000,000 in a blind pool. Eric would raise this capital from past investors who were anxious to invest more money with Redstone. Harry had also identified a commercial property in Laclede's Landing which, when acquired and improved, would cost far less than replacement.

THE ACQUISITION DECISION

In February of 1987, Harry had presented to Eric One Leather Street as an opportunity to acquire a 49,000-square-foot office property in the city of St. Louis for well below the cost of reconstruction.

As the brothers reviewed the investment decision, they identified the pros and the cons of the deal. In addition, they ran some simple calculations to determine the capitalized value of the property after completion.

On the pro side, Harry argued that properties in the Financial District—only a few blocks away—were being built for about $200 per s.f. One Leather Street, at a $3,400,000 purchase price, was only $70 per square foot. Even after the anticipated improvements and carry, Harry estimated that the total cost of the building would be only $100 per rentable square foot. (see **Exhibit 18-1**). The building had been originally built as a parking garage and was structurally sound. In addition, with two elevators, large bathrooms, a marble lobby and attractive exterior moldings, Harry believed the building to have the potential to be B+/A- commercial space.

The market presented both strengths and weaknesses. On the positive side, Laclede's Landing was located near the interchange of both Highway 55 and Highway 70. It's proximity to the Arch and riverfront park generated tremendous foot traffic for its newly renovated restaurant and retail space. The present owner had three applications from prospective tenants at $30 per square foot for the available retail vacancy.

The office market, however, did not appear as strong. Close by, the Financial District was a prestigious market for upscale office tenants, particularly law firms and financial companies and commanded high rents. On the other hand, the Laclede's Landing area still had a low-rent image about it. Although there were other office buildings in the area, there was still vacant warehouse space, light manufacturing and other low-paying tenants. Lawyers, accountants, ad agencies and other prestige tenants had yet to find the area appealing. In fact, the occupants of One Leather Street were indicative of the types of tenants in the area. The Board of Library Commissioners was paying $8.50 per square foot and occupied nearly two floors of the building. Engineering Inc. had nearly one floor and was paying about $8 per square foot. The remaining tenants were all small with short-term leases and low rents. From the look of their operations, these tenants were not highly profitable ventures.

Harry believed that he could renew leases with most of the existing tenants at $15 per square foot, after improvements to the common areas were completed. In addition to the existing fifth floor vacancy, he expected one additional floor would vacate due to rent increases. Harry was pleased that nearly all of the tenancies would roll over within two years. The project, in his mind, was similar to Redstone's residential deals in that the property would never be totally vacant. Because lease renewals were staggered, renovations could only be performed on parts of the building at one time. There would always be some rent coming in and, therefore, soft costs due to interest carry during the development period would be mitigated (see **Exhibit 18-2**).

The brothers, however, were worried about the recent increase in office vacancy. Several new buildings had together added 2,000,000 s.f. to the market. In addition, one of the larger banks was moving many of its back-room operations to the suburbs and would shortly empty nearly 700,000 s.f. in its tower although other areas of the bank were expected to expand to take up most of that space. Even though all of these buildings were charging rents between $25 and $30 per square foot, the overbuilding had pushed office vacancy to 13%, the highest in recent history. The brothers were also nervous that the large vacancy of over 20% in the suburbs might hurt their ability to get solid rents in the building. Still, suburban buildings were quoting $20 to $25 per s.f. (although many developers were reportedly taking deals for substantially less).

On balance, Harry and Eric thought the market would prove to be beneficial. With only a few buildable sites available in the Financial District, Laclede's Landing was a likely recipient of additional investments. Because new building costs were substantially more than their cost of One Leather Street, rents would, they argued, have to move higher.

As a final step to deciding whether the deal was acceptable, the Smiths calculated the capitalized value and cash flow to the investors once the deal was completed (see **Exhibit 18-2**). Although the return on total investment was somewhat shy of what they were accustomed to, they believed that the returns were within a reasonable range. In addition, they had learned not to place much value on financial analysis. They felt that projections of rent had less to do with inflation and more to do with the cost of supplying real estate, the return on that replacement cost, the supply of land, and demand for space.

At the end of February, the Smiths decided to pursue the investment. They placed $100,000 in a nonrefundable deposit to bind a purchase and sale contract. The closing would take place at the end of May.

FINANCING THE PROJECT

Eric had educated his investors as to the development risks and potential rewards of Redstone's strategy. Although Redstone's investors would have been anxious to invest in One Leather Street, they were tapped out with the apartment fund. Eric identified other local syndicators as a potential source of equity capital for this venture.

To his and his brother's dismay, the syndicators were not excited about the project. The common reply was that the deal had development risks and did not produce passive income to offset passive losses from their customers' prior investments in real estate. Since the change in the tax law, passive income generators (otherwise known as PIGS) were the easy deals to sell to the investment community. However, the Crimson Group, a small broker dealer and investment advisor was excited about the deal. They took the numbers that Harry and Eric supplied and restructured them. They insisted on a staging for the equity investment. This, they argued, would raise the investor's after-tax return. Of their investment of $1,939,000, $525,000 was to be paid in cash and the remainder in the form of personally guaranteed promissory notes due in two installments in 1988 and 1989. The developer would be able to borrow from a bank the full amount of these investor notes. Also, to back out a higher return to the investor and generate a fee, the syndicator lowered the reserve for capital cost contingencies (see **Exhibit 18-3**).

Akin to prior deals structured by the Smiths, the Crimson Group allocated 99% of the tax losses to the investors. Investors were entitled to 50% of the pretax cash flow after financing. At the time of sale the investors would receive their investment back first. The remaining cash would follow the aforementioned 50/50 split. The partnership prohibited additional calls for money from the limited partners. However, the general partners could make an unsecured 11% interest-bearing loan to the partnership. The depreciation was calculated at 31.5 years straight line, and investors were expected to be in the 28% tax bracket.

The Smiths were concerned about the level of financial risk this structure created for them and the deal. In the first place, there was less money allocated to contingencies. In a deal like this one, it was difficult to predict the level of vacancy once the rents were raised. Also, the buildout costs were directly related to the vacancy. In the second place, there was more debt to service in this deal. The investor note financing was structured so that the interest was a partnership cost. Therefore, negative cash flow before lease up was higher under the Crimson Group's structure (compare **Exhibits 18-2** and **18-3**). Finally, there was a problem with timing. It was now the first of April. The syndicator indicated that the fastest he could move given the time it took to write the offering memorandum, blue sky it, and sell it to investors would be three months. Although the Smiths were accustomed to raising money in four to six weeks, Eric now learned that this was not the industry standard.

Despite all these problems, the Smiths decided that they would take the Crimson Group's offer. For financing, the seller would be providing a 10-year interest-only first mortgage for $2,400,000 with interest at 10%. Although there were many banks willing to make a second mortgage for $300,000, none were willing to give the extra $832,000 needed for bridge financing between the time of the closing and September when the syndication became final. At that time a loan could be obtained to be repaid from payments by the investors of their stayed commitments.

The Smiths had heard of Mark Gold and his lending company, S.I.C. They made an application to Mark, who agreed to make the loan for the bridge financing. However, as part of the deal, S.I.C. required that the Smiths borrow from S.I.C. the second mortgage for $300,000 as well as the $832,000 bridge loan that would be required until the proceeds of the syndication were received. To induce Mark to make the loan, the Smiths also had to pledge their homes and two notes that they had taken back when selling certain deals. Mark's rate was interest only at 17%, far higher than rates quoted by conventional lenders. The prepayment penalty he charged basically prohibited a prepayment of the $300,000 for nearly two years.

At the closing table on May 30, the Smiths were nervous about the level of risk they were about to undertake. At one point, they almost decided to walk away from the deal when the seller wanted to buy back the agreement by giving the Smiths a $100,000 profit. He had recently been offered $300,000 more than his price to the Smiths and was anxious to break the contract.

CHOOSING AN ARCHITECT AND A CONTRACTOR

During the acquisition period, Harry had begun to interview architects for the project. He was looking for experience in renovating old buildings, creativity and price. Two architects were chosen to submit ideas on design and pricing. Gary Grant and Associates, the first of these companies, was small but accustomed to the smaller renovations of warehouse space near the river. They were highly recommended as architects that kept job costs in mind. Their plan for the building was simple. Panels would be removed from the front of the building on the retail level to allow for more glass, and common area spaces on the office floors would be dressed up with new surfaces and lighting. They suggested that the building be repainted gray from its present yellow and red.

The second architect, Elizabeth Andrews and Associates, was an award-winning company for office designs. The firm was presently designing several large suburban office parks outside the city. Compared to Grant's, Andrews' plan for the building was more exciting. First, she had discovered that through a redesign of the hallways and baths, much of the common tenant space could be eliminated. This would make the floors more efficient and therefore increase the chances of obtaining the desired rent. Second, she showed that through narrowing the main lobby, additional retail space could be created—and, she argued, would not compromise the potential of the main lobby. Besides removing the panels, which limited visibility into the retail spaces, she suggested a design for the storefronts with small panes of glass aligned with the rustications of the stone work. Other ideas for the building included canopies, a light acid wash on the building to bring back the original masonry, and a lobby with a vaulted ceiling.

Andrews also submitted an estimate for fees of $40,000. Grant's price for the same project was $15,000. Grant believed that the budget Harry had submitted was possible with the right type of contractors. Andrews, however, expressed a concern up front that the construction budget for the job was light; she felt that the exterior, main lobby and storefront/glass work were keys to the success of turning the project into a well-respected building. Nonetheless, she agreed that they would work hard on their design to remain within the budget. Harry chose Elizabeth Andrews.

Just prior to his leaving for surgery in July, Harry had instructed Andrews to come up with construction specifications for the office tenant common areas, for tenant improvements, and for the first floor storefronts. Harry wanted these quickly so that he could submit them for construction bids.

At this point, Harry turned the project over to his brother. He introduced the architect to him and gave Eric suggestions as to who should bid the job. They included Richard Harper and Associates; and Bristle and Company, owned by Joe Grogan. The two contractors had worked on other Redstone jobs, primarily involved in painting and minor carpentry. Eric also identified a larger contractor, American Syndicate, to bid on the job. The latter was the construction arm for a major developer of residential and office space nationwide.

Both Harper and Grogan came in with similar prices on the interior work. Each multitenant lobby would run about $25,000 and the tenant space about $75,000 a floor. This price was very close to budget. American Syndicate bid the job at $150,000 for each floor. However, the problem facing Eric was that he believed—despite protests from both Harper and Grogan—that the job was too large for either one of them. Each employed about two carpenters, two laborers, and a handful of painters. On the other hand, the total budget for the three floors—the first floor retail, the fifth floor vacancy, and one unanticipated floor of vacancy, was $300,000. American Syndicate would take the project $150,000 over budget. At the end of July, Eric decided to split the job between Grogan and Harper with Grogan being the general contractor.

Although Eric had breathed a sigh of relief in anticipation of bringing the project in on budget, his problems were just beginning. The $125,000 that the syndicator had funded for negative carry would take the project from July through the end of December. At that point the project would begin to generate cash flow if some of the remaining tenants accepted the higher budgeted rents and the initial vacancy was relet.

Initially, Harry and Eric had not worried about the tight leasing schedule. In May, State University had signed a letter of intent for the entire fifth floor at the projected rent. However, that deal had fallen through at the end of July. The leasing agent felt that a new tenant could not be found, a lease executed, and tenant improvements built by January 1. Each month that the floor lay vacant was a loss of nearly $10,000. In addition to these leasing problems, the architects had fallen behind schedule at least two months on the storefront drawings. Without construction drawings finished by the end of September— which was highly unlikely—construction on the retail space would not be finished until after the first of the year. Interested retailers would lose the all-important Christmas shopping season. Every month that the retail space lay empty after the first of the year also cost the project about $10,000.

To solve the problem with the storefront delay, Eric sent out design drawings to five glass contractors. The architects were furious at him for doing this. They argued that without completed construction drawings, the construction might not accurately reflect their new design for the store fronts and windows in the next floor which now were similar to the other office floors (see **Exhibit 18-6**). More importantly, the materials including glass, architectural glass, moldings, and hardware had not been specified. To Eric's dismay, the prices—subject to review of materials—were coming in at $150,000 compared to a $75,000 budget. In addition, all of the contractors were complaining. The doors, they told Eric and the architects, could not be properly supported, and no glass contractor would guarantee the work.

PROBLEMS WITH CITY HALL

By early August, construction had started on the fifth floor tenant lobby. Grogan's men had demolished the baths and were in the process of rebuilding the multitenant office lobby. Harper's team had demolished the main lobby of the building and was removing the marble panels on the facade. A new boiler was being installed. But there was no building permit on the window of the building.

Eric spoke to Joe Grogan about this. Joe's response was that he was renovating the existing conditions of the building—much as he had done for many of Redstone's apartments where he had not needed to pull permits—and therefore did not need a permit. He had instructed the electrical contractor and the plumbing contractor to take out separate permits for their work. Eric was not satisfied with this response and instructed Joe to get a master permit for the building. This permit could then be amended as the scope of the job changed. Joe then explained that he only possessed a C-Class license. This allowed him to supervise minor jobs. However, Robert Williams, the father of one of his employees, had a B-class license. He would ask Robert to pull the permit.

By early September, a permit had been granted to the building. On the last Friday of the month, Robert Williams had been called by the building inspector, Charley Godbout. Godbout told Williams to shut down the job. He also instructed Williams to meet him at the building the following Tuesday. Grogan told Eric that Williams was frightened. Godbout was reportedly furious at the amount of work that had taken place without a permit, and that much of the work would have to be redone.

Eric met with Williams that Tuesday prior to the arranged meeting with Godbout. Williams was nervous. His license, he told Eric, was at risk. In addition, he told Eric that Harper and Grogan did not know what they were doing. For example, he showed Eric how the two contractors were endangering the tenants by not using proper barricades, demolition lighting, or signs. He also told Eric that Godbout appeared to be looking for trouble.

Williams wanted to know if Eric would pay for 10 $100 tickets that Williams would buy to next month's Big Brother Dinner at which Godbout was to be honored. Williams indicated that without a better relationship with the inspectional services department, the job could be shut down for two to six months. Williams felt that Godbout might be more cooperative if he could be convinced that the Smiths were reasonable developers. In any event, Williams told Eric that he would have to stay on the site to supervise it. His supervision fee would be $600 a week. He threatened Eric that without compensation he would remove his license from the job.

HARRY RETURNS FROM BACK SURGERY

Harry had been back to work for about two days. Eric had told him on his return that he was having very serious problems at One Leather Street. Harry asked Eric if he would put together some numbers to indicate the present financial situation. Although he was not sure they should go this route, Eric organized a new set of numbers assuming a clean break with his contractors and more vacancy (see **Exhibit 18-4**). This Saturday was the first chance they had had to discuss developments at One Leather Street since Harry had left for the hospital.

Exhibit 18-1 *Initial Acquisition Analysis by Smiths (2/87)*
Source and Use of Funds

USE OF FUNDS

Purchase Price	$3,400,000
Capital Improvements[1]	525,000
Contingency Improvements[2]	250,000
Developers Fee	125,000
Leasing Fee	50,000
Mortgage Origination Fees	10,000
Legal Costs	25,000
Interest Carry	100,000
Working Capital	75,000
TOTAL USES OF FUNDS	$4,560,000
Cost per Rentable Square Foot	$ 100

SOURCES OF FUNDS

First Mortgage From Seller	$2,400,000
Second Mortgage	300,000
Equity	1,860,000
TOTAL SOURCES OF FUNDS	$4,560,000

[1]*Capital Improvements*

Three floors of tenant fit up	$300,000
Storefronts	50,000
Main Lobby	22,000
HVAC	24,000
Other Utilities	69,500
Exterior	25,000
Architect	34,500
	$525,000

[2]*Contingency Improvements*

Two more floors of tenant fit up	$200,000
Additional vacancy during construction	50,000
	$250,000

Exhibit 18-2 *Initial Acquisition Analysis by Smiths*

Rental Income Analysis

RENT ROLL	S.F.	LEASE RENEWAL	1987 $/S.F.	1987 RENTS	PRO FORMA $/S.F.	1989 PRO FORMA RENTS
1st Floor						
ATT	2066	1/88	$19.36	$ 39,998	$30.00	$ 61,980
Telemarketing	1366	1/88	15.00	20,490	15.00	20,490
Vacancy	3473	6905	0.00	0	30.00	104,190
2nd Floor						
Board Library	7745	1/88	8.50	65,833	15.00	$116,175
3rd Floor						
S.U.	2250	7/87	11.00	24,750	15.00	33,750
Board Library	4455	1/88	8.50	37,868	15.00	66,825
Vacant	1040		.00	0	15.00	15,600
	7745					
4th Floor						
Engineering Inc.	5380	1/88	8.03	43,201	15.00	80,700
Publicity Assoc.	2445		7.65	18,700	15.00	36,675
	7825					
5th Floor						
Vacant	7745		0.00	0	15.00	116,175
6th Floor						
General Chemical	2500	1/89	9.20	23,000	15.00	37,500
Assoc. Publishing	3107	1/88	8.50	26,410	15.00	46,605
G.R. Publicity	2138	1/88	10.08	$ 21,550	15.00	$ 32,070
	7745					
Total	45710			$321,800		$768,735

Cap Rate and Cash Flow Analysis

	1987 CASH FLOW	1989 CASH FLOW
Rent Roll	$321,779	$768,735
Real Estate Taxes*	(75,000)	(75,000)
Other Operating Expenses @ $2.91/s.f.*	(133,032)	(133,032)
Operating Cash Flow	113,767	560,703
Interest on First Mortgage	(240,000)	(240,000)
Int. on Second Mortgage @ 14%	(42,000)	(42,000)
Cash Flow after Financing	($168,233)	$278,703
Cap Rate on Operating Cash Flow	2.5%	12.3%
Monthly Deficit	($14,019)	

*All expense increases over these levels are assumed to be picked up by tenants

Exhibit 18-3 *Syndicator Analysis (4/87)*

	CLOSING 5/30/87	FUNDING OF SYNDICA. 9/1/87	FISCAL YEAR END 12/30/87	FISCAL YEAR END 12/30/88	FISCAL YEAR END 12/30/89	TOTAL
Sources						
Cash Flow After Financing			($181,500)	$ 62,000	$ 177,000	$ 57,500
1st Mortgage	2,400,000					2,400,000
2nd Mortgage	300,000					300,000
Bridge Loan	832,000					832,000
Loan against Investor Note		1,414,000				1,414,000
Investor Equity		525,000		504,000	910,000	1,939,000
Total Sources	$3,532,000	$1,939,000	($181,500)	$566,000	$1,087,000	$6,942,500
Uses						
Purchase Price	$3,400,000					3,400,000
Legal Costs	69,000					69,000
Mortgage Fees	63,000					63,000
Syndication Costs		258,000				258,000
Developer Fee		125,000				125,000
Leasing Fee			25,000	25,000		50,000
Capital Improvements			262,500	262,600		525,000
Repayment of Bridge Loan		832,000				832,000
Repayment of Loan against Investor Note				504,000	910,000	1,414,000
Total Uses	$3,532,000	$1,215,000	$287,500	$791,500	$910,000	$6,736,000
Surplus/Deficit Cash	0	724,000	(469,000)	(225,500)	177,000	
Cumulative Cash Balance	0	724,000	255,000	29,500	206,500	

Cash Flow from Operations

	1987 (7 months)	1988	1989
Gross Rents	$187,704	$705,545	$768,735
Vacancy (5%)	9,385	35,277	38,437
Net Rent	$178,319	$670,268	$730,298
Expenses:			
Taxes	43,750	75,000	75,000
Operating Expenses	$ 77,600	133,032	133,032
Operating Cash Flow	$ 56,969	$462,236	$522,266
Interest:			
1st Mortgage	140,000	240,000	240,000
2nd Mortgage	29,750	51,000	51,000
Investor Notes	33,359	109,236	54,262
Bridge Loan	35,360		
Total Interest	$238,469	$400,236	$345,262
Cash Flow after Financing	(181,500)	$ 62,000	$177,000

Exhibit 18-4   *Downside Scenario: October 1987*

	CLOSING 5/30/87	FUNDING OF SYNDICA. 9/1/87	FISCAL YEAR END 12/30/87	FISCAL YEAR END 12/30/88	FISCAL YEAR END 12/30/89	TOTAL
Sources						
Cash Flow After Financing			($181,500)	($ 24,063)	$ 146,484	($ 59,079)
1st Mortgage	2,400,000					2,400,000
2nd Mortgage	300,000					300,000
Bridge Loan	832,000					832,000
Loan against Investor Note		1,414,000				1,414,000
Investor Equity		525,000		504,000	910,000	1,939,000
Total Sources	$3,532,000	$1,939,000	($181,500)	$479,937	$1,056,484	$6,825,921
Uses						
Purchase Price	$3,400,000					3,400,000
Legal Costs	69,000					69,000
Mortgage Fees	63,000					63,000
Syndication Costs		258,000				258,000
Developer Fee		125,000				125,000
Leasing Fee[1]			25,000	25,000	12,500	62,500
Capital Improvements[2]			405,000	301,000	175,000	881,000
Repayment of Bridge Loan		832,000				832,000
Repayment of Loan against Investor Note				504,000	910,000	1,414,000
Total Uses	$3,532,000	$1,215,000	$430,000	$830,000	$1,097,000	$7,104,500
Surplus/Deficit Cash	0	724,000	(611,500)	(350,063)	(41,016)	
Cumulative Cash Balance	0	724,000	112,500	(237,563)	(278,579)	

[1]Leasing fee has been increased to reflect additional floor vacancy.
[2]Capital Improvements have been increased from $525,000 to reflect four floors of build out now at $150,000 a floor versus three floors at $100,000 and higher storefront costs.

Exhibit 18-4 *(continued)*

Cash Flow from Operations

	1987	1988	1989
	(7 months)		
Gross Rents	$187,704	$705,545	$768,735
Vacancy[3]	9,385	116,175	58,088
Net Rent	$178,319	$589,370	710,648
Expenses:			
Taxes	43,750	76,875	78,797
Operating Expenses[4]	77,600	136,358	139,767
Operating Cash Flow	$ 56,969	$376,137	$492,084
Interest:			
1st Mortgage	140,000	240,000	240,000
2nd Mortgage	29,750	51,000	51,000
Investor Notes	33,359	109,200	54,600
Bridge Loan	35,360		
Total Interest	$238,469	$400,200	$345,600
Cash Flow after Financing	(181,500)	(24,063)	146,484

[3]Vacancy in 1988 reflects 50% occupancy of two office floors. In 1989, 50% vacancy in one additional floor.
[4]50% of all operating expense increases are assumed to be picked up by tenants, 5% inflation rate.

Exhibit 18-5 *Financial Statement of Harry and Eric Smith, 12/31/86*

ASSETS	
Cash	$ 18,362
Notes Receivable	518,145
Account Receivable	108,452
Investments in Real Estate	2,354,200
Investment in Closely Held Business	233,400
IRA	50,463
Personal Residences	936,500
Personal Property	155,425
	$4,374,947
LIABILITIES	
Income Taxes Payable	$ 46,549
Home Mortgages	387,933
Miscellaneous	12,500
	$ 446,982
NET WORTH	$3,927,965

Exhibit 18-6   *One Leather Street*

19

LYNDON MALL

In September, 1988, Joan Carnevali must decide if MKS should bid to purchase the Lyndon Mall. Lyndon Mall is an older regional shopping center in Mississippi that requires both renovation and expansion to compete against a potential new mall. This case explores the criteria for success in shopping center development. It also looks at the business and ethical issues relating to the acquisition of the mall by its current manager.

Discussion Questions:

1. Evaluate the potential for success of Lyndon Mall both in its current condition and after the proposed modernization and expansion. How would you deal with the existing tenants?
2. What are the market assumptions in the above analysis? Are they realistic? How does Dempsey's announcement affect your thinking?
3. As Joan Carnevali, what would you offer Mutual for Lyndon Mall and why? How would you handle the negotiations with Mutual Insurance?
4. What are the keys to success in shopping center development?

Joan Carnevali was a member of the in-house acquisition team studying the potential purchase of the 566,000 square foot Lyndon Mall by MKS & Associates, a Birmingham-based shopping mall developer, purchaser and manager. Lyndon Mall in Lyndon, Mississippi had been built by Laurel Realty in 1971, then sold to its current owner Mutual Insurance in 1980. MKS had managed the mall since the late 1970s, and engineered its expansion and upgrading in 1981. Now, in September of 1988, MKS considered purchasing the mall to add to MKS's growing portfolio of malls in 14 states. MKS had succeeded during the past five years in changing its business from mall management exclusively to include mall development, acquisition and ownership.

Carnevali saw the biggest risk to Lyndon Mall to be the threat of powerful new competition in the form of the Dempsey Organization, an aggressive mall developer active nationwide. Lyndon Mall was located in the Tri-Cities area of northeastern Mississippi, a triangular shaped regional retail market where local mall sales historically divided fairly evenly among the three mall players: Lyndon Mall, Fort Perry Mall in Kingfisher, MS; and Crystal Mall in Crystal, MS. There was some leakage of mall sales to upper end malls in Memphis and Atlanta. The Dempsey organization announced plans earlier in 1988 to build a one million square foot superregional mall at the heart of Tri-Cities, seven miles from Lyndon Mall. While Dempsey was known for announcing development plans prematurely and not carrying through, his reputation for building successful retail centers could not be ignored.

If developed, a Dempsey mall could completely destabilize the existing retail balance. Carnevali felt that she had to assess this risk before the acquisition team could recommend a purchase decision or decide a purchase price. MKS's hurdle rate for regional malls was a 13% IRR before taxes and financing over 10 years using conservative assumptions. If MKS could achieve that rate, the company assumed it could find a pension fund that would put up 100% of the purchase price in return for the greater of a 9% annual non-cumulative cash return with initial return of its capital on sale or refinancing or 80% of all cash flow and sale or refinancing proceeds.

MKS would want to close a deal by October of 1988 in order to begin upgrading the mall as soon as possible.

Research Assistant Katherine Sweetman prepared this case under the supervision of Adjunct Professor William J. Poorvu as the basis for class discussion rather than to illustrate either effective or ineffective handling of an administrative situation.

CHANGING MALL DYNAMICS IN AMERICA

MKS's negotiations to acquire Lyndon Mall reflected an emerging trend in the regional shopping mall industry in America. Many retail trade areas were mature, even overbuilt, and developers seeking to expand their holdings had to find creative ways to compete. From 1981 to 1984, regional shopping mall sizes had even decreased on average, as seen in **Exhibit 19-1**. The market in general had experienced a shift away from building large malls toward increased activity in building smaller strip centers targeted at a specific market segment, such as designer discount women's ready-to-wear.

More dramatically, some developers began seeing possibilities in controlling a market by vertically integrating, playing the role of both developer and tenant, as illustrated by the Canadian developer Robert Campeau's takeover of the Allied department and specialty store chains in 1987. With the takeover of Allied, Campeau gained control of many major retailers, including Jordan Marsh, Joske's, The Bon, Brooks Brothers, Bonwit Teller, Ann Taylor, Garfinckel's, and Plymouth. In 1988, Campeau's purchase of Federated department and specialty store chains added Bloomingdale's and Rich's, among others. Dempsey had become a major investor in Campeau's new company at Campeau's request.

Developers were also turning to the acquisition of existing malls, purchasing an underperforming mall in a good location and repositioning it by upgrading, expanding, altering the tenant mix, selectively downsizing certain stores and adding new anchors. New interior designs stimulated shopper traffic with atria, sky lights, exotic plants, decorative brooks and fountains, colorful food courts and cultural events. Within the limits of lease terms, stodgy outdated tenants were replaced with new tenants better reflecting trade area demographics. Since shopping mall tenants pay as rent the greatest of a base amount or a stated percentage of their gross receipts, the incentive of any repositioning is to increase the productivity per square foot as much as to increase the size of the mall. Since smaller tenants tend to generate more revenues per square foot, the trend had become to decrease the size of certain stores and to squeeze more stores into a given space.

Complicating any repositioning plan was the power of the anchor tenant in a shopping mall. The anchor acts as a "draw" for consumers and helps generate foot traffic for smaller tenants. Thus, the success of a mall can depend greatly upon the quality of the anchor tenant and the compatibility of the anchors with the smaller mall tenants.

LYNDON MALL

Lyndon Mall is located on North Rhine Street, Lyndon, Mississippi, a busy commercial strip with a daily traffic count of about 38,000 cars, jammed with fast food chains, bank branches, business hotels and service centers. It was about three and a half miles from downtown Lyndon in Jefferson County, Mississippi (see **Exhibit 19-2**). The development of Lyndon Mall in 1971 effectively shifted almost all commerce from downtown Lyndon to this strip, transforming farmland into the commercial magnet of this small city of 52,000. In 1981, an expansion almost doubled the square footage of Lyndon Mall to its present size of 565,741 square feet, with 489,000 square feet of gross leasable area (GLA). Of this GLA, 263,000 square feet were divided among the anchor tenants: Cooper's with 68,000 square feet, O'Neill's with 40,000 square feet, David's with 75,000 square feet, and Ricci's with 80,000 square feet. Eighty other mall tenants ranging in size from 160 square feet to 15,000 square feet occupied the remaining 226,000 square feet. The mall stores grossed an average of $145 per square foot of leased area in 1987, and the anchor tenants averaged $139 per square foot. The site totalled 40 acres and had 2,691 parking spaces or 5.5 spaces per thousand leasable feet. Lyndon Mall was fully enclosed.

MKS designed and constructed the 1981 expansion for Mutual Insurance (see **Exhibit 19-3**). The presence of rocks too expensive to remove required that the new section be built adjacent to and "stepped up" above the existing mall, joined to it by escalators. The awkwardness of this two-tier design for the shopper was compounded by Mutual's budgetary constraints on modernizing the existing wing during the redesign. By 1988, the "new" upper wing was dated but brightened by occasional atria and potted plants; by 1988 the seventeen-year-old lower level had neither skylights nor plants, sported vintage 1970s storefronts and had been refreshed only by a new coat of paint and a lighter shade of linoleum. The traditional tenants in the lower section remained. The newer, more contemporary tenants leased the expansion space upstairs.

TRADE AREA ECONOMICS AND DEMOGRAPHICS

Despite these peculiarities, Lyndon Mall survived economically. Lyndon is the southernmost member of three cities comprising the Tri-Cities region of northeast Mississippi (see **Exhibit 19-4**). The other two points on the triangle, Kingfisher and Crystal, share generally similar characteristics with Lyndon. The three cities are approximately thirty miles from each other, are of approximately the same size, and each has a modest regional mall similar in quality, tenant profile and shopper profile to Lyndon Mall. The Fort Perry Mall in Kingfisher, built in 1977, is anchored by Cooper's, Ricci's, O'Neill's and David's. The Crystal Mall, built in 1979, is anchored by Ricci's, O'Neill's and David's. In addition to these competitors, an estimated 20 percent of the Tri-Cities' retail dollars leak out of the region, to such cities as Memphis, 90 miles away, or Atlanta, 250 miles to the east.

Each of the tri-cities has a distinctive economic base. The Kingfisher economy is almost entirely dependent on Eastman Kodak, while Crystal is supported primarily by Raytheon and Beecham plants. The economy of the Lyndon trade area is more diversified. Included in the trade area is East Mississippi State University with an enrollment of over 10,000 students and recently expanded graduate programs, including a medical school. A large facility of the Veterans'

Administration Hospital is also a significant member of the economic landscape in Jefferson County. Other major employers include Texas Instruments and TPI Corporation.

Overall, population growth in the Lyndon area had been a steady 0.8 percent annually in recent years. Suburban areas closer to Lyndon and Lyndon Mall were experiencing residential growth in the form of attractive, relatively expensive homes. A new development immediately behind the mall had homes ranging up to and over $200,000 in price, a very upscale level for eastern Mississippi. Much of the county, however, is rural farmland planted with tobacco and corn.

EFFECTIVE BUYING INCOME (EBI)

Population and average household income combine to create effective buying power in a trade area. As seen in **Exhibit 19-4**, the trade areas of the tri-cities overlap; the trade areas are competitive at their borders. An estimated 60 percent of the trade area dollars come from the primary trade area; approximately 40 percent comes from the secondary trade area.

		TRADE AREA POPULATION—1987	
TRADE AREA	PRIMARY	SECONDARY	TOTAL
Lyndon	142,200	94,800	237,000
Kingfisher	135,000	80,000	215,000
Crystal	125,000	80,000	205,000
	402,200	254,800	657,000

In the table below, "Retail Dollars Available" represents the consumer spending power available to purchase mall-type merchandise. This category excludes estimated expenditures for grocery, automotive and service items. Having analyzed the highway systems, traffic patterns and location of competition, MKS estimated the primary and secondary trade areas to be as outlined on **Exhibit 19-4**.

The figures below represent the dollars available from primary and secondary trade areas to Lyndon Mall. Because the Tri-Cities are somewhat isolated geographically by mountains and rivers, only a negligible percentage of sales comes from outside the trade area. The Tri-Cities region is a pie fairly equally divided among the three cities:

TRADE AREA	RETAIL DOLLARS AVAILABLE—1987
Lyndon	$201,000,000
Kingfisher	171,170,000
Crystal	192,280,000
Tri-City Region Total	$564,450,000

The market share of a retail shop or center is determined by calculating the percentage of available dollars that the retailer captures. In this case, Lyndon Mall before any additional expansion captures $67,700,000 (226,000 square feet of mall shops less 5% vacancy times $145 gross revenue per square foot plus 263,000 square feet of anchor times $139 gross revenue per square foot in 1987). This translates to 33.7 percent of the retail dollars available to mall-type sales in the Lyndon trade area. Since sales had remained somewhat flat, 1988 revenues were expected to remain the same for the following year.

Retail market studies revealed that the remaining dollars available to mall-type retail sales had been spent either in smaller strip centers (approximately 30 percent), and a few independently located junior department stores and discounters (approximately 15 percent) or had leaked out to larger shopping areas, such as Nashville and Atlanta (approximately 20 percent). Although Lyndon Mall was considered to be the strongest force in the market, it sometimes lost consumer dollars to other competition because its tenants lacked some variety. Although strong, Lyndon Mall naturally lacked sufficient lure to draw all purchasers to its stores all of the time.

At the time of the negotiations, the distribution of market share among these four segments had remained stable since Lyndon Mall expanded in 1981. It was believed that the retail structure of the Kingfisher and Crystal trade areas were remarkably similar to the subject trade area.

EMERGING COMPETITION

MKS had heard through its retail connections that Dempsey expected to gross $180 per square foot in sales revenue in the proposed million square foot mall. Allowing for 5 percent vacancy, Dempsey would have to capture 30.3 percent of the Tri-Cities region's $564,450,000 retail trade area dollars.

THE ACQUISITION

MKS looked at this acquisition in two parts: buying Lyndon Mall as is and upgrading, and repositioning through expansion.

MKS and Associates had to decide on a price to offer Mutual Insurance, a price that would be attractive enough to induce them to sell, yet yield sufficient returns to its own organization. As stated earlier, MKS wanted a pre-tax, pre-financing return of 13 percent within ten years. MKS knew that Mutual Insurance had had discussions with its investment banker, Morgan Stanley, who advised the insurance company to sell at a 7 percent cap rate applied to their 1988 free and clear budgeted cash flow of $2,482,900 or $35.5 million.

MKS's financial people examined the 1988 budgeted cash flow and the ten-year projection of cash flow as a starting point for negotiations. MKS felt that the 1988 budgeted cash flow should be adjusted to reflect items one and two below, then projected out to determine what Mutual Insurance really should be asking as a purchase price:

1. The insurance cost would rise to $100,000 from the $30,000 that Mutual Insurance had paid. MKS could pass through all but 20 percent of the increase in CAM (Common Area Maintenance) contributions. Insurance rates were expected to increase 5% per year.
2. Mutual Insurance had left two items off the Operating Budget which MKS felt should be included under Expenses: $27,749 in Tenant Improvements and $130,000 in Capital Additions.

The adjusted cash flow to Mutual should more realistically be $2,311,151. In addition, MKS figured that they could do a basic redesign to modernize Lyndon Mall at a cost of $1,000,000. This figure includes rents lost during construction as stores were redesigned, relocated or removed. That allowed MKS to do a new 10-year projection as shown in **Exhibit 19-5**. Without the upgrade, there would likely be a deterioration in market share.

THE EXPANSION

The acquisition team at MKS also took into account what it considered to be a conservative but likely expansion plan. The plan included the addition of Margin's department store and more mall shops. Estimates placed the cost to build the expansion at $8.9 million. Sales revenues were anticipated to be $150 to $160 per square foot on the net added rentable area of 205,000 square feet. Higher sales would bring total revenues for Lyndon Mall to $100,500,000, or 50 percent of the effective trade area buying income for mall-type stores.

Margin's had already expressed an interest in the Tri-Cities area and was known to be discussing entering the Fort Perry Mall in Kingfisher. MKS had opened discussions with this popular chain, even though it was a competitor to both O'Neill's and Ricci's who were already in Lyndon Mall. MKS felt that with Margin's as a strong new anchor, and with some exciting updating and trendier mall tenants, Lyndon Mall could wipe out some of the competition.

MKS prepared a preliminary expansion plan (see **Exhibit 19-6**):

O'Neill's had already approached Mutual Insurance with a plan to expand its store. MKS would agree to carve the existing 40,000 square foot O'Neill's store into 28,000 square feet of mall shops plus 12,000 square feet in common area leading to a new 65,000 square foot store which O'Neill's would build (see **Exhibit 19-6**).

MKS would give Margin's five acres of land to build its own 82,000 square foot store. Access to this store would be provided through an existing 15,000 square foot McNamara's discount store whose lease expired in May of 1991 and which had only grossed $66 per square foot in 1987. The former McNamara's would be divided into 9,000 square feet of mall shops and 6,000 square feet of common area.

Rearrangement of other existing space and additional expansion space would add 76,000 square feet of mall-type stores, including an 8,000 square foot court plus 9,500 square feet of common area.

The $8.9 million estimated cost to expand includes the purchase of 15 additional acres of land at $100,000 per acre needed to create the new stores and parking.

In evaluating the economics of the addition, the team assumed that the lease terms would be at least 8 to 10 years, and that the growth would be a modest, steady 3 percent based upon population and economic growth projected for the region. They assumed a sale in the eighth year of operation (tenth year of mall acquisition), the price at that time based on the budgeted free and clear cash flow capped at 7 percent.

Carnevali summarized the changes as follows:

Net addition in mall-type stores	98,000 s.f.
Net addition in anchor stores	107,000 s.f.
Net addition in common area	27,500 s.f.
Net addition to Lyndon Mall	232,500 s.f.

A mall tenant's rental rate is on average the greater of the base rent or 6% of sales. An anchor's rental rate is on average the greater of the base rent or 2% of sales.

Carnevali calculated the additional economic effect on MKS's free and clear of this second expansion as follows:

Net additional anchor stores	$107,000 \times \$150 \times 2\% =$	$ 321,000
Net additional mall stores	$98,000 \times \$160 \times 6\% =$	940,800
Gross additional rental income		$1,261,800
Less: 5% vacancy on mall stores		47,000
Net additional rental income		$1,214,800
Less: expenses not passed through to tenants		70,000
Net additional operating income		$1,144,800

Carnevali based her figures upon the assumption that the $8.9 million construction would begin in January 1989 with the new space filled by January of 1990. The free and clear was expected to increase four percent per year after absorbing a portion of CAM contributions.

To value Lyndon Mall as a whole—as is and with the expansion—the team began to devise a new set-up to add the costs and cash flows of both projects to be able to project whether the combined project met MKS's hurdle rate of 13 percent over ten years after acquisition.

The acquisition team now faced the tough question. Would it be feasible to expand the mall, given the returns and the threat of Dempsey? What were the chances that Dempsey would enter the market? How much market share could they afford to lose and still reach their required return? They considered whether it made sense to buy the mall at all, given the potential local effects from the changing mall dynamics in the nation. Lastly, how should they present their proposal to Mutual Insurance and what were their obligations to that firm?

Exhibit 19-1 *Changing Shopping Center Size*

Median Shopping Center Size

	SQUARE FEET			PERCENTAGE CHANGE	
	1981	*1984*	*1987*	*1984-1987*	*1981-1987*
Super Regional					
Total occupancy area	948,707	855,545	950,579	11%	0%
Mall Shops	352,661	329,214	360,496	10	2
Regional					
Total occupancy area	535,840	479,477	493,050	3	− 9
Mall shops	320,011	252,615	254,736	1	−20
Community	151,857	146,774	151,015	3	0
Neighborhood	62,328	62,525	66,328	6	6

Source: Urban Land Institute, *Dollars & Cents of Shopping Centers: 1981, 1984, 1987.*

Exhibit 19-2

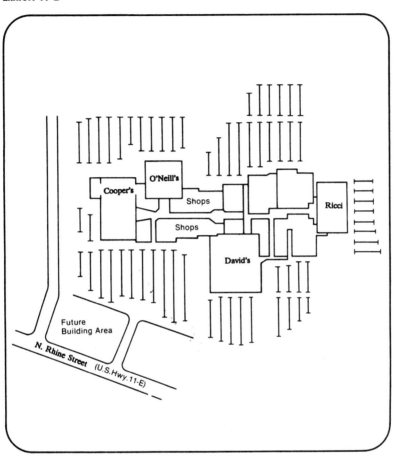

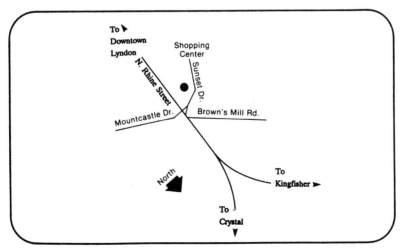

Exhibit 19-3

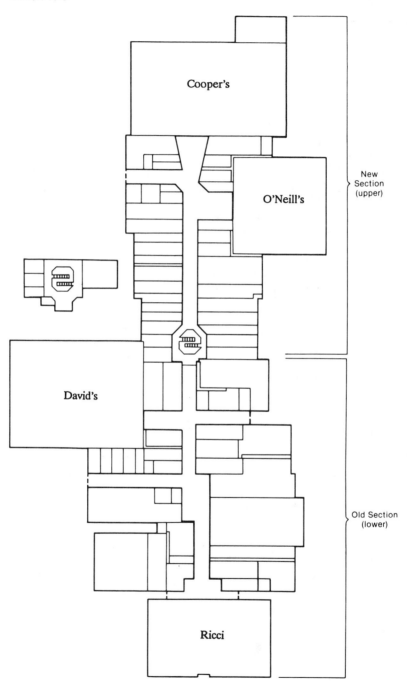

Exhibit 19-4

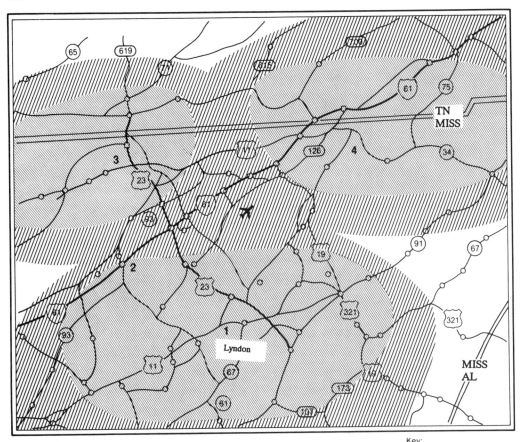

Key:
- ▨ Primary Trade Area
- ▨ Secondary Trade Area

1. Lyndon Mall
2. Dempsey Mall (proposed)
3. Fort Perry Mall - Kingfisher
4. Crystal Mall - Crystal

Exhibit 19-5 Lyndon Mall

1988 Operating Budget and Ten Year Pro Forma after $1 Million Renovation

INCOME	PRESENT 1988 OPERATING BUDGET		10-YEAR PROJECTION AFTER $1 MILLION RENOVATION									
			1989	1990	1991	1992	1993	1994	1995	1996	1997	1998
Minimum rent	$2,304,748	Note 1	$2,339,715	$2,515,005	$2,657,457	$2,697,178	$2,715,227	$2,733,350	$2,974,550	$3,097,984	$3,130,633	$3,142,800
CAM contributions	730,350	Note 2	755,912	782,369	809,752	838,093	867,427	897,787	929,209	961,731	995,392	1,030,231
RET contributions	295,972	Note 3	291,001	317,160	470,291	508,291	550,291	445,291	482,521	520,531	564,091	564,090
Percentage rent	228,200	Note 4	291,770	290,772	336,139	395,135	459,128	523,000	588,000	653,000	718,000	783,000
Miscellaneous income	12,000	Note 5	20,000	22,000	23,000	24,000	25,000	26,000	26,000	27,000	27,000	28,000
Temporary rent	65,000	Note 6	70,000	73,500	77,175	81,034	85,085	89,340	93,000	98,800	103,425	108,600
Total Income	$3,636,270		$3,768,398	$4,000,806	$4,373,814	$4,543,731	$4,702,158	$4,714,768	$5,093,810	$5,358,746	$5,538,541	$5,656,721
EXPENSE												
Management fee (5%)	$ 126,647	Note 7	$ 81,045	$ 86,378	$ 92,123	$ 95,200	$ 97,783	$ 100,371	$ 109,691	$ 115,485	$ 118,562	$ 121,000
Payroll	193,734	Note 8	193,734	203,421	213,592	224,272	235,486	247,260	259,623	272,604	286,234	300,500
Utilities	109,162	Note 8	109,162	114,620	120,351	126,369	132,687	139,321	146,287	153,601	161,281	169,340
Maintenance and repairs	160,169	Note 8	160,169	168,177	176,586	185,415	194,686	204,420	214,641	225,373	236,642	248,400
Security	50,000	Note 8	50,000	52,500	55,125	57,881	60,775	63,814	67,005	70,355	73,873	77,500
General and administrative	22,418	Note 8	22,418	23,539	24,716	25,952	27,250	28,613	30,044	31,546	33,123	34,700
Marketing fund dues	22,550	Note 8	22,550	23,678	24,862	26,105	27,410	28,781	30,220	31,731	33,318	34,980
Legal, audit & professional	15,640	Note 8	5,000	5,000	5,000	5,000	5,000	6,000	6,000	6,000	6,000	6,000
Tenant maintenance & repair	11,000	Note 8	11,000	11,550	12,128	12,734	13,371	14,040	14,742	15,479	16,253	17,000
Insurance	100,000	Note 8	105,000	105,000	105,000	105,000	105,000	105,000	105,000	105,000	105,000	105,000
Real estate taxes	356,030	Note 9	373,710	392,296	490,494	510,114	530,519	551,739	573,809	596,761	620,632	645,457
Tenant improvements[1]	27,749	Note 10	28,145	28,547	28,956	29,370	29,790	30,216	30,648	31,086	31,531	31,982
Capital additions[1]	130,000	Note 10	131,855	133,741	135,653	137,593	139,560	141,556	143,580	145,634	147,716	149,829
Total Expense	$1,325,119		$1,293,788	$1,348,547	$1,484,586	$1,541,005	$1,599,317	$1,661,131	$1,731,290	$1,800,655	$1,870,165	$1,941,687
Free & Clear	$2,311,151		$2,474,610	$2,652,260	$2,889,228	$3,002,727	$3,102,841	$3,053,636	$3,362,520	$3,558,091	$3,668,376	$3,715,034

[1] As adjusted by MKS.

Note 1: Reflects rental income from existing leases and estimated rental increases from renegotiation of expired leases. Existing tenant sales, location, and type of business were considered in estimating renewal rent. Increases in rent were projected for each five-year period of rental with replacement of certain tenants not doing well.

Note 2: Mall tenant CAM clauses allow pass through to tenants effectively 80% of all increases in common area maintenance and insurance.

Note 3: Mall tenant tax clauses are either pro-rata or allow for increases to be passed on to tenants. Therefore, all tax increases are offset by income reimbursements from tenants.

Note 4: In accordance with percentage rent schedules for individual tenants.

Note 5: Primarily represents income from public telephones owned by the mall.

Note 6: Represents rental income from temporary tenants throughout the year.

Note 7: Calculated on minimum, temporary, and percentage rents only. Fee decreased to 3% with new ownership.

Note 8: Assumes increases in these expense categories of 5% per year.

Note 9: We have assumed a reevaluation of the mall in 1990 on the basis of the increase value of the mall after initial upgrade.

Note 10: Does not assume expansion. Tenant improvements and capital additions are included as expenses here to better reflect costs that will recur.

Exhibit 19-6

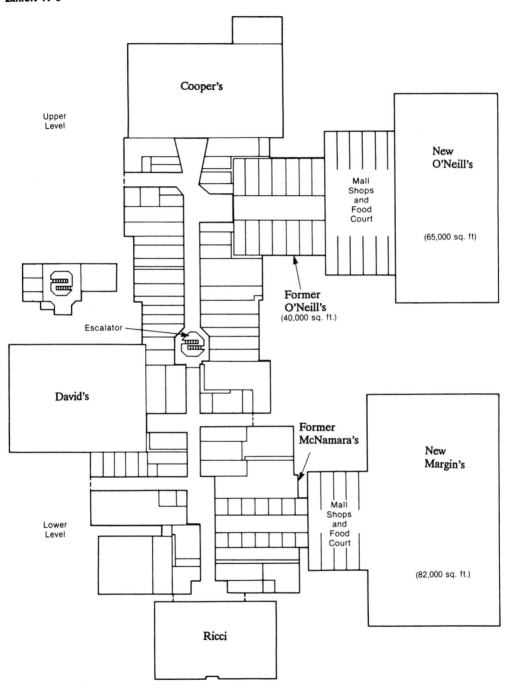

Upper
Level

Cooper's

New
O'Neill's

Mall
Shops
and
Food
Court

(65,000 sq. ft)

Former
O'Neill's
(40,000 sq. ft.)

Escalator

David's

Former
McNamara's

New
Margin's

Lower
Level

Mall
Shops
and
Food
Court

(82,000 sq. ft.)

Ricci

LYNDON MALL

20

PORTLAND ELDERCARE

In September, 1986, Portland, Maine, developer Pam Gleichman is considering entering the field of non-subsidized housing for the elderly. Aware of a national trend toward an aging population, Gleichman wants to investigate the potential of serving the high end of this market. She needs to determine the product which best fits the needs of this segment of the Portland community in terms of location, design, services to be offered and costs. The case discusses the economic and societal implications of three product types—for sale cluster homes, a congregate care development, and a life care facility.

Discussion Questions:

1. Why did Gleichman want to get into the eldercare business? Were her reasons valid?
2. Based upon the economics, what course of action should Gleichman now pursue and how should she fund and manage the project?
3. What are the advantages and disadvantages of the life care, congregate care, and cluster options?
4. What is the impact on the elderly of the proposed options?
5. Who is responsible for the housing and care of the elderly?

INTRODUCTION

In September, 1986 Pam Gleichman, a real estate syndicator and developer in the Portland, Maine area was exploring the possibility of entering into a relatively new form of development—nonsubsidized housing for the elderly.

Gleichman's expertise lay in small government-assisted multi-family projects. However, there was a strong feeling in the Portland area, as in many other metropolitan centers in the country that the windows of greatest opportunity in real estate were likely to be very different in the late eighties than they had been in the past five years. Pam felt that it was important to have a portfolio of complementary investments to ensure continued growth for her firm.

THE MARKET

In the past ten years real estate trends had been impacted by a number of factors in many different sectors. Rapid growth of employment in service industries led to a rush by investors and lenders to participate in that boom. Office space became overbuilt, with supply, at least in the short term, exceeding demand. And though the prices of residential property had been appreciating quite rapidly, many experts felt that the rate of growth was now slowing. With home values appreciating at nearly twice the rate of personal income the rapidly escalating housing prices of the past few years were bound to taper off. Too, significant shifts in national demographics argued for developing a changing market focus. The elderly were becoming a larger and larger part of the population, and many entrepreneurs were beginning to look at a specialized product targeted at this segment of the market.

Political and social conditions seemed to strengthen the viability of this type of concept. The ability of social security benefits to support adequately a rapidly aging population was coming into question. In the next 25 years the elderly would be faced with the question of how to live in an inflationary economy within a system which might no longer fund their needs for the shelter and medical care they had been conditioned to expect. And restrictions on Medicare and other subsidized options were becoming increasingly onerous. There was great

---

Research Associate Elizabeth M. McLoughlin prepared this case under the supervision of Adjunct Professor William J. Poorvu as the basis for class discussion rather than to illustrate either effective or ineffective handling of an administrative situation.

likelihood that particularly upper income elderly (and their children) would have to take a more aggressive posture in providing for independent funding of a final care setting.

Pam felt that this might be an opportunity for the private sector to explore, and at the same time make a contribution to the elderly community.

HISTORY OF PAM GLEICHMAN

Pam had a long history of involvement with multi-family housing, beginning with a directorship of the Maine State Housing Authority from 1974-1977. As one of the prime movers behind the creation of Section 8 and other subsidized housing in Maine, Pam became involved in the development of over 50 government assisted multi-family projects. She was responsible for all facets of development from financial planning and site selection to construction supervision and property management. When she went out on her own in 1977 to found Housing/State of the Art, Pam relied on her public sector experience in financing developments for her own account, using the Farmer's Home Administration, HUD grants, and Section 8 monies for funding.

State and federal subsidies, however, were almost exclusively tied to low and moderate income units and were rapidly being phased out at the federal level. Pam felt strongly that there was a market for a high quality eldercare project, and resolved to pursue the feasibility of such a concept in the Portland area.

THE CONCEPT

Pam envisioned a development community targeted specifically at the elderly segment of the population, a community which assured the senior resident the opportunity of an independent lifestyle, provided medical support, and offered families a dignified option for elderly care.

Pam knew of several developers who had creative ideas for this type of alternate housing for the elderly; at the same time she had doubts about the long term viability of some of the concepts she had read about. Clearly there were some financial considerations which bore greater consideration. Additionally, Pam was proud of her reputation as a developer, had a strong commitment to the Portland area, and wondered how this fit in with her overall personal and organizational objectives.

She wondered, too if her organization possessed the expertise and infrastructure to develop and manage a facility of this nature. And were she to contribute her resources to this endeavor, she was concerned about how readily the Portland market would accept this concept. While her financial position was relatively strong, she was well aware that her pockets were not deep enough to support an inordinately long rent up period.

In light of the above, Pam decided to do a little more research to see if in fact this really was a feasible idea to pursue.

DEMOGRAPHICS

Nationally, the elderly represent a large and rapidly expanding population. Presently there are 26 million people over the age of 65 in the United States, a figure which is growing at an unprecedented rate. Industry experts have placed this figure at nearer to 50 million by the year 2025.

Demographic shifts in the Portland area paralleled that of the country as a whole. Of a total population of approximately 349,000, Portland's elderly represented 13.7%, or 47,813 persons. Census studies predicted a growth rate of over two percent annually for the elderly sector, or nearly twice that of the general population as a whole.

Of this group it was estimated that 25% could afford to enter a continuing care community. Of that 25%, nationwide research suggested that approximately 10% actually would enter such a development, if available. This was consistent with other industry studies which showed the expected market penetration of a life care facility to be three percent of the total elderly population in what is defined as a primary market area.

In the Portland area, Pam thought the most desirable competitive strategy would be to target the high end of the market—hence her calculations of the potential market included minimum income qualifications as well. For the type of high quality facility she wanted to build, she expected that an individual would require a minimum annual income of $35,000. She looked at census statistics for those parts of Cumberland and York counties within a 25 mile radius of Portland (see **Exhibit 20-2**). Historically, it had been found that developments designed for the elderly derived over 80% of their residents from an area within a 25 mile radius of the project.

Exhibit 20-1 shows approximately 4230 people, or 2533 qualifying households with incomes over $35,000 in Cumberland and York Counties. Additionally, because many potential entrants owned a home, and because one presumed that the home would be sold to enter into a lifetime housing arrangement, Pam figured she could expand that base by including a measure of the value of a home in computing qualifying income levels. For example, Pam assumed that if a house were converted into earning assets, it would produce an after tax annual cash flow of approximately 5% of its value. Hence, a resident with an income of $25,000 would income qualify if he or she owned a home with equity valued at $150,000 or more.

After spending some time poring over the data, Pam concluded that approximately half of those elderly with incomes between $25,000 and $35,000 would be eligible, and all of those with incomes over $35,000. This gave her an applicant pool of approximately 6,552 potential entrants. Of those who qualified, it was reasonable to assume that approximately 10% would enter some form of elderly housing arrangement (see **Exhibit 20-1**).

Pam was aware that in Portland, as elsewhere, elderly care fell woefully short of meeting this demand. Elderly housing and nursing care had been historically dominated by the non-profit sector which had been slow to respond to a greatly increased need in recent years. This, coupled with an uncertain political and social environment, a government benefit program having difficulty keeping up with retirement demands, and diminishing resources from the medical sector, served to drive down vacancy rates and increase waiting lists in communities across the country. A typical life care facility, for example, posted a 5-7 year wait to enter. It was projected that over 1800 new elderly facilities were needed simply to meet current national requirements.

While Pam's staff pursued specific market information on comparable facilities in the Portland area, Pam began the process of exploring development options. There were several very different concepts which attracted her interest.

DEVELOPMENT OPTIONS

Cluster Homes

Cluster homes represented the least market specific option, and would offer Pam the opportunity to hedge her bets. Cluster homes were generally attached or semi-attached dwellings built on a large plot of open acreage and sold as condominiums. As in other condominiums, ongoing fees were part of a resident's financial commitment—these fees funded the operating expenses and covered maintenance of outside and common space. Homes were generally small (750-1000 square feet) one story dwellings with many options which appealed to the elderly resident. Emergency call buttons and twenty four hour security, extra wide doors to accommodate wheelchairs, efficient unit layouts, and a centralized community clubhouse were specialized features commonly incorporated into cluster community design.

Though a cluster home concept appealed to "empty nesters" and (particularly upper income) elderly, older persons were not the exclusive target market. Secondly, this type of development usually provided no specialized medical services to assist the elderly resident.

Congregate Care

A more comprehensive option was the congregate care facility. Congregate care facilities provided independent smaller living units with varying levels of support service. Units were generally marketed under one year renewable leases, with an additional all inclusive fee which covered such amenities as at least one communal meal daily, an on premise nurse practitioner, and weekly apartment cleaning (see **Exhibit 20-3**). Agreements were often made with local nursing homes to provide in-patient medical care should that become necessary.

Because of the high level of amenities offered, rents were generally above market levels for comparable units in a cluster home or townhouse type environment, running to approximately $1400-$1800/month for a one bedroom unit (see **Exhibit 20-4**).

Life Care Communities

The most focussed development option was known in the industry as a life care community (LCC). A full life care facility might consist of approximately 300 independent living units, and an attached 60 bed skilled nursing/health care facility (see **Exhibit 20-6**). Prospective residents were required to invest an up-front amount in the order of $150,000 (the "endowment fee") and pay in addition up to $15,000 annually in exchange for which he/she received a lifetime residence contract and guaranteed provision for all medical or nursing services, with the opportunity for stepped up levels of health care that included an on site nursing home.

For a developer to be successful, sophisticated industry knowledge and/or research was paramount. A profitable proforma was based largely on actuarial assumptions as to the duration of a resident's stay and his/her projected health and nursing care needs. Annual dues were set regardless of whether a resident remained in an independent apartment unit or was permanently transferred to the skilled nursing center as a patient (see **Exhibit 20-7**).

Because over 60% of operating costs were fixed, a minimum scale of development was deemed necessary for efficiency. An industry rule of thumb was that a large (20+) acre site would be required to accommodate independent living units, in-patient health care facilities, parking, common areas for centralized services, guest facilities and social amenities. (In fact, in some states such as Massachusetts this minimum was enforced by legislation.)

While mulling over the various options open to her, Pam decided to talk to local brokers and see what land might be available.

Location

Choice of location was not a constraint in the Portland area. Available sites fell into three main categories, each of which posed certain structural determinants and development constraints, and which reflected different operating characteristics. Though land costs varied substantially among the alternatives on a per acre basis, it was expected that land costs per unit would remain relatively constant (for LCC's and congregate care facilities) at approximately $6,600 per unit due to differences in construction density.

An urban option with its physical proximity to retail and cultural amenities, was the epitome of convenience, and offered the aged person an easy way of maintaining involvement with a community outside of the relatively insular congregate care environment. Site availability and premium land prices argued for an efficient layout and a well conceived design which centralized services and maximized the space available. Pam had yet to examine fully the zoning restrictions in the downtown Portland area, but felt that they might have a bearing on appropriate use, especially were she to opt for the LCC, which included an on premise nursing facility. She was unsure, too, whether a sizable enough parcel could be assembled to accommodate an LCC.

Plusses for the urban location included proximity to her own base of operations as well as access to a fairly large pool of qualified applicants. And competition from preexistent elderly housing projects downtown was virtually nil.

Rural Maine land obviously did not command the same premium that downtown Portland did. This was a particularly appropriate choice for a life care facility, with its minimum 20 acre requirement. For the quality development she envisioned, Pam felt that total acreage could run up to 50 or 60 acres, and would cost from $33,000 to $50,000/acre. A spread out townlike atmosphere could be constructed on this site, more on the order of the cluster housing communities which were springing up in suburbs across the country. This option, however, posed its own concerns.

She wondered, were Maine winters conducive to an open space environment? On a gloomy day in February, would isolation be a dominating factor in the lifestyle of an elderly resident? Additionally, the severity of those weather conditions escalated maintenance costs and access to facilities on an emergency basis.

At the same time, Pam envisioned garden plots, particularly waist high raised bed plantings accessible to those wheelchair-ridden, and modest outdoor recreation facilities which offered the physical fitness opportunities an urban location did not.

A third choice of location would be to build in one of the outlying suburbs in the Portland area. This option Pam looked at slightly differently. She envisioned a low rise structure, totally enclosed with central amenities, which incorporated a design consistent with a neighborhood flavor. The success of this option, she felt, was in ensuring town support. Other projects had encountered resistance from abutters who felt that such a development effort would reduce their property values, and incur costs associated with the specialized services offered which would, in the final analysis, increase their taxes. Site preparation approvals, including variances for sewage and other utilities, would be a long and complex process. It was suggested to Pam that initial affiliation with a local church or community group might expedite approval of such a facility.

Three Months Later

By January 1987, Pam felt confident that she had gathered sufficient information to make a decision. She had run all the numbers on her most feasible alternatives, incorporating the recently passed revisions to the tax code, and had come to some tentative conclusions. She looked at her options in turn.

A selling point for cluster home development was that it was not tied to acceptance by a specific sector of the market. By not restricting her target market to a specialized group, Pam could draw on a wider pool of interested applicants, and would be in a more secure position should the optimistic growth projections for the elderly sector not materialize.

However, there were currently a number of competing projects under construction in the Portland area, which made her a little uneasy about a speculative development in the area. Too, cluster homes were most successful in the suburbs, where land costs were appreciating rapidly, and increasingly strict zoning regulations were limiting the number of buildable lots.

Running a few back of the envelope calculations, Pam felt that it was reasonable to assume that she could obtain a 15 acre suburban site for $50,000/acre. She could build 40 attached homes, each with approximately 1000 square feet. Using relatively conservative development costs of $100/foot before land costs, and a per unit sellout price of approximately $125,000, the project would show less than a 10% return on sales. This, Pam felt, was insufficient.

A developer's return from a life care community derives from several sources, which vary in proportion over the life of a project.

1. Entry or endowment fees: Pam's proforma assumed that a prospective resident would put up an average of $144,800 per unit (see **Exhibit 20-7**). Under terms of the agreement between resident and project owner, 90% of that entry fee is refundable to the resident upon termination of the contract and contingent upon resale of the unit. Hence only 10% of fees received are recorded as operating income, with the 90% balance treated as a loan to the developer for the term of the resident's stay, in effect acting as a source of long term financing used to pay off the initial construction loan. Though no interest is actually paid on this loan, some felt that the lender would have to take the imputed interest into current year income. Unfortunately, there might not be a corresponding deduction allowed by the IRS for the borrower or developer.

   Because 95% occupancy is expected to be achieved in the second year of operation, entry fees would be sufficient to repay the construction loan in a short period of time. Under this scenario (per **Exhibit 20-8**), by the end of year one, 228 units would be sold, for total revenues of $33.060 million, with $3.306 million taken into income of the current year (see **Exhibit 20-7**), and $29.75 million contributing to the repayment of the $36 million devleopment costs.

   As the project matures, endowment fees become a much smaller share of revenue. Receipts are contingent upon turnover of units, which is expected to begin in the third year, rising incrementally to a stabilized 6.5% level in year 10. Funds from the resale of units cover the refundable portion of the original owner's entry fee, and are allocated in part to a reserve account. The balance is distributed, and, because of unit appreciation, is expected to add substantially to profits (see **Exhibit 20-8**).

2. A second source of revenue for the project is the ongoing monthly fee for operations and health care paid by residents. Monthly fees are set to cover contract liabilities and operating expenses, and to increase with inflation. A complex actuarial formula is used to project the percentage of residents who will require skilled nursing care, the duration of that care, and the turnover of independent living units. From this, a projection of actual costs per resident is derived, with fee income set to cover that liability. For the developer this income is generally a break even item.

3. In the early years of a facility, the resident population will be younger, and will require less skilled nursing care than will a mature population. Until such time as the residents will require full use of the SNF, the facility may accept outside patients, generating additional health care revenue. These revenues contribute in part to a health care reserve which is set up to cover losses in later years as the maturing population requires more comprehensive nursing.

4. There are two additional sources of return to the developer. The first derives from the noncash expenses associated with the project which provide significant tax

benefits (depreciation). A final contribution to revenue is a 5% development fee built into the construction budget.

Given the assumptions that were made as to rate of sellout, construction costs, and capital appreciation of units, the returns on this project are very high. Because of the high endowment fees all of the initial equity ($5.4 million) is returned by 1990. Secondly, the profit on unit turnover, after repayment of funds to the original occupant, is immediately distributed as an additional cash return to the developer.

In computing this return Pam made several calculations which were different from the way she usually looked at a deal. To determine a terminal value for the project, Gleichman used a p/e multiple of 8 applied to the cash flow after tax and reserve. At the time of sale, however, a tax would be due which she calculated in the following manner.

Initial equity in (incl. $900 initial marketing expenses)	$ 6,300
Cumulative taxable income (from **Exhibit 20-7**)	$ 9,053
Cash distributions:	
Return of original capital	($ 6,300)
Return from operations[1]	($15,090)
Partnership capital before sale	($ 6,037)
Cash proceeds distributed from sale[2]	$14,808
Taxable income on sale	$20,845
Tax due on sale	$ 5,836

[1]Taxable income plus depreciation less reserve from **Exhibit 20-7**.
[2]Assumes sales price of 8 times 1,851 (1997 cash flow after taxes and reserves).

On paper, the project showed a solid return of approximately 33%. However, Pam had some reservations. The large upfront fee restricted the pool of qualified applicants to the high income segment of the target elderly market. And too, the cost volatility of a health care facility argued for low leverage. A budget for a substantial reserve was particularly important if the resident pool required more skilled care than was expected. Many projects had gone under when contract liabilities exceeded expected fee revenues. Another oft cited reason for failure was a too low vacancy projection, which translated into lower endowment fees than expected, and therefore a smaller capital base from which to fund needed capital expenditures and/or debt service (see **Exhibit 20-7**).

Additionally, project financing was inherently more complex; stringent lending covenants often included a 50% presale requirement, significantly increasing upfront marketing costs and lengthening the time line of the development effort.

Recognizing that this posed risks beyond her capability to undertake, Pam had explored the option of a participating development partner who could bring complementary skills and/or resources to the table. There were national organizations who were turning to the development of life care facilities as a natural outgrowth of some other area of expertise. Hotel chains were leveraging their skills in lodging and service management to enter the field. Hospitals and nonprofits had significant health care experience. Insurance companies such as John Hancock were showing a lot of interest.

At this point the field was wide open for the private sector. With a strong partner Pam felt that she could get a preemptive foothold in this market, and garner the experience and credibility to take this concept further afield. She predicted increasingly stringent legislation which would protect the early entrants, with licenses and regulatory approvals hinging on prior experience, effectively creating entry barriers for prospective players in the future. Scarcity of supply, at least in the near term, ensured a favorable appreciation in unit prices, and increasing annual cash flows. And market growth, by even the most conservative projections, was impressive.

By contrast, a congregate care facility was a development effort more consistent with projects she had been involved with in the past. The local savings and loan which had funded many of Pam's past developments had indicated its interest in providing the permanent financing on terms similar to those of her past projects, at a 10.5% interest rate, with a 30 year term, and a 90% loan to cost ratio. With a takeout already lined up, she expected to obtain construction funding at a slightly lower rate—9.5%. She had historically raised the equity portion of development costs through a syndication of limited partnership units. However, with the new tax laws coming into effect, prohibiting the use of so-called "passive" losses against other income, she wondered if she should explore other options for funding—a participating second mortgage, for example.

Though for comparative purposes, she constructed a spreadsheet based on a project identical in size and resident density to the life care community, she felt that the proposed congregate facility could be scaled down considerably to as few as 160 units, and still provide an acceptable return. For a 300 unit project, using a 10% cap rate, and assuming sale in year 10, Pam calculated an IRR for the project of approximately 40.44%.

However, on a broader level, she wondered how she could take this concept one step further. Clearly, the relatively confined Portland area could absorb a finite number of like facilities. Were she to make the necessary investment of time, energy, resources, and reputation to build one congregate or life care community, it followed that she should be prepared to exploit this opportunity elsewhere.

However, Pam's expertise lay in the Portland market; her organization's strength lay in being able to sustain its position through a very impressive knowledge of the local market. She wondered how her reputation would be affected were she to develop such a facility, particularly in light of a number of publicized abuses of the life care system in the recent past. And given a parcel of land, was this the best use of her talents? Could she, or would she have any desire to transfer this concept to another locale?

Exhibit 20-1 Target Market Demographic Analysis Cumberland County and part of York County, September 15, 1986

	AGE 65-74	AGE 75+	TOTAL
People with income $25,000–$34,000			
Number of households:	1,916	865	2,781
× average number of persons/household	1.67	1.67	1.67
Total number of people:	3,200	1,445	4,644
People with Income over $35,000			
Number of households:	1,769	764	2,533
× average number of persons/household	1.67	1.67	1.67
Total number of people:	2,954	1,276	4,230

Calculation of Eligibility/Demand:

Total elderly with incomes $25,000–$34,000	4,644	
50% eligible:		2,322 potential entrants
Total elderly with incomes over $35,000	4,230	
100% eligible:		4,230 potential entrants
		6,552
10% likely to enter = 655		

Housing Demand Analysis
Cumberland County and Part of York Counties

	NUMBER OF ELIGIBLE PEOPLE 1985	NUMBER OF ELIGIBLE PEOPLE 1990 (PROJECTED)
Estimated market area:		
15 mile radius	4,448	7,429
20 mile radius	4,750	7,996
25 mile radius	5,416	9,017
Total market area:	6,552	10,888

Exhibit 20-2   *Portland Eldercare*

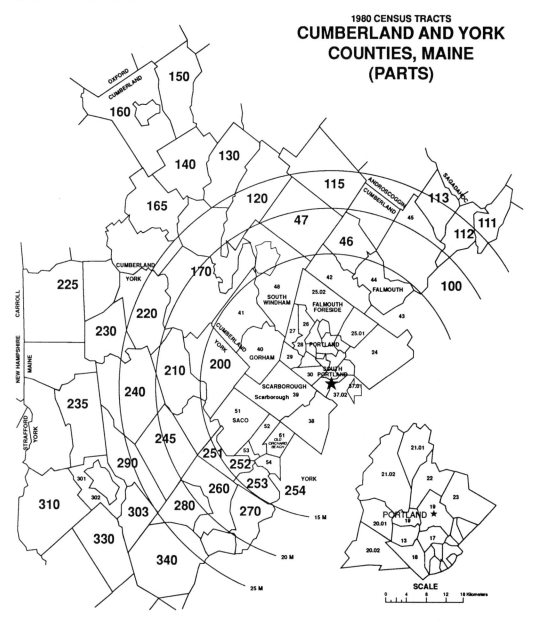

1980 CENSUS TRACTS
CUMBERLAND AND YORK COUNTIES, MAINE (PARTS)

Exhibit 20-3 *Cost of Services Provided: A Comparison of Life Care and Congregate Care*

	TOTAL:	PER UNIT (IN 000's)	PER CAPITA
Congregate Care:			
Stabilized Operating Expenses:			
Food Service	$498	$1,660	$1,194
Housekeeping	268	893	643
Utilities	445	1,483	1,067
Nursing	322	1,073	772
Maintenance	525	1,750	1,259
Mini Bus Transportation	125	417	300
Management Fee	330	1,100	791
Advertising	80	267	192
Insurance	62	207	149
Legal	10	33	24
Wages	55	183	132
Total Operating Expenses	$2,720	$9,067	$6,523
Life Care			
Stabilized Operating Expenses:			
Food Service	774	2,580	1,870
Housekeeping	282	940	681
Utilities	581	1,937	1,403
Nursing	648	2,160	1,565
Maintenance	468	1,560	1,130
Resident Services	168	560	406
Administration	333	1,110	804
Marketing	196	653	473
Insurance	119	397	287
Legal	46	153	111
Total Operating Expenses	$3,615	$12,050	$8,732

Both congregate care and life care communities offer many of the following amenities:

24-hour security	Recreational therapy
Full laundry/linen service	Nutrition programs
Transportation	Resident parking
Apartment cleaning	Auditoriums
Exercise rooms	In-unit kitchens
Emergency call service	Large print book library

Life care, however, offers comprehensive medical care, while congregate offers on-site nursing coverage only.

Exhibit 20-4 *Congregate Care Facility Development Proforma*

Project type	Residential rental
Number of units	300
Unit mix: Studio	60
One bedroom	120
Two bedroom	120
Square feet (gross)	341,538
Square feet (net)	222,000
Hard cost/sq. ft.	52
Construction period	12 Months
Rental appreciation	5%
Expense growth rate	5%
Studio	$1,372/mo. ($45/day)
One bedroom	$1,677/mo. ($55/day)
Two bedrooms	$1,982/mo. ($65/day)
Additional occupant fee	$600/mo.
Number of residents	417

USES OF FUNDS	TOTAL	PER UNIT	SQ. FT.
Acquisition costs	$2,000,000	$6,667	$6
Project hard costs	17,760,000	59,200	52
+Contingency	355,200	1,184	1
Total hard costs	18,115,200	60,384	53
Project soft costs			
Architecture/engineering	888,000	2,960	3
Consultants	60,000	200	0
Legal and accounting	72,000	240	0
Marketing	187,500	625	1
Taxes during construction	52,000	173	0
Financing fees	220,000	733	1
Developer's fee	905,760	3,019	3
Title insurance	148,000	493	0
Construction interest	1,011,000	3,370	3
Total soft costs	3,544,260	11,814	10
Total development costs	23,659,460	78,865	69

SOURCES OF FUNDS			
Investor equity	2,568,091		
Permanent financing	21,091,369		

Exhibit 20-5 *Congregate Care Facility Operating Proforma (in 000's)*

YEAR:	1988	1989	1990	1991	1992	1993	1994	1995	1996	1997
Gross rents	$7,099	$7,454	$7,827	$8,218	$8,629	$9,061	$9,514	$9,989	$10,489	$11,013
Vacancy loss	3,692	1,491	391	411	431	453	476	499	524	511
Net rents	3,408	5,963	7,436	7,807	8,198	8,608	9,038	9,490	9,964	10,463
Less operating expenses:										
Food service	322	367	498							
Housekeeping	177	210	268							
Utilities	306	323	445							
Nursing	181	265	322							
Maintenance	404	485	525							
Mini bus transportation	85	104	125							
Management fee	175	220	330							
Advertising	503	354	80							
Insurance	32	45	62							
Legal	3	5	10							
Wages	23	48	55							
Subtotal operating exps.	2,211	2,426	2,720	2,856	2,999	3,149	3,306	3,471	3,645	3,827
Property taxes	615	646	678	712	748	785	824	866	909	954
Replacement reserve	180	180	180	180	180	180	180	180	180	180
Total operating exps.	3,006	3,252	3,578	3,748	3,927	4,114	4,310	4,517	4,734	4,961
Net operating income	401	2,711	3,857	4,059	4,271	4,494	4,727	4,973	5,230	5,501
Finance charge	2,331	2,331	2,331	2,331	2,331	2,331	2,331	2,331	2,331	2,331
Before tax cash flow	(1,930)	380	1,526	1,728	1,940	2,163	2,396	2,642	2,899	3,170
+ Amortization	116	128	142	157	173	192	212	234	259	286
+ Reserve	180	180	180	180	180	180	180	180	180	180
− Depreciation	788	788	788	788	788	788	788	788	788	788
Taxable income	(2,421)	(99)	1,061	1,278	1,506	1,747	2,001	2,268	2,551	2,848
Tax shelter	678	28	(297)	(358)	(422)	(487)	(560)	(635)	(714)	(798)
After tax cash flow	(1,252)	408	1,229	1,370	1,519	1,674	1,836	2,007	2,185	2,372

Notes
• Depreciation: Development costs-land/27.5 years
• Operating expenses vary as a percent of revenue as vacancy rates decline.
• Vacancy is determined by assuming that 44 units are preleased, with leasing continuing at the rate of 4-8 units/month. Resultant vacancy is 52% in yr 1, 20% in yr 2, and 5% thereafter.
• Income tax rate = 28%.

Exhibit 20-6 *Life Care Community Development Proforma*

Project type:	Life care community		
Number of units:	300 ILU's plus 60 bed nursing facility		

Unit mix:			
Studio	60		
One bedroom	120		
Two bedroom	120		
Sq. ft. (gross)	325,000		
Sq. ft. (net)	233,500		
Construction period	24 months		
Hard cost sq. ft.	$73		
Rental appreciation	5%		
Expense growth rate	5%		
Revenues:	Endowment fee:	Monthly:	
Studio	$98,000	$694	
One bedroom	$138,000	$1,440	
Two bedrooms	$175,000	$1,512	
Add'l occupant fee		$898	
Number of residents	417		

USES OF FUNDS:	TOTAL	PER UNIT	SQ. FT.
Land costs	$2,000,000	$6,667	$6
Project hard costs	23,600,000	78,667	73
+ Contingency	1,180,000	3,933	4
Total hard costs	24,780,000	82,600	76
Project soft costs			
Architecture/engin.	1,180,000	3,933	4
Legal & acct.	485,000	1,617	1
Marketing	1,500,000	5,000	5
Taxes during const.	104,000	347	0
Financing fees	306,000	1,020	1
Equipment	1,500,000	5,000	5
Construction int.	2,906,000	9,687	9
Developer's fee	1,239,000	4,130	4
Total soft costs	9,220,000	30,733	28
Total dev. costs	36,000,000	120,000	111

SOURCES OF FUNDS:			
Investor equity	$5,400,000		
Investor debt	$30,600,000		

*Debt based on 90% construction loan, excluding land costs

Exhibit 20-7 *Life Care Community Operating Proforma (in 000's)*

	1988	1989	1990	1991	1992	1993	1994	1995	1996	1997
Gross Revenues:										
Monthly fees		$4,545	$4,772	$5,011	$5,261	$5,524	$5,801	$6,091	$6,395	$6,715
Nonrefundable entry fee (see Ex. 20-8) (10% of entry fees received)		3,306	866	64	118	158	222	272	326	407
Total		7,851	5,638	5,075	5,379	5,682	6,023	6,363	6,721	7,122
Less vacancies		832	239	251	263	276	290	305	320	336
Net rents		7,019	5,399	4,824	5,116	5,406	5,733	6,058	6,401	6,786
Other income:										
Interest		174	198	239	280	354	465	522	644	693
Health care		879	1,070	963	842	708	557	390	204	0
Residual cash flow to developer (see Ex. 20-8)		0	1,552	54	145	251	432	617	846	1,180
Total		1,071	2,820	1,256	1,267	1,313	1,454	1,529	1,694	1,873
Operating expenses:										
Food service		774								
Housekeeping		282								
Administration		333								
Utilities		581								
Nursing care		648								
Maintenance		468								
Resident services		168								
Marketing	($900)	196								
Insurance		119								
Legal		46								
Total		3,615	3,796	3,986	4,185	4,394	4,614	4,844	5,087	5,341
Property taxes		624	655	688	722	758	796	836	878	922
Subtotal expenses		4,239	4,451	4,673	4,907	5,153	5,410	5,681	5,965	6,263
Cash flow from operations		3,851	3,768	1,407	1,476	1,566	1,777	1,806	2,130	2,396
− Depreciation		1,236	1,236	1,236	1,236	1,236	1,236	1,236	1,236	1,236
− Imputed interest		0	0	0	0	0	0	0	0	0
Taxable income		2,615	2,532	171	240	330	541	570	894	1,160
Income taxes at 28%		732	709	49	67	92	151	188	250	325
Cash flow after taxes		3,119	3,059	1,359	1,408	1,474	1,626	1,718	1,880	2,072
Less reserve additions		841	806	466	427	391	389	348	298	221
Cash flow after taxes and reserves	(900)	2,278	2,253	893	982	1,082	1,237	1,370	1,582	1,851

Notes:
• Health care income: Receipts from leasing unused beds at a daily rate to nonresidents.
• Imputed interest deduction: 10% of entry fees are recognized as income in year received. The 90% balance is treated as a no-interest loan to the developer.
• Assumes a two-year construction period, with $900 pre-marketing expenses.
• Tax rate = 28%.

Exhibit 20-8 *Returns to the Developer: Life Care Communities (000's)*

	INITIAL SALE	TURN OVER	AVERAGE PRICE/UNIT	FUNDS RECEIVED	PAYBACK − OF FUNDS	CASH TO − DEVELOPER	10% FEE + ON SALE	GAIN ON SALE OF UNITS
Year 1	0							
Year 2	228		$145	$33,060	$29,754[1]	$3,306	$3,306	$ 0
Year 3	57		152	8,664	6,246[1]	2,418	866	1,552
Year 4		4	160	640	522[2]	118	64	54
Year 5		7	168	1,176	914[2]	262	118	144
Year 6		9	176	1,584	1,175[2]	409	158	251
Year 7		12	185	2,220	1,566[2]	654	222	432
Year 8		14	194	2,716	1,827[2]	889	272	617
Year 9		16	204	3,260	2,088[2]	1,172	326	846
Year 10		19	214	4,066	2,480[2]	1,586	407	1,179

[1]Payback of construction loan of $30,600 and initial equity contribution of $5,400.
[2]Return of 90% entry fee to original occupant. Assume initially purchased units sell first, i.e., turnover in first ten years is of original units. As an example in year 4 four units turnover at an initial purchase price of $580 (4 units at $145 each) of which $522 (90%) is refunded.

21

THE AMERICAN DREAM

The purchase of a single family home is generally the major investment for most young couples. This case shows in some detail the process the Wellingtons go through in August, 1989, to find, finance, and close on a house in Maryland within what they believe to be their financial capabilities. Students are required to identify all the direct and indirect costs involved in home acquisition and compare these costs with the rental alternative.

Discussion Questions:

1. What is the process for finding, acquiring and financing a home?
2. How much can the Wellingtons afford to spend? What would their monthly payments be if they put either 5% or 20% down towards the purchase of a Devonshire home?
3. What should the Wellingtons do? What are their options?
4. From the consumer's perspective, has Dubin done a good job designing and marketing Grosvenor Park? Will this project be successful?

It was close to midnight on August 15, 1989 as Paula and Alex Wellington finished reading the Purchase and Sale contract. They were considering the purchase of a "Devonshire" single family home in the Grosvenor Park subdivision in Bethesda, Maryland. The base price for this Devonshire model was $255,490 but with extras, financing and closing costs, their total expenditures would probably exceed $300,000. This was a mind boggling number for a young married couple whose largest previous purchase had been a BMW 325 demonstrator for $21,000.

Paula wanted to move quickly. The design and location of the house were perfect and they could, at least for the moment, afford the purchase price. Financing the house would be difficult, but if they didn't buy now, she felt that rising sales prices might push the house beyond their means. Alex was not as certain.

Somehow, during the course of pursuing the American dream of home ownership, a tension had emerged within their relationship. Paula was not sure what she should do. Should she push on or should she give up her dream?

THE WELLINGTONS

Paula and Alex had married in June of 1987, just three weeks after Paula had graduated from the Harvard Business School. Both Paula and Alex had accepted employment in the Washington, D.C. metropolitan area, Paula with a management consulting firm, and Alex with Walt Whitman High School as a science teacher.

Throughout the summer, Paula and Alex had found themselves talking about their goals and about what the future might hold for them. They had always known, in a way, what each wanted in life, but now as they contemplated making a major purchase, these issues seemed to come into sharper focus.

Paula was committed to her career and eventually wanted to run her own company. She wasn't sure how long she would be a consultant but the money, the travel, and the work were all still exciting. Paula was traveling several days a week and she prized her leisure time with Alex.

Alex was glad to be back in suburban Bethesda. He had grown up in the area and he enjoyed both the quieter pace of life and the opportunity to teach

Research Assistant Richard E. Crum and Senior Lecturer Donald A. Brown prepared this case as the basis for class discussion rather than to illustrate either effective or ineffective handling of an administrative situation.

in the local high school. Although a lot had changed in Montgomery County since Alex had gone to high school there, many of his friends and family remained within the area. He missed having a home and yard to work and relax in.

Paula was the more aggressive, outgoing, and impulsive of the two while Alex was more easy going, conservative and patient. They both wanted to have children at some point but that decision seemed far off.

Now, in August of 1989 their combined income was just under $100,000 per year. Primarily as a result of Paula's education expenses, they had debts of $30,000 which required annual payments of $4,500 (see **Exhibit 21-1** for financial statement). Paula hoped to receive a substantial year end bonus but she wasn't sure how much it would be. Alex's parents had offered to help with the down payment in return for a share of the profit when the house was sold but neither Paula nor Alex wanted to give up their new found financial independence if they could avoid it.

THEIR APARTMENT

Shortly before moving to Maryland, Alex and Paula had signed a twelve-month lease for a one-bedroom with den apartment at Grosvenor Towers, a new luxury high rise rental complex located two blocks west of the North Bethesda Metro stop (see **Exhibit 21-2** for a floor plan of the apartment). After an increase of $100, the monthly rental rate was now $1,050 plus about $100 per month for utilities and cable TV. The lease had been renewed until May 31, 1990. The apartment project was developed and owned by the Dubin Construction Company, Inc.

Their apartment was approximately 1,000 square feet. Its finishes were luxurious compared to their rather spartan apartment in Cambridge. The complex had a swimming pool, an exercise room and 24 hour security. They had made many good friends in the complex as they lounged around the pool during the hot Washington summers. When they traveled, they simply locked the door, notified the doorman, and then left.

The complex was conveniently located for both Paula and Alex. Paula took the metro to work each morning and Alex made the five mile drive to Walt Whitman in the BMW. Shopping and recreational facilities were nearby. Traffic in the area, however, continued to worsen.

THE SEARCH

Each month as Paula had filled out the rental check for their apartment, she had become increasingly dissatisfied with being a tenant, and not building up any equity. All around them the Maryland countryside was sprouting new housing developments and the real estate section of their newspaper contained weekly reports of soaring prices and quick sales. Many of their friends had made small fortunes as home values soared.

Paula had begun her search by reading the Saturday real estate section of the Washington Post. After several weeks, she had convinced Alex to accompany her on Sunday drives to look at neighborhoods and houses. At an open house for an older home in a neighboring town, they had met Terri Robinson, a local realtor.

Robinson had sensed almost immediately that Paula was not interested in the house. In a polite but aggressive way, Robinson began to question Paula. Did they have children or pets? How much did they have for a down payment? What was their income? Where were they living now? How many bedrooms did they want? Did they want a garage? When were they thinking about moving? What type of house did she like?

Paula knew that they could not afford their dream house but she felt it was important to buy an interim house and start to build equity as soon as possible. When Robinson had suggested that they get together the following Saturday to look at several houses, Paula and Alex had readily agreed.

FAIRHILL

On Saturday, Robinson had taken them to two fairly nondescript houses. They were terrible. Paula was beginning to feel depressed about their chances to buy a new home when Robinson had pulled into the Fairhill townhouse project.

At Fairhill, a national housing developer was in the process of building 400 townhouse units. The units were new, well designed and well built (see **Exhibit 21-3** for a rendering and floor plan for The Clarendon at Fairhill). They were, however, also somewhat small and the finishes and fixtures appeared to be lower in quality than the ones in their current apartment. Paula had also noticed that most of the other cars in the parking lots were older, more beat up, and less expensive than their BMW. But, at an average price of $200,000 per unit, they could definitely afford to buy at Fairhill.

Robinson had provided them with impressive sales data for the project. One hundred units had sold in the first weekend and prices had already been raised twice. If they got in now, they would avoid the next price increase. Robinson had also claimed that the value of these units would appreciate by at least 20% during the next year. If they wanted to sell at that time, they could sell the unit, pull out their initial investment plus a profit, and invest in a larger home.

Unfortunately, The Fairhill location was not the best. It was on a side road located almost five miles from the metro station that Paula took to work each day. One of them would have to car pool each day or they would have to buy a second car.

GROSVENOR PARK

During March of 1989, Paula and Alex had learned that their landlord was preparing to build 189 houses on the land adjacent to Grosvenor Towers. Now, in August, two model homes were almost complete. Paula had tried to get Robinson to take them through Grosvenor Park but Robinson had been unwilling to show them the project. Prices, she had said, were high, the highway was too close, and the land was essentially swampland. She just didn't think it was worth wasting their time at Grosvenor Park. When Paula had pressed the issue, Robinson had said that she didn't have the time.

Paula had decided to go anyway. The two model homes were sited next to each other. A picket fence connected the two houses. Two large signs at the corner of the site proclaimed "The Grand Opening of Grosvenor Park—Luxury Homes from $200,000". Both houses were immaculately landscaped and the smell of fresh grass and flowers had been in the air.

Upon entering the first model, Paula and Alex had been greeted by Doug Jones, a young sales agent for the Dubin Company. He had welcomed Paula and Alex, had them sign in, and then had given them a brochure with floor plans, prices, and information about the rest of the project (see **Exhibit 21-4** for this material). He had then suggested that they look around on their own and asked that they stop back by on their way out so that he could answer any questions.

Paula had enjoyed the low pressure approach. It had given them the opportunity to explore the model at their own pace and to discuss how they felt without worrying about being overheard. The models were larger and more tastefully decorated than any of the previous homes that they had seen. They were also more expensive.

As they were leaving, they had found that they had to exit back through the original model and sales office or climb over the picket fence. When they entered the sales office, Jones gave them a low key sales pitch. The Dubin Company, he claimed, was a master builder of fine homes and it used only the best materials and appliances. The quality construction and award winning design would make it a wonderful home.

In one corner of the living room, there was a large model of the Grosvenor Park site which showed what the development would look like when the project was completed. The model was beautiful but Alex had a hard time visualizing how the morass of mud and dirt that was outside would someday be transformed into this beautiful oasis. Jones also had a number of samples of the different materials and finishes that could be obtained in each of the models. As he talked, Jones kept referring back to a number of large picture boards that contained colorful renderings and floor plans for the various units.

During their talk, Jones asked a series of questions about the Wellingtons. What type of home were they looking for, what had they liked about Grosvenor Park, what type of amenities were they interested in, which design did they like the most, when were they thinking about moving? He also discreetly inquired about their incomes and the amount that they could afford for a down payment.

The more traditional brick colonial model, which was called the Devonshire in the marketing material, was the most appealing to Paula. It contained 2300 square feet of living space with two bedrooms. Jones mentioned that this did not include the patio and the unfinished basement even though some of the other new home builders often included this type of space in their square footage calculations.

Paula had been pleasantly surprised when a basket of candy and nuts had arrived with a hand written note from Jones. In the note, Jones mentioned that prices were going up 10% on September 1 and that lead times for building a home were six to seven months. If they wanted to move by April 31, they should consider making a decision no later than October 1.

125 MAPLEWOOD ROAD

Later in the week, Alex surprised Paula by asking her to come with him to look at an older house that he had found. The house, at 125 Maplewood Road, was located in an established, upscale neighborhood. The mature trees and well tended yards gave the area a peaceful, prosperous feel.

The house that Alex had found was almost 100 years old and it was beginning to show its age. The owner was asking $175,000 and he admitted that the house probably needed another $50,000 in repair work within the next year. Alex felt that he could do most of the simple carpentry and painting work himself.

Inside, the house was huge. There were almost 3,500 s.f. of space with four bedrooms, three bathrooms, a den, a living room, and a huge kitchen. Unfortunately, most of the interior was poorly laid out for modern uses. It would take a lot of work to turn this old house into their home. It would also take a lot of effort to keep it clean.

THE COSTS

After a substantial amount of prodding by Paula, they had decided to explore the purchase of a Devonshire style house at Grosvenor Park. During their first inspection of the model house they had seen three extras that were tempting. Skylights could be put in the kitchen, hallway, and in the dressing room of their master bedroom at $725 each. Kitchen fixtures and cabinets could be upgraded for $2,000 extra, and three dormers could be added for $3,195. Half the cost of extras had to be paid at the time of authorization and the other half at closing. They had already finished paying for their apartment furniture but Paula knew that they would still need a few new things if they moved up to a house.

In addition, the Wellingtons had also learned that the landscaping installed on the model was not included in the $255,490 price. The purchase and sale contract provided for a landscaping allowance of only $3,000 which would be adequate, but would not cover the $8,000 cost of the mature trees and shrubbery which greatly enhanced the appearance of the model house.

The wallpaper and fancy light fixtures in the model were not included in the sales price either, but the Wellingtons did not feel that these items were essential. The quality of the workmanship in the model was quite good but Alex was concerned that the workmanship might not be as good on their unit. How could they be sure?

Selecting the best lot of the 189 available sites was also confusing. The corner lots were nice, but most of the land was in front of the house. There were 16 large private wooded lots that were clearly most desirable, but they each carried a $20,000 premium. Several other attractive lots backed up to the proposed moderate income section. They both wondered how much these factors would affect resale values.

The contract stated that Dubin would not guarantee anything to the buyers except for a one year structural and mechanical warranty which was required under Maryland State law. He would assign to the purchasers all of the guarantees and warranties that he received from the subcontractors and suppliers. In addition, as a member of the homeowners warranty corporation, Dubin would offer every purchaser the opportunity to purchase a 10-year extended warranty on all work and materials for an additional fee of 1% of the cost of the house.

Paula compiled the following list of costs in order to try and calculate the actual purchase price for a customized Devonshire at Grosvenor Park.

Base Price	$255,490
Premium Lot	20,000
Additional Landscaping	5,000
Skylights	2,175
Kitchen Upgrade	2,000
Dormers	3,195
Extended Warranty	1,439
Purchase Price	$289,299

THE PROCESS

After seeing these numbers, Paula had decided to consult with some specialists. Alex's parents had recommended that they hire a real estate lawyer, a surveyor, and a home inspection specialist to assist them with their purchase.

Margaret Klarman, a social friend whose law practice primarily involved real estate, agreed to meet with them. At their meeting, she explained what took place at a real estate closing. Present at the closing would be a title company representative (who would also act as escrow agent), all buyers, all sellers, and any selling or listing brokers who were involved in the transaction. Buyers and sellers might or might not have an attorney present. All problems involving construction deficiencies would be resolved first. Next, the buyers closing documents would be examined and executed. The buyer would then give the escrow agent the balance of the down payment in the form of "good funds", i.e., cash, cashier's check, or certified check. The seller would then review and sign the deed and any other sellers' closing documents, and would deliver the keys, warranties, guarantees, and equipment instructions to the closing person. The title attorney would then: (1) recheck the title to make sure there had been no last minute liens, (2) record the deed, and (3) disburse the funds. Klarman had filled out a closing statement to show them what their costs might be (see **Exhibit 21-5**).

Paula had then decided to make a second list of all the other fees and expenses that they would have to pay in order to determine what the total cost of purchasing a home would be.

Purchase Price	$289,299
Legal Fee	1,500
Survey	100
Moving Expenses	1,500
Washer & Dryer	800
New Furniture	4,000
State & County Transfer Taxes	5,626
Home Inspection	500
Title Insurance	635
Total	$303,960

FINANCING

By this point, Paula had realized that financing their home would probably be complicated as well. If Paula and Alex decided to proceed, they would still need to determine how much cash to put in as equity. Jones had said that today's prime rate was 11%, but that for qualified buyers, Dubin had locked in an 80%, 30 year adjustable rate mortgage (ARM), with an interest rate of 10% for the first three years. The borrower would also have to pay one and a half points in fees. After that, there would be an annual interest rate adjustment with a cap of 14%. With a down payment equal to 20% of the sales price (i.e., $57,860), the initial monthly payment including taxes would be $2,363.

If they paid 5% down (i.e., $14,465), they would need mortgage insurance (referred to by lenders as private mortgage insurance or PMI) and that would bring their monthly payment to $2,845. A second one and one half point placement fee would also be required.

Some of their friends had bought houses using owner assisted mortgages, graduated payment mortgages, or growing equity mortgages (see **Exhibit 21-6** for a description of the various types of mortgages available). There seemed to be an incredible variety of mortgages available. How should they decide about which type of mortgage to pursue?

Jones had told them to expect the real estate taxes to be approximately

$4,000 per year, payable in September for the prior fiscal year ending June 30. He also said that they should expect the cost of homeowners insurance to be approximately $500 per year, payable in advance. A monthly homeowners association fee for expenses associated with the common areas—taxes, insurance, and maintenance—had to be added in as well. This fee would be $120 per calendar year.

In discussions with some of Paula's classmates, they had heard that the general rule was that home buyers should not pay more than 28% of their gross income for principal, interest, taxes, and insurance (PITI) nor 36% of their gross income for both PITI and other long term debt payments.

THEIR DECISION

During the next three weeks, both Robinson and Jones had called several times. Jones had even gone so far as to fill out a purchase and sale agreement for Paula and Alex to look at.

Paula had recently found out three things that troubled her. First, a friend had told her that the developer of Fairhill was offering real estate agents "incentives" for selling units in his complex. An agent who sold 5 units would get a free trip for two to Hawaii and agent who sold 10 units would receive a car. This seemed to explain some of Robinson's enthusiasm for Fairhill. Second, Paula had found out from Jones that the Dubin company did not "co-broke". This meant that Dubin would not pay an outside leasing agent a commission for locating a buyer. It also seemed to explain why Robinson wouldn't show them Grosvenor's Park. Third, Paula had read an article on local housing sales that had noted that prices appeared to be leveling off and that it was taking longer for homes to sell. Paula wondered who they could trust and how much of their information was accurate.

Paula and Alex had had no idea that a simple house purchase could be so expensive or complicated. After all of their legwork, discussions with various knowledgeable professionals, and general pondering of the information that they had gathered, they still had many questions to answer before they could buy a home.

Which house should they buy? How much could they afford to spend? How much should they put down as a downpayment? What was the correct sequence of steps to follow? Should they try to protect themselves from the possibility that one of them might not be income-producing? What type of loan would be best for them? Did they want a parent as a partner in their home? How would the cost of living in a house compare to the cost of living in an apartment? Would the Devonshire be a good investment? Should they analyze this purchase in the same way as their other investments? Were interest rates going to go up or down? If they felt interest rates were going to come down, should they wait?

Paula was not sure whether there was any one right answer to any of these questions. But the time for academic debates was past. Somehow she would have to decide and then convince Alex.

Exhibit 21-1 *Alex and Paula Wellington's Financial Statement*

ASSETS		LIABILITIES	
Cash, Cash Equivalents	$45,000	Loans	
IRAs	8,000	Automobile, 1986 BMW	$ 3,000
Securities:		Student Loans	
Stock		Alex	1,000
Marriott, 200 shs. @ $30/sh.	6,000	Paula	23,000
AT&T, 150 shs. @ $50/sh.	7,500	Income Tax Liability	3,000
Automobiles:			
1986 BMW, 325	21,000		
Total Assets	$92,500	Total Liabilities	$ 30,000
		Net Worth	$ 62,500
		Total Liabilities and Net Worth	$ 92,500
		Total Estimated Income from Professions and Investments	$100,000

Exhibit 21-2

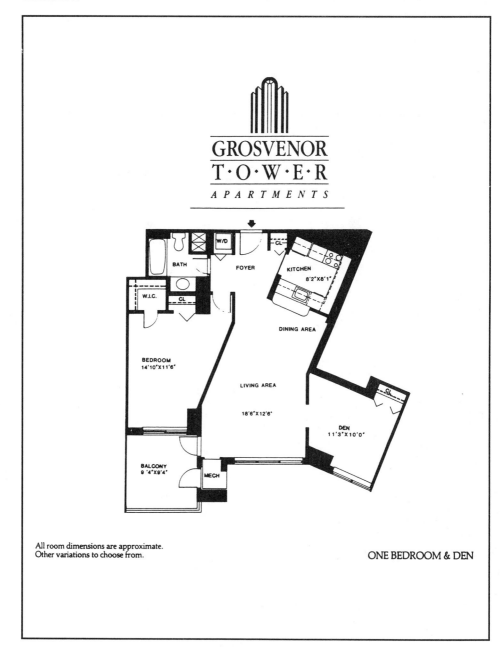

All room dimensions are approximate.
Other variations to choose from.

ONE BEDROOM & DEN

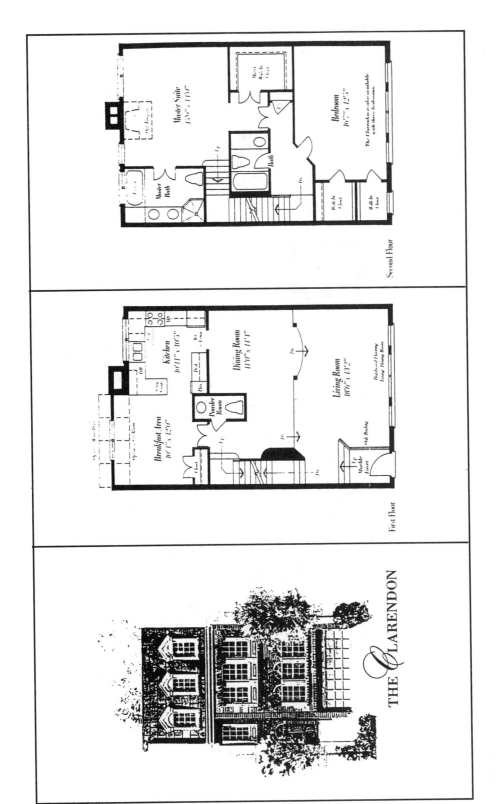

Second Floor

First Floor

THE CLARENDON

Exhibit 21-3

Exhibit 21-4

ith today's very real concerns about travel time
to downtown jobs or how much home you will
get for your dollar, most homebuyers have been
forced to downgrade the importance of quality family living in their
choice of a new home. Until now.

The Dubin Companies are proud to present Grosvenor Park,
where practical reality and important values live comfortably
together.

Located in beautiful, Montgomery County, Grosvenor Park
offers a location that puts you just five minutes from some of the
county's finest shopping, just 14 miles from Capitol Hill and 20
miles from relaxing in the Chesapeake Bay. Churches and fine
schools are close by.

At the same time, Grosvenor Park gives you a rare opportunity
to provide your children with plenty of green open space for safe
play, healthy amenities and opportunities to thrive in a community
oriented around family values. A place that children want to call
home.

The Dubin Companies have been building quality single family
homes, townhomes and apartments in the Washington area for
more than 25 years. We are proud to offer you the exciting opportunity to live in Grosvenor Park–a community for family living.

Exhibit 21-4 (continued)

DEVONSHIRE

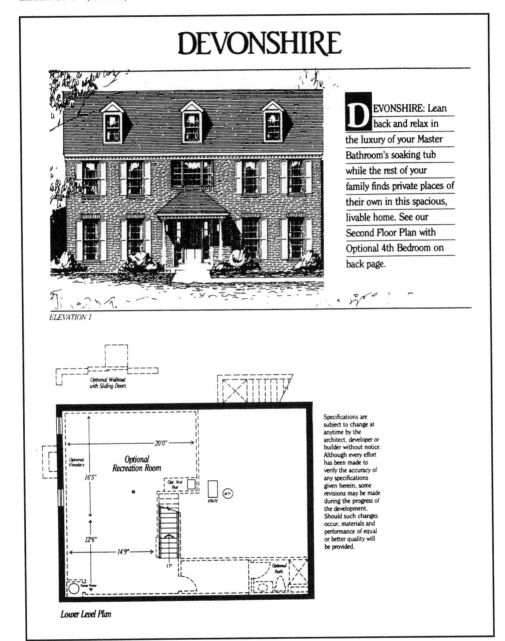

DEVONSHIRE: Lean back and relax in the luxury of your Master Bathroom's soaking tub while the rest of your family finds private places of their own in this spacious, livable home. See our Second Floor Plan with Optional 4th Bedroom on back page.

ELEVATION 1

Optional Walkout with Sliding Doors

Optional Fireplace

Optional Recreation Room

Opt. Wet Bar

H/W H

20'0"

16'5"

12'6"

14'9"

Optional Bath

Specifications are subject to change at anytime by the architect, developer or builder without notice. Although every effort has been made to verify the accuracy of any specifications given herein, some revisions may be made during the progress of the development. Should such changes occur, materials and performance of equal or better quality will be provided.

Lower Level Plan

Exhibit 21-4 (*continued*)

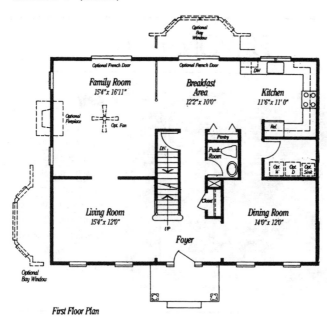

First Floor Plan

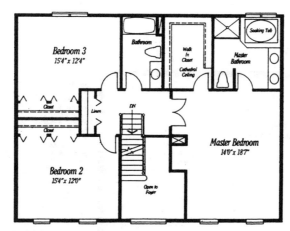

Second Floor Plan w/3 Bedrooms

Exhibit 21-4 (*continued*)

STANDARD FEATURES

AS YOU LOOK AROUND EVERY HOME, YOU'LL FIND . . .

- Traditional design with authentic colonial touches.
- Designer brass hardware throughout.
- Aluminum thermal break windows with double insulated glass.
- Aluminum 6' x 6'8" double insulated sliding glass door.
- Handsome six panel insulated entrance door with dead bolt lock.
- Two car garage with colonial raised panel doors.
- Alcoa vinyl German Lap exterior siding with color scheme preselected by architect.
- Fiberglass shingles.

AS YOU LOOK INSIDE EVERY HOME, YOU'LL FIND . . .

- Oak hardwood flooring in foyer in some units.
- Elegant brass-toned lighting fixtures.
- Dramatic vaulted and cathedral ceilings in some units.
- Drywall walls and ceilings with two coats of flat latex paint.
- Semi-gloss paint on all wood doors, casing, window sills and base boards.
- Authentic 3 1/4" colonial baseboards.
- Comfort underfoot with Armstrong vinyl flooring in kitchens and breakfast rooms.
- Colonial six panel doors with traditional casings.
- Easy care 4" x 4" ceramic tile with ceramic cove base in bath and powder rooms.
- Luxurious carpet with 1/2" foam padding in all carpeted areas.
- Smooth trowel concrete finished basement.
- 3 TV outlets prewired in master bedroom, 2nd bedroom, and family room.
- 5 Telephone outlets prewired in kitchen, family room, master bedroom, 2nd bedroom and 3rd bedroom.

EACH BATHROOM FEATURES:

- Luxurious 42" x 60" acrylic soaking tub in master bedroom suite.
- Comfortable 30" x 60" acrylic tub in hall bath.
- Cultured marble vanity tops in master and hall bath.
- Designer pedestal sink in powder room.
- 14" x 18" medicine cabinet with full mirror over vanity.
- Decorator faucets and elongated water closets.

GROSVENOR PARK KITCHEN FEATURES;

- Beautiful colonial style cabinets with cathedral raised panel wall cabinet doors.
- Formica countertop with single stainless steel bowl.
- General Electric 30" gas continuous clean range with electronic ignition and black glass front.
- General Electric 21 cubic feet frost free refrigerator.
- General Electric 2-level pot and pan cycle dishwasher.
- Quality decorator faucets.

HOME COMFORT AND ENERGY SAVING FEATURES:

- Trane gas furnace with standing pilot for energy efficient heating and air conditioning.
- Energy saving E-7 Insulation Program features R-30 ceilings; R-16 exterior walls; R-19 overhang; special air seal program.
- Double insulated thermal windows and sliding door.
- 50 gallon gas hot water heater.
- A smoke detector on every level.

Exhibit 21-4 *(continued)*

GROSVENOR PARK
• A   C O M M U N I T Y   F O R   F A M I L Y   L I V I N G •

PRICE LIST

ANDOVER I	$228,990
ANDOVER II	$230,990
BENTLEY I	$227,990
BENTLEY II	$229,990
BENTLEY III	$231,990
CAMBRIDGE I	$249,990
CAMBRIDGE II	$255,990
DEVONSHIRE I	$255,490
DEVONSHIRE II	$257,490
DEVONSHIRE III	$257,990

Pre-selected features include:

Cathedral Ceilings in All Bedrooms . . . . Standard

Separate Tub and Shower in Master Bath . . . . . Standard

Fireplace With Slate Surround . . . . Standard

Hardwood Flooring in Foyer . . . . Standard

Director of Sales: Richard Benjamin
Sales Office Phone: (301) 599-0950
Sales Office Hours: 11:00 a.m. to 6:00 p.m. Daily

Prices, Terms, and Specifications
Subject to Change Without Notice

Exhibit 21-4 (*continued*)

GROSVENOR PARK
• A COMMUNITY FOR FAMILY LIVING •

OPTIONAL FEATURES

Brick Fronts:

ANDOVER I	$3,000.00
ANDOVER II (½ Brick)	$2,100.00
ANDOVER II (Full Brick)	$3,000.00
BENTLEY I	$3,750.00
BENTLEY II	$3,750.00
BENTLEY III (½ Brick)	$2,100.00
BENTLEY III (Full Brick)	$3,750.00
CAMBRIDGE I	$3,100.00
CAMBRIDGE II	$3,500.00
DEVONSHIRE I	$4,500.00
DEVONSHIRE II	$4,000.00
DEVONSHIRE III	$4,200.00

Decks: Under $13.00 per sq. ft.

Walk-Out Basement: $2,500.00

Exterior French Door (in Lieu of Slider) $695.00

Whirlpool: $1,295.00

Skylights: $725.00

Bay Windows:
Side $1,595.00
Back $1,695.00

Dormers:
Two Working - Cambridge $2,795.00
Three Non-Working - Devonshire $3,195.00

Finished Rec-Room With Full Bath: $9,995.00

4th Bedroom - Bentley: $8,995.00

Family Room - Andover: $8,995.00

Other Features May be Added at Your Request
Please See Sales Consultants For More Information

Prices, Terms, and Specifications
Subject to Change Without Notice

Exhibit 21-5   *The American Dream*

LOAN TYPE	FEATURES	INTEREST RATE	DOWN PAYMENT	PAYMENTS
30-year fixed rate	Provides stable monthly payments for fixed term.	Fixed	The loan may be obtained as with little as 5% down payment with FHA insurance, but private mortgage insurance (PMI) is required as loans with down payments of less than 20%.	Fixed
10, 15, 20-year fixed rate	Provides more rapid equity buildup than with longer-term fixed-rate mortgage; provides substantial interest savings over 30-year fixed rate mortg.	Fixed	Determined by lender	Higher monthly payments than with 30-year fixed rate because of shorter loan term.
Biweekly fixed rate	Equity builds faster because of increased number of payments annually.	Fixed	Determined by lender	Borrower makes the equivalent of 13 monthly payments in 12 month period. Payments are fixed at one-half of those monthly fixed-rate mortgages and are drafted automatically from the borrower's bank acct.
Adjustable rate (ARM)	Six-month and one and three year ARMs are available, which means that the interest rate will be adjusted after six months or one or three years. Some three-year ARMs feature caps on the level to which the loan may be adjusted during the loan term, 15- and 30-year options, and options to convert to fixed-rate mortgages.	Lenders peg the loan's interest rate to an index, and payments are adjusted according to the movement of the index.	Determined by lender	Some lenders allow (ARM) borrowers to add closing point costs to mortgage payments during the loan's first two years.

Exhibit 21-5 *(continued)*

LOAN TYPE	FEATURES	INTEREST RATE	DOWN PAYMENT	PAYMENTS
Negative Amortization	Borrower's monthly payments fall short of covering the loan's principal and interest. The loan amount not covered by monthly payments is added to the life of the loan.	Fixed	Determined by lender	Allows the buyer to have lower monthly payments.
Graduated Payment (GPN)	Allows the buyer whose income is likely to increase in the future to buy with lower initial payments.	Determined by lender	A larger down payment is often required	Payments increase gradually the first five or ten years and then level off for the rest of the term.
Growing Equity (GEM)	"Overpayments" are applied to the loan's principal creating substantial interest savings over the life of the loan. Typically a 30-year mortgage is paid off within 15 to 20 years.	Fixed	Determined by lender	The mortgage is calculated at a fixed rate on a 30-year basis but payments increase on a regular schedule.
Veterans Administration (VA)	Loans are assumable and can be combined with second mortgages.	Rates are fixed and are typically below conventional levels.	Not required	Determined by lender.
Federal Housing Administration (FHA)	The FHA offers 15- or 30-year fixed-rate mortgages.	Fixed	3% down payments on first $25,000 of the loan value and 5% on the rest.	Fixed
FHA's Shared Equity (SEM)	Allows marginal buyers to pair up with a relative or other investor. Each investor owns a percentage of the home's value. Loans are offered for up to 97% of the home's value.	Determined by lender	Determined by lender	Monthly payments are based on the percent of ownership.
Seller Financing	Often allows marginal buyers the ability to purchase when lenders might consider them poor risks. The	Determined by seller	Determined by seller	Determined by seller

Exhibit 21-5 (*continued*)

LOAN TYPE	FEATURES	INTEREST RATE	DOWN PAYMENT	PAYMENTS
	buyer saves money because there are no discount points and often there are no closing costs or they are less expensive than with lender financing. The sale is treated as an installment sale for the seller's tax purposes. The seller is taxed only on the amount of money the seller receives each year.			
Buy-downs	The seller pays the lender to temporarily or permanently lower the borrower's interest rates.	With permanent buy-downs the interest rate is typically lowered by 1% during the entire life of the loan. The most common temporary buy-down is the 3-2-1 plan, whereby the interest rate is reduced by 3% the first year, 2% the second year, and 1% the third year. Payments then remain stable during the remainder of the loan term.	Determined by lender	Determined by type of buy-downs
Wraparound	The seller makes a money advance to cover or "wrap" the buyer's balance on his/her current home and the new loan.	The interest rate on the new loan is below market rates.	Determined by terms of the loan.	Allows the owner to have a lower monthly payment than if he had taken a new first mortgage at a higher interest rate.

Exhibit 21-6

A.	U.S. DEPARTMENT OF HOUSING AND URBAN DEVELOPMENT DISCLOSURE/SETTLEMENT STATEMENT	B. TYPE OF LOAN

commercial settlements, inc. CASE NO. S–_____

B. TYPE OF LOAN: 1.☐ FHA 2.☐ FmHA 3.☒ CONV. UNINS. 4.☐ VA 5.☐ CONV. INS.
6. FILE NUMBER   7. LOAN NUMBER
8. MORTGAGE INSURANCE CASE NUMBER:

If the Truth-in-Lending Act applies to this transaction, a Truth-in-Lending statement is attached as page 3 of this form.

C. NOTE: *This form is furnished to you a statement of actual settlement costs. Amounts paid to and by the settlement agent are shown. Items marked "(p.o.c.)" were paid outside the closing; they are shown here for informational purposes and are not included in the totals.*

D. NAME OF BORROWER	E. NAME OF SELLER:	F. NAME OF LENDER:
Alex Wellington Paula Wellington	Dubin Construction Company	Bethesda Federal Savings and Loan Association

G. PROPERTY LOCATION	H. SETTLEMENT AGENT:	I. SETTLEMENT DATE:
Lot 45 Block 8 1234 Elm Street Bethesda, MD 20854 Montgomery County, MD	**commercial settlements, inc.** PLACE OF SETTLEMENT: 1413 K Street, N.W., Washington, D.C. 20005 Telephone: (202) 737-4747	April 1, 1990

J. SUMMARY OF BORROWER'S TRANSACTION		K. SUMMARY OF SELLER'S TRANSACTION	
100. GROSS AMOUNT DUE FROM BORROWER:		400. GROSS AMOUNT DUE SELLER:	
101. CONTRACT SALES PRICE	289,299.00	401. Contract sales price	289,299.00
102. PERSONAL PROPERTY		402. Personal property	
103. Settlement Charges to Borrower (line 1400)	15,709.93	403.	
104. Extras ($5400-$2700 POC)		404. Extras (5400-$2700 POC)	
105.		405.	
Adjustments for items paid by seller in advance		Adjustments for items paid by seller in advance	
106. City/town taxes to		406. City/town taxes to	
107. County taxes 4/1 to 6/30	748.02	407. County taxes 4/1 to 6/30	748.02
108. Assessments to		408. Assessments to	
109.		409.	
110.		410.	
111.		411.	
112.		412.	
120. GROSS AMOUNT DUE FROM BORROWER	305,256.95	420. GROSS AMOUNT DUE TO SELLER	290,047.02
200. AMOUNTS PAID BY OR IN BEHALF OF BORROWER:		500. REDUCTIONS IN AMOUNT DUE TO SELLER:	
201. Deposit or earnest money	14,500.00	501. Excess deposit (see instructions)	
202. Principle amount of new loan(s)	230,000.00	502. Settlement charges to seller (line 1400)	8,909.00
203. Existing loan(s) taken subject to		503. Existing loan(s) taken subject to	
204.		504. Payoff of first mortgage loan	
205.		505. Payoff of second mortgage loan	
206.		506.	
207.		507.	
208.		508.	
209.		509.	
Adjustments for items unpaid by seller		Adjustment for items unpaid by seller	
210. City/town taxes to		510. City/town taxes to	
211. County taxes to		511. County taxes to	
212. Assessments to		512. Assessments to	
213.		513.	
214.		514.	
215.		515.	
216.		516.	
217.		517.	
218.		518.	
219.		519.	
220. TOTAL PAID BY/FOR BORROWER	245,000.00	520. TOTAL REDUCTION AMOUNT DUE SELLER	8,909.00
300. CASH AT SETTLEMENT FROM/TO BORROWER		600. CASH AT SETTLEMENT TO/FROM SELLER	
301. Gross amount due from borrower (line 120)	305,256.95	601. Gross amount due seller (line 420)	289,299.00
302. Less amount paid by/for borrower (line 220)	(245,000.00)	602. Less reductions in amount due seller (line 520)	(8,909.00)
303. Cash (X FROM)(__TO) BORROWER	60,256.95	603. CASH (__TO)(__FROM) SELLER	280,390.00

The undersigned hereby acknowledge the examination and approval of this statement and receipt of a copy. Company is directed and authorized to make distribution and payments in accordance herewith and it is agreed that Company assumes no liability for the accuracy or validity of items or charges not imposed by Company or the failure to include on this Statement items or charges not disclosed to Company at settlement.

Buyer: _____   Seller: _____
_____   _____

Exhibit 21-6 *(continued)*

L. SETTLEMENT CHARGES		PAID FROM BORROWER'S FUNDS AT SETTLEMENT	PAID FROM SELLER'S FUNDS AT SETTLEMENT
700. TOTAL SALES/BROKER'S COMMISSION based on price $289K @ 3 %=			
Division of Commission (line 700) as follows:			
701. $ 8,679.00 to			
702. $ to			
703. Commission paid at Settlement			8,679.00
704.			
800. ITEMS PAYABLE IN CONNECTION WITH LOAN			
801. Loan Origination Fee 1 % Bethesda Federal Savings & Loan		2,300.00	
802. Loan Discount 1/2 % Bethesda Federal Savings & Loan		1,150.00	
803. Appraisal Fee $250.00 to Bethesda Federal Savings & Loan		POC	
804. Credit Report $ 40.00 to Bethesda Federal Savings & Loan		POC	
805. Lender's Inspection Fee		100.00	
806. Mortgage Insurance Application Fee to			
807. Assumption Fee			
808. Document Preparation Fee – Bethesda Federal Savings & Loan		195.00	
809. Loan Application Fee – Bethesda Federal Savings & Loan		50.00	
810.			
811.			
900. ITEMS REQUIRED BY LENDER TO BE PAID IN ADVANCE			
901. Interest from 4/1 to 5/1 @$66.52 /day		1,995.60	
902. Mortgage Insurance Premium for months to			
903. Hazard Insurance Premium for 1 years to GEICO –$500.00		POC	
904. years to			
905.			
1000. RESERVES DEPOSITED WITH LENDER			
1001. Hazard Insurance 2 months @ $ 41.67 per month		83.33	
1002. Mortgage Insurance months @ $ per month			
1003. City property taxes months @ $ per month			
1004. County property taxes 9 months @ $ 250.00 per month		2,250.00	
1005. Annual Assessments months @ $ per month			
1006. months @ $ per month			
1007. months @ $ per month			
1008. months @ $ per month			
1100. TITLE CHARGES			
1101. Settlement or closing fee to Commercial Settlements, Inc.		250.00	200.00
1102. Abstract or title search to			
1103. Title Examination to Commercial Settlements, Inc.		250.00	
1104. Title insurance binder to Commercial Settlements, Inc.		15.00	
1105. Document preparation to Commercial Settlements, Inc.		50.00	
1106. Notary fees to Nancy D. Noel		10.00	
1107. Attorney's fees to			
(includes above items numbers;)			
1108. Title insurance to CSI/Chicago Title Insurance Company		635.00	
(includes above items numbers;)			
1109. Lender's coverage $ 230,000.00 ($400.00)			
1110. Owner's coverage $ 290,000.00			
1111.			
1112.			
1113.			
1200. GOVERNMENT RECORDING AND TRANSFER CHARGES			
1201. Recording fees: Deed $ 20.00 ;Mortgage $ 40.00 ;Releases $ 30.00		60.00	30.00
1202. City/County tax/stamps Deed $, Mortgage $ @ 1%		2,900.00	
1203. State tax/stamps Deed $; Mortgage $ @ 5%		1,450.00	
1204. State Stamps @ $4.40/$1000.00		1,276.00	
1205.			
1300. ADDITIONAL SETTLEMENT CHARGES			
1301. Survey $300.00 to –$200.00 – recertification fee		100.00	
1302. Pest inspection to			
1303. Homeowners Association Fee through December 31, 1990		90.00	
1304.			
1305.			
1400. TOTAL SETTLEMENT CHARGES (enter on lines 103, Section J and 502, Section K)		15,209.93	8,909.00

22

GROSVENOR PARK

In September, 1988, Dick Dubin is attempting to gain final approval for a 189 unit single family home subdivision in Bethesda, Maryland targeted to young, upwardly mobile professionals working in the Washington, D.C. area. The case spans the project life cycle from predevelopment to sellout, and addresses issues ranging from land acquisition, construction phasing, finance, design, and marketing, to managing a critical relationship with a powerful local planning board.

Discussion Questions:

1. Evaluate Dubin's performance to date. What are the risks he faces in this project? How has he managed those risks to date? What should he do going forward?

2. Assess the demands of the Planning Department. Are they reasonable? What would you do if you were Dubin?

3. Would Grosvenor Park appeal to you as a place to live? As an investment vehicle?

4. How does the development of single family homes differ from development of multi-family homes?

Dick Dubin loosened his tie and sank exhausted onto the sofa. On this September night in 1988 he was frustrated by yet another negotiation with the Montgomery County Planning Department (PD) over his Grosvenor Park project, a 189 unit single family subdivision in Bethesda, Maryland. The latest demand on the long list of PD requirements was a cool $1 million worth of road improvements. This amount, added to PD demands totaling $2.6 million for developer contributions toward schools, sewers and mitigation of sound pollution made Dubin decide to reexamine some of the assumptions he had made about the best way to go forward with the project. These demands were on top of requirements in Montgomery County which mandated that fifteen percent of the project, 28 units, had to be included at affordable rates to median income families.

The developer had to make some choices soon because he was scheduled to make his financing commitments in one week. He had planned to open model units while construction was underway and offer all 189 units in the same phase, completing the entire project within three and a half years. Dubin's original strategy had been to price the units slightly below market at prices calculated to ensure a quick sellout. The expense of the PD demands, however, tempted him to consider increasing the price of the market rate units to cover fully the additional expenses, raising them slightly above market. Should he fight the PD and delay construction, or should he give in and fold the additional costs into his sales price? How would the bank view the increased uncertainty in the sell-out period caused by increasing sales prices?

THE DEVELOPER

Dick Dubin began his development career soon after graduating from Boston University. After a brief but memorable interlude as a croupier in Las Vegas, Dubin relocated to Maryland and successfully developed over 4,000 residential units, both sales and rental. Over the course of his 20-year career in the Maryland area, he built a variety of residential products ranging from subsidized housing for the elderly to moderate income housing to market rate luxury townhouses.

In 1985, Dubin completed Grosvenor Tower, a highly successful luxury high rise featuring 190 two bedroom units. Grosvenor Tower was located two

Research Assistant Katherine Sweetman prepared this case under the supervision of Adjunct Professor William J. Poorvu as the basis for class discussion rather than to illustrate either effective or ineffective handling of an administrative situation.

blocks from the Grosvenor Park site. The high rise tower rented rapidly and had enjoyed a 98 percent occupancy rate since opening. Dubin attributed the success of the project to its quality and its ability to meet the needs of its tenants. Seventy percent of its tenants were young professional couples who worked in downtown Washington and who took advantage of the building's location near the Metro, Washington's subway system. The remaining thirty percent were mostly single professionals, primarily working downtown, either living alone or sharing apartments. Shopping malls and entertainment were becoming increasingly available along the rapidly developing Route 270 corridor, a short drive away. The building had health club facilities which enabled the tenants to meet each other and encouraged a collegial atmosphere. Rents for the two-bedroom, 1,000 square foot apartments averaged $950 per month in 1988 and had increased at an average rate of 5 percent per year since the building opened.

Dubin knew from the financial data that his tenants had supplied on their rental applications that many of the households grossed about $100,000 in pretax income per year. He also knew from chatting with them that they liked the area and would eventually like to own homes there. The general feeling was that they would like to buy but were in no rush because they felt that their "dream homes" were still out of reach financially. Many of them had in mind homes in sections of Montgomery County which sold for over $400,000.

Dubin felt that he could profitably apply his local experience to market Grosvenor Park to these young professionals as a bridge home priced between the apartment and the "dream house". While the Grosvenor Park site was in a pioneering location for this concept since the immediate neighborhood had been characterized by moderately priced garden apartments for decades, Dubin felt that the success of his rental building indicated that conditions were right for him to take the chance. Dubin would act as land speculator, zoning negotiator, land developer and builder.

SINGLE FAMILY HOUSING

By 1987, 40 percent of America from Maine to California lived in the suburbs. Post World War II economic and population booms rapidly increased the pace of development begun earlier in the century and encouraged wholesale development of large tracts of land in many parts of the country. Sometimes the houses were very similar; sometimes they simply adhered to building and design restrictions; sometimes the purchaser had total freedom over the design of his or her home. By 1987, fully ten percent of all Americans lived in planned suburban communities which were often the product of such large-scale development.

In the late 1980s, most young people were unable to afford a single family home due to rapidly escalating land prices. This economic reality led to a new suburban art of high density planning, where issues of topography (such as slope and drainage) were carefully married to market needs in terms of lot size, building size and landscaping. In the past, suburban planners fit 7 to 8 units per acre; however, with innovative cluster and parking plans, developers were now squeezing 10 to 12 units per acre.

THE OPPORTUNITY

The Grosvenor Park site was located in Bethesda, Maryland, a community of 80,000. Having served as a bedroom community to Washington, D.C. for most of its history, (see **Exhibit 22-1**). Bethesda was newly emerging as a city in its own right. The site was well-located in terms of transportation, with quick access to Interstate 270 and sited across the highway from the newest stop on the Washington, D.C. Metro. The stop was a 17 minute ride from DuPont Circle in the heart of Washington's business district. The surrounding neighborhood was characterized by middle class garden apartment complexes developed during the 1960's and 1970's (see **Exhibit 22-2**). The only exception to this was Dubin's own Grosvenor Tower development.

The 25 acre property in question had been on the market for years at the prevailing rate for garden apartments. Under its R-30 zoning, the site could legally support 426 garden apartments. When Dubin first investigated the site in mid-1987, the owner was asking about $12,700 per zoned unit, or $5,400,000. The property remained unsold because the number of garden apartment units legally permissible could not physically be accommodated on the site. Located at the bottom of a hill, parts of the property collected runoff from the land "up-stream." Legally, the wetlands portion of the property could not be developed, though development rights could be transferred to the dry portions of the parcel. In the case of high density garden apartment development, this would have necessitated building underground rather than surface parking, an expensive proposition.

Dubin saw a better use for the land. His unscientific market survey within Grosvenor Towers fueled his hunch that the time was right for single family homes in that area. With 189 single family homes, the unit density would be greatly diminished, but the unit value greatly enhanced. While a 1,000 square foot two-bedroom garden apartment would rent for $950 per month, a new 2,300 square foot two-bedroom plus convertible study would sell for $250,000. With only 189 units, inexpensive surface parking could easily fit the grounds. The wetlands could be incorporated into the landscaping designs (see **Exhibit 22-3**).

Dubin also took into account that 15 percent of all new construction in Montgomery County must be available to moderate income groups in the form of MPDU's—Moderate Price Dwelling Units. In the case of Grosvenor Park, this translated to 28 units to be sold at an average price of $85,000 each. These units had to be comparable to the market rate units in size, configuration and quality.

With the single family plan in mind, Dubin paid the asking price for the site. A local S&L, the Bethesda Federal Savings and Loan, supplied $7,200,000 for the land portion of the project, based on an appraisal valuing the parcel at

$8,600,000, or $45,500 per single family home. The $1.8 million differential between the purchase price and the loan based on the single family valuation would be advanced for related project costs and gave Dubin a comfortable sum to begin his planning. Dubin gave a personal guarantee for the portion of the loan above the land cost.

THE INITIAL PROCESS

Dubin planned to position Grosvenor Park as an opportunity for young couples to live in a compatible community, enjoy comfortable homes, and build equity toward their dream houses in a residential market currently appreciating at a rate of about ten percent annually. He would offer two designs, a Cape Cod and a brick colonial, each selling for an average price of $250,000 and each containing 2,300 square feet (see **Exhibit 22-4**). Owners could park their cars in the private road in front of their homes. While Dubin did not plan to provide any health club facilities or community amenities of that nature, such facilities were easily available along Route 270.

Dubin would market all the sites during the construction period through the use of models and floor plans. To lower his risk, he would have only six homes in inventory at a time. All other construction would start once a binding contract was signed with a 10% nonrefundable deposit. Dubin would contract to deliver the home six months from the signing of the contract. He figured that the development would take three and a half years to fully build out, and expected that he could have sales contracts for all units within that period. The buyer would select the model and site, and would choose among a variety of options including skylights, customized kitchens and lofts. Purchasers would pay premiums of up to $20,000 for locations with attractive views.

Dubin planned to design a Homeowners' Association similar to those in his other developments which would administer care of the common areas, including the grounds. The Association would be entirely the responsibility of the homeowners once 80% of the units had sold.

AFFORDABILITY

Dubin recognized that a key success factor for this development would be affordability to its target audience. Dubin ran some rough numbers to see if the young couples of Grosvenor Tower could afford new single family homes. In addition to the sales price, Dubin estimated that other costs of ownership including utilities, maintenance, homeowners' assessment and other fees would total about $4,400 annually and increase at about 5% per year. Property insurance would be about $1,500 per year and increase at 5% per year. In addition, property taxes would be 1.25% of the sales price. Closing costs upon purchase would be around $5,000. Dubin also made assumptions based on his knowledge of the requirements banks would place upon purchasers. Most area banks originated their own loans, then sold them in the secondary mortgage markets in bundles. In order for a bank to sell a mortgage, the mortgage had to meet the following strict FNMA underwriting guidelines:

1. A buyer putting less than 20% down must buy mortgage insurance at an extra cost at closing.
2. Monthly principal, interest, real estate taxes and mortgage insurance payments (PITI) cannot exceed 28% of the purchaser's gross monthly pre-tax income.
3. Monthly payments for total long term indebtedness (greater than 10 months left to pay) cannot exceed 36% of the purchaser's gross monthly pre-tax income.

Although not part of the above calculation, payments of interest and real estate taxes were deductible by the buyer for income tax purposes.

HOME MORTGAGE INTEREST RATES

A major factor in affordability is the cost of funds to the purchaser. A favorable mortgage finance climate contributed greatly to Montgomery County's active residential real estate market in 1986. The fixed interest rate for conventional mortgages fell below nine percent by Christmas of 1986. Low mortgage rates began to creep up by the spring of 1987, due to a combination of factors. These factors included a weakening U.S. dollar overseas, balance of trade difficulties, soaring national debt, and increased need for federal borrowing. By September 1987, area home mortgage interest rates had risen to 11 percent and were expected to continue to climb. The Federal Reserve Bank's response to the stock market shock in October of 1987—to increase the money supply—led to a decrease in interest rates by November. By Christmas of 1987, conventional fixed rate mortgages had stabilized around 10.5 to 11.0 percent. Residential mortgage rates in August of 1988 hovered around 10.5 percent in the Washington, D.C. mortgage market. By September, there were as many predictions regarding the future of interest rates as there were experts.

THE MARKET

From 1970 to 1987, the suburban Maryland area of Washington experienced tremendous population growth. This growth was attributable to several factors, including the continued expansion of government facilities into Montgomery County, expanding job markets in the private sector, immigration of new residents attracted by new employment opportunities in Montgomery County, the exodus of former downtown city residents to the more spacious suburbs and the lower crime rate in the suburbs. In the 1970s, the County experienced an annual growth rate of 7,000 jobs. By contrast, annual job growth from

March, 1984 to March, 1985 was 25,000; job growth from March, 1985 to March, 1986 was 23,000. Thirty-nine percent of the job growth was in the service sector.

The trends are expected to continue upward, as seen in the table below:

Montgomery County Long Range Forecasts "Most Probable" Scenario
As of March 1987

	1980	1987	1990	2000
Population	579,000	669,000	710,000	785,000
Households	206,793	256,400	278,000	333,000
Employment	304,600	405,000	455,000	575,000

Source: Montgomery County Planning Board, Research Division.

According to the 1984 Census, the latest Census available to Dubin at the time of his decision, the population was segmented as outlined below:

Montgomery County, Maryland 1984 Census Update

1984	HIGH RISE	GARDEN APT.	TOWNHOUSE	SINGLE FAMILY DETACHED	ALL TYPES
No. Households (HH)	26,223	43,959	25,246	133,008	228,436
HH Population	41,640	86,945	68,071	407,344	604,000
Average HH Size	1.59	1.98	2.70	3.06	2.64
Age 0-4 yrs.	1,256	5,832	7,763	23,813	38,664
Age 5-17 yrs.	2,366	10,097	12,014	83,106	107,583
Average age HH Head	53	41	40	50	48
Average Yrs. in Same House	5.6	4.1	4.4	13.0	9.5
% with Grad. Degree	20.8	14.7	20.1	24.9	22.6
1983 Median HH Income	$24,705	$22,806	$37,772	$49,823	$39,154
Female Workforce Participation (%)	52.3	71.7	70.5	57.5	60.7
Work Location:					
Inside Belt	28.2	22.7	17.2	21.2	21.5
Outside Belt	20.6	40.4	50.4	38.6	39.1
to D.C.	37.9	22.6	18.2	25.2	24.8

Source: Montgomery County Planning Board, Research Division.

RESIDENTIAL ACTIVITY

Since the 1984 Census Update summarized above, the single family housing market continued to grow. Montgomery County experienced completion of 4,125 new single family units in 1985 and 5,175 new single family new housing units in 1986, the highest annual production since 1960. In 1988, the county was experiencing monthly sales of 1,200 units. Virtually all homes offered on the market sold in a reasonable period of time.

Homes also continued to increase in value. The average resale price for a market rate single family home in Montgomery County in 1988 was $214,500. The average price for newly built single family homes was $240,000. Single family housing prices had been rising at a rate of eight to ten percent each year. The Potomac section was the wealthiest section of the county with homes ranging from $400,000 to several million dollars.

Dubin used the following chart compiled by a local real estate research firm as another indicator that housing activity was healthy. No data was available which directly addressed the specific profile of his targeted purchasers.

Montgomery County Housing Market Profile
Sales of Market Rate Single Family Homes First Six Months 1988

| PRICE RANGE | NUMBER OF UNITS SOLD | NUMBER OF MO. ON MKT. | ORIGIN OF PURCHASER | | |
			MONT. CO.	DC	OTHER
$159-$199,000	1,440	2.6	50%	10%	40%
$200-$249,000	2,376	2.5	48%	11%	41%
$250-$299,000	1,944	3.1	52%	12%	36%
$300-$349,000	576	7.1	46%	12%	42%
$350-$449,000	474	8.2	53%	14%	33%
$450-$599,000	360	8.3	47%	11%	42%
$600-$999,000	23	9.0	55%	15%	30%
$1,000,000 plus	7	9.0	15%	30%	55%

INFRASTRUCTURE

The extension and completion of new road systems including the Capital Beltway, Interstate 66 on the Virginia side, Interstate 95, the continuing development of research and development firms along the Route 270 corridor and the construction of a subway system servicing metropolitan D.C. and its suburbs have contributed to the continuing growth of Maryland counties near D.C. Montgomery County's two major residential growth areas are the I-270 and US 29 corridors. Combined, the two growth corridors have, in years preceding 1987, accounted for nearly two-thirds of total housing completions in Montgomery County. Dubin felt that the location of Grosvenor Park near Route 270 was prime.

MONTGOMERY COUNTY DEPARTMENT OF PARKS AND PLANNING

As Dubin moved forward with his plans, he encountered some difficulties with the planning department (PD) regarding his Subdivision Plan. The PD controlled all zoning issues, including the variances which Dubin would require to develop single family homes on a parcel zoned for multifamily units. The PD was known to be a conservative body, dedicated to protecting the existing community and the environment. The Planning Commission of the PD consisted of six board members (three elected and three appointed), whose backgrounds ranged from architecture to law, business, and academics. The Commission had made several demands on Dubin:

1. The PD claimed that the location of the site next to the Beltway resulted in noise pollution which would impair the quality of life of future residents in the development. The PD insisted that noise barriers be erected at a cost of $600,000 to protect future residents.

2. The PD cited the Adequate Public Facilities Ordinance of Montgomery County to show that Grosvenor Townhouses would adversely affect the schools by bringing more children into the system. Dubin was convinced that the demographic profile of his targeted purchasers meant that they would add very few, if any, children to the school system. He felt that the purchasers would wait to have their children until they were more settled. How could he convince the PD that their concerns were unfounded? If he could not prove his case, he could be assessed $750,000 for the Montgomery County School Superfund or be refused a building permit.

3. The PD insisted that Grosvenor Park enlarge the storm water drainage system to accommodate the entire neighborhood. The PD feared that Grosvenor Park's upstream residential neighborhoods might not be handling their drainage well and that Grosvenor Park might find itself flooded by their drain water. The PD wanted Dubin to construct a sediment pond to collect any drainage, settle out the pollutants and, in effect, recycle the water portion of the drainage. Dubin would also be required to maintain the sediment pond ad infinitum. The cost to construct the system would be $1.2 million, and Dubin's soil engineers calculated that annual maintenance costs would approach $50,000. Dubin's soil engineers had also surveyed the upstream neighbors and were satisfied that the PD's fears were unfounded.

The most recent demand was traffic-related. Under a Road Adequacies Provision of the Montgomery County Growth Plan, the PD argued that Dubin should widen 3,500 feet of road providing access to the site, including installing new storm drains for the full two-thirds of a mile, at a cost of $1 million. Dubin's traffic consultants argued back that all that was needed to avoid traffic snarls was a 400 foot deceleration lane at a cost to the developer of $80,000. Dubin felt that this was a disagreement that he could probably win.

FINANCING

Dubin had based his finance negotiations on the numbers he had developed in **Exhibit 22-5** (the costs in Exhibit 22-5 do not reflect the final $1 million demand of the PD). Dubin and the S&L had agreed upon a joint venture for financing Grosvenor Park: a non-recourse loan with no origination fee at prime plus one based on New York bank rates, with the S&L also receiving one quarter of the profit after the repayment of the loan. The bank would lend up to $9 million.

If costs in any quarter exceeded $9 million, Dubin would have to make up the difference out of his own pocket.

As a marketing tool, Dubin negotiated to protect the ultimate purchaser from fluctuations in the mortgage market. Dubin locked in Bethesda S&L's promise to provide 30-year mortgages for qualified purchasers with the rate fixed at 10 percent for the first three years of the mortgage or 10.53% constant plus a fee of 1.5 points payable by the purchaser at closing. The maximum interest rate over the term would be adjusted up or down but not exceed 14 percent. Those purchasers who put less than 20% down would require mortgage insurance at a cost of 4% of the amount borrowed, payment of which would be spread out and payable monthly over the 30-year term of the loan. There would be an additional 1% fee at closing. This package would be available during the first year of the home sales.

THE DECISION

Dubin realized that he had better develop spread sheets for the project, extending the sell-out rate to four years to help figure out the consequences of a slower sales rate (see **Exhibit 22-6**). When should the affordable housing portion be built? Is his pricing appropriate for selling the units? Despite all the work and money that has gone into this project to date, if he cannot compromise with the PD, should he call off the whole project? In that regard, how should he approach the PD?

Exhibit 22-1   *Area Map*

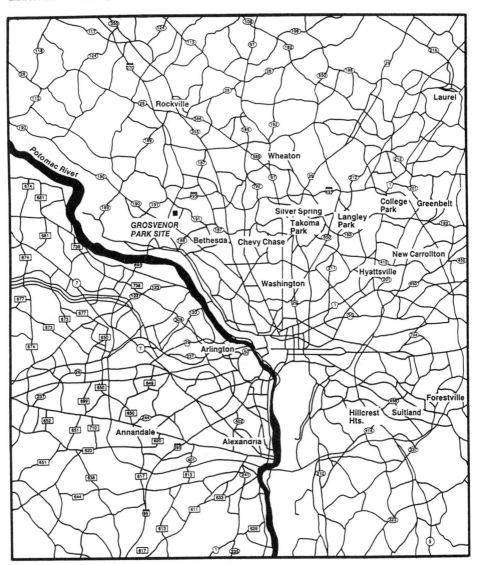

Exhibit 22-2   *Neighborhood Map*

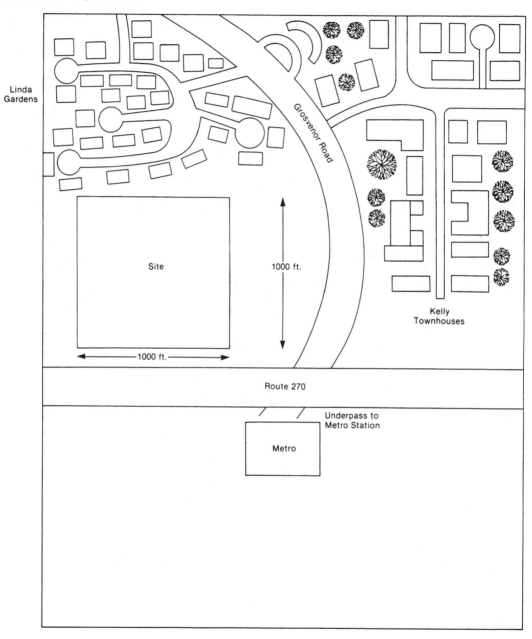

Exhibit 22-3   *Site Plan (as proposed initially.)*

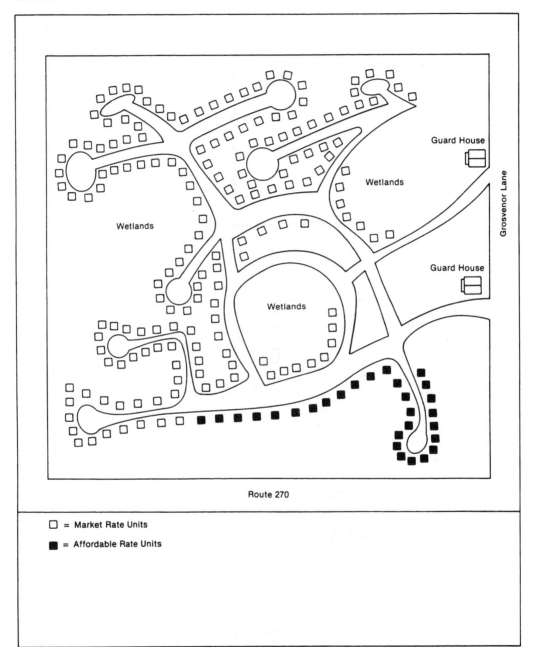

Guard House

Wetlands

Grosvenor Lane

Wetlands

Guard House

Wetlands

Route 270

☐ = Market Rate Units

■ = Affordable Rate Units

Exhibit 22-4 *Devonshire*

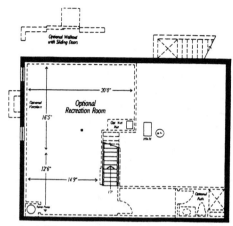

Lower Level Plan

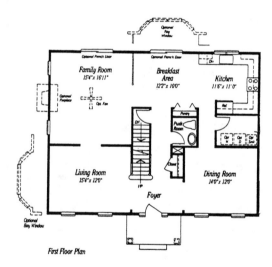

First Floor Plan

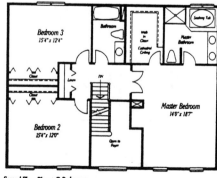

Second Floor Plan w/3 Bedrooms

Exhibit 22-4 (continued)

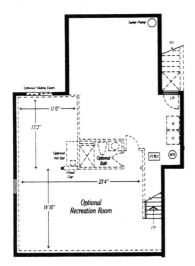

Lower Level Plan

First Floor Plan

Second Floor Plan

Exhibit 22-5 *Grosvenor Park*

	QUARTER 1	QUARTER 2	QUARTER 3	QUARTER 4	QUARTER 5
Quarterly construction starts	0	15	15	15	15
Cumulative starts	0	15	30	45	60
Quarterly sales	0	15	15	15	15
Cumulative sales	0	15	30	45	60
Quarterly settlements	0	0	10	15	15
Cumulative sales	0	0	10	25	40
NET RECEIPTS & REVENUES	0	0	2,500,000	3,750,000	3,750,000
PROJECT COSTS:					
Land acquisition	5,313,000	0	0	0	0
Land development/approvals	0	2,012,500	0	0	0
Direct construction	0	800,626	1,601,250	1,601,250	1,601,250
Onsite OH/indirect construction	0	75,000	75,000	75,000	75,000
Subtotal	5,313,000	2,888,126	1,676,250	1,676,250	1,676,250
Acquisition & Dev. loan interest	0	109,875	172,349	170,879	142,322
Construction loan interest	0	79,564	124,805	123,740	103,681
Subtotal	0	189,439	297,154	294,620	245,382
Marketing, media, and models	0	54,000	54,000	54,000	54,000
Commissions	0	0	50,000	75,000	75,000
Other closing costs	0	0	50,000	75,000	75,000
Subtotal	0	54,000	154,000	204,000	204,000
General Admin./offsite OH	300,000	60,000	60,000	60,000	60,000
Contingency	0	0	37,500	56,250	56,250
Subtotal	300,000	60,000	97,500	116,250	116,250
TOTAL PROJECT COSTS	5,613,000	3,191,565	2,224,904	2,291,120	2,241,882
NET CASH FROM OPERATIONS	(5,613,000)	(3,191,565)	275,096	1,458,880	1,508,118
Working capital reserves	0	0	(200,000)	0	0
Net loans received/(repaid)	5,613,000	3,191,565	(75,096)	(1,458,880)	(1,508,118)
NET DISTRIBUTABLE CASH	0	0	0	0	0
Developer's distribution	0	0	0	0	0
Lender's distribution	0	0	0	0	0
Cumulative loans outstanding	5,613,000	8,804,565	8,729,469	7,270,588	5,762,471

Note: In addition, 28 units of affordable housing had to be built. The fixed additional cost of each of these units was $150,000 resulting in a loss of $65,000 per unit or $1,720,000 in total. The impact of these units are not shown above.

Exhibit 22-5 (*continued*)

QUARTER 6	QUARTER 7	QUARTER 8	QUARTER 9	QUARTER 10	QUARTER 11	QUARTER 12	QUARTER 13	TOTAL
15	15	15	15	15	15	11	0	161
75	90	105	120	135	150	161	161	161
15	15	15	15	15	15	11	0	161
75	90	105	120	135	150	161	161	161
15	15	15	15	15	15	15	16	161
55	70	85	100	115	130	145	161	161
3,750,000	3,750,000	3,750,000	3,750,000	3,750,000	3,750,000	3,750,000	4,000,000	40,250,000
0	0	0	0	0	0	0	0	5,313,000
2,012,500	0	0	0	0	0	0	0	4,025,000
1,601,250	1,601,250	1,601,250	1,601,250	1,601,250	1,601,250	1,494,500	480,376	17,186,752
75,000	75,000	75,000	75,000	75,000	75,000	55,000	0	805,000
3,688,750	1,676,250	1,676,250	1,676,250	1,676,250	1,676,250	1,549,500	480,376	27,329,752
112,800	121,677	91,459	60,221	27,929	0	0	0	1,009,512
81,683	88,111	66,229	43,608	20,224	0	0	0	731,026
194,483	209,788	157,688	103,830	48,153	0	0	0	1,740,537
54,000	54,000	54,000	54,000	54,000	54,000	39,600	0	549,600
75,000	75,000	75,000	75,000	75,000	75,000	75,000	80,000	805,000
75,000	75,000	75,000	75,000	75,000	75,000	75,000	80,000	805,000
204,000	204,000	204,000	204,000	204,000	204,000	189,600	160,000	2,189,600
60,000	60,000	60,000	60,000	60,000	60,000	60,000	0	960,000
56,250	56,250	56,250	56,250	56,250	56,250	56,250	59,000	602,750
116,250	116,250	116,250	116,250	116,250	116,250	116,250	59,000	1,562,750
4,203,483	2,206,288	2,154,188	2,100,330	2,044,653	1,996,500	1,855,350	699,376	32,822,639
(453,483)	1,543,712	1,595,812	1,649,670	1,705,347	1,753,500	1,894,650	3,300,624	7,427,361
0	0	0	0	0	0	0	200,000	0
453,483	(1,543,712)	(1,595,812)	(1,649,670)	(1,426,760)	0	0	0	0
0	0	0	0	278,587	1,753,500	1,894,650	3,500,624	7,427,361
0	0	0	0	208,940	1,315,125	1,420,988	2,625,468	5,570,520
0	0	0	0	69,647	438,375	473,663	875,156	1,856,840
6,215,954	4,672,243	3,076,431	1,426,760	0	0	0	0	0

Exhibit 22-6   *Grosvenor Park*

	QUARTER 1	QUARTER 2	QUARTER 3	QUARTER 4	QUARTER 5	QUARTER 6	QUARTER 7
Quarterly construction starts	0	12	12	12	12	12	12
Cumulative starts	0	12	24	36	48	60	72
Quarterly sales	0	12	12	12	12	12	12
Cumulative sales	0	12	24	36	48	60	72
Quarterly settlements	0	0	8	12	12	12	12
Cumulative settlements	0	0	8	20	32	44	56
NET RECEIPTS & REVENUES	0	0	2,000,000	3,000,000	3,000,000	3,000,000	3,000,000
PROJECT COSTS:							
Land acquisition	5,313,000	0	0	0	0	0	0
Land development/approvals	0	2,012,500	0	0	0	2,012,500	0
Direct construction	0	640,500	1,281,000	1,281,000	1,281,000	1,281,000	1,281,000
Onsite OH/indirect constr.	0	75,000	75,000	75,000	75,000	75,000	75,000
Subtotal	5,313,000	2,728,000	1,356,000	1,356,000	1,356,000	3,368,500	1,356,000
Acq. & Dev. loan interest	0	109,874	169,215	170,766	149,908	128,345	145,449
Construction loan interest	0	79,564	122,535	123,658	108,554	92,939	105,325
Subtotal	0	189,438	291,750	294,424	258,461	221,284	250,874
Marketing, media, & models	0	54,000	54,000	54,000	54,000	54,000	54,000
Commissions	0	0	40,000	60,000	60,000	60,000	60,000
Other closing costs	0	0	40,000	60,000	60,000	60,000	60,000
Subtotal	0	54,000	134,000	174,000	174,000	174,000	174,000
General Admin./offsite OH	300,000	60,000	60,000	60,000	60,000	60,000	60,000
Contingency	0	0	37,500	50,000	50,000	50,000	50,000
Subtotal	300,000	60,000	97,500	110,000	110,000	110,000	110,000
TOTAL PROJECT COSTS	5,613,000	3,031,439	1,879,250	1,934,424	1,898,461	3,873,784	1,890,775
NET CASH FROM OPERATIONS	(5,613,000)	(3,031,439)	120,750	1,065,576	1,101,539	(873,784)	1,109,225
Working capital reserves	0	0	(200,000)	0	0	0	0
Net loans received/(repaid)	5,613,000	3,031,439	(79,250)	(1,065,576)	(1,101,539)	873,784	(1,109,225)
NET DISTRIBUTABLE CASH	0	0	0	0	0	0	0
Developer's distribution	0	0	0	0	0	0	0
Lender's distribution	0	0	0	0	0	0	0
Cumulative loans outstanding	5,613,000	8,644,439	8,723,113	7,658,113	6,556,574	7,430,359	6,321,133

Note: In addition, 28 units of affordable housing had to be built. The fixed additional cost of each of these units was $150,000 resulting in a loss of $65,000 per unit or $1,720,000 in total. The impact of these units are not shown above.

Exhibit 22-6 (*continued*)

QUARTER 8	QUARTER 9	QUARTER 10	QUARTER 11	QUARTER 12	QUARTER 13	QUARTER 14	QUARTER 15	QUARTER 16	TOTAL
12	12	12	12	12	12	12	5	0	161
84	96	108	120	132	144	156	161	161	161
12	12	12	12	12	12	12	5	0	161
84	96	108	120	132	144	156	161	161	161
12	12	12	12	12	12	12	12	9	161
68	80	92	104	116	128	140	152	161	161
3,000,000	3,000,000	3,000,000	3,000,000	3,000,000	3,000,000	3,000,000	3,000,000	2,250,000	40,250,000
0	0	0	0	0	0	0	0	0	5,313,000
0	0	0	0	0	0	0	0	0	4,025,000
1,281,000	1,281,000	1,281,000	1,281,000	1,281,000	1,281,000	1,281,000	679,320	494,932	17,186,752
75,000	75,000	75,000	75,000	75,000	75,000	75,000	55,000	55,000	1,085,000
1,356,000	1,356,000	1,356,000	1,356,000	1,356,000	1,356,000	1,356,000	734,320	549,932	27,609,752
123,736	101,290	78,087	54,100	29,304	3,671	0	0	0	1,263,746
89,602	73,348	56,546	39,176	21,220	2,658	0	0	0	915,127
213,338	174,638	134,633	93,276	50,524	6,339	0	0	0	2,178,873
54,000	54,000	54,000	54,000	54,000	54,000	54,000	39,600	0	741,600
60,000	60,000	60,000	60,000	60,000	60,000	60,000	60,000	45,000	805,000
60,000	60,000	60,000	60,000	60,000	60,000	60,000	60,000	45,000	805,000
174,000	174,000	174,000	174,000	174,000	174,000	174,000	174,000	90,000	2,351,600
60,000	60,000	60,000	60,000	60,000	60,000	60,000	60,000	6,000	1,146,000
50,000	50,000	50,000	50,000	50,000	50,000	50,000	50,000	3,750	641,250
110,000	110,000	110,000	110,000	110,000	110,000	110,000	110,000	9,750	1,787,250
1,853,338	1,814,638	1,774,632	1,733,276	1,690,524	1,646,330	1,640,000	1,003,920	649,682	33,927,475
1,146,662	1,185,362	1,225,368	1,266,724	1,309,476	1,353,670	1,360,000	1,996,080	1,600,318	6,322,525
0	0	0	0	0	0	0	0	200,000	0
(1,146,662)	(1,185,362)	(1,225,368)	(1,266,724)	(1,309,476)	(187,543)	0	0	0	0
0	0	0	0	0	1,166,127	1,360,000	1,996,080	1,800,318	6,322,525
0	0	0	0	0	874,595	1,020,000	1,497,060	1,350,239	4,741,894
0	0	0	0	0	291,532	340,000	499,020	450,080	1,580,631
5,174,472	3,989,110	2,763,742	1,497,0190	187,543	0	0	0	0	0

23

FINANCIAL ANALYSIS OF REAL PROPERTY INVESTMENTS

This note examines some of the methods by which real property investments are analyzed, including those most commonly used and others that will serve for purposes of comparison or illustration. It also offers suggestions about analytical techniques and provides sources of useful information.

The reader should be aware throughout that a successful analysis of a real property investment must consider many critical characteristics that are not easily reflected in the mathematics of a financial analysis. Among these are (a) the extremely long time horizon involved, (b) the lack of liquidity, and (c) the effects an ever-changing environment might have. In short, the investor must temper financial analysis with an understanding of the risks involved before proceeding.

The task of analyzing a real estate investment may be divided into three components:

1. ***Cash flow***   The amount of cash annually received by the investor, including revenues generated and financing proceeds realized, minus all cash expenses incurred, with the exception of income taxes;
2. ***Tax effect***   The amount by which the investment affects the taxes payable in the current year by the investor;
3. ***Future benefits***   The amount by which the capital position of the investor is affected by the sale or refinancing of the property or entity owning the property on an after-tax basis.

Professor William J. Poorvu prepared this note as the basis for class discussion. It was updated in 1992.

This note examines each of these elements of return and their use in establishing an overall rate of return and valuation of the property as well as the effects the passage of time may have on all of the above.

THE SETUP

The term *setup* is real estate jargon for the combination of income statement and cash flow statement. The purpose is to get a better measure of value than either of these statements alone could provide. For the purchaser of real property, the setup provides the basis for a measure of the value of the acquisition. By adjusting the setup, a purchaser can trace the effect on market value of any changes that might be made. Preparing a setup is also useful to the owner of property not currently producing income. It provides a measure of opportunity cost by showing the amount of carrying costs over time and the amount of money at risk in holding the property.

Preparing a setup for a specific piece of real property is a two-step process. The first step focuses on the pretax cash flow. The second measures the effect of taxes. By following the procedure outlined in **Table 23-1**, the pretax cash flow may be determined.

A setup can be prepared using either actual or estimated expense figures. It is critical that a prospective buyer know what kind of information is being shown by the seller because: (1) historical and estimated cash flow may have a

Table 23-1   Determining Pretax Cash Flow

Gross revenues:	Base rentals
	Rent escalators
	Expense reimbursements
	Other income
− Vacancies, collections	
= Net revenues	
− Operating expenses:	Real estate taxes
	Administrative
	Insurance
	Utilities
	Maintenance, supplies, and trash removal
	Repairs
	Replacement reserve
	Other expenses
= Cash flow from operations (also known as free-and-clear cash flow or operating cash flow)	
− Financial payments:	Mortgage interest
	Mortgage amortization
	Land-lease payments
= Cash flow after financing or cash flow before taxes	

direct bearing on one's financial analysis, and (2) lenders use operating cash flow to determine the value of property offered as security for a loan. Lenders examine every expense item very critically.

The portion of the gross rental that goes to each of the expense items varies significantly according to type of property, age of property, its location, and whatever agreements might exist between the lessor and lessee concerning the apportionment of expenses. These factors are subject to careful research besides simple estimation. The allowances for replacement and repair deserve careful consideration; these are especially critical in older properties that may be subject to deterioration or stylistic obsolescence.

ELEMENTS OF THE SETUP

This section looks at each of the elements of the setup, and it discusses the changes in emphasis within the elements themselves caused by dealing with different kinds of property (i.e., apartments, office buildings, industrial space, retail space, and, in some categories, raw land and mobile home parks).[1]

Gross Revenues

The analysis of an income property should start with *base rentals*. As a first step in the analysis of rentals, the investor should attempt to determine *comparables*. Comparables are rents or revenues generated by properties with similar features (e.g., size, quality of construction) and in similar locations. The gathering of baseline data on comparables is generally the first step in the collection of local knowledge required before investing. For apartments, mobile home parks, and some smaller commercial rentals, the daily or Sunday newspaper offers a first source of comparable data. The rental prices generally are quoted in a $-per-month rate and are apt to be at or above market. The primary function of such advertising is to generate demand; some discount may, however, be expected. Once a specific area is selected, the investor should check more localized sources to make certain of the range and distribution of the potential competition for the contemplated investment. The investor should consult the local realtor's listing book and regional weekly newspapers and should make a tour of the area, noting vacancies and other existing buildings.

Rental rates for office, commercial, and industrial space are generally quoted in dollars per square foot. Because of the complexity of these spaces, comparability is more difficult to determine. The primary survey sources are specialized journals such as the *New England Real Estate Review*. In addition, most

---

[1]Fundamental data about the elements can be found in the Building Owners and Managers Association's *Experience Exchange Report*, the Institute of Real Estate Management Experience Committee's *Statistical Compilation and Analysis of Actual Income and Expenses Experienced in Apartment Building Operation*, and *The Dollars and Cents of Shopping Centers*, compiled by the Urban Land Institute.

of the major real estate brokers print listings of available office, industrial, and retail space. Industrial space may also be listed with the state government bureau responsible for commercial development. It is important to remember that the rents and terms noted in these listings are often only suggestive ones. Almost all of the terms will be negotiable, depending upon the market strength, the financial strength of the prospective tenant, the willingness of the tenant to make improvements, and so on.

Two fundamental skills are required to develop significant comparables: (1) the ability to ferret out the greatest amount of useful data, and (2) the ability to put these data together into a meaningful picture of the whole. In dealing with all kinds of properties, the investor must understand the characteristics that make properties comparable: internal features such as layout, ease of maintenance, adequacy of utilities, decor, amenities, and so on—all critical items of comparability. Exterior considerations are also important. Properties that have very similar inside features but that have different locations, access to transportation, views, and so on, can command very different rentals. This can be determined by actually shopping the market.

The prospective investor or developer must determine what the competition is and how effectively a particular property can compete. Once this task is accomplished, a realistic standard can be set for the income to be obtained from the property.

After baseline data are developed for gross revenue potential, the next step is to project the observable trends, such as government policy and inflation. Is rent control a reality or a possibility? Are there public incentives for particular rental groups, locations, or types of property? The impact of trends varies widely according to the type of property involved. In residential and smaller commercial properties, trends are very important. Generally the leases, if any, are of short duration. This provides an opportunity to adjust rents if price levels are rising or, conversely, to decrease rents if the neighborhood is declining.

For commercial and industrial properties under long-term leases, the impact of trend analysis is less important over the short term. The gross revenue figures will be those provided in the lease during the term of the lease. The investor should, however, carefully consider the impact of the observable trends on the willingness of present tenants to renew or, with commercial properties, the impact of the changes in the local market on average rents.

Beyond trend analysis, some of the key profit opportunities occur through the projection of discontinuities in the observable trends. Similarly, major losses may arise through failure to observe unfavorable discontinuities before they occur and to adjust the investment strategy accordingly. Some discontinuities that are of greatest importance are urban renewal activities, new-highway location, entry of national firms into the market, entry or exit of a major industry, and the changing socioeconomic characteristics of a neighborhood.

The critical element in projecting discontinuities is timing. When predicting a favorable change, decisions taken too early tend to be risky. Decisions taken too late, although involving the investor in little risk, usually result in missed opportunities for profit. In predicting unfavorable changes, it is often better to be too early. The opportunities to bail out of a property get worse as the likelihood of the unfavorable event increases. "Holding out for the best price" may be simply an exercise in following the market down.

Analysis of trends and potential discontinuities is possible insofar as the general economic and political data are adequate. Such data are available through local newspapers and also through national journals such as *National Real Estate Investor* and *Real Estate Appraiser and Analyst*. These two publications provide facts useful in making specific projections relative to the properties that an investor holds or contemplates buying.

For commercial properties, the base rental in the lease is only part of the story. There may be built-in *rent escalators*. These may be fixed (such as defined step-ups in rent) or conditional (such as increases tied to changes in the cost of living). In retail leases, percentage-rent clauses tie the rent level to tenants' sales performance. The longer the lease term, the more likely there will be adjustments.

Expense reimbursements have also become common, especially in leases for nonresidential property (for such items as real estate taxes, heat, electricity, water, insurance, and cleaning). Here the tenant will agree to reimburse the landlord either for all such expenses or for changes from a predefined base. In a multitenant building, each tenant's share is often expressed as a percentage based on total space occupied. In acquiring a property it is crucial to analyze the terms of each individual lease and to have a reporting system that takes such complexities into account.

Other income is an item that should be examined carefully in contemplating any form of real property investment. Sources such as laundry rental, furniture rental, parking charges, utility fees, and recreational club dues are often very important profit contributors in housing investments. The investor is cautioned to examine carefully the assumptions underlying such income projections. Similarly, agreements and leases should be examined, and the investor should be aware of local practice regarding the inclusion of certain items when making a forecast. For example, if amenities such as air conditioning are not included in the base rent where such inclusion is common practice in the locality, occupancy statistics may suffer. Other income may, in fact, be an opportunity as well for the investor; charging separately for rental of major appliances or parking can yield a very high return on the marginal investment.

Commercial and industrial buildings offer some opportunities for other income also. Among the possibilities are special janitorial service, parking, and so on. Again, the two factors to consider are the leases or agreements underlying such charges and the local practice. In commercial, industrial, and residential properties, the "other income" category, once established, should be reasonably stable—subject primarily to the vacancy factor. It is important, however, to be aware of the profit opportunities and, in initial analysis, to be certain that those opportunities that are projected really exist. On the positive side, it is often wise to look for some of the unrealized potential that may come from the other income category when contemplating a future purchase or development.

Vacancies

The second element of the setup to be analyzed is the subject of vacancies. The prospective purchaser is often presented with a setup that makes no allowance for vacancies or collection problems. This is especially common with commercial properties. Nevertheless, some reasonable vacancy allowance is almost always necessary for all properties; the art lies in determining what is reasonable. The reader is reminded, however, that even for a property with a 10-year lease, a 3% vacancy allowance implies only a four-month period between tenants at the end of the lease term. With a special-purpose building or an office building, even this may not be adequate. Failure to incorporate such an allowance into the overall scheme may materially distort the potential future return. Commercial properties require other considerations, such as what should be included in the revenue base as well as what is the appropriate percentage allowance to take. Rent escalators, expense reimbursements for charges that will continue even if the space is vacant, and other income should not be forgotten.

Bad debts and concessions are sometimes included in the vacancy allowance. The investor or developer is also cautioned to be wary of the difference between "allowance" and vacancies. In many setups shown to the prospective purchaser, vacancies are shown as an allowance. Such allowance may or may not be related to the actual experience of the building under consideration. The investor should be certain about what is being shown as a basis for further investigation.

Comparable data for vacancies are often difficult to assess. Gross area vacancy statistics are readily available for the Standard Metropolitan Statistical Areas (SMSAs). HUD compiles statistics which are often reported in the *Real Estate Analyst*. Rental boards may also be helpful. In analyzing vacancies on apartment houses, the Census Bureau provides decennial counts. These are not particularly useful, however, in making an investment decision. For housing units, it is often necessary for the prospective builder or developer to cruise the neighborhood looking for empty nameplates on mailboxes and counting "For Sale" signs. Such counts are not statistically reliable, but they may simulate the purchasing behavior of the target consumer.

Commercial, office, and industrial vacancies are harder to pin down. The specialized regional journals cited previously and the *National Real Estate Investor* provide frequent reviews that give a view of the changing market scene. The *Real Estate Analyst* provides historical data for most markets, updated at least annually. Major local realty firms often conduct useful market studies and issue quarterly vacancy reports.

The developer or investor contemplating a project must always be aware of the trends in vacancy rates and the prospective entries into the market, which might adversely affect the developments being studied. Although such trends are never totally reliable, some basis for judgment can be gained from building-permit data, from trade and local business publications, and from direct systematic observation of the local surrounding neighborhood. In examining the possible trends in vacancies, attention should be paid to consumer tastes in habitation and the expansion or contraction of consumer spending patterns. National economic trends such as growth in service industries or cutbacks in defense spending are also important. These are the fundamental data of interest in particular regions and product types.

The prospective purchaser of an existing property should always examine leases and even interview tenants whenever possible to determine that the projected income is, in fact, in line with that required by the lease. The prospective purchaser should also be wary of concessions given to the tenants that might inflate the occupancy statistics on rental payments in the latter part of the lease. Purchasers should also be concerned with leases in which property management provides for special services to the tenant for a higher rent. The type, size, and location of the property often indicate the likelihood of such side deals. For the new development, the prospective developer or investor should be concerned with the normal leasing terms in the area under consideration and with current practices regarding concessions and management absorption of costs.

Operating Expenses

The control of operating expenses is obviously one of the key elements in any real estate investment's profitability. This is also an area in which the buyer is subject to the highest degree of deception and an area in which good information on a current situation is difficult to find and for which reliable projections of the future are almost impossible. The best sources of data on operating expenses for all kinds of properties are the "experience exchange" type of publications such as those mentioned earlier. Using data obtained from these sources, the prospective developer or investor can begin to question intelligently the projections being made and search out sources of difference. Remember that averages for an area do not imply that most properties are at the average.

One of the key mistakes made in analysis of operating expenses is that of leaving out a category of expense. This section will review each category of expense and give indications of some of the factors to be considered. Consideration should be given to the underlying variables to which the expenses are related. Expenses vary in relation to (1) the gross rent, (2) the square feet or cubic feet involved, (3) the number of units, (4) the services provided, and (5) the age, condition, and cost of the property. In preparing forecasts for future profitability it is critical to understand the different natures of the expenses.

The primary categories of expenses to be considered are the following.

    real estate taxes
    administrative
    maintenance, supplies, and trash removal
    repairs
    replacement
    utilities
    insurance

Within each of the above categories there are obviously subcategories. For further information one can consult sources such as the *Building Operators and Management Association* or *National Association of Apartment House Owners* publications, which set up accounting systems for property owners.

Real Estate Taxes Real estate taxes are perhaps the single greatest source of uncertainty in property investment. History shows that they are almost always increased. There is further danger of a major increase if property is sold because of a new market price against which the assessor can make a valuation. In many income properties an agreement with city officials can be reached in which taxes are assessed as a percentage of gross rent. These arrangements are not always legally enforceable.

Before any investment is made, the investor should examine the tax records for the property in question and make an analysis of comparable properties. Tax records are public documents. Histories of the assessments for the town or city in question are available. Changes that may occur in the future can have major impact on tax rates and should offer warning signs. Among these are (1) large population expansion, (2) new-school needs, (3) major public facilities projects, and (4) expansion of municipal services. On the positive side, one can look to a healthy mixture in the industrial base, a community with limited additional population, and the growing voter resistance to tax increases.

Always the prospective purchaser or developer should consider the strength of the tax escalation clause in the leases being used and the willingness of any rent control agency to allow such clauses to be effective. Real estate taxes are a major variable in the profitability of any real property investment. All three forms of analysis—baseline, trends, and discontinuity potential—must be employed.

Administrative Expenses Rental, advertising, and management expenses are often inter-connected. A residential property owner may choose to sign a rental brokerage agreement and a management agreement with a local firm that specializes in handling the particular kind of property and that will manage the property for a percentage of the gross rental. Although the fee is standard for the region or local market, it is often negotiable. If the property is sufficiently large, most investors would do well to consider having both management and rentals taken care of by direct employees of the property. The two primary trade-offs are cost and degree of owner involvement. Unfortunately, common practice in the sale of many properties excludes from the setup both management expense and rental expense. Such an omission materially distorts the return since, for small properties, these may be significant when related to the gross rentals. Even if the intention is for the owner to perform the services, some cost or value should be imputed to the investment of time. If sold, the potential buyer will make an allowance that will reduce the amount offered. Lenders will always input an allowance in considering the building's value.

For commercial and industrial properties, the same caveats apply. It is, however, more critical to examine exactly how the rental function is to be performed, by whom, and at what price. The more specialized the building, the more critical a good marketing-rental program is to the economic success of the development or investment. Where overage rents or percentage leases are involved, there is a further need for management.

Professional fees cannot be ignored. Legal help may be needed in many circumstances ranging from lease or financing negotiations to partnership matters to regulatory issues. The project entity will have to file a tax return normally prepared by an outside auditor. Since real estate ownership has special tax implications, good advice is important. There are other consultants who may be called upon for design or engineering or sometimes even public relations help. The more complicated the entity and project, the higher the allowance should be. As our society has become more litigious and income tax laws have become increasingly complex, the need for outside help continues to grow.

Maintenance, Supplies, and Trash Removal This category often involves uncertainty. Several factors are, however, clear and fundamental. The age of a building is one of the prime determinants of the maintenance required. Even if a building's history is known, simple projection of that history into the future will understate maintenance substantially. The design of a building (including the materials used, the number and sizes of public spaces, and the quality of the original equipment installed) is another critical factor. Whether windows are accessible or must be reached from scaffolding makes a difference. The type of heating and air conditioning equipment and flooring are key determinants. Finally, the previous maintenance history is important since undermaintained assets may require exceptional future outlays.

Contracts for maintenance of major building elements, such as boilers, elevators, air conditioning units, or cleaning, are often obtainable and provide for a program of systematic upkeep. Prices on such contracts often indicate the level of service required, although they are generally high-profit items for companies offering them.

Supplies needed are related to the services provided, such as office, rest room, or common area cleaning. The replacement of light bulbs can be a significant item. With increased environmental awareness resulting in the closing of many disposal sites, trash removal prices have risen considerably in recent years.

Repairs Repairs differ from maintenance predominantly in scope. In this category are such items as painting of apartments; replacement of broken doors and windows; repair of stoves, refrigerators, dishwashers, and disposals; and fixing leaky faucets. Obviously, the age of the equipment in question is going to be a major factor in the amount of money that will be necessary to allocate to this area. It should be possible to obtain comparables as outlined earlier, but considerable annual variations are likely. One should take into consideration the expected level of maintenance by the particular tenants occupying the space.

These items may seem minor to the investor, but are of major importance to the tenants. The ability of responsible management people to learn of and respond to these problems may be a major factor influencing the vacancy rate. For this reason alone (if not also for the old saw "a stitch in time . . .") this area should be carefully researched.

Replacement Reserves   Replacement reserves are part of the setup closely related to the maintenance element. Not all depreciation is simply a tax-oriented fiction. In any property, there are items that are subject to physical deterioration and, therefore, require periodic replacement. Carpets, roofs, paint, and mechanical equipment will not last the economic life of the building. It is critical, therefore, in calculating the cash flow to be derived from an investment, to consider the impact of such required replacement. This is especially true in the purchase of used residential property. Often such property has been purchased on the assumption of operation for five to seven years with sale contemplated as soon as the rental income has been increased. With such an investment strategy, items of major maintenance or replacement are often deferred. Unless such investment is made quickly, the new owner may be faced with either more major repair expense or declining relative attractiveness of the property. Unfortunately, too often, the newer the equipment, the shorter its life cycle.

Replacement reserves are not generally tax deductible. Some items, such as mechanical items or painting, may appear as expenses, but the investor should recognize that these expenses may have to be capitalized and then depreciated, as mandated by the tax code.

Commercial and industrial properties are often not as much affected by such considerations because many commercial leases are written so as to place primary responsibility for replacement of many items on the tenant. The expenditures at the time of lease turnover may be substantial. Normal levels of these reserves are found in the experience exchange reviews discussed previously. The investor/developer can usually also benefit from consulting a person well-versed in property management who is not a broker.

Types of commercial leases vary widely. Leases should be examined for rates, terms, and special options, such as rent concessions during initial months, added buildout allowances, or reduced schedules of pass-through expenses. A major capital expense item for commercial and industrial leases is the expenditure or allowance made when leases roll over or new tenants occupy space. It is rare that a new tenant will want the exact layout of the prior one. Whether the individual tenant or the landlord pays for leasehold improvements will affect the rent charged. Again, because there is no way to predict future needs or market conditions, an allowance is generally taken, based on average length of tenant leases, expected rate of tenant turnover, and the amount of work to be done. Such costs point up the desirability of retaining existing tenants when leases expire.

Definitions of lease terms should be clarified. For example, leases written based on a "gross rentable" basis usually consider the entire gross square footage of a building and prorate it to each tenant. "Net usable" leases measure the actual space allocated to a tenant with no allowance for a proportional share of the waste factor. "Net rentable" includes some but not all of the waste factor. Another variation is commonly referred to as "triple net," in which operating costs and taxes are excluded from the base terms of the lease and are separately charged to the tenant in successive years.

Utilities and Insurance   Both of these items are generally verifiable when purchasing existing properties and are easily estimated by competent professionals for future developments. The key warning for these items is the assurance of the adequacy and consideration of probable future price increases. Considerable expense may be incurred if present utility service is inadequate. Major risk is assumed if insurance coverage is inadequate. A high purchase price may trigger the need for additional insurance. Both should be reviewed before purchase or additional construction. Moreover, operating cost escalators in the leases should be carefully studied.

Other Expenses   Items such as fire protection, security expenses, and "other expenses" items must be specifically related to the property under consideration. All elements of this category are somewhat extraordinary. The requirements in these areas are becoming stiffer; consequently, they are not subject to the same rules of thumb and should be treated as individual elements for analysis when seeking good baseline and trend data. They must be examined carefully for future discontinuities.

Tax Effects   Once the setup and the before-tax cash flow have been established, the second step is to propose a set of measures to find the effect of income taxes. Of prime importance to the real estate investor is the cash flow after taxes (CFAT). This is in contrast to net income, which is the benchmark for stock market investors. CFAT is determined by first calculating the net taxable income and then multiplying by the appropriate tax rate; the tax is then subtracted from the cash flow after financing. Two approaches to arrive at this result are shown in **Table 23-2**.

Mortgage interest   The buyer is cautioned to examine tax effects over time as well as during the initial period. In general, the net taxable income from a real property investment will increase over time even if the operating cash flow

---

[2]Level payment or direct reduction mortgage:

$$pmt = \frac{pv}{\dfrac{1 - (1 + i)^{-n}}{i}}$$

Where: i = mortgage interest rate for period considered
  pv = starting principal balance
  pmt = annual financing payment

Table 23-2 Determining Cash Flow after Taxes: Two Approaches

I. Cash flow from operations	or	II. Cash flow after financing
+ Replacement reserve		+ Replacement reserve
− Mortgage interest		+ Mortgage amortization
− Depreciation		− Depreciation
= Net taxable income		= Net taxable income
× Tax rate		× Tax rate
= Tax		= Tax
Cash flow from operations		Net income before taxes
− Mortgage interest		− Tax
− Mortgage amortization		= Net income
= Cash flow after financing		+ Depreciation
− Tax		− Replacement reserve
= Cash flow after taxes		− Mortgage amortization
		= Cash flow after taxes

remains stable. This is because many real property loans require a constant annual or monthly payment, but the components of that payment change.

Commonly known as a level payment or direct reduction mortgage,[2] the starting principal of the loan (pv) is the present value of an "ordinary annuity," or series of level loan payments. The borrower (or mortgagor) gives to the lender (or mortgagee) a prior claim upon the value of the property as security for the borrowed funds. Equal periodic installments "amortize" the loan, providing the lender with a desired return (i) on outstanding invested funds (pv). Each payment consists of interest on the outstanding principal and amortization or return of principal. As principal is repaid, therefore, the interest component will decline. The remaining principal on a mortgage at any time is simply the present value of remaining payments, discounted at the face interest rate of the note. The level or constant payment varies, depending upon whether payments are made monthly, quarterly, or annually. Most mortgages are written with monthly payments. Tables are easily available giving the constant payment percentages and the breakdown of payments between interest and principal.

Note that in the first year of a 25-year loan at a 9% interest rate, approximately 89% of the financial payment is a deductible interest charge. In the fifteenth year of the same loan only 60% is deductible. Since the financial payment may represent 50% of the gross rental income, this would indicate a change in taxability of 10% of gross rental income, a significant impact that may be 30% to 50% of the cash flow after financing. **Figure 23-1** demonstrates this graphically.

Depreciation The change in tax position shown in **Figure 23-1** is compounded through the use of depreciation. Under the 1986 tax laws, residential property is depreciated over 27.5 years, and commercial property over 31.5 years. This depreciation is treated as a noncash deduction from the depreciable base and is computed as a constant annual amount over the depreciable life (i.e., $100,000/27.5 years = $3,636 annual depreciation). When the depreciation

Figure 23-1 *Deductible Interest Expense as a Function of Time; Constant Annual Payment*

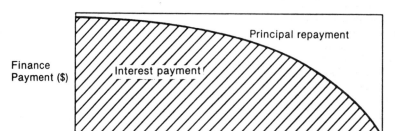

deduction exceeds amortization, tax shelter dollars are created. During the early 1980s, most real estate property had been depreciated over a 15- to 20-year life for tax purposes. Because some bank mortgages lasted for a longer period (usually 25 to 30 years), the tax shelters in the initial years of property ownership have been substantial. With the new tax laws this was no longer the case. (For a more complete discussion of depreciation, see the "Note on Taxation," HBS No. 379-192.)

Net Taxable Income Calculation of the tax effect for a real estate investment involves simply a multiplication of the stream of taxable income by the appropriate tax rates of the investor concerned. Starting in 1991, the maximum marginal tax rate is assumed to be 31% for ordinary income. On this basis, every dollar of losses will reduce taxes paid by 31%. The capital gains tax rate remains at 28%, as set in 1987. This tax savings can then be added back to increase the total return, assuming that the investor has "passive" income to match against the "passive" loss.

Other considerations should include (1) the impact of state and local income taxes, (2) the investor's situation for continued high income and the continuing capacity to use such losses, and (3) the possibility of changes in the tax laws, which might adversely affect the tax benefits. Historically, however, the pattern has been to allow "grandfather clauses" on existing depreciation schedules, even though the tax rates themselves may change.

The investor should always identify the source of the tax benefits. In general there are three kinds of benefits: tax postponement, tax bracket switching, and tax avoidance. A typical real property transaction includes elements of all three. The use of depreciation tends to postpone the payment of taxes even though the total amount payable remains the same. Tax-free exchanges of real property have the same effect. In addition, many types of real estate transactions are attempts to switch tax brackets, although the elimination of the differential for capital gains may reduce that practice. Such transactions include (1) the expensing of heavy maintenance charges to upgrade a property in hopes of a subsequently higher sales price and (2) the sale of limited partnership shares to high-bracket individuals. Tax avoidance is difficult to achieve. Refinancing a property yields tax-free cash: taxes have been previously paid on the portion of the annual payments used to amortize a loan.

Cash Flow After Taxes   The calculation of CFAT is completed by deducting the taxes paid or adding the tax benefit received to the before-tax cash flow. This is equivalent to applying the tax effect to the operating cash flow reduced by financial payments. For many investors, CFAT is the appropriate *annual* cash flow for the evaluation of an equity investment. For analysis purposes, remember that CFAT is composed of two of the three components of a potential return on a real estate investment: cash flow before taxes and the tax effect. The third component, futures, must be estimated to calculate an overall return. This procedure is discussed later in this note.

IMPACT OF FINANCIAL STRUCTURING

With an understanding of the elements that make up a cash flow and the effects of these elements on taxes, the investor is able to begin an analysis of real property investments.

Leverage Concept

A fundamental characteristic of financial leverage (and often not recognized) is that there are two kinds: positive and negative. Positive leverage increases the return on the equity invested; negative leverage decreases the return on such investment. Positive leverage occurs when the cost of debt expressed as a percentage is lower than the percent return on total assets. For negative leverage the reverse is true. The cost of debt expressed as a percentage is the total of interest and principal payments as a percentage of the starting principal balance. Negative leverage is not necessarily bad since it may reflect a more rapid write-off of a mortgage. The percent return on total assets is the operating or free-and-clear cash flow as a percentage of the total cost of the asset. It is a good first-step calculation in determining the most appropriate financial structure for a property.

The size of the mortgage, the time period over which it will be paid off, and the interest rate all affect the cost of debt and subsequently the return on equity. These items, to the extent allowed by the marketplace, can be controlled by the investors and adjusted to their needs. **Tables 23-3, 23-4, 23-5,** and **23-6** indicate the effects of each on the cost of debt and how leverage affects returns.

Table 23-3 illustrates the return on the cost of the asset in the absence of debt.

In **Table 23-4**, the effect of leverage is readily apparent in the return on equity investment column. A 12.5% increase (from 80% to 90%) in the amount of the mortgage brings about a 38.9% change in return. Another way of analyzing the leverage is to note that because there is a spread between the cost of debt

Table 23-3   Relationship of Free-and-Clear Cash Flow to Cost of Asset

Total cost of asset:	$1,250,000	
Setup:	Gross revenues	$270,000
	Vacancies	27,000
	Net revenues	**$243,000**
	Operating expenses	118,000
	Free-and-clear cash flow	**$125,000**
	Return on cost of asset	10%

and the 10% return on total assets, the investor's return is greater than 10%. In a 70% mortgage, the cash return on equity can be broken down in the following way:

10% of the $375,000 investment	$37,500
1.13% (10%-8.87%) of $875,000 mortgage	9,887
Net cash flow to equity investors	**$47,387**

Table 23-4 demonstrates the benefits of arranging a mortgage that is a large percentage of the total asset cost when the financial leverage is positive.

In **Table 23-5** we see once again that the leverage of using other people's money at varying costs is reflected in the return on equity investment. Obviously, there are benefits in having a long-term mortgage. In this case, the 15-year mortgage illustrates negative leverage. The same analysis as used in **Table 23-4** indicates what happened:

10% of the $250,000 investment	$25,000
− 1.13% (10%-11.13%) of $1,000,000 mortgage	11,300
Net cash flow to equity investors	**$13,700**

The investors are not losing money, but compared with the 10% return on assets, they are building up their equity position at the rate of $11,300 per

Table 23-4   Effect of Mortgage Size on Pretax Return
(Variable: Mortgage size; 25 years, 7.5% interest, monthly payments)

MORTGAGE AS % OF TOTAL ASSET COST OF $1,250,000	EQUITY	DEBT SERVICE	BEFORE-TAX CASH FLOW	COST OF DEBT	PRETAX RETURN ON EQUITY INVESTMENT
90%	$125,000	$99,787	$25,213	8.87%	20.17%
80	250,000	88,700	36,300	8.87	14.52
70	375,000	77,613	47,387	8.87	12.64
60	500,000	66,525	58,475	8.87	11.70

Table 23-5 Effect of Payoff Time Period on Cost of Debt
(Variable: Time period; $250,000 in equity: $1,000,000 mortgage; 7.5% interest, monthly payments)

AMORTIZATION PERIOD	DEBT SERVICE	BEFORE-TAX CASH FLOW	COST OF DEBT	PRETAX RETURN ON EQUITY INVESTMENT
40 years	$ 79,000	$46,000	7.90%	18.40%
30 years	84,000	41,000	8.40	16.40
25 years	88,700	36,300	8.87	14.52
20 years	96,700	28,300	9.67	11.32
15 years	$111,300	$13,700	11.13	5.48

year. Because equity buildup cannot be realized until sale or refinancing of the building, it is not included in the calculation of cash return from operations or taxes.

Table 23-6 shows that, as anticipated, lower interest rates lead to higher return on equity investments. In this situation the interest rate of 9.5% creates negative leverage. The investor may be willing to incur the lower return cost to be able to own the asset. Market or other conditions may force this position on an investor, making it a better situation than a total loss, or on the upside if one can anticipate a rise in the operating income, the initial cash return may be less relevant.

Financial leverage offers obvious benefits to the investor who is seeking to maximize return on investment. As a result, the heavy use of leverage is normal in real estate. For the investor, leverage allows control of a greater asset base than would be possible simply through the use of equity. Through the use of nonrecourse clauses in the debt instruments used to purchase the assets, the risk to the equity holder can be restricted to the equity interest held in the particular asset with the creditor having no claim to other assets that the investor may have. A deed of trust can be structured with the same effect. Since the repayment of the debt is a fixed sum, the rate of return on the equity is increased disproportion-

Table 23-6 Effect of Interest Rate on Cost of Debt
(Variable: Interest rate; $250,000 in equity: $1,000,000 mortgage; 25 years, monthly payments)

INTEREST RATE	DEBT SERVICE	BEFORE-TAX CASH FLOW	COST OF DEBT	PRETAX RETURN ON EQUITY INVESTMENT
9.5%	$104,900	$20,100	10.49%	8.04%
8.5	96,700	28,300	9.67	11.32
7.5	88,700	36,300	8.87	14.52
6.5	81,100	43,900	8.11	17.56
5.5	73,700	51,300	7.37	20.52

ately in the event of appreciation and similarly decreased or eliminated if price of the asset should fall (see **Figure 23-2**).

Tax Factors of Leverage

Since the tax base for depreciation is established by the total asset cost, there are potentially large tax losses available due to leverage. Under the 1987 tax laws, real estate losses, except in low-income housing properties, are considered to be "passive" dollars and so are deductible only to the extent that they are applied against "passive" income as such is defined by the law. An impact on the return on investment can be gained through development of syndication packages. In these, a low-tax bracket syndicator or developer teams up with high-bracket individuals who already have passive income from other investments, offering them attractive tax losses in return for their financial backing. Such an arrangement is commonly found in low-income-housing investments. Here, the syndicator or developer obtains front-end cash, which reduces or eliminates all of the initial investment while maintaining both a portion of any cash flow and a major portion of the residual value of the properties. In addition, these properties generate current tax losses reportable both to shareholders and the IRS. For individuals, but not corporations, there is often a dollar limit as to the amount of losses that may be deductible in any one year. One must not forget that leverage is a double-edged sword, and that which can be levered positively can also be levered negatively.

Among the problems that need to be considered are some operational and tax considerations. The use of heavy leverage increases the risk to the equity owner that may force selling at an inopportune time. The heavy cash drain upon operations that results from the use of a relatively large amount of first-mortgage debt can force a property into a negative cash flow position precisely when sale prices for such properties are low.

The extensive use of second mortgages or mortgages with large balloon

Figure 23-2 *Effects of Leverage on Value of Equity*

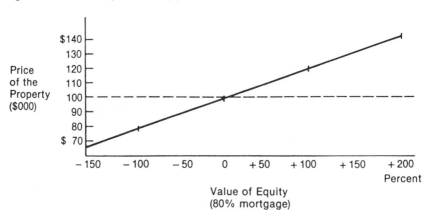

payments can frequently produce similar results. Many buyers of syndications have discovered that the financing that includes second-mortgage debt to the seller absorbs all of the cash flow. Secondary financing increases leverage, but often comes at high interest rates and short maturities, which make a high constant annual payment necessary.

Should problems of cash flow arise, the investor may face another problem created by his or her tax position. As shown in **Figure 23-3**, there may be substantial period of time during which the book value of a property for tax purposes is less than the unamortized mortgage amount. In the event of foreclosure, the sale price would be deemed to be the unamortized amount of the mortgage; a capital gain would be reported even though the investor had lost his or her equity. Thus, the investor could face a tax liability without cash proceeds from the property to meet such liability.

Operating Leverage

In **Figure 23-3**, the analysis of leverage is based on the economic factors existing at one point in time. But with an ever-changing environment, the key factor in investment success is to anticipate correctly changes over time. Fundamental analysis of changes in a real property investment can be divided into three basic steps: (1) development of comparable data, (2) projection of trends, and (3) prediction of discontinuity. Each of these steps is critical to the informed investment decision.

Once the property has been developed and financed, operations become the area most affected by changing economic forces. The investor must be aware that there is such a thing as operating leverage and that it can drastically affect

Figure 23-3 *Book Value of Property vs. Mortgage Balance*

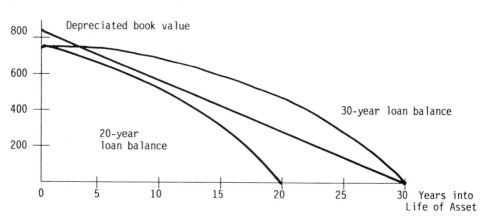

Assumptions: Straight Line Depreciation taken on 31.5-year life.
Loans are for 20-30 years.

the yearly return, the ability to refinance at an appropriate time, and the future or residual value of the investment.

Real estate investments are often made on the basis of the financial leverage. Professional investors, however, are often more concerned in a mortgaged property about the operating leverage available to them. Real property assets are unique in allowing the investor to obtain a high degree of financial leverage while benefiting from major operating leverage as well. Operating leverage arises because a major component of expense (normally the financing payment) in a real property investment is fixed, regardless of the revenue. A small change in revenue produces a large effect upon the rate of return to the equity investor. The example outlined in **Table 23-7** for a typical garden apartment in New England shows the impact of favorable operating leverage.

Table 23-7 Example of Favorable Operating Leverage ($ in thousands)
(Cost of building: $1,100,000; mortgage $900,000; 25 years at 9% interest; constant payment 10.08%)

	YEAR 1	YEAR 2	YEAR 3	YEAR 4	YEAR 5	YEAR 6
Revenues	$200.0	$206.0	$212.2	$218.5	$225.1	$231.9
Operating expenses	90.0	94.5	99.2	104.2	109.4	114.9
Financial payment	90.7	90.7	90.7	90.7	90.7	90.7
Before-tax cash flow	19.3	20.8	22.3	23.6	25.0	26.3
Return on investment	9.65%	10.4%	11.15%	11.8%	12.5%	13.15%

Table 23-7 was prepared on the assumption that operating revenues inflated by 3% annually and that expenses inflated by 5%. Even if the operating expenses increase at a rate 66% higher than revenues, the return on equity still rises significantly. Operating leverage can be negative as well. Since a major portion of costs associated with owning a property is fixed, only a slight decrease in revenues can have a drastic impact on the return to the equity holder. Break-even in **Table 23-7** is 90% capacity.

Another view of operating leverage can be had by holding most of the variables constant. Using the example from the section on financial leverage, we have a setup as shown in **Table 23-8**.

Table 23-8 Basic Setup

Cost of asset	$1,250,000	
Gross revenues	270,000	
Vacancies	27,000	
Net revenue		**$243,000**
Expenses		
Building operations	$ 69,400	
Property taxes	48,600	118,000
Free-and-clear cash flow		**$125,000**
Debt service (7.5% interest, 25 years on $1 million)		88,700
Net cash flow		**$ 36,300**

Note: Above calculations based on 10% vacancies.

If we hold all other costs (except vacancies) constant, we observe an operating leverage as shown in **Table 23-9**. Very obviously, a change of 5% in occupancy levels makes a corresponding change in the return on equity, sometimes to levels that may not be tolerable to the investor. Also note that at 85% occupancy the cost of debt is more than the return on asset, thus putting the investment in a negative financially levered position. It is important in analysis to separate the impact of the additional return that arises from financial leverage from the impact of projected operating leverage. Such separation helps in leaving critical assumptions clear and open for specific attention.

Table 23-9   Operating Leverage with Varying Occupancy Level

OCCUPANCY	FREE-AND-CLEAR CASH	% RETURN ON ASSET	NET CASH FLOW	RETURN ON EQUITY INVESTMENT
100%	$152,000	12.16%	$63,300	25.32%
95	138,500	11.08	49,800	19.92
90	125,000	10.00	36,300	14.52
85	111,500	8.92	22,800	9.12
80	98,000	7.84	9,300	3.72

If the U.S. economy continues to be inflationary, the possibilities to increase returns through operating leverage seem great. But changes in operating cash flows can have further effects on return. To this point, we have assumed that the original financing of an investment is fixed, but it is possible to restructure the debt when more favorable circumstances present themselves. To analyze how operating leverage works in this case, it is first necessary to understand how lending organizations value real property.

MEASUREMENT OF RETURN

Valuation

The primary method of evaluation of income-producing properties is known as the *capitalization of income* or *capitalization rate* technique. For appraisal purposes, this technique is supplemented by an analysis of comparable sales and by an analysis of replacement cost. Even in the area of raw land, appraisals often rely on the value of the prospective income stream to be generated in the future through development.

Capitalization techniques are based upon the following formulation:

$$\frac{\text{Cash stream}}{\text{Capitalization rate}} = \text{Value}$$

The relevant cash stream and the relevant capitalization rate are matters for analysis and dispute.

The two primary cash flows considered to be relevant are the *free-and-clear cash flow* and the *cash flow after financing*. (Cash flow after taxes will be discussed later in this note.) The former is used in determining the value of a property for lending purposes. The latter is most often used in considering the equity value of the property. In most instances, the cash flow is determined by the setup and is a static measure of the value at the particular moment in time with no adjustment for inflation, physical depreciation, operating leverage, tax benefits, or mortgage amortization. Some writers, such as Irvin E. Johnson in his book *Instant Mortgage-Equity Technique*, include such calculations in the development of the capitalization rate to be applied.

For the purposes of a lender, the free-and-clear cash flow is clearly the relevant number since it represents the total funds that would be available to service the debt on the property in the event of foreclosure. The normal practice is to apply a capitalization rate somewhat in excess of the lending rate and then to loan a percentage of the value derived. The following example illustrates the principle:

Cash Flow
Loan to value ratio = $1,000,000
Capitalization rate   = 11%
Loan to value ratio = .75

$$\frac{\$1,000,000}{.11} = 9,090,909 \text{ value} \times .75$$
$$= \$6,818,181 \text{ loan}$$

Note the sensitivity of the loan amount to the capitalization rate. For example, in the preceding example a change in the capitalization rate from 11% to 10% would yield an increase in valuation from $9.09 million to $10 million. Much has been written on capitalization rates. In general, however, these rates are chosen as measures of perceived risk, current and projected interest rates, expected return on equity, and future growth. Lenders normally expect a coverage of cash flow from operations to debt service of at least 110% to 130% or even more depending upon risk. The treatment of the equity value is done similarly. The before-tax cash flow after financing is capitalized at some rate to reflect equity value. The technique of capitalizing cash flow is the basis upon which value is created in real property development. To illustrate, consider a garden apartment complex. **Table 23-10** outlines construction cost information, cash flow, and financing data.

The overall value created as a result of reasonable financing and attention to the operating cost exceeds $1.35 million when the cash streams are capitalized as in **Table 23-10**. The value would not be determined without consideration of both the financial terms available from the bank and the expected return to the equity investor.

The implications of this method of valuation to the investor who is aware of operating leverage are interesting. Future benefits arising from sale or refinancing are the final component of return available to the real estate investor.

Table 23-10   Capitalized Values Before and After Financing

Cost information	
Land	$ 75,000
Improvement	1,175,000
Total cost	**$1,250,000**
Revenues net of vacancies	243,000
Operating expenses	118,000
Free-and-clear cash flow	**$ 125,000**
Capitalized at 9%	1,388,889
Loan at 80% of value	1,111,111
Equity required ($1,250,000-$1,111,111)	138,889
Free-and-clear cash flow	125,000
Mortgage payment 7.5% interest, 25 years	98,555
Before-tax cash flow	**$ 26,445**
Capitalized at 11%	240,400
Value created ($240,400-$138,889)	$ 101,511

Future Values

Because of assumed appreciation, almost all real property transactions anticipate benefits from holding a property. The degree of complexity in calculating the future value depends upon the projected holding period, the nature of the property, the patience of the person attempting the sale or refinancing, and the complexity of the financial structure through which the property was purchased. The value calculated depends upon estimates of many future conditions. These include, but are not limited to, (1) the physical condition of the asset, (2) economic and money market environment, (3) change in the physical neighborhood, (4) consumer preference for the kind of property involved, (5) inflation rate, (6) rate of return on alternative investments, (7) tax position of the seller, and (8) contemplated holding period.

The longer the time horizon, the more difficult it is to calculate future benefits. Probabilities increase for major changes, which may be either for the better or for the worse. In a financial analysis it becomes necessary to make judgments about such changes. These can be categorized as follows:

1. Operating changes
2. Physical changes
3. Financial changes
4. Market changes

Operating changes can be brought about in two ways. First, in the analysis of the setup, projections can be made of operating leverage. These projections should be factored into the final calculation of value as discussed earlier. Second, change can come from operating policy decisions, such as those calling for more efficient operation or for a policy of undermaintenance or those that seek a different market through upgrading the clientele. All of these changes should be reflected in the projected final setup that the buyer and seller use to determine value.

Physical changes are of two primary sorts: those affecting the property itself and those affecting its environment. In both instances, however, the primary impact is made upon the expected revenues to be realized. If the property is physically upgraded, it should be in anticipation of higher revenues. If the property is allowed to run down, lower future revenues would naturally be expected. The impact of the local environment is similar. A major question needing analysis is that of future use. Physical change of both the property and of the environment have an impact on "highest and best use" of the property. Such change is the greatest source of discontinuity in real property analysis.

The prospective developer or investor should be aware of opportunities to use the purchase as a holding action anticipating future uses. Often duplexes or small commercial buildings are purchased in anticipation of the opportunity to develop them later either for higher-density dwellings or for more intense commercial uses. The purchase of a mobile home park is often a high-yield way of holding land for future high-density commercial or residential development. In these situations, however, it is probably wise to make alternative analyses showing the impact on return of both the change and no-change options. What is permissible zoning now may change with the political environment.

Financial changes affecting future value are projections relating to the future financial market conditions and the simple calculation of the changed financial structure of the deal as loans are repaid and other obligations, such as below-market leases or limited-partnership responsibilities, are met. A projected financial change that assumes more favorable financial market conditions at the time of sale than are currently prevalent is generally a trap set for the unwary. If the major source of return comes from refinancing a property with a long-term mortgage at below present market rates, the investor might have a long wait. Such an assumption in an analysis has considerable favorable impact on the equity value of the project. However, it also is beyond the control of the principals and, therefore, realistically should be excluded from hard analysis unless the current situation is highly unusual.

Market changes derive from the assumption that at the time of sale someone will be willing to pay more for the same cash flow and associated benefits of ownership than the present owner is. This assumption, although bearing certain resemblance to the "greater fool" theory of investing, often stands up under analysis. Among the factors contributing to such changes in attitude are the effect of aging upon the perceived risk from a property, the changing tenant mix brought about through a well-defined property strategy, changes in government tax policy, and simply a better selling job brought about through greater patience.

In conclusion, the reader should be aware throughout that a successful analysis of a real property investment must consider many critical characteristics of the investment. Among these are (a) the extremely long time horizon of most investments, (b) poor liquidity, and (c) uncertainty concerning the valuation of the property. Valuation of property is subject to vagaries caused by competition, changes in financial market conditions, physical depreciation, government action, and changes in the microenvironment. Any of these may seriously revalue the property. In addition, historical information on a particular property may be unavailable or, if available, either irrelevant or intentionally misleading.

Despite the uncertainties, future benefits should be estimated when evaluating a real estate investment. Sources of future benefits are mortgage amortization, return of initial equity, and sales price appreciation. As always, benefits should be evaluated net of taxes.

Table 23-11 illustrates the benefits available to the investor who can refinance opportunely.

In the example shown in **Table 23-11**, the investor will have (without immediate tax consequences) all the original equity returned, as well as that paid in by mortgage payments, plus an additional $418,000 from refinancing. The investor will have obtained some of the potential future benefits without sale of the property and will have no cash still invested, but will retain ownership. Because the new cash flow after financing will be $37,862, the investor will be receiving more income than in year 1 and will be building equity once again. The importance of improving the free-and-clear cash flow is obvious. The possibilities here and the effects of leverage are great. But the reader must remember that al-

Table 23-11 Setup Showing Benefits from Refinancing
(Cost of asset: $1,250,000; mortgage: $1,000,000)

	PRESENT	RATE OF INFLATION PER YEAR	YEAR 10
Gross revenues	$270,000	4.14%	$405,000
Vacancies	27,000		40,500
Net revenues	**$243,000**		**$364,500**
Operating expenses	118,000	4.14%	177,000
Free-and-clear cash	**$125,000**		**$187,500**
Debt service (7.5% interest, 25 years)	88,700		88,700
Cash flow after financing	**$ 36,300**		**$ 98,800**

At the end of 10 years, if the free-and-clear cash flow of $187,500 were capitalized at 9%, the property might be worth $2,085,000. An 80% mortgage on this is $1,668,000.

Net mortgage	$1,668,000
Less: Balance of old mortgage	792,000
Cash proceeds	**$ 876,000**
Less: Prior mortgage amortization	208,000
Original equity	250,000
Net new cash	**$ 418,000**

though refinancing is usually optional, leverage can be negative and refinancing can be forced on the investor inopportunely with disastrous effects.

   To calculate the future benefits of sale, one again must face the added complication of computing the net cash to seller *after* taxes. To predict the future sales price of an income-producing property, the capitalization-of-income method previously discussed is generally used. Note that assumptions of future operating results are required and provide an area of much discretion. Alternatively, a simple growth assumption may be applied to the original purchase price. Once sales price and holding period assumptions have been made, the net cash to seller can be calculated:

Table 23-12   Calculation of Net Cash from Sale

1. Calculation of book value
       Purchase price
     + Capital improvements
     − Accumulated depreciation
     = Book value

2. Calculation of gain on sale
       Net selling price
     − Net book value
     = Gain on sale

3. Calculation of tax
       Gain on sale
     × Tax rate
     = Tax liability

4. Calculation of net cash to seller
       Net selling price
     − Mortgage balance
     − Income tax
     = Net cash from sale

The net cash from sale is the appropriate cash flow in the year of sale to use when evaluating an equity investment. Note that the net cash from sale is composed of the three potential elements of future benefits, adjusted by taxes:

	Return of initial cash equity
+	Return of mortgage amortization
+	Increase in sales price
−	Income taxes
=	Net cash from sale

METHODS OF CALCULATING RETURN

The preceding sections have focused upon development of basic data for analyzing the profitability of a real property investment and upon elements that lead to change in such investments. This section shows how these data may be used to measure return on investment in such a property. There is extensive literature on evaluation and return, but space does not permit an in-depth review of it here. This section simply reviews the various methods of evaluation as they apply to real property assets. A cardinal rule of financial analysis that the investment decision be made apart from the financing decision does not hold for many real estate decisions. Although the operating cash flow may be used to determine the project value for mortgage purposes, the after-tax cash flows will determine the return on equity to the investor. Since the cash-flow-after-tax calculation requires financing assumptions and since mortgages by definition are property specific, it is necessary to consider financing effects when comparing alternative investments in real estate.

The measurement of return on investment in real estate is a subject of great dispute and sales expertise. The careful builder or investor must be aware of the measures being used since one person's 28% return is another's 6%. The major differences occur in the elements of return that are included in the measurement and in the time horizon which the measurement is made. The measures will be examined on the basis of the time horizon and with the inclusion of the three elements of return.

Capitalization Rate Basically, this measure of return may be defined as follows:

$$\frac{\text{Free-and-clear return}}{\text{Property cost}}$$

This measure of return is static in that it assumes the same cash flow throughout time. It ignores the tax consequences of the investment and ignores the capital change brought about by disposing of the investment.

Before-tax Cash Return on Equity This measure of return may be stated thus:

$$\frac{\text{Before-tax cash flow}}{\text{Equity}}$$

In this case, the before-tax cash flow is the equivalent of cash flow after financing, and equity is defined as the initial cash investment. This measure is also known as "cash on cash" return and is frequently applied by seasoned investors in the real estate field. The measure looks at return statically and omits both tax effect and capital change. The argument made by investors using this measure is "if a deal will stand up under this, everything else is a plus." It is perhaps the most rigid measure applied because it ignores all elements of return that are not reflected in the end-of-the-month checking account balance. The preceding two measures are commonly used by professionals.

The following measures are often shown to induce purchase. In general, they have major flaws that limit their usefulness. Either the simple measures or a full internal-rate-of-return calculation should be used.

Before-tax Cash Flow + First Year's Amortization Return on Equity This measure is defined in the following way:

$$\frac{\text{Before-tax cash flow + Mortgage principal payment (year 1)}}{\text{Equity}}$$

This measure is the same as the previous one except for the addition of the amount paid on the mortgage as an element of return. This return measure and the one that follows are often used by aggressive real estate salespeople. Assume an 80% mortgage at 8¾% interest and a 20-year amortization schedule. The first-year reduction in loan balance amounts to 1.9% of the original balance. Thus it represents a 7.6% return on the equity investment. That 7.6% return is not available without either refinancing or selling the property subject to the mortgage. These events are considered only as future possibilities rather than as certainties, so some portion of that return should be discounted. This measure of return is appropriate only for the initial year. It considers neither the tax effect nor the bulk of the change in capital position that will arise through change in value of the property.

Before-tax Cash Flow + Tax Effect as Return on Equity This measure is defined as follows:

$$\frac{\text{Before-tax cash flow + Tax effect (year 1)}}{\text{Equity}}$$

This measure gives the cash value of the investment to the investor in the first year of ownership. It ignores the change of after-tax cash flow over time and the impact of sale on the capital position of the investor.

Average Returns All of the last three measures are sometimes shown as averages based upon an estimated holding period. It is wise to look carefully at the components of these averages rather than to accept the average figure. For example, in the tenth year alone of an 8¾% 20-year loan, approximately 4.2% of the original loan balance is paid off. For a property purchased with 80% debt, the loan amortization alone accounts for a 16.8% return on the original equity. Unless there are plans for the realization of the equity built up through loan amortization, the inclusion of such a large annual figure may materially distort the average and mislead the potential investor. This is especially critical given the long time before that portion of the return is to be realized.

Averaging the projected returns (cash flow, tax effect, and future benefits) gives considerable effect to the returns to be realized in the sale. The rate of gain is the arithmetic mean rather than the compounded rate of return; mortgage amortization, which is considerable in later years, is considered to be achieved at an average rate rather than in the progressively growing fashion that is the actual pattern. Such a measure, therefore, will show a rate of return considerably higher than one calculated by computing an internal rate of return.

Payback Period   This simple benchmark return measures the number of years required for the investor to recoup the cash equity invested. Discounted payback applies the investor hurdle rate to the future stream of after-tax cash flows. These measures are of limited value because they ignore benefits beyond the payback period.

Net Present Value (NPV)   The net present value for a real estate investment may be found by applying the following formula:

$$N = \text{holding period}$$
$$NPV = \text{Equity} - \sum_{n=1}^{N} \frac{1}{(1 + i)^n} [\text{CFAT year}_n]$$

Where: i = investor hurdle rate.
CFAT = cash flow after taxes in year N
   (= the sum of: before-tax cash flow in year n + tax effect in year n + futures in year n).

In other words, a stream of cash flows is discounted back at a predetermined discount rate, totaled, and then subtracted from the initial investment.

The NPV calculation considers all of the components of return available to the real estate investor. The relative sizes of initial investment are not explicitly accounted for by the NPV method; therefore, projects cannot be directly compared unless they are of the same size. This failing may be accounted for by the use of a profitability index, which is simply the ratio of the NPV to the amount of equity invested.[3]

Internal Rate of Return (IRR)   The internal rate of return for a real estate investment may be found by solving the following equation for i:

$$N = \text{holding period}$$
$$\text{Equity} - \sum_{n=1}^{N} \frac{1}{(1 + i)^n}$$
$$[\text{Before-tax cash flow (year } n) + \text{Tax effect (year } n)$$
$$+ \text{Future benefits (year n)}] = 0$$

Thus i is the rate of return that will set the discounted present value of all cash flows equal to zero. All of the standard caveats regarding discounted values apply. Arduous trial-and-error algorithms solve for the IRR and are best left to calculators or computers. Care must be taken in remembering the critical assumptions underlying the calculation of the IRR. The primary critical assumption is that the cash thrown off by the investment can and will be reinvested at the calculated internal rate of return. This assumption is often not true in practice. This is particularly invalid with the cash saved on taxes. For a project with a pattern of large initial tax losses and then considerable taxable income,

[3]The NPV calculation is useful when the investor's cost of capital is known, when projections are made that involve many changes from positive to negative cash flows and might therefore produce multiple IRR solutions, and when investments with widely varying lives are compared.

the tax savings must be reinvested or the project in its later years may actually have a negative cash flow. For example, the following stream has approximately a 12% internal rate of return but a negative total return:

−	$1,000	Year 1
+	500	Year 2
+	500	Year 3
+	500	Year 4
+	500	Year 5
	0	Years 6 through 11
−	$2,000	Year 12

The unwary investor who dealt with the $500 as though it were real return (as is often done in tax-shelter investments) will have a financially troublesome shock in Year 12.

SUMMARY

Analysis of real property investments is complicated. It is not, however, impossible. Since it most often involves projection of future events, it is well to err always on the conservative side. Projections of compound growth over the periods involved in real estate must always be considered to contain a risk. The key tasks that need to be performed for all investments are the following:

1. to develop baseline data,
2. to project trends, and
3. to search out sources of discontinuity

These tasks, adequately performed, will yield opportunities. One must understand what assumptions have been made. The number calculations themselves are not very complicated. Basing the future on projections of the past may be the most logical way to start, but as any investor knows, events rarely work out that way. Fortunately, over time real estate has been one of the securest and most profitable forms of investment. However, it is crucial to realize that the ability to sustain and take advantage of short-term downturns and to hold property for the long term has generally been the key to success.

24

NOTE ON TAXATION

INTRODUCTION

Every real estate transaction is affected substantially by the tax consequences which result from its form and substance. Structuring a transaction without a thorough understanding of its tax considerations is likely to reduce the transaction's potential value. The failure to utilize the available tax benefits eliminates one of the major reasons for real estate investment.

This note provides a broad overview of the income tax factors most relevant to real estate ownership and operation. It is not intended as a definitive guide to the area, but to help the student better understand the basic factors and their interrelationships.

It cannot be overemphasized that all transactions should receive competent professional review. The application of the law is affected by the particular circumstances of the taxpayer and the property. The field is highly technical with many interacting considerations. Most rules have variations and exceptions, and many exceptions have their own exceptions. The governing tax law changes frequently.

Some of the more recent acts were the Tax Equity and Fiscal Responsibility Act of 1982 (TEFRA), the Tax Reduction Act of 1984, the Tax Reform Act of 1986 and the Revenue Reconciliation Act of 1990. Whereas the 1982 Act expanded the tax benefits of real estate ownership, the 1986 Act substantially curtailed such benefits. The 1990 Act altered the tax rates imposed on individuals, with special treatment for long term capital gains.

This note was prepared as the basis for class discussion. It was updated in 1992.

This note deals with taxation at the federal level. In most cases states have income tax laws affecting real estate that are significant factors. However, because of local variations, the state laws will not be considered in this note but will be left to the individual investor to investigate. State taxes are deductible from federal income for tax purposes. Investors should be aware that state taxes are not deductible for taxpayers in the alternative minimum tax position (AMT). AMT is a complicated area and will not be discussed in this note.

The major distinction between real estate and other fields relates to the differences between cash flow and income tax accounting. Real estate operations may generate a positive cash flow while also showing a loss for income tax purposes. As shown in the statement below, federal income tax law permits the deduction of noncash allowances as expenses in calculating taxable income. When the *noncash* depreciation allowance exceeds cash expenditures for principal amortization and replacement reserves, taxable income is less than the pretax cash flow for the period.

The relationship can be seen in the following diagram. In effect, the income tax due must be calculated first to determine the cash flow. The starting point is the before-tax cash flow *or* the cash flow from operations. The taxes due or saved depends on the individual or entity's actual tax rate.

Cash Flow from Operations

INCOME EFFECT		CASH EFFECT
	— Interest	— Interest
	— Depreciation Allowance	— Principal
		— Replacement reserves
	= Net income before taxes	= Cash flow after financing
	— Income taxes	— Income taxes
	= Net income	= Cash flow after taxes

In a capital transaction, to determine gain or loss on sale, the depreciation previously taken by the seller must be considered. Calculations are done in a similar manner to that shown above.

$$\begin{array}{r} \text{Gross Sale Price} \\ - \underline{\text{Selling Expenses}} \\ \text{Net Sales Price} \end{array}$$

− Book value after depreciation	− Debt outstanding
= Net income before taxes	= Cash flow before taxes
− Income taxes	− Income taxes
= Net income after taxes	= Cash proceeds from sale

The owner-investor can judge the economic merits of a transaction only by reference to the sum of the total after-tax cash flow during ownership and the after-tax cash proceeds from sale. Both provide the input for calculating the internal rate of return on investment.

Tax planning critically affects both the timing and the amount of income recognized. As the tax tables below indicate, as spelled out in the 1990 Act, the federal government in 1991 can be up to a 31% partner in real estate operations. The 1990 Act also includes personal exemption phaseout provisions and limitations on itemized deductions, which can increase the marginal tax rate above 31%. The alternative minimum tax rate was increased from 21% to 24%. The maximum tax rate imposed on long term capital gains remains at 28%.

1991 Federal Income Tax Tables

Unmarried Individuals
Taxable Income

OVER	NOT OVER	PAY	+ TAX RATE	ON AMOUNT OVER
$ 0	$19,450	$ 0	15%	$ 0
19,450	47,050	2,918	28	19,450
over 47,040		10,646	31	47,050

Married Individuals Filing Separate Returns
Taxable Income

OVER	NOT OVER	PAY	+ TAX RATE	ON AMOUNT OVER
$ 0	$16,225	$ 0	15%	$ 0
16,225	39,200	2,434	28	16,225
over 39,200		8,867	31	39,200

Married Individuals Filing Joint Returns
(and Qualifying Widows and Widowers)
Taxable Income

OVER	NOT OVER	PAY	+ TAX RATE	ON AMOUNT OVER
$ 0	$32,450	$ 0	15%	$ 0
32,450	78,400	4,868	28	32,450
over 78,400		17,734	31	78,400

This note assumes the perspective of the individual taxpayer, or the recipient of "passed through" partnership income. The decision as to the form of real estate ownership is discussed in the Note on Forms of Real Estate Ownership (9-373-148). Factors which contribute to the general preference for the partnership form are: the statutory complexity of corporations, the "double taxation" of corporate income and dividends and the treatment of losses in excess of annual corporate income.

This note is organized into four principal sections. Each section focuses on the major concerns affecting the taxation of the property investment—both the factual determinations required and the special problem areas encountered.

THEORY OF INCOME TAXATION AND ACCOUNTING

This section introduces the income tax concept of matching the timing of recognition of costs and revenues. It emphasizes the importance of clear and accurate records and discusses the difference between "cash" and "accrual" methods of tax accounting.

TAX CONSIDERATIONS IN THE ACQUISITION AND DEVELOPMENT OF REAL PROPERTY

This section focuses on the determination of the taxpayer's tax basis in a property; the allocation of that basis to the property's various components; the determination of the taxpayer's holding period of a property; the role of prepaid interest; the alternatives of capitalizing and expensing costs during property development; and the application of the investment tax credit to real property.

TAX FACTORS IN REAL PROPERTY OPERATION

This section discusses the nature of income, and the types of and eligibility for deductions in computing the tax liability from real estate operations. Particular attention is given to the concept and the calculation of the depreciation deduction.

TAX FACTORS IN THE DISPOSITION AND SALE OF REAL PROPERTY

This section discusses the calculation of the gain on the sale or other disposition of property, the factors which determine ordinary income and long-term capital gains treatment, and the methods by which to defer the recognition of that income.

THEORY OF INCOME TAXATION AND ACCOUNTING

Theory of Taxation

The federal income tax treatment of real estate has two basic, but sometimes conflicting, goals: the generation of revenue to support government, and the encouragement of private real estate investment relative to other investments. The incentive aspects have caused much investment in real estate. For example, hundreds of thousands of subsidized housing units have been built to take advantage of favorable tax incentives. Heated debate continues, however, over the costs of providing these incentives in terms of the loss or deferral of federal revenue.

The basic principles of tax law and accounting aim at taxing income as it is generated while granting offsetting deductions for valid expenses incurred in producing that income. The Internal Revenue Code (Code) requires that the taxable income be determined, in general, in the same manner used by the taxpayer in computing income for financial reporting purposes and that differences be reported on the tax return. It requires consistency in the manner in which the taxpayer reports from year to year. In all cases, the Internal Revenue Service (IRS) requires the taxpayer to maintain clear, written records to justify the deductions claimed. The taxpayer has the burden of documenting the logic underlying transactions so as to show both the business purpose of each expense and that the accounting procedures have not "materially distorted income."

Methods of Accounting for Income

A real estate business must select one of two basic methods of accounting. The most commonly used is the "cash receipts and disbursements method," often called the "cash method." The other is the "accrual method."

Under the cash method, income is recognized in the taxable year in which payment is received. Expenses are recognized in the year in which paid. The cash method offers much flexibility in timing billings, and accelerating expense payments; income can be increased by delaying payment of bills and by encouraging prepayment of rents or accounts receivable.

This control of reportable income has led many private individuals to choose the cash method. In addition, it limits the practical ability of the IRS to challenge the taxpayer's position. The major contestable issue is whether the taxpayer is in constructive receipt of income where funds have not changed hands. The doctrine of constructive receipt holds that a cash basis taxpayer who possesses an unqualified right to property, and the power to exercise that right, is to be treated as if in actual receipt of that cash.

The "accrual method" aims at matching income and expense through noncash accounting. Income is recognized in the year in which all conditions are met which determine the taxpayer's right to receive it. The items recognized must be determinable with reasonable accuracy; unsubstantiated estimates usually are inadequate to trigger recognition. Most public companies use accrual accounting in order to reflect more accurately the financial condition of a company and to provide greater comparability among corporations.

It should be noted for income tax purposes, rental income is taxable when received without regard to the taxpayer's method of accounting. In other words, an accrual basis taxpayer who receives rental income prior to the time that income has been earned, i.e. prepaid rents, must still recognize that amount as income in the year received.

The decision to use the cash or accrual method of accounting is made by each taxpaying entity, whether that entity is an individual taxpayer or an intermediary business vehicle such as a partnership. Once adopted, the method must be consistently applied and cannot be changed without the consent of the Internal Revenue Service. The long term consequences of this decision make it important that the taxpayer get competent advice before selecting an accounting method and that the search for simplicity or tax gimmickry not be allowed to impede the development of a sound accounting or management information system. The 1986 Tax Act eliminated the decision making for certain entities by requiring all tax shelters and many C corporations, partnerships having a C corporation as a partner and tax exempt trusts having unrelated business income to use the accrual method of accounting for years beginning after 1986. There is an exception to this rule for entities other than tax shelters so that the cash method can be used if the entity has less than $5,000,000 in gross receipts.

TAX CONSIDERATIONS IN THE ACQUISITION AND DEVELOPMENT STAGE

A long-term tax plan should be formulated during the acquisition and development of a project. Interactions will occur with the income tax on the owner/investor's other income during the development period. This is so despite the fact that acts of purchasing or developing a property do not usually give rise to taxable income, because they involve merely the creation of a capital asset rather than income or loss generation. Many decisions made at that time affect the seller in the short run and the buyer throughout the period of ownership.[2]

Determinations Which are Primarily Factual

The primary factual determinations involve the amount of the taxpayer's tax basis in the property, its allocation to the components of the land and buildings, and the length of the holding period for the property. Other important factors include the allocation of future payments between principal and interest,

---

[2]Considerable real property is being purchased today as investments by pension funds and other entities that do not pay income tax. Although the tax factors discussed in this note are not applicable to them directly, indirectly the lack of tax consequences could be advantageous or disadvantageous to them in competing for individual real property investments.

and the expensing or capitalization of items, such as real estate taxes, interest, loan fees, etc.

Determination of Basis The Cost of the Property. The first factual determination to be made is that of the tax basis of the property. The fundamental rule is that a property's tax basis is its cost. For tax purposes, cost is not limited to the cash paid by the purchaser but includes any mortgages or notes assumed. This is illustrated by the following example:

> A taxpayer purchases a building for investment purposes for a price of $300,000. The buyer gives a $75,000 down payment and obtains a $225,000 mortgage from the bank. The buyer's basis is $300,000. The existence or nonexistence of a mortgage does not affect the basis. If the mortgage were repaid, the tax basis would still be $300,000.

Among other costs included in the tax basis are the following:

> Attorney's fees
> Appraisal costs
> Land survey
> Title examination and title insurance
> Option payments
> Brokerage commissions
> Delinquent *ad valorem* taxes
> Tax stamps

The tax basis may change during the period of ownership. For example, capital improvements made by an owner increase one's basis, and the depreciation deductions reduce it.[3]

[3]*Other Forms of Acquisition:* The basis of properties acquired other than by purchase deserves special consideration. Common transactions include inheritance, gift, the satisfaction of a debt, payment for services and the exchange of other properties.

a. *Inheritance:* An owner's property becomes part of one's estate upon death. It is valued for the estate tax purposes at its fair market value on the date of death (or, at the option of the estate's representative, six months later). The recipient of the property takes that fair market value as a new basis in the property.

b. *Gift:* Property acquired by gift receives a basis equal to the lesser of the donor's basis or the fair market value of the property on the date of the gift. The donee's basis is increased by the federal gift tax paid on the gift; but the total cannot exceed the fair market value. If the property is later sold for less than the donor's basis, the loss is computed by reference to the lesser of the carry-over basis or the fair market value on the date of the gift. Note that there is now a combined transfer tax system for gifts and estates.

c. *Debt:* The basis in property acquired in satisfaction of a debt or other claim is determined by the fair market value and the previous ownership of the property.

If the debt holder did not own the property previously (i.e., the debt is not a purchase money obligation), the basis is its fair market value at the time of transfer or foreclosure. If that value differs from the amount of debt satisfied by the transfer, the transferee and transferor recognize a capital gain or loss.

Otherwise, the basis is the face value of the debt plus any other consideration paid. For example, where a creditor purchases property from a debtor by using the claim as the payment

Basis allocations reflect the fair market values of the separate elements. For new construction, actual cost serves as the basis for components. In contrast, the price of an existing property is usually arrived at on an overall basis, and any separation into parts is done after the fact.

The most commonly used method is to allocate between land and buildings by reference to the ratio of assessed valuations placed upon those components by the local tax assessor. Sometimes an appraiser is hired to evaluate the components if the assessed valuation method does not give a satisfactory result.

The IRS may accept an allocation which the parties make in the purchase and sales contract. Acceptance occurs most often when arm's-length negotiations have been conducted between parties with adverse interests; for example, when certain items sold, such as personal property, give rise to ordinary income to the seller, but permit rapid or high tax write-offs for the purchaser. Even the most reasonable approach may be affected by hindsight. Artificial allocations which produce unrealistic tax results are always subject to challenge.

Holding Period The concept of holding period was a much more important consideration prior to the 1986 Tax Act when capital gains received special tax treatment resulting in an effective tax rate of no more than 20% of the gain. The rate for capital gains from 1987 to 1990 was 28%, regardless of the holding period. Beginning in 1991, the maximum rate for long-term capital gains remains at 28%, and applies to capital gain property held for more than one year. Short-term capital gains (and ordinary income) are taxed at a maximum rate of 31% beginning in 1991. The starting date of the holding period of property varies depending on the means used to acquire the property.

The holding period of property acquired by purchase commences usually with the day following that on which the sale is closed and title transferred.

For property acquired by gift, the holding rules follow the basis rules for gifts. If the donor's basis is carried over, the recipient's holding period includes that of the donor. If the basis is the fair market value on the date of the gift because a loss is realized, the date of the gift governs.

---

at a sale by auction at foreclosure, the basis is the price bid at the auction, including any unforeclosed items.

The original property owner will recognize a gain or loss if the original owner's basis differs from the face amount of the debt transferred.

d. *Services:* The basis is property acquired for services is the fair market value of the property at the date of transfer. A person paid in property services includes that value as earned income.

e. *Exchange:* The basis in property acquired in exchange is dependent upon the tax treatment of exchange. If the exchange is tax deferred, the basis of the property transferred carries over to the property received. Adjustments are made when the exchange is partially taxable. These are discussed later under the heading *Sales Transactions.*

In a fully taxable exchange, the basis is the fair market value of the property acquired at the date of transfer. The taxpayer's gain or loss on the transfer is taken into account. The transaction is like a purchase at fair market value.

The holding period of the property acquired in a tax-free exchange includes the taxpayer's holding period in the property transferred. Both basis and holding period are carried over from the original asset.

Property acquired by bequest, devise or inheritance usually acquires a holding period dating from the date of death. The holding period for improvements made by an owner begins with the date of construction of each item. Thus, a single sale can include both short- and long-term assets.

Areas for Management Decision-Making: Tax Treatment of Certain Expense Items at Time of Acquisition

The discussion to this point has been concerned with relevant factual determinations. Although some of the "facts" are subject to judgment, established rules usually determine their validity. Nonetheless, there are also managerial decisions which must be made during the acquisition and development period which also have major tax implications. Not all are under the control of a single decision maker. Good decisions may result in long-run payoffs. This section of the note will consider several important areas for managerial decision-making.

Much flexibility inheres in the real estate investment vehicle. Buyer and seller often reach agreement largely as a result of structuring a transaction so as to create a more beneficial total tax picture for both parties. Negotiating upon, and sharing in, the tax trade-offs from allocating the total purchase consideration can allow both sides to come closer to objectives which otherwise would conflict.

The partnership as a form of ownership probably offers the greatest amount of flexibility but this flexibility has been reduced in recent years as a result of perceived abuse. Two major areas where flexibility has been curtailed include special allocations and retroactive allocations. Current law requires items of income, loss, gain, deduction or credit to be allocated according to the partners' interest in the partnership unless a special allocation to the contrary has substantial economic effect.

The second area of reduced flexibility comes through prohibition of retroactive allocation of income and loss. A partner who acquires a partnership interest during the year must be allocated income or loss for that portion of the year during which the interest was held. This allocation can be made either by determining actual income or loss for the period or by prorating the year's income or loss to the period the interest is held.

A major change in the 1986 tax law is the passive activity loss rule, which prohibits claiming most real estate losses against income not derived from real estate or other specified passive activities. Individuals, estates and trusts, S Corporations and personal service corporations will not be able to use losses from real estate to offset active or earned income, or portfolio income such as interest, dividends or gains from the sale of securities. Payments earned by partners for providing management or other services are considered earned income for the recipient and a passive deduction for the payer. Interest or guaranteed payments paid on capital accounts is also deemed portfolio income. The operation of nursing homes, hotels or other transient lodging facilities where substantial services are rendered is active, not rental, income for the owner who materially participates in the activity. It should be noted that a limited partner cannot, by law, materially participate.

There is an exception to the passive activity rule for up to $25,000 of losses by individuals who materially participate in real estate rentals. A similar exception is allowed for tax credits from qualified rehabilitation expenditures and low-income housing projects. The exception is phased out for individuals with adjusted gross incomes between $100,000 and $150,000 in the first case and $200,000 and 250,000 in the second.

Prepaid Interest, "Points" and Contract Interest   Interest is deductible only in the year to which it relates, irrespective of when paid. Similarly "points" paid on a loan must be deducted ratably over the loan period. An exception is made for points paid on a secured loan for the purchase or improvement of a taxpayer's principal residence if the charge is typical for one geographical area.

In earlier periods, for cash method taxpayers, interest could also be deducted for the next year. In that situation, the flexibility of prepaid interest could be advantageous to a seller. Investments were often structured for continuing prepayments of interest for future periods. The conversion of a capital asset to ordinary income could preserve the tax benefits of a large loss carry forward which was expiring. The logic was that since the interest was income to one and an expense to another there would be no loss of revenue to the Treasury. For public corporations, ordinary income is often more highly valued by securities analysts than capital gains; the latter may be treated as nonrecurring and discounted in evaluating performance.

Care must always be taken that some interest rate is stated in a contract. Contracts which specify no interest rate or annual simple interest rates of less than the market are subject to restatement under tax regulations which impute a market rate compounded semi-annually. The change made by the Tax Reform Act of 1984 extends original issue discount (OID) rules to obligations issued for nontraded property and require the interest rate be compared to 110% of the "federal rate" effective for taxable years beginning in 1985. Most leveraged real estate purchases will be subject to the OID rules in cases where adequate interest is not provided for or cases where adequate interest is charged but not payable annually. The IRS commissioner has the right and does, in fact, change these rates from time to time. The applicable federal rate is published monthly. There are special rules about interest rates for transactions involving related parties.

Election to Capitalize Normally Expensed Items   The investor may elect, under detailed rules, whether to capitalize or expense separately for each kind of expense. An owner of many projects may make different elections for the various kinds of expenses of the different projects.

After 1986, individuals, partnerships, trusts, and corporations are no longer allowed to deduct interest and property taxes or related administrative expenses on real property under construction. Those costs must be capitalized and amortized over the life of the property. Prior to 1986, interest and property taxes incurred during the construction period could be amortized over a ten year period.

A tax credit is used to offset income tax payable on a dollar-for-dollar basis.[4] Prior to the 1986 Tax Act, an owner was eligible for a tax credit of 10% of rehabilitation costs for work done on a nonresidential building built prior to a particular date. For several years prior to 1987, the owner of a certified historic structure, which can be either residential or nonresidential, was eligible for a tax credit equal to 25% of the rehabilitation costs. These tax credits can be carried back 3 years and forward 15. A lessee may also be eligible for these tax credits if the remaining lease is at least 15 years. Starting in 1987, only certified historic structures are eligible for the tax credit, and the amount has been reduced to 20%.

In all situations, to qualify for a tax credit the renovation must be substantial, basically defined as at least equal to the purchase price of the property. The renovation, especially for historical structures, must also meet certain technical requirements. The rehabilitation tax credit reduces the basis of the property eligible for depreciation. Thus, if $1,000,000 is spent renovating an historic structure, the owner receives a tax credit of $200,000 when the work is complete, but for depreciation purposes the basis of the building only goes up by $800,000. If the building is sold within five years of the rehabilitation work, a portion of the tax credit will be recaptured according to the following schedule:

YEAR OF DISPOSITION	RECAPTURE PERCENTAGE
Within one full year after placed in service	100%
Second year	80%
Third year	60%
Fourth year	40%
Fifth year	20%

If an owner receives one of these investment tax credits, the rehabilitation expenditure must thereafter be depreciated on a straight line basis. In addition, the rehabilitation work associated with the investment tax credit is not eligible for other tax credits, like an energy tax credit.

The 1978 Energy Tax Act permits businesses or owners of income-producing properties to obtain a 10% or 15% (depending on the property classification) energy property tax credit. Energy property must have a recovery period of at least three years and must provide alternative energy sources, recycling capabilities, energy conservation or other benefits.

[4]Actually, the tax law provides a dollar-for-dollar offset only for the first $25,000 of tax liabilities. Liabilities in excess of $25,000 are offset at a 75% rate.

For renters or owners of principal residences, the Energy Tax Act provided tax credits for expenditures on energy conserving and renewable energy source property.

For low income housing, the special depreciation schedules and other benefits have been eliminated for projects placed in service after 1986, and replaced by tax credits for certain expenditures. The credit is claimed annually for ten years. The new credits are 4% for acquisitions and 9% for new construction and rehabilitation unless financed with tax-exempt bonds or similar Federal subsidies, in which case the credit is 4%. The credits are phased out for individuals with adjusted gross incomes of $200,000 to $250,000 and only $7,000 per individual investor can be used against "non-passive activity income." Corporations do not have these restrictions.

TAX FACTORS IN THE OPERATION OF REAL PROPERTY INVESTMENTS

It is also critical that the potential investor understand the tax factors which are relevant to the operating phase of a building's life. The primary activity of most people who are active in the real estate field is in its operation. This section considers three principal areas: eligibility for tax deductions; recognition and characterization of income; and determination of deductions.

Eligibility for Deductions

The federal income tax deductions which arise from real estate ownership fall into two classes: those available to all owners, even for property held for personal use; and additional ones available only to owners of property "used in a trade or business" or held for the "production of income."

Deductions Generally Available Owners of a principal residence or a single second home may deduct interest on debt secured by a security interest and real estate or property taxes. However, for loans incurred after August 16, 1986, interest deductions are limited based on the lesser of the purchase price of the property plus the cost of improvements or the fair market value of the home at the time the debt is incurred. with maximum limitation amounts of $1 million for original acquisition indebtedness and $100,000 for home equity indebtedness. There is an exception for loans used to pay certain medical and educational expenses. For second homes, personal use must exceed the greater of 14 days or 10% of the total number of days for which the unit is rented at a fair value. Although the lower current tax brackets reduce the benefits of these deductions, even after taking into account lost income from the downpayment on a house, there is usually an after tax cash flow advantage to ownership versus rental of one's home.

All owners of real property are allowed itemized deductions for real estate taxes and interest expenses. Holding mere legal title is insufficient to render an expense deductible to the taxpayer. The taxpayer must "bear the burdens and risks of ownership." Deals can be structured to take advantage of differing tax brackets or need for reporting earnings of buyers and sellers.

It is important to note that whereas interest payments are deductible for tax purposes, principal payments are not since the payer is reducing a liability and theoretically increasing net worth. Therefore, the term of the mortgage which with the interest rate determines the allocation of mortgage payments between principal and interest has important tax implications.

Deductions Available with Respect to Property Used in Trade or Business or Held for the Production of Income   Income or business properties generate not only deductions for interest[5] and property taxes but also additional deductions. Among these are deductions for operating expenses, repairs and maintenance, and depreciation. All will be considered in this section of this note.

There are two primary requirements for taking deductions for these items: First, the taxpayer must have a legitimate business purpose for incurring the expense, in contrast to mere personal benefit. Second, the taxpayer must have the benefits, burdens and risks of ownership. Allocation of deductions among partners and other joint owners of a property is subject to complex limitations which are based on the view that the benefits and burdens of ownership must be spread reasonably among the owners by reference to their economic interests in the property. Certain limitations on these deductions are footnoted below.

Recognition and Character of Income

The owner or lessor may receive compensation for the use of a property during its operating phase. This compensation is called *rent* and results in ordinary income to the lessor. In determining the owner's taxable income, the ordinary income is reduced by the operating expenses incurred in connection with the property. The rent payments are deductible by the lessee if the property is used in connection with a trade or business or for production of income.

Although defining reportable income is generally straightforward, issues are often raised as to advance rents, security deposits, lessee improvements, payments made under leases with options to purchase and payments made to cancel, extend, or modify a lease. The primary determinants are the intent of the parties, the economic substance of the transaction, and any written agreement.

Advance rents protect a lessor against default by the lessee during the lease term. These are usually applied to the first or last periods of the obligations, but may be applied in any fashion which is agreed to in the lease. They become taxable income to the landlord upon receipt of cash or a marketable promissory

---

[5]Interest on debt used to purchase or carry investment real estate may be subject to investment interest limitations. This is a complicated area and will not be discussed in this note.

note. The lessee does not receive a deduction for advance rent payments until the period for which the rent is actually due or the payment is applied as rent. Thus, the deduction may be separated from the recognition of income by many years.

Security deposits may be used in place of advance rentals. These differ from advance rentals in that the lessor is obligated to hold and account to the tenant for the monies advanced. There is no recognition of income until the deposit can be used without a duty to account for or repay it. Many states require that the security deposits on residential rental properties be placed in interest-bearing escrow accounts for the benefit of the tenants. The tenant is not allowed a deduction for a security deposit unless and until the deposit becomes rent under the lease terms.

Lessee improvements are a complicated area of income recognition. There are three basic categories of improvements: those made by a tenant which reduce the rental cost; those made to property owned by an unrelated party; and those made to property owned by a related party.

The fair market value of improvements made by a lessee in consideration of a rent reduction results in income for the lessor. The fair market value may differ from the cost of the improvements because the lessor does not receive the right to immediate use. The mere enhancement of the ultimate value of the property of the lessor does not automatically generate taxable income.

In a more usual case, the cost is treated as a capital expenditure for the tenant, and does not constitute additional rent or add to the lessor's basis. The tenant must recover the cost through either depreciation over the recovery period of the improvements or amortization over the term of the lease including option periods whichever is shorter. Leases between related parties are more likely to be scrutinized by the IRS since transactions by them are more likely to be entered into primarily to minimize the total tax due: the improvements must be depreciated over the recovery period of the improvements rather than the shorter period of the lease term.

Leases with options to purchase are especially complicated. The combination is usually made with the intention that during the lease all payments will be ordinary income to the landlord and deductible to the tenant. Upon exercise of the option, the payments become capital if the economic reality appears to be that some of the "rental" payments are in reality payments for the purchase of the buildings and that the sale in fact occurs before the option is exercised. Inflated rents, below-market options and uneven payments over the lease indicate a nonstandard transaction.

Revenue received by the landlord as payment for *extending, canceling or modifying a lease* is ordinary income in the year of receipt. The landlord may deduct related expenses against the income generated; these costs include the unamortized portion of any lease acquisition expense. The payments are deductible by the tenant in the year in which paid, except that payments made to extend or modify a lease are amortized over the lease term.

Determination of Deductions

Although the general rule is that expenses incurred in the generation of income in an operating business are usually deductible, an awareness of the specific nature of deductible expenses can often mean a major difference in the after-tax return available from a project. This section discusses the following kinds of expenses: cash operating expenses; depreciation and amortization expenses; and financial expenses.

Cash operating expenses affect the cash flow from operations. The following table is presented to recapitulate:

	Gross Rental Income
+	Other Income
	Gross Revenues
−	Vacancies
	Net Revenues
−	Operating Expenses
−	Real Estate Taxes
	Cash Flow from Operations

Several areas are of primary concern: vacancies, real estate taxes, repairs and maintenance, and rental expenses.

An allowance for vacancy is not a deductible expense. Vacancies result in a reduction of income in the year in which they occur. No provision is made for estimates.

Real estate taxes are deductible in the year in which payment is made or the assessment comes due, whichever is later. In the years in which the property is purchased or sold, however, there is mandatory allocation between the purchaser and seller of the real estate taxes attributable to the year. Payments on overdue assessments due from the seller are capitalized by a purchaser.

The deductibility of repair and maintenance costs is often a gray area. Deductibility is generally allowed for expenses which maintain the operating efficiency of an asset over its useful life. There is a narrow line, however, between expenditures which maintain a property and those which add to its value, extend its useful life or adapt it to a different use. This distinction has been the subject of much tax litigation, with the taxpayer usually seeking to deduct as many such items as possible and the IRS seeking to capitalize borderline expenditures. Although nondeductibility does not preclude an item from being expensed or depreciated over the benefit's recovery period, it does defer the tax benefit over a longer period. The fundamental categories of expenditures and their tax treatment are shown in the following table. It is especially important to keep records in order to apportion the costs properly where repairs are combined with replacement or modernization.

EXPENDITURE TYPE	ORDINARY EXPENSE	CAPITALIZED ITEM
Carpentry	Repair of minor damage	Replacement of major structure
Plumbing	Minor part replacement and regular maintenance	Major replacement or addition
Roofing	Leak, repair, patching	Significant replacement
Cement, Plaster and Paving	Repair of cracks, holes and minor damage	Renovation, remodeling or complete resurfacing
Electrical	Minor replacements and repair	New addition or general replacement of serviceable but obsolete equipment

Expenses which are incurred incident to obtaining a lease are deductible ratably over the life of a lease. These include the expense of obtaining a specific tenant, such as attorney's fees and broker's commissions. More general items, such as advertising, can be deducted in the year incurred. When a lease terminates prior to the complete amortization of related capitalized expenses, unamortized amounts can be deducted in the year of termination.

Depreciable allowances form much of the foundation of tax shelter in the real estate industry. The concept of depreciation grew out of the recognition that man-made property has limited physical and economic useful life. It has been the primary vehicle through which businesses recover the cost of a capital investment. The Internal Revenue Service allows an owner to recover the capital costs of an investment in a depreciable asset through periodic deductions of a portion of the costs.

This section addresses several critical areas with respect to depreciation: To whom is depreciation available? What property is depreciable? What methods of depreciation are allowed?

Depreciation deductions are available only on depreciable property held or used either in a trade or business or for the production of income. This precludes depreciation deductions for personal residences or other property used solely for the personal benefit of the owner.

A lessee may take depreciation on improvements which are made to a leasehold interest, where the improvements are subject to declining value. If the recovery period of the improvements exceeds the term of the lease, the improvements are amortized by equal deductions over the lease term. Otherwise, they are depreciated over their own recovery period. There are special rules to determine the amortization period if the lease contains renewal options, assuming the recovery period exceeds the length of the initial period in the lease.

Property is depreciable if it has a limited useful economic life. Improvements to land are depreciable since they wear out, but the land itself is not depreciable since it either has or is deemed to have continuing economic utility.

The depreciation allowance is computed so that the total amount set aside through depreciation charges over a certain number of years plus the cost of the land equal the initial cost of the real estate. As an incentive to spur investment in tangible assets, the 1981 Economic Recovery Tax Act shortened the time period over which real estate could be depreciated to 15 years. Subsequent acts lengthened the cost recovery period to 18 and later 19 years.

The 1986 Act expanded the number of classes of depreciable property from five to eight. Generally, real property will be depreciated using the straight line method over 27.5 years for residential rental property (where 80% or more of the gross rental income is derived from dwelling units) and 31.5 years for non-residential rental property. A 40 year period is required for assets used abroad, by tax exempt entities, or if financed with tax exempt bonds. Most personal property connected with real estate is depreciated over seven years, using the 200% declining balance method.

Prior to ACRS, owners of real property were entitled to depreciate their properties using accelerated methods. At the time of sale of such property, however, the excess of the accelerated depreciation over straight-line depreciation would be recaptured and taxed at ordinary income tax rates.

An important point that follows from the emphasis on cost recovery is that generally no distinction is made for depreciation purposes between new and used real property. Prior to 1982, there was such a distinction in order to stimulate new construction in the form of shorter depreciable lives and the use of more accelerated methods to calculate depreciation.

Two methods of calculating depreciation were available to owners of property prior to ACRS: straight-line and declining balance. The second method is known as accelerated depreciation because it permits larger deductions in the early years of asset ownership. Prior to the 1981 Tax Act, four methods of calculating depreciation were available to owners of property: 1) straight-line; 2) declining balance; 3) sum-of-the-years-digits; and 4) any other consistent method which during the first two-thirds of the asset's useful life does not exceed the amount allowable under the declining balance method. Prior to the 1981 Tax Act the availability of depreciation methods was, however, limited and determined by the class of property being depreciated and its use, as the following table illustrates:

METHOD OF DEPRECIATION	TYPE OF ALLOWABLE PROPERTY	NECESSARY LIFE
Straight-line	All properties	No restriction
125% declining balance	Used residential rental property	20 years or more remain
150% declining balance	All new depreciable property	
200% declining balance	New residential property where 80% or more of the revenue is derived from nontransient residential units	3 or more years
Sum-of-the-years-digits	—same as (200% declining balance)	

Under previous tax law, an owner could separate the building into components and, for example, depreciate the roof over 10 years, the elevator over 15 years and the building shell over 40 years. Now the building and all its systems must be depreciated as a whole. In doing rehabilitation work, if the addition is not substantial the cost can be added to the basis of the building and depreciated over the cost recovery period appropriate for that type of addition. If the addition is substantial, it must be depreciated separately. If the addition to the building is a stand-alone piece of equipment, that equipment can be depreciated separately using the appropriate cost recovery rate for that kind of equipment.

Owners who chose accelerated depreciation were entitled to depreciate their property using 175% (200% for low-income housing) declining balance method. An important distinction, however, was drawn between residential and nonresidential property. Should the owner of residential property choose accelerated depreciation and then sell the property in less than 15 years at a gain, the difference between the depreciation taken by the owner and the amount for which the property would have been eligible using straight-line depreciation was recaptured at ordinary income tax rates.

With passage of the 1990 Tax Act, the maximum difference between ordinary and capital gains tax rates is 3% for most situations, so the penalty for recapture is no longer as significant.

Summary of Tax Factors in Operating Real Property

The major tax factors in the operating stage of a property's life cycle relate to the determination of income and of deductions. The timing of income recognition may vary depending on whether the taxpayer is on a cash or accrual basis. The availability of the depreciation deduction is the principal factor which makes real estate more attractive than other investments. It allows the owner of real property to deduct a non-cash charge, which reduces taxable income but not cash flow. The taxable income often can be negative, while the cash flow is positive. This is most frequently the case with highly leveraged properties. It produces a tax shelter for the taxpayer's other income although there are limits as to the deductibility of such losses except against other "passive activity income" as discussed.

TAX FACTORS IN THE SALE AND DISPOSITION OF REAL PROPERTY

When the taxpayer sells or otherwise disposes of real estate, there is an accounting of certain tax benefits received during the earlier operating stage. Factors, such as good records, proper form of ownership, and sound economic judgment come together to affect after-tax profit maximization. The most relevant tax considerations fall into three categories: calculation of gain or loss; income tax treatments of the gain or loss; and deferring taxation of any gain realized on the transaction.

Calculation of the Taxable Gain or Loss

Two factors determine the amount of taxable gain or loss: the selling price and the tax basis of the property. The gross selling price is the sum of the following:

Cash received by the seller
Determinable amounts receivable from the purchaser
Liabilities against the property owned by the seller where the buyer assumes the obligation or takes the property subject to the pre-existing liability
The fair market value of other property received by the seller.

From this amount, the seller is allowed to deduct the expenses of sale, such as the following:

Selling commission
Legal fees
Recording fees
Tax stamps
Capital expenses incurred within 90 days of sale which have not yet been capitalized.

The taxpayer's basis in the property sold is the original basis established upon its acquisition adjusted by the following (a) increased by any capital expenditures made during the period of ownership; and (b) reduced by the depreciation and other capital charges which have been deducted. The following sample illustrates the calculations made:

Sales Price	
Cash Down Payment	$ 65,000
Purchase Money 2nd Mortgage	255,000
Mortgage Assumed by Buyer	1,296,000
Total Price	$1,616,000
Less Deductions	
Legal Fees	$ 5,000
Recording Fees	3,000
Brokerage Fees	60,000
Total Deductions	$ 68,000
Net Sales Price	$1,548,000
Tax Basis	
Basis upon Purchase	$1,200,000
Capital Additions	90,000
	$1,290,000

Less

Depreciation Taken on Original Purchase:
100% S-L, 7 Years of 15-year Life   560,000

Depreciation Taken on Capital Additions:
4 Years of 15-year Life   24,000

Tax Basis on Sale $ 706,000

Gain on Sale $ 842,000

The calculation determines the amount of gain or loss realized. As the discussion which follows indicates, additional information is required in order to determine each taxpayer's tax liability.

The Importance of the Character and the Tax Treatment of Gain and Loss

The Different Characters of Income   The 1990 Act reintroduced a difference in tax rates between capital gains and ordinary income. Therefore, the tax system still differentiates among ordinary, capital, and Section 1231 income as follows:

> Capital gain or loss arises from the sale or other disposition of a capital asset, which is defined to include property held for investment purposes.
>
> Ordinary gain or loss arises from the sale or other disposition of property held for sale in the ordinary course of business, so-called dealer property.
>
> Section 1231 gain or loss arises from the sale or other disposition of depreciable real property which is used in the conduct of a trade or business, such as a store used by its owner. Section 1231 gains are treated as capital gains if they exceed Section 1231 losses, but otherwise they are treated as ordinary gains. Section 1231 losses are always treated as ordinary losses.

The application of these definitions generates uncertainty and controversy for investors, who on occasion may inadvertently assume dealer status.

The importance of this distinction related to the beneficial treatment accorded long-term gains on capital assets and certain long-term gains on Section 1231 assets. Where these assets have been held for more than one year, the gain or loss on them is treated as more than long-term. The effective tax rate applied to capital transactions provided an important incentive for investment in capital assets.

The 1981 Tax law provided that 60% of net long-term capital gains be excluded from income and that the remaining 40% be subject to tax at ordinary rates. In addition, the Act reduced the tax on investment income from 70% to 50%, thereby reducing the maximum tax on long-term capital gains from 28% to 20%.

The 1986 Act eliminated the distinction between ordinary income tax rates and capital gains tax rates, except for some taxpayers with incomes above a certain level in 1987, a transition year. As discussed earlier, beginning in 1991, the maximum tax rate imposed on capital gains remained at 28%, while the maximum tax rate imposed on ordinary income increases to 31%.

Deferring the Tax Consequences of Sale

It is often desirable to seek ways of deferring the tax consequences of a sale by spreading the recognition of income over a period of years. For example, the sale of real estate often generates a large liability which must be paid in cash, but the seller may not receive payment of the sales proceeds until a subsequent year. Moreover, a large gain can cause an individual to pay taxes in a higher marginal tax bracket than would otherwise be applicable to that taxpayer.

Deferral of tax on a sale may be achieved by five general methods: the first involves delaying receipt of the total proceeds by an installment sale; the second involves the qualified reinvestment of the proceeds in a tax free exchange; the third arises out of the involuntary conversions; the fourth involves the sale of low and moderate income housing primary residence; the fifth involves sale of a personal residence. In all five cases, the seller benefits by keeping tax monies working for himself or herself. Tax deferred transactions must be carefully structured to meet all the requirements. When they are met, the benefits can be substantial. Each method of deferral and the associated requirements will now be considered in greater detail.

Under the installment sales method, the seller may report a pro rata share of the profits from a transaction over time as the cash proceeds are received. In order to qualify for the installment sales treatment, the sales price must be payable to the seller over two or more years. This reporting method has two primary advantages. First, the seller's tax liability can be timed to correspond better with cash receipts, thereby eliminating the need to borrow funds to pay taxes. Second, the seller does not recognize the full amount of the income in a single tax year; thus, the marginal tax bracket applied to the income is likely to be less.

The following example illustrates calculations made for an installment sale:

In 1987, an investor sells a plot of land, subject to a pre-existing mortgage of $30,000 for $150,000 with a down payment of 20% of the purchase price. Interest on the purchase money mortgage will be 10%. Semi-annual payments of principal and interest will be made, with the former in equal installments of $10,000. The expenses of sale are $8,000. The seller's basis in the property is $30,000. The computations are as follows:

Sales price	$150,000
Selling expense	− 8,000
Net selling price	$142,000
Seller's basis	− 30,000
Gain on sale	$112,000

Sales price	$150,000
Mortgage assumed	− 30,000
Contract price	$120,000

Ratio of gain to contract price $112,000/$120,000	= .933%
Payments received in year of sale	= $30,000
Gain taxable in year of sale .933% x $30,000	= $28,000

The Tax Reform Act of 1984 provides that any gain on sale attributed to depreciation recapture will be recognized in full in the year of sale, even if no payments are received in that year.

During the first year principal payments will be $2 \times \$10,000$, of which 93.3% will be recognized as taxable gain. Interest income will be 5% of $120,000 for the first six months and 5% of $110,000 for the next six months, for a total of $11,500. The interest will constitute ordinary income to the seller.

It should be noted that the selling expense in this example is reflected over the life of the contract. This treatment differs from that accorded to a dealer in real estate who can deduct selling expenses separately in the year of the sale.

Selling the installment contract triggers recognition of the entire gain deferred. Pledging the contract can have similar results. Installment sales among related parties are subject to particular scrutiny. The 1986 Act also has developed a complex formula to deal with taxation of certain installment sales, requiring recognition of some or all of the gain based on the taxpayer's outstanding debt. This is true even if no payments have been received on the installment note.

Tax-deferred exchanges provide a technique for disposing of real estate investments and reinvesting the proceeds in other investment assets without incurring a tax liability on the disposition. By deferring the tax, up to 28% or more dollars can be kept at work. This method is often used where there may have been major appreciation in value and where the original owner wants to continue to be an investor in real estate.

For an exchange to qualify fully for tax-deferred treatment, it must meet several requirements:

1. The property must be held for use in a trade or business or for investment purposes. Fully passive investments such as corporate stocks and bonds do not qualify. Property held for sale or resale does not qualify; if the property is sold too soon after the sale, it may be found that no investment intent was present.
2. There must be an exchange of property for property rather than a sale, repurchase or reinvestment.
3. The property exchange must be of like kind.

If those conditions are met, deferral is mandatory for both gains and losses. Thus, a loss cannot be recognized even if it would be to the taxpayer's advantage to recognize it.

A qualifying exchange need not be limited to two-party transactions. Multi-party exchanges are allowable, so long as every transaction provides an exchange of properties. The "like kind" requirement has historically applied to real property so liberally that it covers almost every property. Office buildings, apartments, city lots, undeveloped land, warehouses, and many other kinds of real estate have been held to be "like kind" with other real estate interests. Recent tax court cases have significantly broadened this interpretation of "like kind." A taxpayer contemplating an exchange must seek competent counsel for both the mechanics of the transaction and the most recent ruling.

An exchange can be partially tax deferred where assets of a different character are included. Assets which do not qualify for a tax-free exchange are called "boot." These include cash, notes, personal property, and the assumption or transfer of liabilities. In a partially tax-deferred exchange, the amount of realized gain which is recognized is limited to the sum of the money and the fair market value of other nonqualifying property received.

In all transactions, the gain realized, the gain recognized and the new basis must be determined. Examples of the calculations follow:

Mr. Star and Mr. Ackerman negotiate the following exchange:

		STAR	ACKERMAN
A.	Tax basis of properties exchanged	$350,000	$200,000
B.	Fair market value of properties	450,000	500,000
C.	Mortgages	400,000	400,000
D.	Net equity	50,000	100,000
	Gain realized if sold (B-A)	100,000	300,000
	Gain recognized upon exchange	0	50,000

Mr. Star acquires control with no immediate tax consequences of a larger but less highly leverage property with an additional cash outlay of only $50,000, the difference between the net equities of the two projects. Mr. Ackerman receives a more highly leverage property, $50,000 in cash and the continued deferral of all but $50,000 of the $300,000 gain that would have to be recognized if he sold his property outright.

After this transaction is completed, the two individuals must compute their tax basis on the property acquired. If no boot is received, the basis in the property acquired becomes the adjusted basis in the property given. But, since in this case Mr. Star paid $50,000 in cash and Mr. Ackerman recognized gain in that amount, each could increase his original basis by $50,000.

Involuntary conversions generally arise out of the compulsory or involuntary loss of property through condemnation proceedings, theft, seizure or destruction. In contrast to "like-kind" exchanges, losses as well as gains must be recognized immediately and cannot be deferred unless reinvested according to specific rules.

Not all forced dispositions fall within the involuntary conversion rubric. Among those excluded are sales in foreclosure and in satisfaction with governmental assessments or liens. The exclusions can prove costly: if a property was purchased for $1 million, was depreciated to $800,000, and then was foreclosed with a mortgage balance outstanding of $900,000, the owner would realize a $100,000 capital gain, subject to possible depreciation recapture at ordinary rates.

In a qualifying involuntary conversion, the entire gain is deferred if the full amount of proceeds is reinvested so as to satisfy the rules for replacement. If only partial reinvestment is made, the treatment of that part which is not reinvested is similar to that accorded to "boot" in a tax-free exchange, i.e. it is taxable.

Replacement must take place within two years after the taxable year in which any part of the gain on conversion is realized. For condemnation awards, the period begins with the earlier of the date of the award or that on which condemnation first becomes imminent. The IRS has the discretion to grant extension periods.

Qualification of property as replacement property depends upon the cause of the conversion. For condemnations, the test has been the liberal "like-kind" rule which also governs tax-free exchanges. For other causes, stricter tests apply. Some look to the same end use (such as warehouse or factory) and others to the same business purpose (such as investment or rental of land).

Sales of low and moderate income housing built under certain financing programs can have their tax consequences deferred. The sale must be made usually either to a qualified not-for-profit corporation, cooperative organization or tenant group. The proceeds must be reinvested within one year in another subsidized housing project.

The sale of a principal personal residence can also yield wholly or partially deferred gains. One provision allows taxpayers to elect to defer the full gain on such a sale when the entire proceeds are reinvested in another principal residence purchased within a prescribed time period. Multiple deferral in a succession of qualified purchases and sales is possible.

There are three basic requirements of the general provision. First, the property must satisfy the sometimes ambiguous definition of the taxpayer's "principal" personal residence. Units in cooperatives and condominiums are included, as well as single family homes. Second, the new residence must be purchased within 24 months before or after the disposition of the old residence. The taxpayer is allowed more than one rollover, or deferral, during the 24 months if the taxpayer is required to relocate by an employer. When replacement is through construction, the construction must be started within 24 months. The acquisition of the new residence requires primary use or occupancy as well as acquisition of title. Third, for the full amount of the gain to be deferred, the amount reinvested (or expended on construction within the replacement period) must be at least equal to the "adjusted sales price" of the old residence. This amount is the gross sales price reduced by selling expense and fixing up expenses. The cost of the new residence includes its purchase price, construction costs, capital improvements, and various expenses, such as nondeductible finance

CHAPTER 24/NOTE ON TAXATION **421**

charges, legal fees, survey costs, and the taxpayer's liabilities on the property. To the extent the proceeds are not thus reinvested, any gain realized is recognized. For married taxpayers, the exemption applies if the requirements are satisfied by either spouse as long as the property is held jointly or as community property and a joint return is filed for the year of sale.

Taxpayers, age 55 and over, are allowed a one-time elective exclusion of up to $125,000 of gain from the sale of a principal residence. The taxpayer must have owned and occupied the principal residence for three of the last five years immediately prior to the sale. Gain above $125,000 may also be rolled over by the purchase of a new principal residence at a higher price.

GENERAL PRECEPTS

This note has attempted to establish some attitudes and major themes regarding taxation of real estate: careful planning, good advice and thorough records. The economic importance of taxes cannot be overstated. The federal government is always a major partner in every real estate transaction. The tax collector participates at every stage: during acquisition, during operation and at sale. The area is dynamic: assume that Congress will periodically revise the tax treatment of real estate.

Good planning in tax matters means knowing the taxpayer's whole tax and cash flow picture and that of any intermediary entity involved in the transaction. It means detailed analysis of the effective average and marginal tax brackets on both current and future incomes. It means understanding the sources of the income and their stability. It further means understanding the objectives and tax structure of the other parties involved. Deal structures which optimize the overall tax situation can emerge only from this type of planning.

Good advice is perhaps most critical. It seeks out the unique and protects the unwary. The consequences of bad decisions can come back many years later to haunt the investor. It takes preparation, however, to be able to use good advice effectively. The principals must prepare themselves well enough to ask the right kinds of questions. Good advisors can answer good questions, but it is up to the individual to ask those questions, and to translate the answers in a way that maximizes profits.

Good records are crucial in all tax situations, and often are clearly required. These include not only documentation of the numerical data which support claims, but also the deal structure itself, the economic reality, and the intent of the parties. Unambiguous written documentation of the terms of any agreement can significantly reduce future problems and provide unforeseen economic benefits. Good records imply good planning, and a pattern of activity that has been consciously thought through in order to achieve a specified result. Much tax litigation occurs many years after the operative transaction, when many key parties are often unavailable and the interests, memories and view of others are in conflict. Timely and complete documentation enables better resolution of any dispute, whether it be between taxpayer and the IRS or between direct parties to the transaction. The presumption must be that a later review will occur in an adversary proceeding.

The following ten guidelines should prove useful in practice if only for their simplicity:

Taxes are only one of many elements which contribute to the return on an investment—be certain to consider all of them and their interrelationships.

Cash, financial accounting, and taxable income are not the same—be certain to know the difference.

Tax laws are designed to show reasonable relationships between reported income and the expense incurred in generating it.

An expense is currently deductible when it relates to current usage.

The person who pays the cost gets the deduction, unless it is a gift.

Unless otherwise provided, an expense must be capitalized.

Tax basis is the cost of an asset adjusted by all taxable transactions relating to the asset.

If a transaction is not at arm's length, expect fair market value to govern; but fair market value does not mean the same thing to all people.

Depending upon the tax code of the time, long-term capital gains may be more beneficial than ordinary income, but long-term capital losses are less beneficial than ordinary losses.

A foreclosed property does not result in tax benefits—remember the underlying property value.

The real estate professional must adjust the form and substance of all business activities to the recognition that the tax treatment is an increasingly important element in managerial decisions. Beyond a general knowledge, the mechanics of a transaction are critical to its tax success. These aphorisms provide merely a basis for understanding the tax game. Be careful to consult your tax advisor before making your decision. Remember also that tax laws change. The assumptions as to taxation you make upon acquisition of a property may alter not only the after-tax return you achieve while holding the property, but the price that a new buyer will pay you if you want to sell that property.

25

NOTE ON FORMS OF REAL ESTATE OWNERSHIP

INTRODUCTION

This note addresses the question of the advantages and the disadvantages of various legal forms of organization used in owning and operating real estate properties.

Each of these forms should be approached from two different directions: from the general business management point of view and from the tax point of view. General business management is concerned with questions about formality of organization, continuity of existence, degree of liability and ease of transferability. Tax questions deal with the issues of taxation during the operation of income-producing property and during the sale or liquidation of real property assets.

For someone active in real estate, this note is especially important in that each real property investment is normally held in a separate legal entity as opposed to that of other businesses where it is customary to expand through existing corporations. The prime reasons for this difference are that most real estate financings both at the debt and equity levels are property specific; that it is common to have different lenders and investors in different projects; and that separation of ownership makes it easier to limit risk. Also, by having a separate entity it is possible to tailor the nature of the relationships among the parties to

---

This note was prepared as the basis for class discussion. It was updated in 1992.

their specific needs and contributions. For income tax purposes, most investment properties are held in a partnership format.

It should be emphasized that this discussion is general and introductory in nature. It is therefore essential to consult with competent legal and tax advisors before deciding upon the vehicle through which property is to be purchased and managed.

THE SINGLE PROPRIETORSHIP

General Description

The legal concept known as "single proprietorship" is exemplified by the individual who opens up a store front and begins to do business without further formality. The single proprietorship is literally a form of business organization where there is no separate form of organization: the business and the individual are one and the same. All proprietorship property is owned directly by the proprietor. All management decisions are the responsibility of the single owner. All the debts of the business are owed directly by the individual.

The creation and operation of a single proprietorship require, by and large, no form of official approval except for the filing of a certificate if the individual wishes to do business under another name.

Tax Situation

A single proprietorship does not pay taxes as a separate entity, nor does it file a return. If an individual buys, holds, operates and sells property as a single proprietorship, the results of the transactions are reported on the individual's tax return.

Advantages and Disadvantages

In general, the proprietorship form of organization is well adapted to the purposes of the individual property owner. It is an inexpensive way to do business. It also offers flexibility and sensitivity, since the legal power and the responsibility are vested in a single person.

The disadvantages of a single proprietorship, like many of its advantages, stem from the unity between the business and the individual. The owner/operator is subject to unlimited liability on account of the debts of the organization. This exposure to risk for the owner can be reduced through the use of "exculpatory clauses" in leases, loans or other contracts which means that recourse is taken solely against specified assets of the business. Negotiating such an agreement depends upon the respective bargaining-powers of the parties.

The proprietorship form of organization suffers from a lack of continuity of existence, since the proprietorship ends with the death, insanity or bankruptcy of the owner. In some ways tax laws do not favor single proprietorships since the cost of pension plans, health and life insurance and other fringe benefits for its employees are not deductible.

THE GENERAL PARTNERSHIP

General Description

A partnership is "a voluntary association of two or more persons to carry on as co-owners a business for profit". There are two categories of partnerships: (1) general and (2) limited. In a general partnership, all the partners have a voice in the management and are subject to unlimited liability.

A general partnership can also be created without any legal formalities; however, this approach is neither the typical one, nor is it the most sound. A preferred procedure is to hire an attorney to prepare a partnership agreement specifying: (1) the name and the nature of the business, (2) the term of the agreement, (3) capital contributions, (4) the allocation of profits and losses and cash distributions, (5) the salaries and drawings, (6) the sharing in initial expenses, (7) management duties and restrictions, (8) the banking arrangements, (9) the accounting books, (10) the consequences of the retirement, disability or death of a partner, and (11) the means of sale of an interest or dissolution and liquidation of the partnership. In effect the agreement establishes what provisions shall apply among the partners. The expense of organizing a partnership is usually not a controlling factor in selecting this form of ownership.

Tax Situation

For tax purposes a partnership is not considered to be a separate entity but a conduit. Although the income is earned or the losses incurred by the partnership as a whole, the partnership itself does not pay taxes. Rather, the profits and losses flow through the partnership to the partners, who compute and pay the taxes as separate individuals. The apportionment of tax profits and losses generally follows whatever the partnership agreement specifies. There must, however, be an economic or business purpose to the allocation of tax profits and losses.

In order to make this scheme operable, the partnership keeps records analogous to those of an individual or corporation and files an annual tax return.

This tax situation makes the partnership form of ownership an attractive business form. This is especially true in comparison with the corporate tax situation where the taxation of corporate profits and the taxation of distributed dividends combine to produce the effective tax. The single tax levied upon members of a partnership is, in all instances, substantially less. The ability to utilize taxable losses from real estate to offset other types of non-real estate income has been limited by recent legislation. It is limited as to the amount that can be applied and by the income bracket and business interests of the partner.

A general partnership is allowed to hire one or more general partners as employees and pay them fixed compensations which are tax deductible. However, like a proprietorship, a general partnership is not allowed to deduct the expense of fringe benefits such as pension plans, health and life insurance.

Advantages and Disadvantages

The main attraction of the partnership arrangement is that although it is based on a formal legal structure, it is an informal, flexible one.

A crucial weakness of the general partnership arrangement is that the partners are exposed to unlimited liability for partnership debts. Given the substantial power of any general partner to make financial commitments in behalf of the partnership within that partner's actual or apparent authority, the feature of unlimited liability creates a real risk for all of the general partners.

A general partner is free to assign shares of the profits to a third person at any time. However, unless the unanimous consent of the other partners is obtained, this third person assignee will enjoy none of the other privileges of partnership. Like a sole proprietorship the partnership is extinguished by the death or insanity of any of the general partners. However, this defect can easily be corrected by the formation of a successor partnership or by providing in the original partnership agreement that, upon the termination of the original partnership, a new partnership is immediately reformed by the remaining partners to carry on the business.

THE LIMITED PARTNERSHIP

General Description

A limited partnership is a partnership which contains one or more general partners and one or more limited partners. The status of the two groups is radically different. The general partners in a limited partnership have essentially the same relationship towards their fellow partners and towards the partnership as do the partners in a general partnership. By contrast, the limited partners are passive investors and are legally precluded from participating in day-to-day decisions of the partnership.

A limited partnership may only be created in accordance with certain statutory formalities. The limited partnership agreement governs the relationship between the partners. Sound practice recommends that an expert attorney be employed to draw up this agreement.

Tax Situation

For the purposes of taxation a limited partnership is treated the same as a general partnership and therefore is protected from the double taxation of a corporation.

Advantages and Disadvantages

The advantages of the limited partnership are a function of its hybrid status somewhere between a corporation and a general partnership. It shares with the corporation the appeal of centralized management and limited liability for some of the investors. At the same time, it offers the opportunity for tax savings which are available through the conduit treatment granted to all partnerships.

Exculpatory clauses can serve to reduce the risk borne by the general partners. Continuity of existence can be written into the partnership agreement by providing that the remaining general partners may elect a replacement for any among their number who might retire or be disqualified.

As noted earlier the partnership agreement will spell out the allocation of profits for tax purposes as well as the priorities for cash distributions from operations, refinancing or sale of assets. The ordering is not always the same, but generally, the apportionment should correspond closely to the contributions made by different partners to the partnership. The I.R.S. will reject an apportionment of profits and losses in a partnership agreement when it concludes that the formula used is designed solely for tax avoidance and does not have a valid business purpose.

The I.R.S. has issued regulations stipulating the minimum net worth requirements of individual and corporate general partners.

THE CORPORATION

General Description

A corporation is an artificial legal entity created for the purpose of carrying on a business. As a creature of statutory law, a corporation can be established only by careful adherence to statutory requirements and may not commence operation without first receiving state permission.

Tax Situation

For tax purposes, a corporation is considered a separate taxable entity and is taxed at both state and federal levels. Unless the corporation qualifies as a Subchapter S corporation, double taxation occurs upon distribution of income. Under Subchapter S, tax treatment is similar to that of partnerships. Tax deductible fringe benefits such as deferred compensation schemes, health and life insurance and pension plans may change the timing of employees' income.

Advantages and Disadvantages

The most important reasons for selecting the corporate form of organization are: (1) limited liability, (2) perpetual existence, (3) ease of transferability of shares, and (4) control of the timing and nature of income. The value of these different features will depend, of course, upon the situation. The use of multiple corporations to own separate properties may be appealing from a general management point of view. The disadvantages in the corporate form of organization are related to double taxation, the expense involved and the formality required.

THE JOINT VENTURE

General Description

A joint venture is an association of two or more individuals, corporations or partnerships for the purpose of participating in a specific and limited business enterprise. A joint venture is a general partnership for a single special purpose. Operationally an agreement will generally cover the same points as in a partnership agreement.

Tax Situation

The tax code provides specifically that a joint venture is taxed to the participants in proportion to the respective interests. The tax affect is substantially the same as a general partnership.

Advantages and Disadvantages

The reasons for accepting or rejecting the joint venture format are the same that apply to partnerships. A joint venture has particular appeal because it is designed specifically for one-shot propositions. This explains its common occurrence in the field of real estate development and acquisition.

THE BUSINESS TRUST/REAL ESTATE INVESTMENT TRUST

General Description

A business trust is an unincorporated association established for the purpose of carrying on a business by declaration or deed of trust. Business trusts were first developed in Massachusetts in order to circumvent restrictions on the power of a corporation to acquire and develop real estate. For this reason they are often referred to as "Massachusetts trusts."

A business trust is created when capital is conveyed to a group of trustees who then execute a deed of trust to the effect that they hold this property, and any subsequent trust property, for the purposes stated and for the benefit of the shareholders of the trust. The contributors to the trust then receive shares, represented by certificates, in numbers proportionate to their respective contributions to the capital.

An important difference between corporations and trusts is that the latter may not have perpetual existence. The maximum life span of a trust is the length of a designated life in being, plus twenty-one years. Although trustees have a fiduciary responsibility, the trustees can be indemnified by the beneficiaries.

As a hybrid creation of both corporate and trust law, Massachusetts trusts have always occupied a slightly ambiguous position, particularly in geographic areas where they are infrequently used as a form of business organization. In different states and in different circumstances, business trusts have been variously treated by the courts as general partnerships, limited partnerships, and corporations. This leaves the question of the beneficiary's protection against unlimited liability a little uncertain. Even in those jurisdictions where limited liability has been accepted, it is unclear at what point excessive involvement in the affairs of management will strip the beneficiary of protective privileges.

Tax Situation

For tax purposes, a business trust is considered as a corporation. By virtue of certain revisions in the Internal Revenue Code made in 1960, business trusts are entitled to elect tax treatment as a modified conduit, similar to the treatment given to the different forms of partnership. This election will be discussed in detail under the topic of the Real Estate Investment Trust.

Advantages and Disadvantages

In those states where business trusts were initially developed or where they have become a familiar form of business organization, their advantages are virtually those of the corporations they were designed to resemble. In those states where business trusts are still unfamiliar, there is a certain risk involved in choosing this form, and it is more prudent to seek the clear-cut status of a corporation or some form of partnership. Because business trusts are relatively uncommon, the use of a specialist in planning and creating one is particularly appropriate.

REAL ESTATE INVESTMENT TRUSTS

In the 1960 amendment to the Internal Revenue Code, Congress created a new category of business trust, the Real Estate Investment Trust (hereafter REIT). This is a business trust which is organized to invest in real estate and which pays out virtually all its income in the year earned. Congress wanted to create a vehicle analogous to a mutual fund which would allow a small investor with little money and experience to participate in a large, diversified and professionally-managed portfolio of real estate assets. At the same time, Congress wanted to avoid the penalty which comes from double taxation of corporations. To all qualified REITs, as defined in the statute, Congress gave conduit treatment with regard to income distributed in the year earned. With regard to income which is retained, the trust is treated like an ordinary corporation.

In order to be treated as a REIT a trust must meet specific requirements regarding its income, assets and business conduct. These requirements are described in Appendix A.

POINTS TO REMEMBER IN SELECTING A FORM OF REAL ESTATE OWNERSHIP

In an actual situation the process of selecting the most appropriate form of ownership for real property assets should include consideration of: (1) the formalities of organization and operation, (2) the capital and credit requirements, (3) management and control, (4) profits and losses from tax and cash standpoints, (5) extent of liability, (6) transferability of interest, (7) continuity of existence, and (8) income tax considerations, primarily federal but also state.

This note has made a rapid survey of the more salient features of the various legal forms of ownership as they can be used to organize real estate ventures. The reader is warned that the picture painted here is no more than a brief rough outline made with broad brush strokes. Under actual conditions, the assistance of an experienced attorney, especially a tax expert, and/or an accountant is essential to any successful planning for the ownership of real property assets. The attached checklist may be an oversimplification, but may provide a general road map in helping you in making your decision as to which form of ownership is most appropriate for your venture.

APPENDIX A   REQUIREMENTS FOR QUALIFICATION AS A REIT

The **income qualifications** restrict the acceptable sources of income:

1. At least 75% of gross income must be derived from property rents, interest on obligations secured by a mortgage on real property, property tax refunds and abatements, gain from the sale or other disposition of real property interests, and gain from the sale of shares in other qualified REITs;
2. An additional 15% must come from these sources plus dividends and interest or gain from the sale or other disposition of stock or securities;
3. Less than 30% of the gross income must be in the form of short-term capital gains which are defined here as including gain on the sale or other disposition of stock held for less than six months and real property held for less than four years.

The effect of these restrictions is that 10% of the gross income can come from sources which are tainted. Many REITs use this allowance to cover income which comes from commitment fees, discounts paid out of loan proceeds and technically usurious interest where present.

There are **investment qualifications** which restrict the form and amount of acceptable investments. Likewise, there are conduct and cash distribution requirements in order to remain qualified as a REIT.

At least 75% of an REIT's assets must be invested in real estate interests, government securities, cash or cash items, and of the remainder not more than 5% of the trust assets can be invested in the securities of any one issuer. A REIT may not hold more than 10% of the outstanding voting stock of any one issuer.

A third set of restrictions applies to the **conduct of a REIT**. A REIT must pay out at least 90% of its income in the year earned (recent legislation permits certain exceptions to this rule for trusts that have experienced financial difficulties), must issue certificates of beneficial interest and have at least one hundred beneficiaries. A REIT should remain "passive", which means that it should not act as a property manager and that it should not acquire property as a broker/dealer. Normally an advisory company is hired to perform these functions.

Checklist for Forms of Ownership

	LIABILITY	TRANSFERABILITY	FORMALITY	TAXABILITY
The Proprietorship	unlimited	easy	informal	conduit
General Partnership	unlimited	limited	informal	conduit
Limited Partnership	limited	limited	formal	conduit
The Corporation	limited	easy	formal	double
Joint Venture	unlimited	limited	formal	conduit
Business Trust	limited	easy	formal	conduit